The Autobiography
of
WILLIAM JAY

REV. WILLIAM JAY.

(In his 48th year)

The
Autobiography
of
WILLIAM JAY

Edited by
George Redford
John Angell James

The Cottage in which M.ʳ Jay was born.

The Banner of Truth Trust

THE BANNER OF TRUTH TRUST
3 Murrayfield Road, Edinburgh EH12 6EL
P.O. Box 652, Carlisle, Pennsylvania 17013

*

First published 1854
First Banner of Truth Trust edition 1974

ISBN 0 85151 177 5

*

Printed in Great Britain by Offset Lithography by
Billing and Sons Ltd, Guildford and London

PREFACE.

THE Editors have a few words, and but a few, to express—and those chiefly for the satisfaction of the reader—that in the following pages he may feel assured he will read what Mr. Jay left for his perusal. It was the anxious wish of his family, and especially of his executors, that the manuscripts here published should pass, precisely as he left them, into the hands of the Editors, one of whom was selected by Mr. Jay before his death, and the other subsequently by his family. To them the papers were committed entire, and without alteration, restriction, or condition, to edit them for the press, according to their best judgment, and to make such additions as might seem desirable to complete the narrative; carefully, however, distinguishing, as they have done, between such additions and the original work.

In undertaking this task they did not feel that they were required to write a Memoir, but simply to complete an Autobiography, which was necessarily left, as to time, unfinished; and to gather up such other portions of information, respecting Mr. Jay, and his course through life, as might seem desirable for the purpose of perpetuating the memory of so much excellence, usefulness, and wisdom. It has, therefore, been their main object to let Mr. Jay speak for himself; and to preserve such specimens of his mind and genius, piety and usefulness, at different periods of his long course, as might prove both gratifying and instructive.

They are well aware that a large circle of friends are waiting, with eager expectation, for a work which its author had often promised should be forthcoming after his death, and which it was well known he had long been preparing. To such they trust it will prove all that they had anticipated from the pen of their esteemed friend; and that to a still wider circle, though now dead, he will yet speak. Some persons may wonder at the delay of the publication; but when they are informed that the whole of the manuscripts have had to be rewritten, from a handwriting requiring no little skill and patience to decipher, and then to be carefully compared and examined; and that much new matter had to be collected to continue the thread of the narrative, and to carry it through the closing scene,—it will be evident that no time has been lost, and that greater haste could only have been attended with defects and incompleteness.

To the numerous friends of Mr. Jay, who have obligingly contributed copies of letters, and other valuable and important documents, the cordial thanks of the Editors are due, and are hereby respectfully pre-

sented. It would be invidious to particularize individuals, and inconvenient to enumerate all who have
thus kindly aided the work. It is hoped, therefore,
that this general acknowledgment will be accepted.

The Editors have now only to commend the work
to the candid attention of the reader; and the blessing
of Him who alone can make this monument his servant
has inscribed to the glory of His divine grace, eminently
subservient to the edification of His Church universal,
and encouraging to the rising ministry, who have in
Mr. Jay an example which they may do well to emulate,
and an instance of success which they will scarcely
hope to surpass. The portraiture and the history are
now before them, and with equal talents, superior advantages, similar motives, diligence and devotedness,
while they have the same Gospel to preach, the same
world to preach it in, and the same Great Master to
serve, why may not the Church yet be blessed with
many a young preacher who shall begin as auspiciously,
proceed as successfully, and terminate as honourably,
as William Jay?

CONTENTS.

PART I.

THE AUTOBIOGRAPHY.

PART II.

SUPPLEMENT TO THE AUTOBIOGRAPHY.

BY THE EDITORS.

PART III.

REMINISCENCES OF DISTINGUISHED CONTEMPORARIES.

PART IV.

SELECTIONS FROM THE CORRESPONDENCE OF THE REV. W. JAY.

CONCLUDING OBSERVATIONS
BY THE EDITORS.

PART I.

THE AUTOBIOGRAPHY

OF THE

REV. WILLIAM JAY;

WITH A GENERAL INTRODUCTION BY THE EDITORS.

GENERAL INTRODUCTION

TO

THE AUTOBIOGRAPHY, REMINISCENCES, ETC.

———

"THEY that be wise shall shine as the brightness of the firmament, and they that turn many to righteousness as the stars for ever and ever." So speaks the Oracle of Sacred Truth, and all history elucidates and confirms it. When such moral benefactors of the world pass away from the scenes and labours of time, a lustre gathers around their memory purer and steadier than that which attaches to conquerors, statesmen, and princes. Even the honoured names of poets, patriots, and philosophers, though sounded forth more loudly and widely by the trump of fame, are not so dear to mankind, nor do they exert so benign and extensive an influence upon the heart and character of survivors. This happy result seems to be secured by a law in the moral government of God which conserves, for the benefit of future ages, whatever in human character is most redolent of heaven's own goodness and purity. That law may be clearly traced in the history and experience of mankind, but is fully read only in the words of inspiration, "the righteous shall be in everlasting remembrance, but the name of the wicked shall rot." Even the world itself, true, in this case, to its moral instincts, cannot help reverencing the one character, and despising the other, though unconscious of the law by which it is influenced.

Hence the fragrant memories of the good and great are claimed as the common property of mankind. They are the specimens of itself in which humanity glories; the types of what men ought to be, and living examples of what the grace of God can do with even a fallen nature. Men will not let such memories perish. They are the lode-stars of life to many : luminaries to all eyes that never sink beneath the horizon. Or, in another view, they become sacred spoils rescued by their own inherent immortality from the power of the universal destroyer, and consecrated by the pen of history to embellish and enrich future and distant ages. Humanity would feel itself poor without them; and history would want its greatest lights and best lessons.

These intellectual and spiritual treasures may remain embodied in the writings which such pre-eminently wise and good men bequeath to the world; or they may consist in the records which others preserve of their bright example, wise instructions, and useful lives; and sometimes partly in their own writings, and partly in those of others concerning them. It is only occasionally and rarely that such persons embalm their own memories, for the benefit of their successors, in an autobiography; and probably it is chiefly due to the rarity of this species of composition, that the desire to peruse it has become so strong.

It is a difficult and a delicate thing for a man to write memoirs of himself, and the world is curious to see how he can perform it. There is strong reason, however, to doubt whether any artist could produce so good a portrait of himself as he could of some other person, or some other of him. At any rate, we have seldom seen an autobiography which conveyed so correct and complete a conception of the character of its subject as might have been conveyed by another hand; though in some lineaments it might have been more accurate and striking. There are doubtless many things in a man's experience and feelings which no one can understand and explain so well as himself—many facts in his history which no one can describe so well as himself—and perhaps some traits and some phases of his character which no one can harmonize with his individuality so well as himself; and if he be so thoroughly honest and simple-hearted as not to fear being "known and read of all men," and so devout a worshipper of truth as to sacrifice pride and fame upon its altar, then he may produce an autobiography the accuracy of which would command the approving verdict of all competent judges, and the value of which every reader would appreciate. In that case we might place the portrait in the picture gallery and moral treasury of the mind, to be studied for imitation, as well as reverenced and guarded by honour and love. When the memory of the just has thus embodied itself in form, and embalmed itself in our affections, it only remains for us to give to it that vital force and influence which shall enable it to reproduce its like in ourselves and future generations.

Whether our esteemed friend, Mr. Jay, showed more wisdom in writing memoirs of himself than he would have shown in leaving materials by which some other hand might have traced his history, and described his character; or whether he has comprised in his Autobiography as much of himself and his history as his friends and the world will care to know, are both questions, we suspect, on which there will be a diversity of opinion, and which as editors it does not become us to decide. It is, however, quite certain that many interesting facts in his history are not noticed in the Biography, and that some of the most important and instructive come out in his Reminiscences of other persons : so that the reader must not expect to find anything like a complete narrative of Mr. Jay's life in his Autobiography.

While it is probable that many readers of this volume will feel some disappointment that Mr. Jay has not left us a history of his life at once more comprehensive and minute yet the record of his matured opinions on various important subjects connected with the cause of Evangelical Religion, will by men of sound judgment be accepted as ample compensation for the lack of historic detail. Of how much greater value, in other memoirs of eminent persons, would such expressions of opinion have proved, than many of those ordinary instances of every-day life which, as they convey no important information, and elucidate no principle, serve only to swell the bulk, without enhancing the worth of the volume, or it may be *volumes*. In the one case we are listening to the decisions of wisdom and experience, while in the other we are entertained with facts without interest, or garrulity without amusement.

Mr. Jay's *Reminiscences* often bear no inconsiderable relation to himself, and show the influences of early connexions. But there are many interesting and memorable facts relating to his personal history which he has failed to record in either section of his work, and which we have felt it our duty to supply as far as we have been able to collect information. In the matter of dates also in the Autobiography, where they were most essential, our friend has been totally negligent. There is scarcely one from the beginning to the end. Most of those, however, which were of any importance, we have been enabled to supply.

To us, moreover, it appears an inauspicious circumstance that Mr. Jay should have left his Autobiography to so late a period of life. The undertaking was frequently urged upon him by his children, but it was not until a very earnest Letter, in the name of the rest, was written by one of his sons, that he commenced it resolutely and at once. This was about August in the year 1843. He then wrote as follows :—

"At length I have begun in good earnest, having such good health and some leisure, besides what relaxation requires, to write the memoir. The sight of the Letter you wrote, dated August 6, 1842, urging it, fell in my way, and I yielded to it. My plan is to address it in a number of Letters to yourself,* like Mr. Winter's to me, as I can go on by easy degrees. I have already written seven, but I send them not (not having copies), lest they should be lost; and I may like to revise them as I proceed. I am so happy I have hit upon this method, and begin to feel an interest in it. The fragments I wrote some years ago will occasionally come in with alterations and additions. Now tell no one this but your wife, till I give you leave. Should my health continue I hope to bring together a good number of these Letters; but I find I must not apply too closely, as it affects my head and my stomach."

At this period Mr. Jay was in his seventy-fourth year, and though, as to his preaching abilities, possibly as lively and popular as ever, yet as to his recollection of dates, and the order of circumstances, it was scarcely to be expected that he could avoid some confusion, even if he retained vivid recollections of events and persons through so long a series of years. It does not appear that he had kept any diary or memoranda, and most probably had nothing to aid him but his memory when he first commenced his work. This, however, we believe applies solely to the Autobiography.—The " Reminiscences " were committed to paper much earlier, at least in part. Some of them were evidently written soon after the demise of the subjects of them. Many of these were persons of note and eminence in their day, whose friendship Mr. Jay highly prized; and all of them had some influence in the formation of his character, or in directing the events and circumstances of his life. Several of the most distinguished subjects of his Reminiscences have had copious and separate biographical works devoted to them. This,

* This was addressed to one of his sons, but he afterwards changed his purpose, and addressed these Letters to all his children.

however, will not lessen but rather heighten the interest attaching to his recollections. They are entirely his own, and for the most part will be clear additions to the facts already known concerning those eminent and excellent persons. In some instances a clearer light will be thrown on certain facts, some obscurities will be removed, and some mistakes or misrepresentations corrected. We are quite sure Mr. Jay's anecdotes will be highly relished by the admirers of those characters to whom they relate.

Concerning his correspondence we have only a very few observations to offer. It appears that Mr. Jay felt a great reluctance to engage in letter-writing. He refers to this so early in his history as the commencement of his acquaintance with Miss Davies, afterwards Mrs. Jay. The reader will find it confirmed in an early section of his Autobiography. He frequently alludes to it in the course of his correspondence, and in several other parts of his writings; sometimes alleging conscious distaste and incapacity, though at other times charging neglect and failure to the pressure of other claims and the multiplicity of public engagements. Yet we have had a very considerable mass of letters submitted to our examination, a fair proportion of them being long letters.

In a paper containing directions and suggestions to his literary executors, he writes thus: "With regard to my Correspondence I now see I never laid sufficient stress upon letter-writing as the means of promoting social affection and moral pleasure and profit. I had naturally an aversion to letter-writing. My letters were therefore few and imperfect, and written in haste, as if occupying time taken from more serious engagements. I therefore think none of them entitled to publication. Yet I would leave this, after my own expressed opinion, to the judgment of my executors."

While using the liberty here conceded to us for the

gratification of friends, we have at the same time respected Mr. Jay's own opinion by making a comparatively small selection.

It would seem from Mr. Jay's high appreciation of the epistolary style of both Newton and Cowper, that he felt it difficult to realize his own *ideal* of excellence in this department. This may explain his reluctance to make the effort, while the eagerness of his correspondents to be favoured with his letters attests how successful he was when he did make it. His own style in his letters scarcely yields in simplicity, playfulness, and ease, to the eminent examples at which he aspired. The frequent excuses and apologies he makes for delay clearly prove that he was not what is conventionally termed a good correspondent. In this respect he contrasts himself with his admired and beloved tutor, who was distinguished for the excellence as well as for the extent of his epistolary correspondence. Mr. Winter, he says, "frequently cautioned his young men not to follow his example. In one case, at least, this advice, I fear, was pursued to the extreme, and this he equally censured. The writer is the guilty individual. When, therefore, I had my last interview with my venerable friend, he asked me—for he was willing, if possible, to learn of those he had taught—to sketch the outline of a sermon from the words, 'His letters, say they, are weighty.' I complied; but in presenting it expressed my wonder at the choice of the subject, and intimated that I could hardly deem it important enough for the edification of an audience, many of whom could not write at all. He smiled, and I saw he had gained his object. In this way he had insinuated a mild reproof. He had drawn from me some reflections on the utility and importance of letter-writing, by which I own I was condemned." *

An indiscriminate publication of a man's letters is not to

* Mr. Jay's Life of Winter, p. 313.

be applauded.   A considerable proportion of all letters, written by men of such publicity as Mr. Jay, must be letters upon business or domestic occurrences, or entering into details of family matters or interchanges of friendship, in which strangers can feel no interest whatever, and from which they can extract no improvement.   It is but rarely that men engaged in public life can sit down to discuss set subjects with their friends; and it is but very seldom indeed that such persons can afford time for more than prompt and brief replies to their correspondents.   But sometimes their letters to their afflicted friends are highly valued, and may be appropriate to many besides those to whom they were first addressed.   We have made a selection of those letters to Mr. Jay's friends, and of some of theirs to him, which we have thought would be read with interest by others.

We trust the perusal of the whole work will gratify Mr. Jay's numerous friends, and through the Divine blessing promote that great and good cause to which our venerated friend devoted his long life and earnest endeavours.

THE AUTOBIOGRAPHY

OF

THE REV. WILLIAM JAY.

LETTER I.

MY VERY DEAR CHILDREN,—I duly received your kind and respectful letter. The contents were both pleasing and humbling. I could not but feel gratified by the expressions of your filial affection and piety; yet my conscience told me while reading them, how far short I came in fully exemplifying the qualities and excellences which your regard has led you to attach to your father.

The letter is too partial and flattering to be here introduced. But what can I say to the proposal it brings, in pressing me to write some account of myself, and the leading events of my life? The application has a powerful claim in coming from those who stand in a relation so near; and it acquires additional influence when, as you affirm, it is accompanied and enforced by the earnest wishes of my other relatives and friends, and church and congregation, and of many of the public.

But before I could determine on refusing or complying with the proposal, I had four things to consider :—

First, Whether such a memoir ought to be secured?

This was a delicate question for the individual himself to answer, and some might suppose that *he* could not answer it in the affirmative, without betraying self-importance. But humility is not founded in ignorance. A man may know and own what he is, without vanity or pride, if he can say, " By the grace of God I am what I am ;" " Not I, but the grace of God which was with me." It would have been mere affectation (and it must have been *deemed* so), had I *seemed* unacquainted with my rise from an obscure condition; the earliness of my preaching; the degree of popularity attending my first efforts; the undiminished continuance of the favour shown to my labours; the candid respect I have received from the various religious denominations I have occasionally served; the friendly notice taken of me by some very significant personages; the number of my publications, with their acceptance and enlarged circulation at home and abroad; and the portion of usefulness, in serving my generation for more than half a century, which is generally attributed to my endeavours.

A *second* question was, Whether, if I refused this proposal, everything of the kind would be prevented from other quarters? The present rage for biography is excessive and notorious, Such is the voracity of its appetite, that it frequently waits not for the license which death is supposed to give. It falls upon its prey, and devours it *alive;* and many a man may be himself the reader of his own character and history, furnished by some anonymous or even known writer. A number of different sketches of myself have already appeared in periodical or separate publications in England and America. It is not, therefore, impossible or improbable but that some notices after my death may be attempted, either by the mercenary or needy grasping at gain, or by real friends, meaning well, but labouring often in the dark.

Thirdly, It was to be asked whether autobiography in some respects is not more desirable and preferable than information derived from extraneous sources? "Those relations," says Johnson, "are commonly the most valuable, in which the writer tells his own story." With regard to a man's talents and productions, and also those attributes and habits, the result and fame of which form so much of what we mean by character, the pen of another may be better than his own. But yet, respecting many things of an interesting nature, he himself must be the best witness, the best judge, and the best recorder. By a competent writer, the *public* life of an individual is easily supplied; but people are seldom satisfied without some insight into his more private retreats and recesses. They would know not only what he did, but why he did it. They would know, not only the direction in which he moved, but whether he was led into it by design or accident, and what retarded or aided his progress. They would not only contemplate his elevation, but learn by what degrees and efforts and instrumentalities he reached it; for there is nothing really unaccountable in such cases. The thing wondered at is, under Providence, the natural consequence of a series of events and circumstances. What appears a kind of impassable depth and distance between the early and later condition of the man is owing to an ignorance of the intermediate connexions in the passage. We see him on the opposite sides, but have not accompanied him in the transition from the one to the other; but he himself knows that he passed, not by miracle, but by means; that he was not supernaturally borne across, but gained his position by many alternations of hope and fear; by many a weary step, and by many a painful struggle.

But how is a man's more personal and interior experience; his original disadvantages or helps; what chilled his ardour or animated his diligence; what in his intellectual, or spiritual, or official career was found to be his bane or his benefit; with many other interesting and useful things; — how is all this to be known, unless from the communications of the individual himself?

A *diary* will not fully subserve the purpose. A diary regards chiefly a man's intercourse with God; and the variations of his religious views and feelings there recorded are designed to promote self-acquaintance, and not to divulge himself to others. Such a work is devotional rather than narratory, and will abound with much that is not proper for public observation.

Fourthly, I had to inquire whether, in such an undertaking, I could trust my own views and motives? While I knew how hard it is to be honest where self is concerned, and that nothing is perfectly pure that comes from man; yet I felt that I ought to be conscious of being so far actuated by a principle of truth, rectitude, and usefulness, as to be able to commend my work unto the Lord; and not only to implore his assistance in the performance, but also to hope for his blessing in the perusal of it.

These considerations I have endeavoured fairly to examine; and though I do not say that I am perfectly satisfied as to the conclusion, yet there is nothing in it that, upon the whole, constrains me to decline attempting the engagement you urge upon me. Yet I fear I shall find the execution no easy enterprise. Some difficulty will be found in the selection. When a man looks back upon a life of seventy-four years, he sees a very extensive field; and what he is to detach for the notice of others asks for the exercise of judgment and prudence. Much *may* be, and much *ought* to be, passed over. Some love to eke out pages and volumes; but a brief account will generally comprise all that ordinary biography requires.

Two things should not be forgotten in the choice of articles. 1st, The influence they are likely to have on the reader, in a way of innocent gratification, instruction, or improvement. And, 2ndly, Their appropriateness to the character of the individual.

The insertions, therefore, should serve directly or indirectly to develop *him*—for it is of *him*—of *his* condition—of *his* changes—of *his* opinions, attachments, and doings, the reader wants to be informed.

But besides the selection of materials themselves, there

must be some arrangement; and this also has occasioned thought; for here various modes have been employed, with perhaps equal propriety and success. *You* have neither recommended, nor suggested, any particular method. I shall therefore throw my narrative and reflections into a series of Letters to yourselves. In this I shall conform to the example of my honoured tutor, Cornelius Winter, in the Life of him which I have published, and which has met with so much success. This mode will best suit a man of years and engagements, as it will allow of freedom in the expression, enlargement or contraction in the statements, and easy gradualness (not much affected by breaks and pauses) in the progress. The number of Letters the series will contain, must depend on the uncertainties of circumstances. But whether I shall live and be able to accomplish the design wholly or partially, rests with *Him* " in whose hand our breath is, and whose are all our ways." " But this will we do if God permit."

N.B. I had no sooner written the above than I was favoured with a call from my esteemed brother, the Rev. John Angell James, of Birmingham. Upon being informed of my purpose, he not only very much approved of it, and zealously urged its execution, but begged that I would not limit myself, by aiming at too much conciseness ; especially as to any parts and circumstances that would bear usefully upon the rising ministry—that ministry for whose improvement and excellency he has shown much anxiety. Hence, some things which otherwise would not have been introduced, must plead this excitement and sanction.

LETTER II.

MY DEAR CHILDREN,—In commencing this Letter I have one advantage which saves me time and trouble. I have not to trace a long and proud lineage. If any great and illustrious individuals have been found among my ancestors, they have not been ascertained in my family, in my own time.* But were I mean enough to feel any mortification here, I could not console myself. Lord Bacon has remarked that they who derive their worth from their ancestors resemble "potatoes, the most valuable part of which is under ground." When one of Lord Thurlow's friends was endeavouring to make out that he was descended from *Thurloe*, Cromwell's

---

* Through the courtesy of the Rev. J. Ward, Rector of Wath, near Ripon, we have been favoured with a considerable list of persons of the name of Jay, baptized, married, and buried at Milton Lislebon, in Wilts. There is one marriage that may have been that of Mr. Jay's father and mother: "1751, May 13, William Jay and Sarah Smith;" but we have no means of deciding the question. Mr. Jay has said very little of his parents. A Rev. Charles Jay was vicar of that parish in the year 1733, and died there 1761.

Mr. Waylen, of Etchilhampton, has also furnished many notices of the family of Jay in Wiltshire, extending back for nearly three centuries; but from which of them Mr. Jay of Bath descended, or whether from any of them, all authorities are silent, and probably William Jay was as ignorant as ourselves.

Secretary, who was a Suffolk man,—"Sir," said he, "there were two *Thurlows* in that part of the country, who flourished about the same time; *Thurloe* the Secretary, and *Thurlow* the Carrier:—I am descended from the last." We have read of a man who, in respect of his promotion, being asked concerning his pedigree, answered that "he was not particularly sure, but had been credibly informed that he had three brothers in the ark;"—but one of our most distinguished poets of obscure origin surpasses this in his epitaph:—

> " Princes and heralds, by your leave,
> Here lie the bones of Matthew Prior;
> The son of Adam and of Eve,—
> Can Nassau or Bourbon go higher?"

My parents were very respectable, that is, they were *poor* and *religious: religious*, not precisely according to the theory and discipline of a particular party (for as yet there was in the place no society formed on professedly evangelical principles, nor had the preaching of such doctrines as yet been heard there); but really and practically religious; exemplifying the morality of the gospel under the influence of piety, or the fear and love of God; *poor*, not abjectly and dependently, but able, by frugality and diligence, to support themselves, and to bring up a family in the decencies and even comforts of village life.

My father was the son of a small farmer, but he himself was a mechanic, working at the business of a stone-cutter and mason. There was nothing remarkable in him as to talent, nor in my dear mother. They were both persons of slender education, but of good solid understanding, and of much common sense; upright, conscientious, kind, tender, charitable according to their means; and much beloved and esteemed in all the neighbourhood. I was their fourth and only male child;* but there were four daughters, all of

* Mr. Jay was born May 6, 1769.

whom are " gone the way of all the earth." Three of them
married in humble life, but to husbands sober, industrious,
and much more affectionate and attentive to their wives
than many I have seen in superior conditions, and among
those who are often called (for what reason God only knows)
" *the better sort of people.*" The other, who had a considerable share of wit and cleverness, was united to a man
of property. She possessed more capacity and knowledge
than perhaps half the whole population of the place beside.

The presbyterian minister on whom we attended was a
Clarkean Arian, (but he never dealt much in doctrine,) a
very dry and dull preacher, but a lovely character, and exceedingly tender-hearted, kind, and generous; denying himself almost to a fault, that he might have, out of his contracted income, to give to him that needeth; and wherever
misery was, there was he. From my earliest remembrance,
he kindly and gently noticed me; and when I was able to
read, he presented me with the two first publications I ever
called my own. These were " Watts's History of the Old
and New Testament," and " Bunyan's Pilgrim's Progress,"
and never shall I forget my feelings at the receipt of them;
for books (what a change has since taken place!) were then
very scarce in villages; at least few came in my way. The
schooling of the village was of course very limited, and had
nothing to awaken or expand the mind beyond the common
elements of reading, writing, and vulgar arithmetic. In this
humble education I shared; but I can say nothing more:
to any literary or intellectual advantage or excitement I was
a stranger.

It is perhaps commonly supposed that if a man is destined
to make a little figure in the world, he gives some indication
of it in childhood and even in infancy. Is this always true?
or is it true generally? It is said the bull-calf and the he-
lamb begin to push and to butt before their horns appear.
But metaphors alone prove nothing. Our Saviour speaks

of some seeds, which fell on superficial soil, and forthwith they sprang up *because* they had no *deepness of earth* : but the larger and more solid and durable trees are slower in their growth than more common ones. Thus the oak is longer in its rearing and maturing than the poplar or osier. Does not *mind* both act and show itself according to particular periods, or rather occurrences, which seize and press and excite it ?

However this may be, to compare little things with greater, I know both from report and experience, that your father exhibited nothing like this early precociousness. I can well remember with what pains I acquired reading ; and my eldest sister observed, when questioned concerning my first years, "We thought he never would have learned." But when the difficulty by which I was depressed, and for which I was often reproached, was overcome, and I felt *encouragement* and praise, I soon made some progress, and soon wished to make more : but what opportunities or helps did my situation afford ? It may be asked if I remember whether, at an early season, I had any workings of mind not growing naturally out of my condition, but having a seeming reference to my subsequent rising in life ? I answer, I had, and not a few ; though it would not be easy to describe them.   But I always felt a strange love of withdrawing myself from my playmates and roving alone ; and, while pausing among the scenes of nature, of surrendering myself to musings which carried me away, and often left me lost, in doing or enjoying something indistinctly different from what I had ever actually witnessed. Our dwelling, which was my father's own property, consisting of a double tenement, too large for a cottage, had attached to it a proportionate garden and orchard. It was situated about an equal distance from Wardour Castle, the seat of Lord Arundel ; Pithouse, the seat of Mr. Bennet ; and Fonthill, then the splendid mansion of Mr. Beckford. The village in which it stood was wide and varied, and abounded with lovely and picturesque aspects—

" And the sweet interchange of hill and vale and wood and lawn."

It is impossible to express the intense pleasure I felt from a child, in the survey of the rural scenery, while standing on the brow of an eminence, or seated upon the upraised root of a branching tree, or walking through a waving field of corn, or gazing on a clear brook with fish and reeds and rushes. How vividly are some of those spots impressed upon my memory still; and how recoverable, at this distance of time, are some of the rude reflections so early associated with them!

Yet what probability was there that such a change as I have experienced would ever take place? No effort, no purpose of my own, or of my relatives, had the least concern in it. It resulted purely and entirely from the providence of God; and as it was not only so unlikely in itself, but so eventful, and such consequences hinged upon it, I will endeavour to state the case as it *was*, fairly and simply, without straining to magnify the remarkable into supernatural, or the extraordinary into miraculous. But this must be the subject of the next Letter. In the mean time,

I am, &c.

LETTER III.

MY DEAR CHILDREN,—Mr. Thomas Turner, the memoir
of whose eminently pious wife has been long before the
public, and a second edition of which was published by
Dr. Bogue, left Tisbury while young. He was then possessed of no substance; but he gradually succeeded in
business at Trowbridge, and gained more than a com-
petency. Being a truly religious man, he wished to do
something to evince his gratitude to God, and promote the
welfare of his fellow-men. He, therefore, determined to
introduce the preaching of the gospel into his native village,
and, if possible, to awaken attention to the one thing needful, in those he had left behind him in ignorance and carelessness. He took a house and licensed it, and opened it
for preaching. After some length of time, he built also a
neat chapel entirely at his own expense; and a very considerable congregation and church were raised there, which
have continued ever since; and recently a new, commodious
and beautiful chapel has been erected, which I had the
pleasure of opening, and at the dedication of which more
than £100 was collected, after more than £700 had been
subscribed among the people themselves.

Some persons love to talk of their being born again, and
of their being made new creatures, with a kind of physical
certainty and exactness; and refer to their conversion,—not

as the real commencement of a work which is to continue
increasing through life, but as something which may be
viewed as a distinct and unique experience, immediately produced, originated and finished at once; and perfectly deter-
minable, as to its time and place and mode of accomplishment; but I hope this is not necessary, for I have no such
narrative or register to afford.   A distinction is not always
made between depraved nature and actual transgression.
All are sinners, and all have come short of the glory of
God; but all are not profligate, nor in *this* sense do all
speak of themselves, as if they had been the chief of sinners.   Restraint from evil is a mercy, as well as sanctification and good works.   I cannot speak as some do of going
great lengths in iniquity, and thereby rendering a work of
grace more sure and more divine.   I bless God I was from
my childhood free from immoralities.   I remember, indeed,
one act of gross transgression (it pains me now in review);
it was the uttering of a known and repeated *falsehood*,
accompanied with an *oath*, to carry a point, as I was intensely at play.   For this my conscience so smote me that
I was soon constrained to withdraw from my companions,
and went home, and retired to implore forgiveness.   But,
though free from vice, I now began to see and feel
deficiencies with regard to duty, and to be dissatisfied with
the state of my heart towards God.   I also felt my need of
something more than was held forth by the preaching I
heard.   Without knowing the nature of this good, I was
just in the condition of mind that would welcome and
relish the truth commonly called evangelical.   Our minister, too, from some things which I had said (for he always
allowed and encouraged me to speak freely), strangely put
into my hands a letter, which, he said, had been written to
a father by a young man who had (these were his own
words) become a *Methodist*, and wished to *convert* him.
I had never heard the name before; but when, soon after,

persons of this description were reported to be coming to preach in the village, my curiosity was the more excited; and, from the instruction and impression of the letter (which was a very striking one), I longed to hear them, conceiving and hoping it would relieve my concern of mind.

The private dwelling which Mr. Turner had purchased and licensed was first used for worship on the Saturday evening. I attended. The singing, the extemporaneousness of the address, and the apparent affection and earnestness of the speaker, peculiarly affected me: and what he said of "the faithful saying, and worthy of all acceptation, that Jesus Christ came into the world to save sinners," was like rain upon the mown grass, or cold water to a thirsty soul. I scarcely slept that night for weeping, and for joy; and as the preaching was to be renewed the next morning at seven o'clock (not to interfere with the service of the Established Church), I happened to be the first that came. Mrs. Turner, who had come from Trowbridge to superintend things for the time, opened the door herself, and taking me by the hand, benignly asked, "Are you hungering for the bread of life?" She continued talking to me most winningly for some minutes, till others began to enter. But this seemingly casual and trifling circumstance was important in the result; for from that day forward she particularly noticed me; and, as I had been recently apprenticed, and was returning from my work, which was then at Fonthill House, in the evening, she often met me, and conversed with me till I reached home; and her information and addresses were more useful than many of the sermons I heard, as she adapted herself to the state she found I was in, and to the present kind of knowledge which I required.

[Reluctant as the Editors are to divert the reader's atten-

tion for a single moment from Mr. Jay's interesting narrative, they yet judge that this is the most suitable place for
introducing a few facts which they feel assured will add
interest to the narrative, and increase the gratification of
the reader.   The mention of Fonthill House a page or two
before, and of Mr. Beckford, its accomplished proprietor
and builder, is followed by the statement, that when the
lad William Jay was first noticed by Mrs. Turner, he was
not only working as an apprentice to his father, but both
father and son were actually working at the erection of
Fonthill House; and further, that it was on his return,
evening after evening, from that place, that Mrs. Turner met
him, and talked with him in that instructive way recorded
by himself in this letter.   We suppose William Jay to
have been then little more than fourteen years of age, and
but recently apprenticed to learn the art of stone-masonry.
It was just at this time that Mr. Winter came to preach at
Tisbury, and was struck with the comely countenance of
the lad.   About a year after, when Mr. W. came again to
preach at Tisbury on a week-day evening, there was William
Jay in the chapel, with his flannel-jacket and his white
leather-apron, just as he had left his work at Fonthill
Abbey, listening to the good Cornelius Winter.   After
that sermon he was introduced to Mr. W. for the first time,
and, no doubt, wondered what the minister could want with
him.   Let the reader realize this scene, and connect with it
the fact that he had been that day working at the mansion
of a gentleman who afterwards, most probably with an
utter unconsciousness that Mr. Jay had ever been in his
employment, passed upon him as just and elegant an eulogy
as perhaps ever was passed upon him; and frankly recorded
the fact that he had been himself a learner from the eloquent piety and wisdom of William Jay.   In proof of this
we present the following interesting statement, which ap-

peared in the Bath Herald immediately after Mr. Beckford's decease:

"*The Christian Contemplated* had been perused with much interest by Mr. Beckford, as appears from his numerous notes, written on its leaves; and from which the following is extracted: 'This man's mind is no petty reservoir supplied him by laborious pumpings—it is a clear, transparent spring, flowing so freely as to impress the idea of its being inexhaustible.   In many of these pages the stream of eloquence is so full, so rapid, that we are fairly borne down and laid prostrate at the feet of the preacher, whose arguments in these moments appear as if they could not be controverted, and we must yield to them.   The voice which calls us to look into ourselves, and prepare for judgment, is too piercing, too powerful to be resisted; and we attempt, for worldly and sensual considerations, to shut our ears in vain."

" Beckford told me that Jay of Bath, whom he had gone to hear *incog.*, was one of the finest preachers he had ever heard, and showed me his sermons; and, curiously enough, he had a correspondence with Jay about the bad poetry, both in the church and among the dissenters, as exhibited in the hymns and psalm versions which they used."—*Closing Scenes, Second Series.   By Rev. E. Neale.**

* We have received the following letter from a gentleman at Bath, whose intimate acquaintance both with Mr. Beckford and Mr. Jay entitles his communication to our entire confidence, and to insertion in the present edition of our work.   It places Mr. Beckford's character in a more pleasing light, especially during his latter days.   It corrects the mistake into which Mr. Neale, or his authority, fell respecting Mr. B. having heard Mr. Jay *incog.*, and having had some correspondence with him.

(TO THE EDITORS.)

GENTLEMEN,—Some particulars mentioned in the extracts inserted in your first edition of the Rev. W. Jay's Autobiography, respecting

It will not be deemed irrelevant by those readers who have no knowledge of Mr. Beckford, if we state a few facts

Mr. Beckford, from a work by the Rev. E. Neale, entitled the "Closing Scene," are so incorrect, that I have thought it desirable to put you in possession of some facts which have come under my own observation, and which will modify and correct the statements made by Mr. Neale and quoted by you.

During a period of nearly twenty years, I enjoyed the pleasure of constant and familiar intercourse with Mr. Beckford, and, being professionally employed as his architect, frequent were the opportunities afforded me of knowing his sentiments. I presume, therefore, on your kindness for the insertion of the following brief account.

In the many hours spent in conversation with that highly-talented individual, theological and religious subjects were frequently introduced. Mr. Beckford knew I was an admirer of Mr. Jay and a constant attendant upon his ministry. His texts, the treatment of his sermons, and their divisions, were sometimes alluded to; and being on one occasion at the Horticultural Exhibition at Sidney-gardens with Mr. B., Mr. Jay being there also, I pointed him out, and as Mr. B. was desirous of seeing him, we walked towards the place where he was standing, and I exchanged salutations; but there was no introduction: nor did Mr. B. at any subsequent period become acquainted with Mr. Jay: so that the statement of his corresponding with him, on hearing him preach, is wholly incorrect and unfounded.

On the publication of his "Recollections of Alcobaca," Mr. Beckford presented me with a copy, which I lent to Mr. Jay; and mentioning the circumstance to Mr. B., he inquired if he had been pleased with the perusal; on my answering in the affirmative, he withdrew to his chamber, and returned with a copy, inscribing, "*From the Author*," on its pages. "Take this," said he, "to the good and holy man; say all that is kind from me to him, and beg his acceptance of it." My commission was duly executed, Mr. Jay observing, I am indebted to you for this: and then addressing his son, said to him, "I will send him *my* book," meaning "The Christian Contemplated." I immediately responded, it would afford me much pleasure to be the bearer. He then wrote "*From the Author*," and forthwith it was conveyed by me to Mr. Beckford. I drew his attention to the preface, recommending the perusal as developing the character of the man. At my next visit, Mr. B. almost imme-

concerning him and the famous Abbey which William Jay and his father helped to build.

diately reterred to the book, saying, he had not only read the preface, but the work itself. The whole of his numerous notes he then read to me, among which was the memorable passage inserted in your work at p. 25. It was inserted by myself in the Bath papers, after Mr. Beckford's death. So pleased was Mr. Beckford with Mr. Jay's book that, on the next visit of his daughter, the Duchess of H——, to Bath, he informed me that he had placed the book in her hands. Some time prior to this he had read Dr. Dick's "Philosophy of a Future State," lent him by myself; and not many months previous to his death, he had been engaged in writing a poem, the subject of which was "The Temptation of our Saviour in the Wilderness." This he read to me in manuscript. The expression and tone of voice added much to it. The awful and dignified reply of our Saviour I never shall forget. In sublimity of conception it reminded me of Milton's Paradise Lost; and had I not known who had written it, might have supposed him the author. I much regret it has never been published.

Preceding his illness, he had commenced a perusal of "Strauss' Life of Christ," from which, at times, he read to me extracts, commenting on the blasphemous character of the work. Indeed, had his life been prolonged, the Duchess was anxious he should have published his strictures on that work. Mr. Beckford's religious belief was Orthodox; but he had been much disgusted by the sacred calling having become too professional, and characterized by a greater regard for the fleece than the flock. His observations were repeated on several occasions and in very strong terms.

Speaking of religious opinions he remarked, "If a man was a Trinitarian he could not be very far wrong;" and Socinianism he denounced, calling it a Christless Christianity, cold as the grave. His penetration into the thoughts of those he conversed with was extraordinary. He observed that he could read men's minds by their countenances. From my earliest acquaintance I have heard him speak severely on the vicious habits and follies of many of the aristocracy. His " *Liber Veritatis*," to which he often alluded, and which he intended should be published after his decease, was so cutting a sarcasm that it has been withheld from the eye of the public. One day he said that he had murdered Lord ——. I observed I could not comprehend his meaning. He repeated it. I asked an explanation. He replied—" Having in vain endeavoured

William Beckford, Esq., was the proprietor, designer, and builder of the splendid Fonthill Abbey, which cost in its

to get rid of the Fox-hunters in my neighbourhood, I ordered notices to be fixed in different parts of my estate at Fonthill, that, after a certain time, I should sink pits :"—which he accordingly did. "Lord —— fell with his horse into one of them; he broke his leg and died. I, therefore, murdered him."

On his Tower on Lansdown being robbed of some most rare articles, which from their antiquity could not be replaced, I naturally expected he would have been greatly disturbed; but, to my surprise, on meeting him there, he remarked, with inconceivable equanimity —that "they were only toys for our amusement for a short time." His memory was remarkably retentive. Any author being quoted, he would almost immediately refer to the part. Although eighty-four years of age, his eyesight was good to the last, reading without the assistance of glasses.

The last interview I had with him was on a Sunday, when he seemed much surprised to see me, as I had invariably refused meeting him on that day. He asked, on my entering, what brought me there. My reply was, to inquire after his health. We conversed for some time. He was calm and self-possessed, manifesting no anxiety as to the result of his illness, and apparently had not the least apprehension on his mind. The Duchess of H—— shortly after arrived; her physician from London, also, came down to see him, being the first time medical advice had been sought. The attentions rendered by the Duchess were most affectionate, devoted, and incessant. In conversation with her Grace, reference was made by her to his religious belief, as she had doubts that he was a Roman Catholic. I informed her to the contrary. As the prospect of recovery became very doubtful, the Duchess asked him to see a Roman Catholic priest, but to that proposal, as well as for the rector of the parish to visit him, Mr. B. objected. I suggested to her Grace that she should ask Dr. B. (who was then visiting him as a physican) to draw his attention to the near approach of death; which she did; —and he very kindly undertook to do so. Dr. B. informed me, that when speaking to him on our common depravity—that we had no merits of our own—but must all come as guilty sinners to a crucified Saviour, whose atonement alone was sufficient for a penitent, he listened with much calmness and attention, clasping his hands with evident approval and acquiescence. He died the following day.

Mr. Beckford's character underwent a great change after he came

erection £273,000, and the pictures, library, and furniture of which were valued at more than a million. He was the son of the famous Beckford, twice Lord Mayor of London, who reproved King George the Third on his throne, when he insulted a deputation of the citizens. Mr. Beckford, the son, who was placed, at his father's death, under the care of the first Earl of Chatham, became a most accomplished man and distinguished author. His gorgeous tale, entitled "Vathek," was written in French when he was barely twenty-two, at one sitting of *three days and two nights*. Byron said of it, that " even Rasselas must bow before it." He wrote also " Letters on Spain and Italy," " Observations on Celebrated Painters," &c. &c. He was universally

to reside at Bath. His paroxysms of passion, when first I knew him, were most fearful ; but, in his latter years, he had obtained a wonderful mastery over himself, and which was seldom broken through. He used to say he could not now afford it. The resources of his mind were vast. He said he never knew what *ennui* meant : being always occupied, he was not its subject. Persons in distress were very frequently relieved by him, but he never would allow any one to know it, or permit his name to appear as a donor or subscriber. I have been the bearer of a handsome subscription to a neighbouring church, and for charitable and other purposes.

He directed by his will that his body should be embalmed and deposited in a solid granite tomb, previously erected in his garden, on Lansdown, but the inscription, said in your extracts to have been chosen by himself from " Vathek,' was selected by his executor ; and that on the other side from verses written by himself, I suggested, being subsequently approved by the Duchess.

I cannot forbear, in conclusion, introducing two very striking aphorisms of Mr. Jay, not noticed in your work ; and being so peculiarly characteristic of him should have a place in it.

Faith he described as " Conviction in motion and action ;" *Despair*, as "locking the door of heaven, and throwing the key into the bottomless pit."

I remain, Gentlemen,
Yours most truly,
H. E. GOODRIDGE.

Bath, Nov. 17, 1854.

esteemed a man of exquisite taste and of keen discernment. His splendid fortune was spent in the gratification of his taste for the fine arts and literature. Over his mantel-piece, in his dining-parlour, was a picture of St. Catherine, by Raffaelle, which cost him £3000. One who knew him well says, "I had many conversations with him upon the subject of religion; for he was rather fond of controversy. I should say that he was an orthodox Catholic; but, like many, professed a faith he did not practise."

He was famous for a most sumptuous entertainment which he gave to Admiral Lord Nelson. But though he was accounted in his day the richest commoner in England, yet he sustained, long before his death, immense losses of property, and the Abbey was sold to Mr. Farquhar for £330,000. The sale of its contents created an excitement throughout the nation, and during its continuance of thirty-three days, such was the influx of visitors, that not a lodging was to be had for many miles round. It is recorded that between seven and eight thousand catalogues were sold at a guinea each.

After this calamity Mr. Beckford retired to Bath, where he ended his days at very nearly the same age as Mr. Jay, and where that mutual recognition took place, in the interchange of their respective publications, which has been recorded in the letter of Mr. Goodridge, and which, in some particulars, corrects the statement given by Mr. Neale in his "Closing Scenes."

Of Mr. Beckford, his friends have recorded that he battled manfully at first with his malady. When he saw that the struggle was vain, not before, and that life was rapidly ebbing, he wrote to his affectionate daughter* in town his last laconic note: "Come,—quick, quick,"—and expired a day or two after the arrival of the duchess.

"He spoke to no one about his belief or his hope. In-

* The Duchess of Hamilton.

deed, he was one of those whose thoughts would have communed only with God at such a crisis. He used to say,
What are forms ? The heart is everything A clergyman
came. He thanked him for the offer of his services ; but he
could do no more : it was his last effort." This was the
testimony of one of his friends. Mr. Neale says : " From
another source I learned that in his parting hour, the truly
estimable rector of his parish attended at Lansdown (the
name of his mansion). He assembled Mr. Beckford's whole
establishment for prayer, in the room adjoining that in
which the dying man lay. . . . . . Mr. Beckford
himself made no confession of faith. . . . .
His was a silent death-bed as to the mighty future.

"Beckford was a very proud man, of violent passions.   .
. . . . He adopted a certain line of policy towards his
fellows ; and his haughty spirit bravely supported him. He
said just after Lord Byron's death : ' So Byron is gone ! He
cared about the world, affected not to care, defied it, and was
unsuccessful. I have defied it and succeeded. I have resources if I should live centuries !'   . . . .

" He directed by his will* that his body should be embalmed, placed in a chest, and deposited in a tomb, erected
in that part of his garden adjoining Lansdown Tower ; that
on his mausoleum should appear the following inscription :
on one side,—' William Beckford, Esq., late of Fonthill,
Wilts, died 2nd May, 1844, aged 84,' with this quotation
from ' Vathek ' :—

" ' Enjoying humbly the most precious gift of Heaven to man—hope ! '

" On the other side the same obituary, followed by these
lines, from a prayer written by himself :—

" ' Eternal Power !
Grant me through obvious clouds one transient gleam
Of thy bright essence on my dying hour ! '

* Mr. Goodridge says that the *inscription* was not chosen by
himself, but by his executor.

"Was this gifted and wealthy man a faithful steward?
What did he for his kind? *Mighty trusts were confided to
him!* Blest with ample means, highly cultivated intellect,
and unusual length of days, what permanent blessings did
he confer on his fellows? . . . . What hospital did he
build? What asylum endow? What school did he originate? What sanctuary did he raise for the worship of the
Most High? What cloud of heathen error did he seek to
dissipate? What memorial has he left behind him to cheer
and gladden, during life's weary pilgrimage, the aged, the
sorrow-stricken, the suffering, the desolate, or the bereaved?
What charity did he munificently support during life, or
place beyond the reach of failure by his testamentary dispositions at death? What widows' grateful tears or orphans'
murmured blessings will the casual mention of his name
arouse? Was his a mere religion of the imagination; and
his reverence for sacred subjects bounded by his admiration
of 'The Madonna,' 'The Infant Saviour,' 'The Salvator
Mundi,' when placed on the canvas by the limner's art?"
—*Closing Scenes*, &c.

Between William Beckford and William Jay how wide is
the difference! What a contrast in their outward fortunes
and original conditions! What a contrast in their characters,
their achievements, their services to mankind, and the memoirs that now survive them! And, above all, how affect-
ingly contrasted were the closing scenes of their two lives,
—both in the city of Bath!

Mr. Beckford's own verses, a part of which were inscribed
on his splendid monument, though they display and perpetuate the exalted genius and exquisite taste of their author,
yet afford no trace of Christian hope or peace. He calls
them a prayer:

" Like the soft murmur of the secret stream,
    Which through dark alders winds its shaded way,
    My suppliant voice is heard :—Ah, do not deem
    That on vain toys I throw my hours away.

" In the recesses of the forest vale,
  On the wild mountain, on the verdant sod,
  When the fresh breezes of the morn prevail,
  I wander lonely, communing with God.

" When the faint sickness of a wounded heart
  Creeps in cold shudderings through my shaking frame,
  I turn to Thee,—that holy peace impart
  Which soothes the invokers of thy awful Name.

" O All-pervading Spirit—Sacred Beam !
  Parent of Life and Light !—Eternal Power !
  Grant me through obvious clouds one transient gleam
  Of thy bright essence on my dying hour."

Let our readers compare these lines, which no doubt
expressed the last solemn, but yet gloomy, feelings of their
author, with the account of Mr. Jay's last hours, which will
appear in its proper place in these pages ; and then let him
say which was the happier man while they both lived, and
which is now the most honoured and the most illustrious,
after the long career which they both enjoyed; the one in
the full blaze of worldly splendour, or in luxurious seclusion
from it, gratifying and improving his intellectual powers
with everything refined, except *the one thing needful;* but
the other, from the day that he left off working at Fonthill
Abbey, till the day of his death, in the full hope of eternal
life through the grace of our Lord Jesus Christ, devoting all
his energies to the service of God and man, and deriving all
his pleasures from doing the work which his Heavenly
Father gave him to do.]

Mr. Jay's narrative thus proceeds :—
And here occurred, what is mentioned without a name, in
the life of Mrs. Turner, concerning "a lad who, after hearing
a discourse enforcing family worship, besought his father
upon his return home to undertake it; and upon his refusing, on the ground of inability, offered to perform it
himself. The offer was accepted with tears, and he became

a kind of domestic chaplain." This lad was the writer. A little while after this, he was urged to pray at the private meeting in the chapel, which he did with no little backwardness, and also with no little difficulty. Connected with this, he cannot but mention a circumstance, as it affected him at the time with a shock of amazement, and has since aided him in not laying an improper stress on the figurative language of Scripture; and made him careful to avoid such views of the doctrines of grace as should exclude *any* from hope of salvation. It was this :—He had prayed that our names *may* be written in the Lamb's *book* of life; but a high-toned brother, from a neighbouring congregation, *who saw things clearly*, took him aside, and rebuked him for the impropriety of his expression, saying, "You know that book was filled up from eternity; and if our names *are* not written there, they never can be now."

Bless God, my children, that from your infancy you have been familiar with a testimony too plain to be mistaken. "The Spirit and the bride say, Come; and let him that heareth say, Come; and let him that is athirst come; and whosoever will, let him take of the water of life freely."

I shall soon resume the relation, and notice another link in the chain of occurrences which drew me from my native condition to set my feet in a large place.

I am, &c.

LETTER IV.

MY DEAR CHILDREN,—For several years there was no
fixed minister at Tisbury, but the service was supplied by
preachers of various denominations, each officiating for one
sabbath only, but always coming early enough to preach also
on the Saturday evening; and these men, after perhaps a
long and trying journey, had not only to preach on that
evening, but they had the following day to preach at seven
in the morning, and at six in the evening, and also to go in
the afternoon five miles to preach at a place called Ebs-
bourne; yet had they nothing to remunerate their toilsome
but willing efforts. Among these supplies came the excellent Cornelius Winter from Marlborough, a distance of near
forty miles. A year after the first time, he came a second;
and calling on Mrs. Turner at Trowbridge on his way, he
told her that when at Tisbury before, he had been particularly struck with the aspect of a lad in the congregation; that
the impression had not worn off; and that he felt a strong
desire to have an interview with him before he should
return. Not knowing however his name, he could not
inform her who was the youth he intended. She immediately said there was a lad in the place she also much
wished him to see and converse with, mentioning my name,
that he might inquire for me. Accordingly on the Saturday evening he desired the doorkeeper to ask for

Billy Jay to come to him in the parlour after the service.
Again, while in the pulpit he was equally attracted by the
appearance of *the* lad who had so impressed him before; and
was eager to know who he was, and to have some talk with
him.   When the preaching was over, as desired, I followed
him into the house, and was presented to him.   I was in my
simple village dress, with my apron drawn around me.   He
then perceived that the youth Mrs. Turner had mentioned,
and the youth he had remarked, were the *same*.   He was
affected even to tears, and immediately kneeled down and
prayed.   I was of course amazed at the strangeness of all
this; nor could I for one moment conjecture the design.
He then began to talk with me, and in a manner which
disarmed me of fear, concerning several things, and especially
of my religious views and feelings.   At this interview he
proceeded no further, but desired me to come to him again
after the service on the morrow evening.   I again waited
upon him; he again immediately prayed for a few moments;
and then began to inquire whether I should not like, and
did not long, to communicate to others what I felt myself.
He observed that he had a small academy of young men for
the ministry; and kindly invited me to join them, if after
reflection and prayer my heart should be inclined, and my
parents should be disposed to give their consent.   The
invitation was after some time accepted; and I went to
Marlborough, where for some years (they were far too few)
I was privileged to live under the tuition and care of that
incomparable man (Bishop Jebb calls him in a Letter, *that
celestial creature Cornelius Winter*), whose life I have published; written indeed under a grateful sense of my obligations to him; but yet with no exaggerated praise, as all
who knew him intimately have acknowledged.

[The Editors conceive that the following document will
appear so interesting, as the only existing relic of William

Jay the pious youth, just invited to enter the Marlborough Academy, that, though it shows rather painfully the defects of his village education, yet by the contrast it affords with the productions of the same pen only three years after, it will strikingly illustrate his rapid improvement, and afford pleasure by showing the reader, first the jewel in its rough state, just being drawn out of the mine, and emitting a gleam of that lustre which it shed after it came from the hands of that skilful workman his tutor.   This document is the only one that remains of all his letters to Mr. Winter, so far as we are aware ; and it is very remarkable that it should be both the first and, in a literary sense, the worst of his letters.   The autograph is before us, and we give it *verbatim et literatim*, that our readers may form a little acquaintance at this point with William Jay, the stonemason, before he went to Mr. Winter's Academy, or had doffed his leather apron and quitted the lowly home of his boyhood.   The letter was preserved by an old and valued servant of Mr. Winter's, and it fully verifies all Mr. Jay says of himself.

To Mr. Winter, Marlborough.
                    Tisbury, January 30th 1785.

DUTIFULL FREIND,—this comes with my kind love to you hoping It will find you in good health as it Left me and all my friend at tisbury thanks be to god for his mercy and Goodness in preserving us to this present moment in health and strength, health is the hony that Sweetens every temporal mercy to be well in body is a great blessing but to be well in Soul is a much greater Blessing than this what is the body when compar,d with the Soul it is no more than the Candles Slender Light to the great illuminary the Sun in its meridian Splender and beauty.

I received your Letter and was very thankfull for your kindness to me in it. You Desired to hear from me by Mr. Serman's return and if I could write you something of

my Christen Exprience.   my experience is that I Desire to
Love the Lord above all and Desire to live more to his Glory
and honour.   I hope I can Say that he is the Cheiftest to
my Soul of ten thousand and altogether Lovly I Desire to
know nothing but Jesus and Desire to be found in him not
having on my own Righteousness which is pulluted with sin
and impure but the Righteousness which is of god which is
for all and upon all that Believe in him.   my father says he
will find me in cloths as much as he is able I can come at
any time when you think proper So I conclude with my
father and mother's Love to you I am your humble servant
WILLIAM JAY.]

In what I have stated I cannot be mistaken; and there
are some still living (there were once many) to whom Mr.
Winter related the transaction; for he was pleased to advert
to it, especially after the encouraging success of his undertaking.   Various things at first seemed unpromising and
discouraging; my deficiencies were great.   Mr. Winter had
no certain provision for my support, his own income was
very limited.   He had, therefore, largely to draw upon the
providence of God; and he was enabled to trust without
fear or doubting.   But he always affirmed that at the time
he hardly knew how to justify the step he took, but from
impression and impulse he could not decline it.

I leave the fact, having stated it accurately, to the candid
judgment of my readers.   The command is, " Let thine eyes
look straight *on*, and let thine eyelids look *straight before
thee*."   " Ponder the path of thy feet, and let all thy goings
be *established*."   And it is well for a man to feel the firmness
of the ground he treads upon; and be able to give, to himself at least, a reason of his conduct in any measure of
moment.   And in general, no one laid more stress on prudence, and did more honour to the use of proper means,
than the man of God before us.   Yet he always had this

sentiment, (and I have often heard him avow it,) that there may be cases in which Providence, having a particular end in view, will not, by some excitement or other, *allow us* to give up, or pass by the thing, though for the present we walk by faith rather than by sight.

Must we *always* condemn such faith as presumption ? Is it enthusiasm to suppose, that there may be cases in which the secret of the Lord is peculiarly with them that fear him, and fear him above many ? Is there any rule that admits of no exception ? Might not that which looks like a deviation from a principle, be found to be compatible with it, if we had knowledge to penetrate further, and to comprehend more ? Let us not judge one another. " Happy is he that condemneth not himself in that thing which he alloweth." " Let every one be fully persuaded in his own mind."

It will naturally be supposed that no one could have gone to an academy more destitute of many advantages than myself. But I had a thirst for knowledge, and a valuation of it, which would ensure *application* when opportunities and means were afforded. Mr. Winter's library was not large, but it was large to me; and every moment I could spare from my studies I was searching it as for hidden treasure. It may seem strange, but the authors I was most struck with then, have continued to be my favourites ever since, and my views and tastes with regard to sermons and preachers have not otherwise changed than as they have been enlarged and improved.

As our tutor rated learning very high, I was obliged to fag hard. At first, the difficulties were not only trying, but seemed insuperable ; but in a little time I felt encouraged, and soon found pleasure in even the languages. But my progress was not considerable; and the literary acquisitions of the students were not a little impeded by what the tutor deemed justifiable. The state of the country then was very different from what it now is, as to an evangelical ministry.

The real labourers were few. The spiritual condition of
many of the villages was deplorable, and the people were
perishing for lack of knowledge. No one cared for their
souls. So it was with the vicinages all around Marlborough;
and their spiritual wants, if not their wishes, cried aloud,
" Come over and help us." Mr. Winter, therefore, obtained
and licensed various private houses to preach in, and not
only went as often as he was able himself, but also sent his
young men to instruct these poor creatures, and show unto
them the way of life. In the milder seasons which would
allow of it, we often addressed large numbers out of doors;
and many a clear and calm evening I have preached down
the day, on the corner of a common, or upon the green turf
before the cottage door.

These neighbourhoods were supplied sometimes weekly
and sometimes fortnightly, both on the week days and on the
sabbaths. We always on the sabbaths avoided, if possible,
the church hours; and on week days we commonly omitted
the services during the hay and corn harvests, that we might
not give reasonable offence to the farmers, or entice the
peasants away from their labour before their usual time.
I would also remark, that we did not always in these efforts
encounter much opposition; indeed, I remember only a few
instances in which *we* suffered persecution from violence or
rudeness. This was much owing to the students being
always recommended to avoid needless provocation. Our
tutor enjoined us never to rail at others, or to *say* the gospel
was not heard there till *we* came; but leaving the hearers
to learn this of themselves by comparison; and also to speak
the truth in love; being always affectionate and kind, and
endeavouring by our manner to show that we loved those we
addressed, and were only concerned for their welfare—not
anxious to make proselytes but converts. Yet Mr. Winter's
horse was cruelly cropped and maimed at Ablington, where
he had preached on the sabbath. And there were places,

and not a few out of *our* own circuits, where, though there was little or nothing exceptionable in the preaching, the carnal mind showed itself not only in secret malignity, but in open outrage. The excitement of the ignorant populace was commonly produced by the clergyman, the squire, and some of the stupid and intemperate farmers.

The injuries inflicted on the preachers, and the houses in which the people assembled, might have been sooner terminated had the sufferers (as they ought to have done) more readily availed themselves of their legal rights; but they often yielded to unwilling concessions and apologies; and were backward to prosecute, forgetting that the trespasser was a burglar; and that though we are to forgive private and personal offences, it is otherwise with the violation of the laws of the land, established for the public safety and welfare. The best regard we can pay to a law is to obey its precepts ourselves—the next is to see its penalty executed upon transgressors. But in general, the village peasantry (and of them only I am now speaking) were disposed, *if left to themselves,* to receive and hear us; and it was truly interesting and delightful to see how, after a little curious observation and surprise, they seemed to drink in the word, as rain on the mown grass, and as showers that water the earth. The testimony to the Messiah was, " the poor have the gospel preached unto them; " and what right-minded and right-hearted man is there, but would rejoice that those who had so little of this world's goods and comforts should be able to realize " the unsearchable riches of Christ," and " walk in the comforts of the Holy Ghost ? "

I am, &c.

LETTER V.

My dear Children,—Great attainments and qualifications were not necessary in those rude villages where we made our first attempts to minister. But we knew enough from scripture and our own experience to " shew unto men the way of salvation; " and to say, "Behold the Lamb of God that taketh away the sin of the world."

This early preaching unquestionably broke in much upon our studies : but the tutor did everything in his power, by rule and restriction, to lessen the injury, while there were some rather compensatory advantages arising from it. *First*, Hereby good was done in the conversion of sinners in many instances, some of which were very striking ; and what is the gain of the whole world to the value of one soul ? And, *secondly*, The usage tended, by its exercise, and by the preparation for it, to keep the minds of the students in the things of God; and it is well known, that literary application, and the free mingling of young men together, do not much befriend spirituality of mind. *Thirdly*, It was of great advantage to the young pupil to begin, before he knew too much, to feel certain difficulties, and to gain confidence and facility by practice. And thus, though the scholar was injured, the preacher was benefited.

In the review of the case, I cannot see how a man of God, (whatever his zeal for learning might be,) circumstanced as Mr. Winter was, could have conscientiously acted otherwise than he did; and much as I have always lamented, in addition to my original want of education, the loss of some literary advantages, I not only submit to what appears to have been the will of God, but upon the whole am even thankful for such a course of things as I passed through. God has not only a right to choose for us, but as he appoints us our stations and offices, and foresees all they will require, he arranges our trainings, and renders all our previous circumstances and experience preparatory to our fitness.

> " Thy method cross'd my way, and young desire,
> Which did to academic eminence aspire.
> Fain I'd have sat in such a nurse's lap
> Where I might long have had a sluggard's nap,
> Or have been dandled on her reverend knees,
> And known by honoured titles and degrees;
> And there have spent the flower of my days
> In soaring in the air of human praise.
> *   *   *   *   *
> My youthful pride and folly now I see,
> That grudged for want of title and degree."

Some may be surprised at the *earliness* of my preaching; for I began a few months after I was placed at Marlborough. Some, also, will doubtless censure it, and it is easy for them to say much in support of their censure. Yet I cannot in this case blame myself. It was not from my own forwardness, or of my own choosing; but I was under the authority and direction of another, and bound to obey, even if I could not entirely acquiesce. How sad is a spirit of resistance, especially in students for the ministry! They are best prepared to rule and govern who have previously learned to obey and serve. Why do not tutors expel for insubordination, as well as for error or vice?

I remember a circumstance hardly worth relating. Soon after I had begun my early career, I went to supply for a sabbath at Melksham. At this time was residing there an old gentleman from London, a very wise man, at least in his own conceit. I called upon him on the Monday morning. He received me rather uncourteously. He did not, indeed, censure my preaching, but rudely said, he had no notion of *beardless* boys being employed as preachers. " Pray, sir," said I, " does not Paul say to Timothy, ' Let no man despise thy youth ? ' And, sir, you remind me of what I have read of a French monarch, who had received a young ambassador, and, complaining, said, ' Your master should not have sent me a beardless stripling.' ' Sir,' said the youthful ambassa- dor, ' had my master supposed you wanted a beard, he would have sent you a goat.' "

The first sermon I preached was at Ablington—a village near Stonehenge. The text was 1 Peter ii. 3 : "If so be ye have tasted that the Lord is gracious." The division was, 1. The Lord is gracious. 2. The best way to know this grace is by tasting it. 3. Such knowledge will have an in- fluence over the possessor; for *if* we have tasted that the Lord is gracious it will induce us to love him—it will draw out our desires after more—it will make us anxious to bring others to partake with us, saying, " That which we have seen and heard declare we unto you, that ye also may have fellowship with us." " O taste and see that the Lord is good, blessed is the man that trusteth in him."

I was little more than sixteen when I began; and from this period I was called to preach with no little frequency; and before I was of age, I had preached, I believe, near a thousand sermons ; * for in all our places, then, we always

* The Christian Observer, for June, 1855, contains a Review of the Autobiography which is at once so candid and kind towards Mr. Jay, that we feel disposed to thank the writer for the truly Christian spirit which characterises the article, and especially to offer a few explana-

preached three times on the Sabbath, with some week-day services.

While I was at Marlborough, and after I had begun preaching, with considerable acceptance and success, it was inquired by some of those who had contributed to my educational support, and who were themselves moderate Episcopalians, whether it should be proposed to me to go to the University, and enter the church; but Sir Richard Hill and John Thornton the philanthropist* decided against it, saying,

tory words in reference to the strictures he has passed, not improperly, upon the forcing system of education under which Mr. Jay was introduced to the ministry; as if that were the approved and usual system pursued by the Dissenting churches. The fact is, the system followed at the Marlborough Academy was not the system patronized by dissenters generally, but by some few zealous and good men, both churchmen and dissenters, who wished to supply with all speed the thirst for evangelical preaching that was then felt through the country, and that had been awakened by the preaching of Whitfield and Wesley: and to take this Academy as a specimen of what was then, or is now, the average of Dissenting Educational Institutions, would be to fall into a great mistake. The education afforded in the dissenting colleges at the time when young Jay was at Marlborough is not to be estimated by this particular case, which was an exception; and that enjoyed at the present day by candidates for the ministry among dissenters is not inferior to that enjoyed in any of the institutions of our country.

* Had Mr. Jay personally known Mr. Thornton, he would no doubt have given us a sketch of that eminent philanthropist. In an article furnished by Sir James Stephen to the Edinburgh Review for July, 1844, and entitled "The Clapham Sect," is the following allusion to the subject of this note:—"John Thornton was a merchant renowned in his generation for a munificence more than princely, and consecrated to the reverence of posterity by the letters and poetry o Cowper. He was one of those rare men in whom the desire to relieve distress assumes the form of a master passion; and if faith be due to tradition, he indulged it with a disdain, alternately ludicrous and sublime, of the good advice which the eccentric have to undergo from the judicious. Conscious of no aims but such as may invite the scrutiny of God and man, he pursued them after his own fearless

" God has opened the young man's mouth, and for years to come we dare not shut it, while there are so many immediate and pressing calls for exertion." But for this I have reason

fashion, yielding to every honest impulse, relishing a frolic when it fell in his way, choosing his associates in scorn of mere worldly precepts, and worshipping with any fellow Christian whose heart beat in unison with his own, however inharmonious might be some of the Articles of their respective creeds."

Mr. Thornton was an Episcopalian, and an intimate friend of the Rev. John Newton, of St. Mary Woolnoth. His benevolence was as unsectarian as his general habits, and "he stood ready," said Mr. Cecil, "to assist a beneficent design in every party, but would be the creature of none." Hence, in conjunction with Mr. Newton, and some excellent men among the Dissenters, he was mainly instrumental in establishing, and for a while supporting, a Dissenting Academy at Newport Pagnell, which was placed under the tuition of the Rev. William Bull, whose son the Rev. T. P. Bull, and grandson the Rev. Josiah Bull, continued till its recent extinction to conduct its studies ; and who exhibited the very rare occurrence of men of three generations being pastors of the same church, and tutors in the same college. Mr. Thornton, as intimated above, extended his patronage and pecuniary assistance to the institution at Marlborough, under the direction of the Rev. Cornelius Winter, and thus was brought into connexion with Mr. Jay, towards whose support he contributed while passing through his academic course.

Mr. Thornton spent myriads of pounds in the purchase of livings for Evangelical preachers ; in the erection and enlargement of places of worship, both in the Church of England and among Dissenters ; in sending out Bibles and religious books by his ships to various parts of the world; and in numerous other ways. Nor was his beneficence confined exclusively to religious objects. " Mr. Newton," says Mr. Bull, in a letter I lately received from him, " told my father, that while he (Mr. N.) was at Olney, he had received from Mr. Thornton more than £2000 for the poor of that place. He not only," continues Mr. Bull, "gave largely, but he gave wisely. He kept a regular account (not for ostentation or the gratification of vanity, but for method) of every pound he gave, in a large ledger, which he once showed me. I was then a boy, and I remarked on every page was an appropriate text. With him, his givings were made a matter of business, as Cowper says in an Elegy he wrote upon him—

to believe Mr. Winter would have had *then* no objection to the proposal. As it was not made to myself, I was neither required to consent nor refuse; though, had I been, the latter I am persuaded would have been the result. My views upon some subjects have always been *firm*, though *moderate*,—allowing me to distinguish between preference and exclusion, and leaving every one to follow his own conviction.*

One of the advantages of a smaller academy like that at Marlborough was its assuming a kind of domestic character, and associating us more with the tutor himself. A freer and more intimate access to the tutor is sadly wanting in some, yea, I fear, in all our public institutions. It is not enough for the student to hear his tutor regularly and formally lecture. There are things of great importance, especially to his experience, and conduct, and character, some of which are too delicate, and many of which are too minute, to be here brought forward. These can only be supplied properly by personal intercourse and converse. In

> " Thou hadst an industry in doing good,
>   Restless as his who toils and sweats for food."

Such was the man to whom Mr. Jay stood indebted in part for his support during the term of his education. The good Churchman, and the eminent Nonconformist, have met in that world where these designations have no place ; and does the one regret that he lifted his hand above the ecclesiastical barriers to extend his beneficence to him that stood on the other side of it ? Or does that other blush to recollect that he stood indebted to the Churchman for his love and liberality ?—Such mention as this is due to Mr. Thornton in the present volume.

* Referring to this subject many years after in a letter, he says,—
" Our preaching is too commonly of a cast I am sorry to say not the most calculated to do good. The mathematics and classics are good in their places ; but unless men have something else, they will never make ministers of the New Testament. How thankful I am that I did not, when a student, (as some of my Episcopalian sup-

this respect (oh that I had profited more by it!) I had a
peculiar privilege; for, as I was so young, Mr. Winter felt
a more parental relation towards me ; and, besides the freedom we all had in the family, he never walked out in the
morning or evening but I was always by his side.   I frequently also accompanied him when he took an excursion
for a few days from home.   With what gratitude do I look
back to these hours, and thank God for my distinguished
intimacy with such a celestial spirit, and how often has it
led me to exclaim—

> " When one that holds communion with the skies,
> Has filled his urn where those pure waters rise,
> And once more mingles with us meaner things,
> 'Tis even as if an angel shook his wings :
> Immortal fragrance fills the circuit wide,
> That tells us whence his treasures are supplied."

I am, &c.

[As an appendix to this letter, we should have been happy
to supply notices of some of those who were in the Marlborough Academy along with Mr. Jay.   But his allusions to
them are neither clear nor numerous.   We are not informed
how many students at a time were under Mr. Winter's care.
Several of those who were there during Mr. Jay's term, or
afterwards, became ministers of great excellence ; and one
at least of the number attained a degree of popularity and
usefulness only inferior to that of Mr. Jay.   We refer to
the late excellent Mr. Griffin, of Portsea, of whom a separate
Memoir was published some years since.   The following
List of Students in Mr. Winter's academy is most probably
incomplete ; but it is the best we can furnish :—

porters recommended,) leave Mr. Winter's to go to Oxford, where I
must have been five or six years before I could be ordained; when
during that time I was preaching the gospel to thousands, and saving
souls."   Bath, July 14, 1846.

Rev. W. Jay . . . . . Bath.
  ,, Mr. Surman . . . Chesham, Bucks.
  ,, ,, Yockney . . . Staines, Middlesex.
  ,, ,, Wood . . . . Died while a Student.
  ,, ,, Hogg . . . . Entered the Church.
  ,, ,, Cliff . . . . . Frome.
  ,, ,, Sloper . . . . Plymouth.
  ,, ,, Golding . . . Fulwood.
  ,, ,, Griffin . . . . Portsea.
  ,, ,, Underhill . . .
  ,, ,, Richardson . . Frampton.
  ,, ,, Daniel . . . . Kingswood.
  ,, ,, Lane . . . . Wells.
  ,, ,, Higgs . . . .

Mr. Jay remained in the Academy from the early part of 1785 till Midsummer, 1788, in the autumn of which year he settled at Christian Malford.

LETTER VI.

MY DEAR CHILDREN,—I hardly know how it was that I
succeeded in preaching from time to time in such a degree
as I did. But I could not be ignorant of the acceptance I
met with, and the numbers who followed me; nor did my
too fond and partial tutor keep from me so often as he
should have done, the applications he had for "the boy
preacher." I am convinced my motives at this time were
right; for gain and fame seemed perfectly out of the question. This simplicity of intention much helped me in
studying and speaking; for it is only as the eye is single
that the whole body is full of light.

After having for some time been confined to village efforts,
I was *elevated* to preach occasionally in some of the respectable congregations, both in the neighbouring and remoter
towns. Here also I found favour; and from report and
observation I began to think I possessed something *more*
than I had formerly been aware of; and I supposed (I trust
I may say this without arrogance) what it was, and that it
might be improved; and that it would be my wisdom to
adhere *chiefly* to it. I knew some attainments were not in
my power; and that few individuals ever had talent enough

to excel in *many*, or even in *several* things. A remark had struck me in reading Johnson's Life of Watts, in which he says, "The reason why the ancients surpassed the moderns was their greater modesty. They had a juster conception of the limitation of human powers; and, despairing of universal eminence, they confined their application to one thing, instead of expanding it over a wider surface."

I cannot deny that even at this time I felt enough to excite and encourage a moderate hope that, by the blessing of God in the diligent use of means, I might become a preacher of some little distinction. The work also appeared the noblest under heaven, and to be a sufficient employment in *itself*. To this, therefore (not entirely neglecting other things), I resolved more peculiarly to *dedicate* myself, keeping as much as possible from encroachments, and endeavouring to make every thing not only subordinate, but subservient to my chosen and beloved aim.

Nor, though it may seem vain, could I state things truly and fully unless I observed, also, that I perceived some common failings in preaching which I thought might be avoided, and some sources of attraction, impression, and improvement, that might at least be essayed with propriety. Of course I refer more immediately to the state of the pulpit in the religious connexions in which I moved. It is probable my meaning will be explained and exemplified before the close of these letters. But in what I have here intimated I am certain I judged from my *own* views and feelings. I also left nothing to mere speculation. I tried the case, in some humble degree, and my conviction was increased by a measure of success.

As I was now leaving Mr. Winter, after too short and imperfect a course of preparation, I came in contact with the Rev. Rowland Hill, who, with the permission and approbation of my tutor, engaged me for a season to go to London, to supply Surrey Chapel. This was indeed a formidable

engagement, but I was carried through it far beyond my
expectations. The place, though so large, was soon crowded
to excess; and when I preached my last sermon, the yard
before the dwelling-house was filled with the lingering
multitude, who would not disperse till I had bidden them
farewell from the window.*

This visit to London was, with regard to myself, a very
important and influential event. It gave me an enlarged
publicity.† It led to a friendship between Mr. Hill and
myself which continued till his death. It involved me in an
engagement to supply Surrey Chapel for a number of Sabbaths annually. It brought me into a very intimate
intercourse with, and subserviency to, that extraordinary
character, the Rev. John Ryland, of Northampton, the father
of the late Dr. Ryland, of Bristol. It placed me under the
notice, and gave me a share in the affection, of that most
estimable man of God, the Rev. John Newton, rector of St.
Mary Woolnoth; and it also laid the foundation of my
acquaintance with, and admiration of, your entirely beloved
and esteemed mother.

Before I left town I received applications to settle; but
owing to my youth, and being anxious before I became a

---

* This first visit to Surrey Chapel, which had so important an influence upon the subsequent career of Mr. Jay, took place in July,
1788. This is determined by a very interesting and most appropriate
letter on the occasion, from his friend and tutor, Mr. Winter.—See
Jay's Life of Winter, p. 195, Edit. 1843.

† In the Preface to the Sermon entitled "The Wife's Advocate,"
Mr. Jay relates the following fact relative to this visit:—

"When the author, if he may be excused a reference to himself,
quite a youth, first went to London, and was all anxiety to hear the
preachers of the famed metropolis, he was told by a friend, that if he
wished to hear a good doctrinal sermon, he must hear Mr. —— ; if
an experimental, he must hear Mr. —— ; and if a practical, he must
hear Mr. ——. And he well remembers simply asking, 'But is there
no minister here who preaches all these? I should rather hear him.'"

pastor to secure more preparation for the office, I declined them all, and retired to Christian Malford, near Chippenham. This was a small, but to me an interesting village, as I had often preached there while a student, and as here Mr. Winter himself for some time had resided, and laboured in his earlier ministry, as may be seen in his memoirs. My salary was to be £35 a-year; but my wants were few, and a considerable tradesman (who had married Mr. Winter's niece) promised to board me gratuitously. Here I was rich compared with the prophet in the house of the Shunammite, who had only " a little chamber on the wall, and a bed, and a table, and a stool, and a candlestick." I was therefore as to accommodation and provision perfectly satisfied, and free from all worldly care.

Here (it was much my wish in going there,) I hoped to find abstraction, and to pursue my improvement. But my design and expectation failed me in no small degree. My own stock of books was very scanty, and there was no public library to which I could have access. My purse did not allow me to buy, and there was no one from whom I could borrow. I had also become previously too well known in most of our neighbouring congregations to be left unsolicited when they had a lack of service. I was, therefore, urged constantly to preach abroad, and I had not the courage and firmness which time gives one, to say "*No*," to importunity ; for, as Mr. Cecil remarks, " A minister should never be to be had."

Here in my little volume of life you will ·have to turn over another leaf. In the mean time,

I am, &c.

[The reader will, we trust, not be displeased at an interruption here for the purpose of introducing to him some extracts from the sermon which Mr. Jay preached and published on the occasion of quitting this his first station. The fact of the very early appearance of this sermon in print, is of itself interesting; but the great excellence of the farewell words from so young a minister, will gratify all who admire Mr. Jay's character and writings, but few of whom can ever have seen that sermon. It so pleased Mr. Winter, that, though he had before dissuaded him from printing when urged by partial friends, yet he not only consented to the publication of this sermon, but himself wrote a prefatory address to the reader, which, as it is an expression of affectionate regard for Mr. Jay and a relic of the excellent tutor, we shall insert it entire, together with so much of Mr. Jay's sermon as refers to the solemn farewell.]

Mr. Winter's Address to the Reader.

" Soon after Mr. Jay's public appearance several of his friends were desirous of reading some of those sermons which they had heard with pleasure. I had influence enough with him to overrule the motion, and my reasons for interfering may easily be conjectured. The subjects were common, and in a variety of forms had been treated by the most able ministers, whose years and experience gave weight to their observations.

" The sermon preached at the opening of Mr. Tuppen's Chapel at Bath, however, found its way to the press, through the request of many who heard it. The subsequent sermon is published at my particular desire. On being informed of the impression it made at the time of delivery, I desired to read it. I cannot but think it will gratify some, as it did me,—no doubt it will those who heard it preached. It was the production of a Saturday evening, and the writer had not the most distant thoughts of its coming abroad. A special notice taken of, and an address made to, individuals of a congregation in the body of a discourse such as Mr. and Mrs. Prior received, is unusual; but local circumstances justified it on the present occasion; and it may serve as a specimen of the difficulty with which the Gospel is supported in many of our villages. My principal design in this advertisement is to take the blame of the publication to myself, if it deserves any, and to screen the youth from reflection. Whether it will be thought wise or weak by the speculatist is not, I am persuaded, what Mr. Jay will be concerned about, so much as whether it may conduce to answer the end he had in view when he preached it,—the profit of many that they may be saved, and for which he is willing to renounce the praise of man. If I mistake not, the sermon is expressive of a proper spirit, and may safely be imitated by young men, who too frequently break their first connexions with acrimony and reflection, that betray resentment of injuries, either real or imaginary, and impatience of contradiction.

" Like all other congregations, that at Christian Malford has those in it who are not properly sensible of the blessings of the Gospel,—are prone to cavil at what they have, and to want what they have not. But the best and the greatest part are otherwise minded. It is a poor congregation, which has undergone many revolutions, and includes a small society over which I was ordained; and with which, from my great attachment to rural retirement, I had a desire to live and die. Though I left them of necessity, I intended to give them all the assistance I could, and when I opened my little seminary, I had my eye upon them as a proper people with whom my young friends might with advantage make their first exertions. They have shared as largely in Mr. Jay's affections as they have in mine, but I never supposed he would continue with them. He who stations the stars, has the disposal of his ministers; and in subordination to his wise and righteous appointment, the qualification of ministers should determine the propriety of their situation.

"Men of the most distinguished ability, if disposed to exert themselves, might diffuse their light where it would be improper for them to fix their residence; and by their occasional services might help such indigent country congregations as that at Christian Malford to advantage. The necessity of raising and preserving such societies is obvious to a thinking man, influenced with proper zeal for the spread of vital godliness. Parochial instruction is, in general, too superficial and abstruse. It does not enough respect the first principles of religion; and what it does inculcate is without that solemnity, fervour, and perspicuity that is necessary to render it effectual. As the poor want more condescension than in common is shown to them, so their minds require more labour than in general is bestowed upon them. An attention to this I always inculcated upon Mr. Jay; and, blessed be God, he has learned to stoop to the child. If I detain the reader a moment longer from the sermon, it is only to add a hint on the importance of my brethren in the ministry making such congregations as that we refer to, the object of their benevolent attention, as far as circumstances will admit. The tedious hours of many old people are hereby well employed; and their minds fed with knowledge. Mothers of young children, who by maternal duties are prevented from going far distant from their habitations, partake of the benefit; and servants who are restricted in their time find their advantage from it. The glory of God and the salvation of souls are concerned in it. By this means living expositors supply the place of printed expositions; and a proper attention being paid to the narrow capacity of the poor illiterate peasants, their understanding is informed, while their affections are animated. By the blessing of God upon our endeavours, they acquire proper ideas of a church, and without engaging in the clamours of controversy, silently and modestly organize themselves into such societies as they have examples of in the Sacred Records. Though they may be destitute of the splendour of the world, they have the sanction of God, and the neighbouring minister or evangelical student—for they are incompetent to support a pastor—finds pleasure and profit. But every such village has not the advantage of a student disposed or permitted to lay out himself and bestow the first fruits of his studies upon its inhabitants, and the accomplished academic thinks it too great a stoop for him to make. The luxuries of the study, the laborious attention given to the turning of the period, the ceremonious time-wasting visits, and the large portion of time spent in decorating his person, prevent attention to the pursuit after souls in this humble way. We admire, then, the providence of God that selects from the laity, men of genius and spirituality more than sufficient to supply their place, nor do we startle though they should be called Methodist. By the effect of their labours, we perceive them to be the servants of the Most High God, who show unto men the way of salvation, and contribute to the common cause of Christianity. That a reserve of such a blessing may be always made for the people who heard, and now may read the subsequent sermon; and that the word may be preached in power, and in the Holy Ghost, and in much assurance, is the prayer of their affectionate and devoted friend,

" CORNELIUS WINTER."

Conclusion of Mr. Jay's Farewell Sermon at Christian Malford.

"We are now dissolving a very tender connexion, and it yields matter for mutual humiliation. My success has not equalled my acceptance. It becomes you to inquire what on your part has prevented it; and with sorrow to lament that you have not improved the help you have enjoyed. But all the blame is not yours, and upon a review of my labours, I need not wonder that so little good has been done. Pride and levity—the want of spirituality of mind, zeal for God, and love for souls, have corrupted my services, and rendered them unsuccessful. Infirmities, natural and sinful, I have had many. I repent that I have had no more fervency and importunity with you about the concerns of eternity. O, eternity! eternity!—that thou hast been no more on the lip of the preacher, and in the ear of the hearer! Yet, blessed be God, I have the testimony of my own mind, and I hope of yours also, that I have not walked in craftiness, nor handled the word of God deceitfully; but by manifestation of the truth commended myself to every man's conscience in the sight of God. Those principles only have been inculcated upon you which I believed to be consistent with the oracles of truth. Having explained the doctrine, and enforced the practice, of the gospel—having paid equal regard to the moral and spiritual part of the Word—and having kept back nothing that was essential for you to know or do, 'I have not shunned to declare unto you the whole counsel of God.' Having described the guilt of sin, warned the sinner of his danger, directed him where to flee for refuge, and testified repentance towards God, and faith in the Lord Jesus Christ, 'I take you to record, that I am pure from the blood of all men.' What my doctrine and manner of life have been is known to you; and what my aim and intent has been is known to God. Respecting the former, I have endeavoured 'in simplicity and godly sincerity, not by fleshly wisdom, but by the grace of God, to have my conversation in the world; but more abundantly to you-ward.' Respecting the latter, I have had the salvation of your souls at heart; 'for God is my record, how greatly I long after you all in the bowels of Jesus Christ. Brethren, my heart's desire and prayer to God for you is that you may be saved.' With this view, I would now close the subject by reciting

a few doctrines, giving you my thanks, and expressing my
wishes, fears, and advice.

"The doctrines which you have heard, and which we pray
God may ever sound from this pulpit, include man's depravity, the redemption of the soul by the blood of Christ,
justification by his obedience, and sanctification by his Spirit
—or faith and holiness. 'Without faith it is impossible to
please God,' and 'without holiness no man shall see the
Lord.' Where there is faith there will be holiness, and true
holiness always springs from faith in Christ. The believer
disclaims merit, but delights in obedience, and walks before
God in newness of life. It would be easy to prove of what
importance such doctrines are. Be well grounded in them,
and pay more attention to *them*, than to those which are of
less moment, and which have furnished the world with matter for endless controversy. 'Contend earnestly for' these
important articles of 'the faith once delivered to the saints,'
and beware of hearing or receiving a man who opposes them,
lest ye be partakers of his evil deeds. 'Be ye not carried
about with divers and strange doctrines, for it is a good
thing for the heart to be established with grace.'

"My thanks are due for the respect you have paid me,
and for your desires of my continuance. While the love of
many cannot be overlooked, it would be very remiss, were I
not to notice the kindness of some present, which reflects
the greatest honour on them, and lays me under peculiar
obligations. Our united thanks are due to our dear friends
with whom I have resided. Under God, we have been indebted to them for my coming and continuance here. Being
unable to support a minister yourselves, I could not have
lived among you, had they not generously invited me to
their house, and given me my comfortable subsistence.
Nor are they unwilling for my continuance; but have
earnestly desired me to continue my connexion with their
family. 'That which was lacking on your part, they have

supplied; for they have refreshed my spirit and yours; therefore acknowledge them that are such.' There can be no impropriety, my honoured friends, in making this public acknowledgment, 'for this thing has not been done in a corner.' You have exerted yourselves to the uttermost in the cause of your Redeemer; yea, and beyond your power you have been willing to discover the sincerity of your love. 'Now he that ministereth seed to the sower, both minister bread for your food, and multiply your seed sown, and increase the fruits of your righteousness.' Remember, 'God is not unrighteous to forget your work of faith, and labour of love.' Beloved, I wish above all things that you may prosper in your body, soul, and family. May your dear children 'know the Lord God of their parents, and serve him with a perfect heart and willing mind!'

"My wishes respect your welfare as individuals, and a society; that you may order your conversation aright, and love one another with a pure heart fervently; that there may be no root of bitterness springing up among you; no divisions and contentions; but that you may live in peace, and the God of peace be with you; that religion may be visible in the power and practice of it, and that you may neither be barren nor unfruitful in the kingdom of God! May the seed which has been sown yet spring up, and bring forth much fruit; may the Lord provide a supply for you, and render future labours more successful! While I am thus expressing the wishes of my soul, may you be able to say, 'The Lord grant thee thy heart's desire, and fulfil all thy petitions!'

"My fears are great and many. I fear lest I have bestowed labour upon you in vain. I fear you have been instructed, warned, exhorted, to no purpose. I fear that while you have been hearing of an inheritance incorruptible, undefiled, and that fadeth not away, there are many of you who have no part nor lot in the matter, but are still in the

gall of bitterness and bond of iniquity. If our Gospel be
hid, it is hid to them that are lost. And are there none
among you to whom this Gospel is hid ? Hid as to the light ?
Hid as to the power of it ? Are there not many blind minds,
hardened hearts, ungodly lives ? But, God be thanked ! there
are a few, who, though they were the servants of sin, have
obeyed from the heart that form of doctrine which was delivered them.   O that it was the case with you all ! I would
not leave one unconverted person.   O how happy would it
be to leave you all in a fair way for glory ! But I cannot
depart from you so.   O, then, ye blind souls, upon whom
the light has shined in vain; ye hardened souls, upon whom
the Word has made no impression ; ye deluded souls, who
have a form of godliness, but deny the power thereof;—I
fear for you, and I will weep in secret, when my tongue cannot reach you.   Let my concern be yours.   How is it you
are so unalarmed ? Can you rest secure under such a load
of guilt ? Can you expect a certain fearful looking-for of
judgment, and be unconcerned ? What ! are there so many
Sabbaths, sermons, exhortations, gone never to be recalled,
and not afraid ? Like the jailor, may you fear, and tremble,
and cry, ' What shall I do to be saved ? ' But this is not the
case.   I have then another fear, that I must rise up in judgment to condemn you.   Dreadful ! What ! be the means of
increasing their condemnation whom I would gladly save ?
Soon we must all stand before the judgment-seat of Christ,
to give an account of our preaching and hearing ! May
each of us then be able to do it with joy, and not with
grief ! It would yield a minister much pleasure had he reason
to conclude that all the people now committed to his care
would then prove his joy and crown of rejoicing. But, should
he be unsuccessful, yet if he be faithful he shall not lose his
reward. 'Though Israel be not gathered, yet shall he be
glorious in the eyes of the Lord.' 'For we are unto God a
sweet savour of Christ, in them that are saved, and in them

that perish; to the one we are a savour of death unto death, and to the other a savour of life unto life.'

"My advice respects you as sinners and saints. If you are sinners of any description whatever, I exhort you to inquire into your true state, your heinous guilt, your dreadful danger. Lay yourselves open to your inspection. View yourselves in the glass of the law. Believe that you are what the word of God represents you to be,—'miserable, and wretched, and poor, and blind, and naked.' Pray for the wisdom that cometh from above, and that you may know the value of your immortal souls, and the excellency of Jesus Christ. Search the Scriptures with prayer for an understanding heart. Depend on Christ alone for salvation. 'Tis at your peril you neglect Him. There is none other name by which you can be saved. But in Him you will find plenteous redemption. Come, and welcome. He will not cast you out. He waits to be gracious.

"And you, my dear young friends, what shall I say to you? My heart feels for you. The enemy of souls eyes you as his prey: disappoint his hope. Beware of the snares of the world, and particularly of an evil heart of unbelief, in departing from the living God. Give up yourselves to the Lord by an early dedication, and you will find that his ways are ways of pleasantness and all his paths peace. Your tears now at my departure show your affection for me. You have given many evidences of it. Give one more. 'Tis my parting request. Recollect the many exhortations I have given you. Remember your Creator in the days of your youth. Seek him early, and you shall find him.

"I can rejoice with those of you who know the Lord. You have begun well, but you must go forward and hold out to the end. Pray for an increase of grace. Set the Lord always before you. Converse much with him, and keep up a holy, happy communion. Live in continual dependence on his mercy and power for every supply you

need. Act for his honour and praise. Prefer this to all
pleasure and interest of your own. Whether you eat or
drink, or whatsoever you do, do all to the glory of God.
Grow not indifferent in his service, but be zealous for every
good word and work. And, as you would be happy in time
or eternity, be ye holy in all manner of conversation and
godliness, looking for the blessed hope and the glorious
appearing of the great God and our Saviour Jesus Christ.

"Herein I give my advice. Were these to be my last
words, I know not what I could press upon you of greater
importance. Let me prevail with you to have a proper
regard to what has been said, and remember it has been
given out of love to your best and eternal interest. 'Tis
not because I seek myself, but your salvation, that I thus
speak. I utter the dictates of affection. Let, then, the
parting advice of one who sincerely loves you be received
and followed. 'Wherefore, my beloved brethren, be ye
stedfast, unmoveable, always abounding in the work of the
Lord, forasmuch as ye know that your labour shall not be
in vain in the Lord. Only let your conversation be as
becometh the Gospel, that whether I come and see you, or
else am absent, I may hear of your affairs, that ye stand
fast in one spirit, with one mind, striving together for the
faith of the Gospel. And now, brethren, I commend you to
God, and the word of his grace, which is able to build you
up, and to give you an inheritance among them that are
sanctified. Finally, brethren, *farewell*. Be perfect; be of
good comfort; be of one mind; live in peace, and the God
of peace shall be with you.'"

LETTER VII.

MY DEAR CHILDREN,—After more than a year in the situation I have described, and where my improvement was not small (though it might have been greater with more prudence and diligence), I met with Lady Maxwell in Bristol, to whom now belonged Hope Chapel, at the Hotwells. I hardly know how it was (for I did not feel entirely convinced of the propriety of the measure,) but she prevailed upon me to supply this chapel, which had not been very long opened. My preaching always filled the place, and I hope good was done. I not only heard of various instances of conversion, but three of those who were awakened by my labours while there became preachers themselves, were ordained over congregations, and died in the faith of Christ.

Here I continued about twelve months, and here it is probable I should still have continued, (as I was pressed both by her ladyship and the people to become the stated minister,) but a difference with the sub-governess, who managed, during her ladyship's absence in Scotland, the temporal concerns (and who had no objection to interfere with the spiritual), actuated me to resolve to withdraw. Perhaps there was mutual blame, as there generally is in such cases ; and therefore the apostle says, "forgiving one another," as if it were necessary for the pardon to pass from side to side. However this was, I certainly considered Mrs. C. an excellent woman, and I respect her memory, and am not ignorant how God blessed her endeavours with her children. But, with all my regard for the sex, and submission in domestic affairs, I do not plead for female ecclesiastical rule, whether supreme or subordinate.

The Lord determines the bounds of our habitations ; and the events that move us from one place to another are as much under the direction of his providence, as the fiery cloudy pillar which was the conductor of the Israelites in the wilderness. But on what apparently casual and slender causes do consequences the most interesting in our history often hinge! At the very time of this difference came an invitation from the Independent Church at Bath, then destitute by the death of their very able and worthy pastor, the Rev. Thomas Tuppen. This (as I was no stranger to the place and the people, having several times preached there during their pastor's indisposition) I soon accepted; and so my residence was fixed in that far-famed city.

I know not whether it is common for persons not to seem to themselves at home till they are in the proper places designed for them. I know it was thus with me. I never felt that I was where I *ought* to be, or was likely to remain, till I became, as a preacher, an inhabitant of Bath ; but from that time I said, ' This is my destination, whatever be its duties or trials ;' and it was additionally satisfying to understand that this was the conviction of all my friends and brethren in the Gospel. This being the case, and as I have been there for more than fifty-three years,

" Preliminary to the last retreat,"

and as so much of my ministry is connected with it, it may
be expected that I should notice what led to it.

Here, again, I am not going to insinuate anything supernatural, but several rather striking circumstances concurred
to produce the result; and "whoso is wise and will observe
these things, even he shall understand the loving-kindness
of the Lord."

During my first visit to Surrey Chapel, already mentioned, Mr. Tuppen happened to be in London, and frequently heard me there. After his return to Bath, he spoke
of me with much kindness of manner to many of his people.
Hence, when he was laid aside by sickness, the deacons
applied to me (being then at Christian Malford) to supply
for a season their lack of service. I complied; and considering what was to follow, my first text has been since
frequently remarked: it was,—"What I do, thou knowest
not now, but thou shalt know hereafter." Mr. Tuppen
after a short time revived, but soon relapsed again, and his
illness was severe and long; yet some fond hope was entertained of his recovery, and this occasioned delay in the
opening of Argyle Chapel, which, encouraged by the promised help of Lady Glenorchy, and excited by his growing
success, he had been induced to build; for he naturally
wished (and his hearers also), that he who had been the
instrument to rear it, should open it himself. At length,
however, it was deemed expedient to wait no longer for the
dedication. I was therefore applied to for this purpose,
and preached both parts of the day. The sermon, particularly suited to the occasion, was from the words, "The
hour cometh, and now is, when the true worshippers shall
worship the Father in spirit and in truth: for the Father
seeketh such to worship Him. God is a Spirit: and they
that worship Him must worship Him in spirit and in truth."
—John iv. 23, 24. This sermon was, by desire, published.
The service took place Oct. 4, 1789.

[The insertion here of two or three extracts from this sermon, will not be displeasing to the reader. It was the first of all his publications, and displays a maturity and correctness of judgment, as well as earnestness and simplicity of manner, truly admirable in a minister so young, being then little more than twenty years of age. How gratifying is the consideration that this early promise of excellence was so fully realized, and so long, in the very place the opening of which so unexpectedly devolved upon him! Little did he conceive or imagine that that was the beginning of days to him,—that he was opening his own and his only chapel, and commencing a pastorate unusually long, happy, and useful!]

Extracts from the Sermon at the Opening of Argyle Chapel.

" When that universal revival and spread of religion shall commence, by which the earth shall be filled with the knowledge of the Lord, as the waters cover the seas; we may expect to come nearer to the worship of the inhabitants of the upper world, and more intimately partake of their joys. Before that eventful period, 'tis more than probable, many congregations of worshippers will successively occupy this house. Those who at present use it should be concerned to know that they are in the number of the *true* worshippers, lest they should be repulsed when most sanguine about their acceptance, and be denied admission into the company of those ' nations who are appointed to worship God before the throne.' "

*   *   *   *   *

" You will soon change your place, but not your employment; only you will worship without weariness, imperfection, or end. If now you can turn to God and say, ' Lord, thou knowest all things, I have loved the habitation of thine house, and the place where thine honour dwelleth, your souls will not be gathered with sinners, nor your lives with

bloody men.' God will receive you to himself, advance you
to his temple above, that where he is, there his children
may be also. His gracious properties recorded in his word,
are not only descriptive of what he has been to his people
of old, but of what he is, and of what he will be to his
children for ever."

*   *   *   *   *

" God is not confined. He is no respecter of places or
persons; 'but in every nation he that feareth God and
worketh righteousness, is accepted of him. There is now
neither Jew nor Greek, barbarian, Scythian, bond nor free,
but Christ is all and in all. For in Christ, neither circumcision availeth anything, nor uncircumcision, but faith which
worketh by love.' It argues our exceeding ignorance when
we would limit the Holy One of Israel to temples made
with hands; and when our bigotry and attachment to any
particular society lead us to exclaim, 'The temple of the
Lord, the temple of the Lord are we!' Nothing makes a
people dear to God but their conformity to him! nor a
place of worship sacred, but the Divine presence. In point
of external sanctity, all places are equal to Him who hath
said, ' The heaven is my throne, and the earth is my foot-
stool; where is the house that ye build unto me,' &c. &c.
Isaiah lxvi. 1, 2."

" O thou God of all grace, send out thy light and thy
truth, that all may know thee, from the least even to the
greatest! When the Jew shall be called in, with the fulness of the Gentiles, and when neither in this nor that place
only shall men worship the Father, but all shall worship
him in spirit and in truth."

" Let us bless God for revelation, and the extent of its
discoveries; for the predictions and promises yet to be accomplished; for the Gospel which sounds in our ears; for the
ordinances upon which we attend; for every convenience for
his worship; and that we can sit under our own vine and

fig-tree, none daring to make us afraid. He hath not dealt so with any nation ; and as for his judgments, they have not known them. Praise ye the Lord."

*   *   *   *   *

" This being the house of prayer, and the place where the attention of sinners is called to the living God, we have reason to bless the Providence by which it has been raised; and the expression of our gratitude must be enlarged, when we reflect upon the blessing and success that have attended the ministry of our honoured but afflicted friend ; by whom a worshipping assembly has been collected, and for whose convenience this building has been erected. We by no means confine the Lord and his work to this house, or suppose the place has any holiness in it, any more than 'tis dedicated to God, and appropriated to his service.   'Tis not built in opposition to our fellow-christians of different persuasions, but to promote the common interest of Christianity. The population of this respectable city increases, and with it, blessed be God, ' the numbers of believers are multiplied.' Should this house be one of the nurseries of heaven, the end of its erection will be answered. We take it for granted, that the grace of God will prevent our fellow-christians from looking upon it with an envious eye, and lead them to pray for its prosperity ; and that ' if Christ is preached, they do rejoice and will rejoice.'   To the lovers of Catholicism, and those who regard the honour that cometh from God, it must be pleasing to find here a house where the minister of Christ may deliver what he has received from the Lord, though he does not choose to appear under episcopal sanction. May the man of God, through whose instrumentality it was first begun, and whose eyes see it occupied, live long to sound his Redeemer's praise therein, and find the fruit of his labours in the conversion of sinners, and increase of grace to all that believe."

[Mr. Jay continues his narrative thus:]

When Mr. Tuppen's recovery was quite despaired of, the deacons of the church repaired to his dying chamber, and expressed a wish to have his advice and recommendation with regard to his successor, observing that though his opinion might not absolutely determine the choice of the people, it would tend much to influence, unite, and guide them. He only and instantly mentioned my name; and as this fell in with the conviction and wish, both of the members and the attendants, I was immediately invited to take the pastorate. I accepted the call; and was in due time ordained over them in the Lord. At this solemnity my venerated tutor prayed, (I think I hear that prayer now,) and gave me the charge; while the Rev. John Adams of Salisbury preached on the duties of the people. Some things usual on such occasions were waived, and the order of the service altered as well as curtailed. For this some of my brethren censured me; and for which I have, nearly ever since, censured myself. The alteration originated in nothing commendable,—I was for the moment improperly influenced by the friendship and talents of a man who was wanting in sobriety of mind, and often affected singularity. But it is better to gain distinction by regularly going in " the king's highway," than by tumbling on the road, or breaking through the hedge. I much approve of the usual method of ordination among our dissenters and their fathers before them. It is lawful, it is expedient, it is profitable; and falls in with the spirit and principles, and rule and mode of the New Testament. I have long been afraid of whims and vagaries, and new discoveries in religion; and have been content to go forth by the footsteps of the flock, and to walk in the good old way. I have felt increasingly disposed to tolerate rather than innovate. I may not admire everything I find in my own party or denomination; but I would not divide from them for every trifling difference of opinion. I must

not, indeed, sin in violating the convictions of my conscience;
but in how many cases may the question and the admonition
be safely applied, "Hast thou faith? have it to thyself
before God."

I am, &c.

[This is the proper place for introducing into the narrative
some extracts from the very interesting service of Mr. Jay's
ordination—particularly his address to his congregation,
which is prefixed to the pamphlet—and his own statement
of principles, technically called the Confession of Faith. As
both these documents have an intimate connexion with his
autobiography, are not now to be obtained, and possess
great intrinsic excellence, we have thought it desirable to
preserve them entire, with a short extract from the charge
by Mr. Winter.]

AN ADDRESS TO THE CONGREGATION, PREFIXED TO THE ORDINATION SERVICE.

DEAR AND HONOURED FRIENDS,—Though I was as forward as yourselves for the publication of the other parts of
the service, I was averse to the publication of the several
thoughts I delivered on the same occasion; nor should I
have sent them abroad, had it not been for repeated solicita-
tion, and for the sake of those important instructions which
were not to make their appearance without them. My
reluctance did not arise from an over-nice delicacy, or from a
fear of the discovery of my creed; but from a persuasion of
its inutility, my sentiments having been all along fully
known, and the design of the work of the day equally
answered without it. The intention of it was not to bring
to light our proceedings—it was not to make a pastor or
declare a person to be one—it was not to unite us or to
ratify such a union—much less was it to invest with any

new power, or authorize an administration of the ordinances. The simple design of it was to receive instruction, in order to impress us with a sense of our mutual duties, and to implore the God of all grace to bless us "with all spiritual blessings in Christ Jesus."

As I had taken no minutes of what I delivered, I feared I should be unable to recollect it so far as to give satisfaction; however, I may venture to say from several testimonies, that the address which you now see is the same which you lately heard. I did not absolutely determine to say anything on the occasion. I left it to the freedom of my mind, and finding inclination and liberty, I spake freely, regardless of the studied plan of confessional system.

The glorious Gospel of the blessed God our Saviour is the great object of our attention as minister and people; this only am I allowed to preach, this only are you allowed to hear. If I mistake not, the substance is to be found in the following pages. Some, probably, will deem my creed deficient; such should remember that I have not here delivered all my sentiments, or everything relative to one of them. It is enough if I believe in my heart and confess with my mouth Jesus Christ and him crucified. The apostle determined to know nothing in comparison with it. He began his ministry by delivering "first of all, that which he also received, how that Jesus Christ died for our sins, and was buried, and rose again according to the Scriptures." And it is more than probable he ended in a similar manner, saying "God forbid that I should glory, save in the cross of our Lord Jesus Christ." He is "the author and finisher of our faith;" his obedience and sacrifice the alpha and omega of the Gospel. "No other foundation can any man lay than that which is laid. Now if any man build upon this foundation gold, silver, precious stones, wood, hay, stubble, every man's work shall be made manifest, for the day shall declare it, because it shall be revealed by fire." Blessed be God, many of you know and are assured that the fall of man, the redemption of Christ, the work of the Spirit, and many other things inseparable from them, far from being opinions, are facts—facts which may be opposed—facts which can never be overturned. Perhaps some of you are poor and illiterate, are not able to dispute their truth, or solve the objections with which they have been loaded,—but you are as satisfied of their reality as those who may possess a capacity competent to both. While others are controverting as a *notion*, whether you are disordered, and whether you are incapable of action, you do not hesitate for a moment: it is a fact you see, you feel, you groan beneath the sad effects of your deep-rooted malady. While others are controverting as a *notion*, whether there is such a thing as the sun in the firmament, and whether he benefits the earth, you entertain no doubt it is a fact: you see its light, you feel its heat, you rejoice in its pleasant influence. To drop metaphor, you are not captives to a blind belief, nor is your faith the child of folly. You do not receive your religion without proof; for while others who are able may judge from outward, you judge from internal, evidence ;—while others who are able may determine from the conviction of the mind, you judge from the conviction of the heart.

If you " hold the Head," you will not be " carried about by strange doctrines." While others are "ever learning and never able to come to the knowledge of the truth," " as you have received Christ Jesus the Lord, so " you will continue to "walk in him, rooted and built up in him, and established in the faith as ye have been taught, abounding therein with thanksgiving." A disposition for novelty in religious truth is the spring of error running through the flowery field of speculation into the gulf of apostasy. It is the mark of a bad palate when a man is for ever seeking fresh food; and it is an indication of a corrupt mind to despise and neglect common truth. Happy in the possession of what others seek for in vain, you will be satisfied with the word of life which you have known, handled, and tasted. Content with this provision, you will feed and "grow thereby," and be nourished up in the words of faith and sound doctrine. While others are strangers to a peace of understanding, their understanding being perpetually on the search, not knowing where to settle, you will come to a point, and be able to make an absolute, unhesitating conclusion. And while their mind, "like a wave of the sea, is driven to and fro and tossed" on the ocean of uncertainty, till dashed on the rocks of scepticism or infidelity; you will "continue in the things which you have heard, knowing of whom you have learned them;" and "your hearts will be comforted, being knit together in love, unto all the riches of the full assurance of understanding, to the acknowledgment of the mystery of God, of the Father, and of Christ."

You will remember, that by the things which you have heard you are saved, " if ye keep in memory what has been preached unto you, unless ye have believed in vain." They are the chief sources of comfort and the principal motives to duty. "Ye shall know the truth, and the truth shall make you free." It unbinds the captive soul from the chains of sin, and releases him from the bondage of misery. Other doctrines may bring a few persons on the cold legs of custom to a place of worship, and keep them from some enormous crimes; but they are not effectual "to turn a sinner from darkness to light, or the power of Satan to God;" nor can one instance be proved of any nation, society, or individual, experiencing a moral change of nature where these truths have been renounced. Therefore, we do not plead for them as mere notions, but truths; we do not plead for them as mere truths, but as truths essential to our holiness and happiness. If people will show us other doctrines which will better answer the purpose of reforming the wicked, of purifying the heart, of supporting the mind under the sor-

rows of life, and of enabling the soul to rejoice in the dark
valley of the shadow of death " with joy unspeakable and
full of glory," we will believe.

But you will observe, that no system of doctrine will
serve in the stead of that grace by which the heart is to be
renewed, and the life sanctified. Purity of sentiment, followed by wicked practice, is only "holding the truth in
unrighteousness." "Faith without works," is as the body
without the spirit, "dead, being alone." He that cherishes
it is a "vain man." Would God we knew not where to
find such a character! But alas! how numerous are the
instances of professors discovering immoderate attachment
to "the present evil world;" and instead of confessing
themselves to be "strangers and pilgrims upon earth,"
seeking a naturalization into its prohibited customs and
delusive honours! Hence so little savour of grace in their
conversation—so little spirituality in their devotions—so
little holiness in their lives! Be not conformed to them.
"Adorn the doctrine of God your Saviour in all things."
Let your practice praise your creed, and your lives do
honour to your heads. "Walk worthy of the vocation
wherewith you are called," as "heirs of the grace of eternal
life;" "joined together in the same mind and in the same
judgment, striving together for the faith of the gospel." In
our present connexion let us never forget our duty and
privilege. " O house of Israel, trust thou in the Lord: he
is their help and their shield. O house of Aaron, trust thou
in the Lord: he is their help and their shield. The Lord
hath been mindful of us, he will bless us, he will bless the
house of Israel, he will bless the house of Aaron." "Except
the Lord build the house, they labour in vain that build it.
Except the Lord keep the city, the watchman waketh but in
vain." "Commit thy way unto the Lord, trust also in him,
and he will bring it to pass." "O satisfy us early with thy
mercy, that we may rejoice and be glad all our days. Let

thy work appear unto thy servants, and thy glory unto their children.   And let the beauty of the Lord our God be upon us; and establish thou the work of our hands upon us, yea the work of our hands establish thou it."

Mr. Jay's Confession of Faith delivered at his Ordination, January 30, 1791.

A VIEW OF THE GOSPEL ; OR, THE PRINCIPAL MATTER OF AN EVANGELICAL MINISTRY.

" Moreover, brethren, I declare unto you the Gospel which I preached unto you, which also ye have received, and wherein ye stand ; by which also ye are saved, if ye keep in memory what I preached unto you, unless ye have believed in vain."—1 Cor. xv. 1, 2.

The sacred business in which we are engaged is to commemorate, solemnize, and sanctify by prayer and instruction, the union which the minister and people of this church, for a considerable time, have formed.

Such a union should always be formed with a cautious regard to the Divine will, an affectionate concern for immortal souls, and a pleasing hope of being helpers of each other's joy.   It is a work of the greatest importance because of its consequences, for it is not so much a natural as a spiritual connexion; not so much designed for time as eternity ; not so much to be approved, judged, or censured in the present state, as in the future day, when we must all, in our individual, relative, and public capacity, " give an account of ourselves unto God."

" To save us with a holy calling, not according to our works, but according to his purpose and grace given us in Christ Jesus before the world began," has been the one grand aim of Jehovah, adhered to in every age, in every state of the present system, and universally pursued through all the course of nature and order of Providence.   " Salvation belongeth unto the Lord."   It is his own work.   Nor

does he detract from his glory as the Author by using instruments to accomplish it. He could have easily done
without men, but he is pleased to act with them, and hence
some of them are called saviours, the salt of the earth, and
the light of the world, because under his Divine influence
they communicate spiritual advantage. To make us love
one another, which is a great design of religion, God has
appointed us to be the means of communicating his blessings,
and under the law made men priests, and under the gospel
made men ministers, " having infirmity."

He has not commissioned any of the higher orders of in-
telligences, " thrones or dominions, principalities or powers,"
" the angels that excel in strength and do his commandments, hearkening unto the voice of his word," but descending to earth he has sent forth the sons of men ; " Go ye
into all the world and preach the gospel to every creature :
and, lo ! I am with you always, even unto the end of the
world." " He gave some apostles; and some prophets ;
and some evangelists ; and some pastors and teachers ; for
the work of the ministry, for the perfecting of the saints,
for the edifying of the body of Christ."

He will never fail in his instruments while he has any
purpose to bring to pass. He may and he does produce
changes in his church, removing one and another ; yet he
has always a reserve of instruments in his secret intention,
and in the due time they are made manifest. He will never
leave his work without witnesses, or suffer those to perish
for want of provision who " commit the keeping of their
souls to him in well doing."

I hope, my beloved, that you have seen the truth of this
remark in the several steps you have taken since your social
connexion, and that on the present occasion you are ready
to utter the memory of his goodness, in the words of the
restored Jews, " The Lord hath done great things for us,
whereof we are glad."

Indeed it becomes me to speak with proper modesty on this subject. I am not going to intimate that the Lord has fully repaired your late and deplorable loss.* I am not about to flatter him who now addresses you by placing him on an equality with your dear departed pastor. No. As I am inferior to him in years, so I am inferior to him in grace. As I come behind him in succession of labour, so I come behind him in every natural endowment, in every acquired help, in every spiritual qualification, that can make the shining man, or adorn the illustrious minister.

I hope, therefore, none will consider the hint which I am going to drop, as in the least tending to make you insensible of your affliction, in the death of the great man who has fallen in this Israel. While creatures decay and die, " the Creator of the ends of the earth fainteth not, neither is weary; there is no searching of his understanding." Immutable in his nature, unfrustrable in his designs, " his counsel shall stand, and he will do all his pleasure." The loss of no instrument, the loss of no set of instruments, shall render his purpose of none effect; " the thoughts of his heart endure to all generations." Separate from his blessing no good can be done ; and, as all success depends on him, he can work with one as well as with another. " Who then is Paul, and who is Apollos, but ministers by whom ye believed, even as the Lord gave to every man ? So then neither is he that planteth any thing, nor he that watereth, but God that giveth the increase. Now he that planteth and he that watereth are one ; and every man shall receive his own reward, according to his own labour."

On this occasion I suppose it is expected that several things will be delivered relative to myself; and believing that it is not only looked for but desired, I have no objection to it.

* The Rev. Mr. Tuppen, Mr. Jay's predecessor.

Fully satisfied that personal religion is necessary to perform every office in the church with propriety, I should not
have entered on the ministerial work in general, or the
pastoral charge in particular, without some satisfactory hope
that God had called me by his grace, and revealed his Son
in me.   An early dedication to God made way for an early
dedication to the work of the ministry.   I cannot help
tracing the hand of God in the whole of this affair.   Born to
no secular honour, possessed of no fortune, bred up in the
shades of obscurity, I had not the least qualification for the
work, or the least probability of being brought into it.   But
the Lord by providential circumstances opened the door,
and I was placed under the care of my dear and honoured
tutor, Mr. Winter, the best friend I ever had ; to whose
character I would bear my public testimony ; whose amiable
temper, generous disposition, condescending carriage, un-
ceasing friendship, I could enlarge upon with pleasure, were
I not forbid by his presence ; properties which, having been
displayed in general, and in particular towards me, will ever
render his memory dear, and apologize for my feelings on
the present occasion.

By him I was gradually introduced to the ministry, and
went out preaching from place to place as opportunity
offered, refusing offers of settlement on account of my age,
and satisfied that in due time the Lord would make plain
the way, and open a door for stated labour.   And I cannot
help concluding that he has made the way plain to, and
opened a door in, this place ; our attachment has been
mutual from the beginning, our affection has increased upon
acquaintance, and I hope our love will flourish through
time, and shine bright to all eternity.

As I have believed, so have I spoken.   I have advanced
no doctrine from the pulpit which I was not satisfied of in
my mind ; nor have I kept back from you anything that I
conceived profitable for you to know.   I never aimed to

deliver my ideas in ambiguous terms. I never thought I had a tongue given me to cloak my creed and puzzle people. What I have embraced as true, I have without fear or shame openly avowed. Therefore you must fully know my doctrine already; however, ready "always to give an answer to every man that asketh a reason of the hope that is in me with meekness and fear." "Moreover, brethren, I declare unto you the gospel which I have preached unto you, which also ye have received, and wherein ye stand, by which also ye are saved, if ye keep in memory what I preached unto you, unless ye have believed in vain."

"He that cometh unto God must believe that He is." This is the foundation of all religion. If there be no God, there is no divine law; if there be no divine law, there is no difference between virtue and vice; and if there be no difference between virtue and. vice, morality can only be, considered in the highest light, a civil thing established by human authority.

Without an overruling providence we can have no confidence in the Supreme Being: if saints, we shall want the principal solace in adversity; if sinners, we shall want the principal restraint in prosperity. If we pervert this necessary doctrine by denying a particular providence, we destroy a particular confidence, a particular source of comfort, a particular motive to duty, and give our actions only a general rule of reference.

As we "believe in God, we must believe also in Jesus Christ." Man stands related to God and his neighbour. The Divine law considers him in this light, and requires him to love the one with all his heart, and the other as himself. By considering his relation to God as his Creator and Preserver, he may discover how destitute he is of that love, reverence, gratitude, and obedience he owes to him as his Benefactor. By considering his relation to his neighbour, he may discover how destitute he is of that charity and justice which he owes to him as a brother. Thus he finds himself a transgressor, is led to acknowledge his desert, and is brought to perceive those doctrines by which the religion of Christianity is distinct from, and superior to, the religion of nature.

The religion of Christianity, in whole and part, respects man as fallen ; by which I mean a blind, weak, guilty, miserable creature. Therefore, the depravity of man is a very material article in an evangelical creed; and it is an article no less necessary to be believed, than easy to be proved, demonstrated through every age, in every country, by every person. The corruption is universal,—no part remains uninjured. It is the cause of all actual transgression. The evil practice of the life proceeds from the desperately wicked and deceitful heart; the tree being bad, the fruit is bad; the spring being corrupt, the streams are corrupt also. Our pride is the cause of all "the filthiness of the spirit," and the dominion of sense—of all " the filthiness of the flesh." By the one we are alienated from God, by the other attached to the earth. From hence arises that impotency which the Scripture attributes to us, by which we are incapable of faith, repentance, and holiness. If we give up the doctrine of the Fall, we preclude all possibility of recovery, like a disordered man who imagines he is well, and therefore refuses the medicine which would recover him from the sad effects of his malady. But if we are truly convinced that we are sinners, and are unable to deliver ourselves, we shall be suitably disposed for " the excellency of the knowledge of Christ Jesus the Lord."

This knowledge relates to what he *is*, and represents him to us as "the true God and eternal life," as made in "the form of a servant," and "manifested in the flesh." Hence his name is " Wonderful," because, while he is the " Child born," and the " Son given," he is also "the Everlasting Father, the Prince of Peace." He is divine, as well as

human ; and the same thing which proves him to be the one
proves him to be the other; allowing the word of truth to
be judge, I could as well deny that he was man, as that he
was God.   To deny the deity of Christ is the same in
revealed religion as to deny the being of a God in natural
religion. It is the foundation : remove it, and the superstructure falls : the doctrines are unintelligible, the promises vain, the precepts weak in their motive, impertinent
in their application, and inoperative in their influence. But
that he is the " Lord God Almighty" is the belief of my
mind, and the rejoicing of my heart. There is no name by
which " the living and true God" differs from "false and
dumb idols ;" there is no perfection by which the " God
over all" is known from " the lords many, and the gods
many ;" there is no act of worship by which the " Most
High" is distinguished from " the powers which are" receiving ceremonious respect and civil adoration ; there is no
work by which " the Creator" can be discriminated from
" the creature," as to nature, providence, grace, or glory,
that is not ascribed to the Lord Jesus Christ.

The Gospel relates to what he *did*. It contains his history
from the throne to the cross, and from the cross back to the
throne. It represents him as undertaking to remove our
sins, according to his address to his Father as he comes into
the world : " Sacrifice and offerings thou hast not required ;
then said I, Lo, I come to do thy will, O God :" " by the
which will we are sanctified through the offering of the
body of Jesus Christ." It discovers him to us as " wounded
for our transgressions, bruised for our iniquities, delivered
for our offences, and raised again for our justification." He
has realized what the various victims under the law only
typified. They made their appearance to show their ineffi-
cacy, and to convince "the comers thereunto" that they
stood in need of a better sacrifice, because they could not
take away sin. But he, by the once offering up of himself, has

for ever perfected them that are sanctified, so that "there remains no other," and there needs no other, "sacrifice;" by him all that believe "are justified freely from *all things.*"

The doctrine of the Atonement, not in the reserved, ambiguous way in which many use the term who deny the thing, but "Christ dying for our sins," in the proper sense of the expression, I consider as that which constitutes the good news, or glad tidings, which the word "Gospel" signifies. It is a great advantage, that by the Gospel we have so plain and perfect a system of duty; but it is a degradation of it to suppose it was only designed to republish the law of nature. The intent of the Gospel is indeed to recover us to true holiness; but for this purpose there was need of something more than a revelation of moral obligation, which is set forth by the apostle : " Our Saviour Jesus Christ gave himself for us that he might redeem us from all iniquity, and purify unto himself a peculiar people, zealous of good works." Restoration to the Divine favour was the first thing to be provided for, and would, of course, be the first concern of every man as soon as he found he was " guilty before God." To what purpose to lay before a convinced sinner a rule of duty without giving him a ground of hope ? Discover to him pardon for past sins, and assistance for future obedience, and then such a rule would be seasonable; and this is the order in which the Gospel proceeds, as preached by the apostle: " And all things are of God, who hath reconciled us to himself by Jesus Christ, and hath given to us the ministry of reconciliation, to wit, that God was in Christ reconciling the world unto himself, not imputing their trespasses unto them. Now then we are ambassadors for Christ, as though God did beseech you by us : we pray you in Christ's stead, be ye reconciled to God. For he hath made him to be sin for us who knew no sin, that we might be made the righteousness of God in him."

There is no other scheme of doctrine which deserves even the name of the *Gospel*. Suppose the Gospel to be only a system of morality requiring that we should "be holy and without blame before him in love." Here is no good news for the sinner. He has no inclination or ability to be sanctified throughout, body, soul, and spirit. Suppose the Gospel treats principally of the resurrection. Here is no good news for the sinner. He is not delighted with the idea of rising again—he would rather remain in the grave for ever. Suppose the Gospel only brings "immortality to light." Here is no good news for the sinner. He is not pleased with the thought of eternal duration—he would rather cease his continuance. Suppose the Gospel only a promise of pardon and life, on condition of faith and repentance. Here is no good news for the sinner. It is bad news; his desire is only irritated to be disappointed—like a person engaging to give me an estate if I will fly to the moon. Or suppose the Gospel to be a revelation of absolute mercy as ready to pardon iniquity. Even here is no good news for the sinner, unless he can see a way in which it can come to him agreeably to the character which the Scripture has led him to entertain of God. "God is holy in all his ways, and righteous in all his works." Whatever favours he confers as a benefactor, he must preserve his claims as a legislator. Therefore, when I begin to be delighted with the glad tidings of Mercy, saying, 'Spare him, bless him;' I am terrified again by the language of Justice, 'Cut him off, destroy him.' It is evident the one, as well as the other, exists,—the one, as well as the other, has its claim. In this case, Mercy shows me the tree of life: Justice stands with flaming sword to guard it from approach. If we say, that we should take the declaration of God, that he will *pardon* iniquity, without any other consideration, and be satisfied of his doing it; why may we not say, that we should take the declaration of God, that he will *punish*

iniquity, without any other consideration, and be satisfied
of his doing it? Shall we make the Divine perfections
anything or nothing, magnifying one and depreciating
another? Is the Divine law to vary in its demand and fail
in its execution? Shall we weaken its authority by dis-
pensing with its penalty? We cannot do this; for if the
penalty be founded in the fitness of things, and agreeable
to the Divine perfections, (and unless it was so, God would
never have appointed it,) it follows, that not only we, but
God himself cannot dispense with it, any more than with
the whole law. I think no man can rationally hope for
pardon unless he can see a way in which God can do it *as
God*, and be "*faithful* and *just* to forgive us our sins, and
to cleanse us from all unrighteousness." Such a scheme is
the Gospel; it reveals a free, rich, righteous salvation through
Jesus Christ, "set forth to be a propitiation, through
faith in his blood." Hence it answers its name: it is good
news, glad tidings. It would be easy to illustrate this view
of the Gospel. If there was a man in debt, and I told him
a surety had discharged him,—if there was a man perishing
for want, and I told him of provision,—if there was a man
destitute of clothing, and I told him of raiment,—or if there
was a condemned man, and I told him of liberty and life ;
who does not see in each case that here would be good
news? Sinner, "behold, I bring thee glad tidings of great
joy." Sinner, indebted to Divine justice, having nothing
to pay, behold "the Surety of a better covenant," "the
Lamb of God, that taketh away the sin of the world."
Sinner, perishing with hunger, behold "the bread of life,
whereof if a man eat he shall never die." Naked soul, here
is "fine raiment that thou mayest be clothed; that the
shame of thy nakedness may not appear." And thou, poor
wretch, writing bitter things against thyself, condemned by
the holy law, crying, Where shall I flee for refuge? "Believe on the Lord Jesus Christ, and thou shalt be saved."

In order that the Gospel might be of advantage to us, faith is necessary. In whatever way the blessings of salvation are represented, faith is requisite to a proper enjoyment of them. One should imagine that benefits calculated to relieve our wants, and make us eternally happy, presented to us in the Gospel, would be eagerly embraced. But this is far from being the case. The pride of the human heart scorns to stoop, it hates obligation, it affects an independence. It will not submit to the righteousness which is of God; it would rather patch up a shelter than "flee for refuge to lay hold on the hope set before it in the Gospel."

Therefore the operation of the Spirit is necessary. This is one of the principal glories of the evangelical dispensation; and it shall be my endeavour to show my hearers that their regeneration, advance in holiness, support under trouble, final perseverance, everlasting triumph over all the cursed effects of sin, depend on the agency of the Holy Spirit. Revelation is no sooner admitted than reason confirms this truth. We allow that the miraculous operations of the Holy Spirit have ceased, because their necessity has ceased—but we affirm that his ordinary operations continue, because the necessity of them continues. Why was the Spirit given forth upon the followers of the Apostles? To sanctify them. Have we less need or more ability for sanctification than they had? It was given to "shed abroad the love of God in their hearts." Have we more spiritual, more fervent affections? It was given to help their infirmities. Have we less weakness? It was given to bear witness with their spirits that they were the children of God. Have we no need of this testimony to assure our hearts before Him? To deny the influences of the Spirit is to relax the energy of the Gospel, and turn the church into a valley of dry bones. To suppose an innate efficacy in the word to produce faith, is to suppose an innate virtue in the sun to produce a plant. The seed must be there previously before the one or the other can bring forth fruit. To talk of the fitness of things, the beauty of virtue, the union of moral and natural good and evil, is good in its nature and true in its fact; and upon men who are truly wise and well-disposed may have influence; but this is not forcible enough to disentangle the heart which is already an enemy to reason, allied to vice, sunk in sensuality, enslaved by appetite and passion. To produce faith is solely the prerogative of God; we own, indeed, that the word is a means in his hand, but deny that it possesses any power to do it independently of the Holy Ghost. The Gospel, therefore, is called "the ministration of the Spirit," because his influence renders it efficacious, and continues to make it an instrument of operation to the end of the world.

Holiness is necessary to present peace and future glory. "Without it no man shall see the Lord;" and so far is the doctrine of the cross from opposing this truth, that Jesus Christ crucified is the principle and end of it. The man who believes in him, believes in him for righteousness. While he disclaims merit he delights in gratitude; and it is his desire and endeavour to "walk before God in holiness and righteousness all the days of his life." He is as much distinguished by his practice as by his creed—his works are evidential of his faith, and his faith is the spring of his works; for in order to all true holiness, pride and the dominion of sense must be destroyed. And what can destroy the one or the other? Nothing ever has, nothing ever will, nothing ever can, but faith in Christ crucified. Every other scheme of doctrine which has spread in the world, has tended to promote one or the other. But the believer, from his union with the Saviour, experiences the gradual destruction of both, according to the words of the Apostle, "I am crucified with Christ, nevertheless I live, yet not I, but Christ liveth in me: and the life which I now live in the flesh, I live by the faith of the Son of God, who loved me and gave himself for me."

As it is the work of God, and he does nothing in time which he did not design to do from eternity, salvation is his own eternal purpose, and the effect of his gracious sovereignty; "according as he hath chosen us in him, that we should be holy and without blame before him in love; having predestinated us unto the adoption of children by Jesus Christ to himself, according to the good pleasure of his will, to the praise of the glory of his grace." And as his purpose, and the promises which are the discovery of it, cannot be broken, "the righteous shall hold on his way, and he that hath clean hands shall wax stronger and stronger."

[Mr. Winter's Charge followed this Declaration of Faith.]

LETTER VIII.

HIS RESIDENCE AT BATH :—PREDILECTIONS FOR IT :—CIRCUMSTANCES OF THE CONGREGATION :—HARMONY :—ADMISSION OF MEMBERS.

MY DEAR CHILDREN,—You have seen me inducted into my new, and which has proved my permanent, and is likely to prove my final, ecclesiastical connexion. Though the charm of novelty soon wore off, the congregation still increased. The place has three times been enlarged, yet in its present extent it is too small to meet applications for pews and sittings. During the lengthened period of my pastoral relation how many have I admitted into the church who have adorned their profession! How many have I also attended to the house appointed for all living! How much precious dust is reposing in my burying-ground! "The fathers, where are they?" and our brethren too? yea, and the sons, "as plants grown up in their youth?" and the daughters, "as corner-stones polished after the similitude of a palace?" where are all these? I, too, can "go to the grave to weep there—I also—."

"My soul desireth the first-ripe fruit;" yet we have no reason to despond, but much cause to be thankful. Instead of the fathers are the children. As many in the ranks have fallen, others have been baptized for the dead. The house is filled with inhabitants. The table is furnished with guests. Peace is within the walls, and prosperity within the palace.

It is worthy of grateful acknowledgment, especially considering the restless and disorganizing times in which we have lived, and the discords and divisions in so many churches, that the harmony of this religious interest has never been broken. Yet there have been considerable differences of judgment with regard to some measures; and we have not only had mixed communion, but have extended full membership, and even office-bearing, to our Baptist friends. Yet there has been no jar. "The dipped and the sprinkled *have* dwelt in peace." Bigotry on either side is not to be conquered by bigotry on the other, but by an opposite disposition. This continued state of things is very honourable to the members and deacons of the church, and shows that *their* religion has reached the temper as well as the understanding, and inspired them with the meekness of wisdom to pursue "things by which one may edify another." Should it, in any degree, serve to commend the pastor, it may perhaps, under God, be ascribed to his preferring influence to authority, and resolving to take no share in any party difference whatever.

You know, I always loved peace as well as truth, and liberality, and order. I hardly think I could have taken the charge of any church that *indispensably* required a candidate for communion to deliver before them an oral account of his conversion and experience, or to send in a written one. This mode of admission keeps back many who ought to be encouraged to come forward. Such are many females; such are the weak and timid in spirit; and such also are those whose religion has been so gradual as to yield none of those striking circumstances which a narrative loves and seeks after. And how often is this the case so;—that the convert can hardly describe anything but the result; like a man with a plant, who sees indeed the growth, while the growing escapes him. With us, the minister, or one of the officers, or one of the members, converses alone with the individual, and reports the nature and ground of his satisfaction at the church-meeting, when the matter is left for a month, during which inquiries are made after his moral character and deportment; at the end of which, if no objection is advanced, he is admitted. We are not qualified to judge the heart. We are to be influenced by favourable appearances, and should always lean to the side of charity rather than of suspicion. Some may think this rather dangerous, and affect to be alarmed for the purity of the church; but we have had from the beginning few, very few instances of excommunication or suspension, compared with the exactors of more rigid church-discipline. The truth is, *their* requisition never keeps back any improper person who wishes and is resolved to enter. The condition is a cheap passport which he can easily procure, so many accounts of conversions and experiences being published and sold.*

A little before my ordination an event took place the most interesting to my happiness, character, and usefulness. I was united to one of the best of women. This was Anne, the eldest daughter of the Rev. Edward Davies, a pious and evangelical clergyman of the Establishment, first rector of Bengeworth, Worcestershire, and afterwards of Coychurch. My acquaintance with her commenced on my first visit to London. Mr. Winter being acquainted with her excellent father, and knowing that he then resided near Surrey Chapel, wrote a letter to introduce me to him, and to beg that he would kindly notice me, and give me any hints of improvement he might deem necessary. I soon called and delivered it. It was then for the first time I saw Miss Davies. During the eight weeks I was preaching at Surrey Chapel, I was often invited to the house, and you will not wonder if sometimes I contrived to call without an invitation, for I felt a pleasing and powerful attraction. Yet I was able to act under the impression with some prudence. I concealed my affection as much as possible, till I had

---

* This subject is noticed again in Letter XVII., where we have added an explanatory note.

more fully observed, and found that observation justified an increased attachment. Yet I returned into the country, and paid another visit to Surrey Chapel before I ventured to make any direct advances. I had some reason to hope that my regard would not be contemned by the young lady herself. But there were *parental* difficulties to be overcome, which I can much more easily appreciate and excuse now than I could then. I had no patrimony: as yet I had nothing like an official provision, or even proper settlement. I was indeed much followed as a preacher, but it was justly said that popularity was very dangerous and corrupting; that many had fallen by it; that I was very young, and my character unformed, and as yet untried. Waiting, of course, was therefore recommended; and, as an absolute refusal was not given, the counsel was more easily followed.

My intended must have deemed me rather an awkward lover, and not a very satisfactory correspondent, for I always disliked letter-writing, and I had little leisure for courting by post. A part of what some of her sex would have deemed wanting with me, was, I can truly say, the effect of design and principle. I always felt for women who are flattered to adoration before marriage, and obliged to put up with at least comparative neglect and indifference afterwards; and I resolved to raise no expectations which I could not hope to realize, and not to suffer the husband to belie and disgrace the suitor.

I am, &c.

LETTER IX.

MY DEAR CHILDREN,—It is one of the peculiar circumstances which, without any contrivance and purpose of my own, have attended me through life, that, after another year of faith and patience (neither of these graces being very perfect), and just as I was going to settle in Bath, Mr. Davies having a dispensation for non-residence at his living, accepted the curacy of Batheaston, a pleasant village only two miles from Bath. Nothing could have been more gratifying to the feelings, and more friendly to the intercourse of the young parties, than this wholly unexpected approximation of residences. Things being now more favourable, Mr. Davies soon gave his consent; and some time after I went to London, where the elect was on a visit to her most intimate friend, Mrs. Rowland Hill. We were married at St. Peter's, Cornhill, January 6, 1791, Mr. Hill performing the service. In returning to Bath we paid our first visit to Mr. and Mrs. Winter at Painswick.

How much has resulted from this auspicious connexion for which I can never sufficiently praise the providence of my God and Father! How far I have succeeded, it does not become me to attempt to determine; but of this I am conscious, that I was always desirous and anxious to be a good husband; nothing in my estimation and remarkings ever being able to atone for the want of consistency and

excellency here, especially in a *minister*. But I must have
been one of the basest of men had I not always endeavoured
to act worthily towards the wife of *my* youth, to whom I am
under so many obligations. It was she (for we always
judge of the whole by parts, and chiefly by those parts
with which we are most acquainted), it was she who contributed so much to give me that exalted idea of the female
character which I have always entertained and expressed.
She excluded perfectly the entrance of every notion and
feeling of submission or authority, so that we had no rights
to adjust, or duties to regulate. She possessed every requisite that could render her a helpmate. Her special
qualities were admirably suited to my defects. She had an
extemporaneous readiness which never failed her, and an
intuitive decisiveness which seemed to require no delibera-
tion. Her domestic virtues rendered my house a complete
home—the abode of neatness, order, punctuality, peace,
cheerfulness, comfort, and attraction. She calmed my brow
when ruffled by disappointment and vexation; she encouraged me when depressed; she kept off a thousand
cares, and left me free to attend to the voice of my calling.
She reminded me of my engagements when I was forgetful,
and stimulated me when I was remiss, and always gently
enforced the *present* obligation, as "the duty of every day
required."

I mention this the more distinctly, not only to express
my own gratitude, but that my church and the public, if
they have derived any little advantage from my labours,
may see how much of it they owe to this wise and good
woman. She now stood in the additional relation of a
mother; and in process of time furnished me with a most
lovely family of six children, three of each sex, who "rose
up and called her blessed."

My first-born was a daughter, and named Anne, after her
mother. She seemed one of those who are sanctified from

the womb; and, instead of being averse to any of the duties required of her in her training, she appeared naturally and without admonition to fall in with them. She never gave us pain but by her own pain. When she was only seven years old, and we went abroad for a few days, not waiting for any intimation from us, the little creature read a chapter and a prayer every morning and evening with the servant and the nursemaid. At the age of sixteen she impressed a young American who was travelling through England, and, bringing letters of introduction, abode for a short time at our house. To him she was early married, and brought him a family of no less than thirteen children. They are all yet spared;[*] they are all walking in the truth, adorning their profession, blessing their generation, and showing what education, by the grace of God, may accomplish. After some years Mr. Bolton returned to the United States with the whole of his family. This separation, which could not be viewed but as probably a final parting as to this world, was one of the greatest trials of my life. Yet there were things which prevented my opposing it, and made it appear to be the path of duty. The dispensation has already had issues which serve in a great measure to explain it, while it seems also pregnant with future consequences of much importance. The marriage itself was strange and marvellous. What probability was there that a young gentleman from another quarter of the globe, first passing through Bath, and casually seeing her, should have been united in marriage to my daughter?

One thing struck me much in this affair from its beginning. It was my learning that he who asked to become my

---

[*] Abby Wolsey, the fifth daughter, has since been gathered to her rest, at the age of 21; a memoir, written by her sister, was published, entitled "The Lighted Valley," to which her grandfather added a preface, the last production of his pen which, we believe, has been given to the public.

son-in-law was himself the grandson of the pious and worthy
Mr. Bolton, merchant of Savannah, mentioned with so much
respect by Mr. Winter in one of his letters to me, to be
seen in my Life of him; for when this man of God was not
only neglected but despised, *because* he had gone to America
purposely to teach and Christianize the poor negroes, Mr.
Bolton received and encouraged him, and accommodated
him with a room in which he could instruct his sable charge
free of expense.

After a while my son-in-law joined the Episcopalian
Church, and is now the rector of St. Paul's, East Chester,
New York, where his labours are crowned with much
acceptance and success.*

My second child was a son, named after myself. From
the turn of his mind, when he had fulfilled his schooling, he
was apprenticed to an architect and surveyor in London,
where, after his time had expired, he continued for a while,
and then went to Savannah, in Georgia. There he was
employed for a few years; when, leaving many proofs of his
professional ability behind him, he returned to England.
After several attempts to succeed at home, he went out, by
the appointment of Lord Glenelg, on government service,
to the Mauritius. There his taste and talents met with full
encouragement, and his prospects were very promising; but
he was cut off by a premature death. A little before his
own dissolution he had buried a most pious and interesting
child, whose remains lie in the same grave with those of
Mrs. Newell, the wife of the American missionary. An

* Mr. and Mrs. Bolton, with part of their family, returned to
England some years before Mr. Jay's death, and had the melancholy
satisfaction of attending him in his last days. Two of his sons are
ministers in the Episcopal Church of England, and one in the
American; viz., Rev. William Jay Bolton, curate of Christ Church,
Cambridge; Rev. James Bolton, minister of St. Paul's Chapel,
Kilburn; Rev. Cornelius Winter Bolton, assistant minister of
Christ Church, Baltimore.

account of him has been published and widely circulated, called "Little Willy," drawn up by his mother, to which I prefixed a preface. Many, as well as myself, can testify that what is said of him is not maternal lavishment, but truth. My son had married a very estimable wife, Miss Louisa Coulston of Henley, by whom he had two other children besides "little Willy." These were left to be the care and comfort of the widowed mother, now keeping a school in her native place. My son, besides professional talent and cleverness, had a large share of wit and humour, qualities always dangerous and commonly injurious to the possessor. So it was, alas! here. His comic powers drew him into company, not the most friendly to youthful improvement. He was led into expense by his admirers and flatterers, and for a while left the path in which he had been taught to go. But the principles which had been early sown revived, especially under the teachings of affliction, and the conjugal influence of gentle, wise, and consistent piety. He sought the Lord God of his fathers, walked soberly, righteously, and godly, and finished his course in peace. And I record it to excite my gratitude and praise, and to encourage others who may be tried for a time in the same way. It has been delightful to my sorrowing spirit to read the testimonies concerning him which I received from two ministers, the one a missionary of the London Society, the other of the Church of England Missionary Society; as also from Mr. Alexander, the Keeper of the King's Stores.

My third-born was a daughter, whom we called Arabella, after a step-mother of Mrs. Jay's of uncommon piety, whose letters to her children were published, and of whose character an account is found among Gibbons' "Pious Women." She was early married to Garfit Ashton, Esq., a solicitor at Cambridge, and now also Clerk of the Peace. She has no family, but has been the most devoted of children, and has so attached herself to the comfort of her afflicted mother, as to entitle her to every endearment of my heart.*

My fourth-born was named Cyrus. As I always admired the Friends, and they seemed exemplary in training their youth to habitudes of order, and self-control, and disregard of ridicule and reproach, I was induced to place him for a considerable time at one of their schools. But I was not entirely satisfied with the result. The want of more *express* evangelical instruction, and the comparative deficiency of *instrumental* religion, were a disadvantage which I found it was not so easy to remedy. He fixed in London as an attorney, and married a daughter of my inestimable friend, the pious and benevolent Robert Spear, Esq. of Manchester.

My fifth child was named Edward, after his maternal grandfather. When quite a child he had nearly perished. His nursemaid had, by reading herself asleep, set fire to the curtains. I had just time to snatch him from a flaming bed, which was nearly all consumed, with other furniture in the room. He was at first educated for the ministry, and preached for some time with much approbation. But a timorousness and even dread with regard to his appearing and officiating in public, instead of decreasing by use, so grew upon him, and so threatened and even affected his health, that I was constrained to acquiesce in his importunity to leave the pulpit and enter secular life.

The last of my family was a daughter, named Statira after an eminent female of Grecian extraction, to whom my preaching had been useful in drawing her from the world into the way everlasting. She was not endowed with those personal attractions which some children possess, yet was

---

* Mrs. Ashton was suddenly removed by death shortly after the funeral of her beloved father. The particulars of this mournful event will be given in the Supplement to the Autobiography, in connexion with the account there inserted of the interment and funeral service of Mr. Jay.

pleasing to the eye of parental affection. She was a child of a very lovely and obliging temper, and apt at learning. She was also truly pious, and like her two sisters had early come to the table of the Lord. But at the age of nineteen I was summoned to resign her. She had been always free from ailments. I left her in perfect health, to go and preach at the opening of a new chapel at Tavistock in Devonshire; but I had not proceeded farther than Totness before a messenger overtook me with foreboding intelligence. I hastened back in anxious, trembling suspense, and reached home only just in time to see her dying of typhus fever. She was incapable of knowing the father around whose neck she had so often clung. I turned away, and was led by her mother into the solitude of my study. We kneeled down hand in hand to pray; but not a word was uttered. At such a season, how poor is speech; and how surprising is it that persons should employ it, and not yield to the devotion of silence and tears!

This was the first time death had entered our indulged dwelling. Till now I knew not what it was truly to be a parent. My heart was desolate within me; and there was danger that weeping would hinder sowing. As my ministry had always been very much of a consolatory kind, I began to dread the application of the address of Eliphaz to Job, " Behold, thou hast instructed many, and thou hast strengthened the weak hands; thy words have upholden him that was falling, and thou hast strengthened the feeble knees. But now it is come upon thee, and thou faintest; it toucheth thee, and thou art weary." What in a measure prevented this ?

" Oh, woman!   .   .   .   .

. . . .

When pain and anguish wring the brow,
A ministering angel thou!"

As being not only her husband, but her pastor, I ought

to have solaced and supported my wife under the loss, but she solaced and supported me.

One thing I peculiarly remember as arising from our affliction. Though I was not wanting in love to my wife before, yet now I felt her the more singularly endeared. No thought of her seemed so sacred and tender as that of the mother of my beloved and glorified daughter; and so I commonly addressed her in my letters.

I am, &c.

LETTER X.

MY DEAR CHILDREN,—I return to the notice of one connected so intimately, so importantly, and so influentially,
with my character and history; and so interesting to yourselves also. But now, alas! the narrative becomes as painful
as it was pleasing before.

Though in her early youth, and before I had the privilege of knowing her, your mother had been twice supposed
to be in a decline, for about thirty years after our marriage
she enjoyed continual good health. Her first complaint
was a degree of oppression in breathing, affecting her at
first occasionally, but rather growing, upon the whole, and
at length frequently returning with painful violence. From
some symptoms attending the suffering, (though I might
have mistaken them, and was afraid to inquire,) I feared
there was water on the chest. But this apprehension was
proved to be groundless, and her complaint was removed by
a sudden, painful seizure. My dear and invaluable friend,
Dr. Bowie, was instantly sent for, and did everything that
skill and unrelaxing attention could accomplish. Mr.
Wilson Brown, also an eminent surgeon, was peculiarly
kind and attentive.

About a year after her first attack she had a second,

though not attended with any paralysis. She was then at Clifton, with a dear friend, and her devoted servant, while I had gone to London for a few days on preaching business —not only with her full consent, but even recommendation. The seizure was violent, and left her for two hours and a half insensible; but professional assistance was close at hand. She was profusely depleted, and again revived. I hastened back, and again embraced her as one a second time given me from the dead.

Years have elapsed since this last attack without anything like a return; but I have always been constrained to rejoice with trembling. I have also long ceased to hope for any further improvement, especially as age was so gaining upon her. Yet much mercy has been mingled in my great trial; and I ought to have been, and I trust I have been, thankful for alleviations.

I know not whether the case is peculiar, in the reality or the degree, but I state the matter accurately; and I have been too long accustomed to the effect to be mistaken. As deviations and exceptions, instead of disproving a rule, sometimes only render it the more observable, in the case before us, owing to the frequency of the result, one might have been led to suppose that there was some kind of physical law in the operation where there was a contrariety, whether in nature or custom; her manner was nearly invariable. Thus she spoke of a drop of bread and a thin bit of water; she called the black white, and the white black; the cold heat, and the heat cold; preaching was hearing, and hearing was preaching; in the morning she wished you good evening, and in the evening good morning. Besides these *obvious* contrarieties, how many instances were there in the course of the day or hour in which the opposite did not strike you, till you reflected or examined, and then you perceived them. She is in a considerable measure apprehensive of this, and feels the greatness of the trial; and often complains, that though she knows everything she cannot command the right words. To relieve her embarrassment, at her own desire, she has ingeniously had written for her the names of a number of persons and things of which she is likely to speak; and often, after a pause or effort, she takes out the little book, which she always carries about with her. Till of late, her attempts to be again able to read, especially the Scriptures, have been great and incessant, and when she could succeed with a verse, she was much pleased with the achievement, and would often repeat it; while she was always craving for some one to read to her in the word of God, or books of experience and devotion.

Thus when the companion, so delightful and edifying by her discourse, was almost entirely removed,—the friend, the helper, the comforter was, in a considerable degree, yet graciously continued. And now that she has become in the course of nature more infirm and dependent, she is indescribably interesting. I cannot for a moment forget what she has been, and what she has done; or be insensible of my obligations to her. She needs and she occupies much of my attention, but attention endears her the more. My affection has now infused into it an unselfish tenderness, and I have learned by experience that the happiness of love results principally from its disinterestedness. And we know who has said, " It is more blessed to give than to receive."

Health is an unspeakable blessing, not only on the score of enjoyment, but of usefulness. Job called the season of his sickness " months of vanity," during which, as nothing was enjoyed, so nothing was pursued or accomplished. While disease deprives us of our liberty, and weakens our strength in the way, the hands of the workman are no longer sufficient for him—the eyes of the handmaiden no longer look to their mistress—the mother leaves her infant

charge to less tender care—and the preacher, whose lips fed
many, ceases to deal forth the bread of life. Paul, therefore, not only instructs his son Timothy as an apostle, but
prescribes for him as a physician : " Drink no longer water,
but use a little wine, for thy stomach's sake, and thine often
infirmities." Next to our spiritual welfare is the good
estate of the body; therefore John says of Gaius, " Beloved,
I wish above all things that thou mayest prosper and be in
health, even as thy soul prospereth." A word, therefore,
concerning the degree, the interruption, the recovery, and
the preservation of my health, may not be improper or
useless.

I had never a very strong constitution, or, at least, a
remarkable freedom from slight indispositions. For a
great length of time I had almost incessant headaches,
which rendered my preaching difficult, and my studies painful. Many will remember the several seizures in my head
with which I was visited, and which more than once befell
me in the pulpit. They were very sudden. They momen-
tarily confused my sight, and nearly deprived me of all
consciousness. The faculty, who then attended me, viewed
these attacks as serious and perilous; and I was bled, and
cupped, and reduced in strength and size, till I seemed a
shadow hastening to the grave. This I could not have
borne much longer. In this state, Mr. Wilberforce, being
in Bath, called upon me, and urged me to see Dr. Baillie,
whom he extolled as his friend and physician. He expressed
the greatest confidence in his judgment, and offered to write
me a letter of introduction. I gratefully accepted his kindness, and repaired to town. The doctor favourably received
me ; paid (in consequence of the recommendation) a good
deal of attention to my case ; and to the kind and seasonable advice of the negro's friend, I am fully persuaded, I
owe, under God, the prolongation of my life and labours.
And I cannot but here remark two things—*First,* " A word

fitly spoken how good is it!" and what important consequences may arise from a single instruction or admonition!
Secondly, We see the propriety of sometimes varying medical authority. No man is infallible. What does not
strike one may strike another. When a physician is called
in, he may immediately form and express his opinion of the
case, and then go on looking, not for what corrects but confirms his conviction, till every doubt or suspicion of the
possibility of mistake is lulled to sleep.

I should have mentioned before, that at rather an early
period of my ministry I suffered very considerably from a
nervous malady, and which threatened for the time to lay
me aside from my work. This was of *my own procuring*, in
neglecting for a season early rising, and proper air and exercise, and confining myself to long and sedentary reading
and writing. From a firm conviction of my own, I threw
off, by degrees, but not without difficulty, this affecting and
deplorable complaint, to return no more. Yet, as every
kind of experience is useful to a minister, the suffering has
been overruled for good, as it has enabled me to sympathize,
where otherwise, perhaps, I should have felt nothing; to
warn and admonish any of my brethren likely to err in the
same way; and to regulate my own applications, and to
blend action with thought; and to do much of the work of
the study in the open air. In vain we talk of the value of
health, or expect to enjoy the blessing, unless we use the
rational means for preserving it. These means will not
deliver us from the sentence of mortality, but they may
lengthen our days, and render them more tolerable, delightful, and profitable. With few exceptions, I have always
practised early rising, being seldom in bed, summer or
winter, after five o'clock; and this has been with me, not
as with some, who say they rise because they cannot sleep;
for it has been always an act of self-denial, since I could
enjoy more; but I felt a conviction that it was morally

right, as it redeemed time and aided duty; and also that it
was physically right, as it was wholesome and healthful.
How does it refresh and invigorate the body, revive the
animal spirits, and exhilarate and elevate the mind! Yet
how many are there, and even ministers, and young ministers, not too much qualified for their work, who can sacrifice all this advantage to the lazy, low, debilitating, dis-
reputable influences of a late indulgence in bed!

In looking back upon the years I have passed through,
for nothing am I more thankful than the cautions I was led
to exercise with regard to *drinking*.*   I knew the danger of
increase with regard to spirituous liquors; I knew what

---

* In the year 1839, Mr. Jay was solicited to attend a Festival of
the Teetotal Society in Bath, but as this was not convenient, he
conveyed his sentiments to the meeting in the following letter, which
was afterwards published extensively both in this country and in
America:—

" My dear Sir,—Circumstances will prevent my accepting your
invitation to attend the Teetotal Christmas Festival on Friday evening. I am thankful that all through life I have been a very temperate
man, and for more than twenty-five years *generally*, a Teetotaller,
but for the last six years I have been one constantly and entirely.
To this (now I am past 70) I ascribe, under God, the glow of health,
evenness of spirits, freshness of feeling, ease of application, and
comparative inexhaustion by public labours, I now enjoy.

" The subject of Teetotalism I have examined physically, morally,
and christianly; and after all my reading, reflection, observation,
and experience, I have reached a very firm and powerful conviction.
*I believe that next to the glorious Gospel, God could not bless the human
race so much as by the abolition of all intoxicating liquors.*

" As every man has some influence, and as we ought to employ
usefully all our talents, and as I have been for near half a century
endeavouring in this city to serve my generation, by the will of God,
I have no objection to your using this testimony in any way you
please. I am willing that both as a *Pledger* and a Subscriber you
should put down the name of,

" My dear Sir,

" Yours truly,

" *Percy Place, Bath, 24th December.*   " W. Jay."

temptations a young minister of some considerable popularity is exposed to in his frequent dinings-out, especially in great town and cities, and at the table of professors who vie with each other in extravagance; for the faithful do not always add to their faith "temperance." As far as it was in my power, by word and deed, I always discountenanced such needless and improper "feastings of themselves without fear." I commonly used water, *principally*, and, for years back, *only*; and I am fully persuaded that it has befriended my digestion, preserved the evenness of my spirits, and added to my comfort, especially in my feeling cool and fresh in the relaxation and lassitude of warm weather, while others were deservedly panting, and burdens to themselves. My natural wants were so many, that I never thought of adding to them the cravings of fictitious appetites equally importunate. I had, therefore, no trouble or expense from the wretched habits of snuff-taking or smoking. I have often found perspiration produced by a brisk walk or working in the garden, or cleaving of wood, the means of relieving me from many a slight ailment, especially headaches. To which I may add that I have often also derived benefit of this kind from preaching; but then it has been, not by dry discussions, or laboured recollections, or stale repetitions, but by animating subjects, producing a lively frame, and fine glowing emotions; then I have often come from the engagement with renewed strength, and "anointed as with fresh oil." Perhaps the thing can be physically accounted for; if not, I have experienced the effect too often to question the truth of it. I ought to bless God, not only that my life has been continued so long after some menacing appearances, but that I have been laid by so few Sabbaths upon the whole, and can now perform my usual and occasional services with as much vigour and pleasure as ever.

I am, &c.

LETTER XI.

HIS AUTHORSHIP :—FIRST VOLUME OF SERMONS :—MONTHLY REVIEW :—
SUCCEEDING PUBLICATIONS :—HYMNS, ETC.

MY DEAR CHILDREN,—My authorship is too important
an article in my little history to be overlooked. I had
early, too early, published several single sermons; but they
neither excited nor deserved much notice. I have not,
therefore, perpetuated them in the list of my works. But
having delivered a discourse on "The Mutual Duties of
Husbands and Wives," at the nuptials of a gentleman who
married his lady immediately from my house, I was impor-
tuned to publish it. It rapidly went through six large
editions, and was not a little commended in several of the
periodicals of the day, and by Mr. Hall from the pulpit.
This encouraged me soon after to venture before the public
a volume of sermons on various subjects. This also was
favourably received, and was spoken well of even by the
"Monthly Review," then a work of much authority. Not
long after this I published a second volume, with similar
acceptance and success. I should, perhaps, *now* deem some
of these sermons not sufficiently evangelical; but I then
expected them to be read principally by those who were
already acquainted with the doctrines of the Gospel, and
some of whom were more familiar with doctrinal than practical theology. It was also at the same time my intention
to add a third volume, containing subjects of a more doctrinal character.

I next published, in succession, four volumes of "Short

Discourses for the Use of Families." These, too, were kindly received, and went through repeated editions, and procured for me a diploma of D.D.,—a dignity I never used, except once in travelling, when I left a case of manuscripts at a large inn, the better to ensure attention to the recovery; and it answered my purpose. Who, then, can deny the usefulness of such honours? I also sent forth two works of a biographical kind: "The Life of the Rev. Cornelius Winter," and "Memoirs of the Rev. John Clarke." The first of these sold well; the sale of the second was slow and limited; yet it occasioned me more pains than any other of my publications; and in America they have published extensively my remarks and observations, *detached* from the narrative itself, furnished by the Diary of the deceased.

I also published two volumes of "Morning Exercises for the Closet," which soon reached a tenth edition; and, three years after, I yielded to importunity, and produced two more volumes of similar exercises for the "Evening." I cannot but hope, from the wide circulation of these "Exercises," and the testimonies I have received from so many quarters, that they have been owned of God, and will continue to be useful after my decease.

Between the Morning and Evening Exercises, I preached and published a work, called "The Christian Contemplated," in twelve lectures. To these I afterwards, by desire, and as a kind of application of the whole, added another lecture, from the words, "Almost thou persuadest me to be a Christian." This work also sold rapidly, and has now reached the eighth edition.

But the work which has had the largest sale, next to the Morning and Evening Exercises, and is still in demand, is, "The Domestic Minister's Assistant." It consists of morning and evening prayers for six weeks, with additional ones for particular seasons and occasions. Some of my brethren were rather disposed to be displeased with this publication, and accused me of aiding what they called the cause of formality; but I bless God that I ever was led to undertake it. I only herein followed the example of some very eminent ministers of our own body, such as Baxter, Henry, and Watts, &c. And are we not commanded, "as we have opportunity, to do good unto all men?" Is there no difference between preference and exclusiveness? Is the assistance of the weak any injury to the strong? There are persons who pray spiritually with a form; and there are persons that pray very formally without a form.

The smaller publications were, "An Essay on Marriage," "A Charge to a Minister's Wife," "A Preface to Mrs. Savage's Memoirs," some Funeral Orations, with a large number of single Sermons, preached on particular occasions. I also published an Appendix of Hymns, but the contents are principally selections from other authors; and I am only answerable for about twenty new composures, and some introductory remarks on psalmody. I have not mentioned all the publications in the order of time in which they appeared; but this could easily be ascertained by their dates, were it of any importance.

There has been no complete edition of these works in England till that which is now forthcoming; but a very handsome one was published some years ago at Baltimore, in America; and there have been several since; for *there* God has much smiled upon my labours.

Many of my publications, especially the principal ones, were begun, or completed, or much advanced, when I was taking an annual excursion by the sea-side, and had a little more leisure than necessary relaxation and occasional preaching at those seasons required. I have given some account of this in the preface to the last volume of the Morning and Evening Exercises.

I have not been able to do justice to any of these works,

or even to the degree of my comparative ability, for want of more time and abstraction, in composing and revising, than could be obtained from a large congregation, four services a week at home, and numerous calls to preach on special occasions abroad. I have rarely been at liberty to transcribe, and have frequently written from short and imperfect notes, to supply the immediate demands of the printer. I do not mention this to boast anything like great readiness in composition, or to justify haste where it could be avoided; but to intimate that among engagements and interruptions I did what I was able. At an earlier period I might, perhaps, have pleaded this, to soften, if not to disarm, critical censure; but my advanced years remind me that I ought to think only of the approbation of God, regardless of being "judged of man's judgment."

Since the Lord has so favourably disposed the public mind to receive my writings, notwithstanding their defects, I need not lament that I have published so much, as it enables me to do a little good in many places at the same time, and may lengthen a degree of usefulness beyond natural life. I hope it makes me humble rather than proud, (I am sure it ought,) to think how many, in particular, I am continually attending in their most sacred moments of retirement, and aiding at the family altar, as well as helping in their general religious concerns.

I am also thankful, that though a man's writings will always have a tinge of his own opinions, I have published nothing that can fairly or justly give offence to any religious parties among those who "hold the Head." Let a man, if he please, state and defend his own peculiar views in a work of *itself*, and professing its own purpose; but I always disliked the smuggling of particular sentiments into a subject designed and adapted to general usefulness.

I do not consider my Sermon on the Reformation as an exception to this remark. The occasion was singular, and

allowed and required me to speak freely. If any suppose
that because I conceded to the Catholics their civil rights, I
was too candid towards the doctrines and superstitions of
Popery, they have but to peruse the Sermon to see that
they were mistaken. If any members of the Established
Church were offended, it was only those who did not hear
the Sermon, but only heard of it, in connexion with a gross
misrepresentation, which ignorance reported and bigotry
spread, and which was soon rectified by public denials.
These denials, however, the author never called for, having
always followed an advice early given him by a very wise
and good man, viz., never to notice anything said of him in
newspapers and periodicals. There were witnesses enough,
in the numbers that attended the discourse, who could
vouch for his innocency of the charges which were malici-
ously and eagerly circulated.   The libel was, that he
affirmed the only difference between the Church of Rome
and the Church of England was the same as between a
toad and a tadpole. The preacher was applying this coarse
image to another subject; the liars transferred it to this.
It was also an Episcopalian, and not a member of his own
congregation, who drew up the application for him to publish the sermon.   One thing said gave offence to some, who
have since seen it abundantly explained and exemplified—
The Popery of Protestantism. How truly and forcibly has
Dr. Chalmers enlarged on this !

I am, &c.

LETTER XII.

MY DEAR CHILDREN,—While musing with what I should
fill this sheet, it struck me that I would notice the disadvantages arising from my original state in life, and see
what there has been in any degree to counterbalance them.
I have nothing to lament on account of it physically ; yea,
I was more likely to inherit a purer blood, and a sounder
constitution, by being born of healthful, robust, and active
peasants, than if I had descended from the enervating and
disease-breeding habitudes and indulgences of higher life.
But my early condition painfully affected my ease and confidence in company. I, therefore, rarely ever felt myself at
home, or in my element, unless in some very special instances. This, however, was overruled for good, by keeping
me much out of society, and giving me more time for reading and study, which I both wanted and desired. Hence,
also, in a measure, arose my backwardness to speak at
public meetings. For the sacredness of the temple I had
been accustomed privately to prepare, and the presence of
God seemed to reduce creatures to their proper level.

Thus when I had to preach before the Duke of Sussex, at
the opening of Hanover Chapel, instead of dining with His
Royal Highness and a large company previously to the
service, I passed the time in retirement ; and when I left
it, to enter the pulpit, I felt no more than if I had been

going to preach Christ in a poor-house. One of the papers
of the day abused me for the freedom of my address; but
as I never had been accustomed to speak evil of dignities,
so I was not likely to insult greatness to its face. The case
was, retirement had awakened conscience, and conscience
accompanied me in the pulpit, and bade me speak, "not as
pleasing men, but God who trieth our hearts," and with
whom "there is no respect of persons." I never consider
myself as chargeable with personal reflection, when I am
conscious I should deliver the same things from the same
words, in any other place or to any other audience. But
I could never (so modelled and governed are we by habit
and circumstances) realize this frame in a town-hall or an
assembly-room. There, notwithstanding the object of the
meeting, it seemed to be a kind of civil proceeding; and
I felt as only among men whose presence and manner
confounded me. The expectation of being called upon to
propose or second some motion has crucified me in the
prospect, for the whole preceding night; and it sometimes
induced me to abstain from places and assemblies, which
I should otherwise have delighted to attend. I have also
felt impressed with an invincible apprehension that I did
not succeed when I made the attempt. After my first
speech on occasion of the first meeting of the Bible Society
in Bath, I was desired by a rude member of the committee
to furnish for publication in the provincial papers, "as
much of what I had delivered as had any relation to the
business of the day." This so completely chilled me, that
I spoke but once after, and without any of that freedom
which would give it grace or effect. Then I came to a
determination, that, to prevent importunity, I would refuse
all future applications. I the more readily adopted this
resolution, as I had a plenitude of other pressing claims.
I was also afterwards confirmed in the propriety of it
by Dr. Chalmers, who, when I was at his house in

Glasgow, remarked, "The pulpit is the preacher's appropriate station; and he can there be most influential and useful, by touching a number of springs which will set all in motion." Observation also has kept me from repenting of my resolution. I have seen that ministers, who, as platform orators, have figured much at these meetings, have been sadly drawn off from keeping their own vineyards. Nor, in general, are preachers on these occasions the best or the most acceptable speakers. They are too professional —too sermonic. Laymen, who speak more briefly, more simply, and apparently more from the heart, are commonly more effective, and are heard to more advantage. My esteemed friend Mr. Hughes, one of the secretaries of the Bible Society, also confirmed this; and he had the best opportunities to judge.

"Every man in his own order:" we have all our particular dispensations under which we should be content to labour, and getting above which, we soon appear to be out of our place. Genteel life lays restraints on the expression of feeling, and gives a softness to the manners, and a courtesy to the speech, especially in differences of opinion. Here, I fear, I also have sometimes, if not frequently, erred, having been hasty of spirit in conversational disputes, if not rudely decisive. But the great disadvantage arising from my original condition was the want of an early and good education. As this was not placed within my reach, I have no feeling of shame or of blame on account of wanting it; but I am persuaded I should, had the opportunity been afforded me, have seized it with avidity; and have made that progress which depends on some degree of talent, accompanied with much application and diligence. I say nothing, therefore, in depreciation of schools and learning;—but it becomes me to dwell on any consideration that tends to reconcile me to the will of God in denying me, what I shall ever deem a privilege; and, viewing things in their bearing

on my ministry, I was, perhaps, by my previous circumstances, more acquainted with the lower ranks in the community, and could better accommodate myself to their modes
of thinking and feeling.   And may not this be one reason
why God takes so many of his labourers from common life?
And how was it with the great Teacher sent from God?
We are aware of a grand speciality in his case.   He had
knowledge by intuition—but he communicated it naturally.
His teaching was unlike that of the doctors of the schools,
—"He spake as one having authority, and not as the
scribes."   He did not soar above vulgar apprehension.   He
did not abound in learned allusions.   His images were all
taken from familiar scenes.   Other teachers were very fine
—he was very simple.   They were mechanism—he was
nature.   "The poor," therefore, had "the gospel preached
unto *them*," and "the *common* people heard *him* gladly."
Was this recorded of him who "spake as never man spake"
in a way of commendation?   Why then do we not seek to
resemble him?

Cromwell always ordered his soldiers to fire low; and
what execution would they have done had they fired high?
Such are the effects of *their* preaching who shoot over their
hearers' heads.   Have we never seen an audience gaping
with admiration at what they did not understand;—nor
perhaps their wonderful and astonishing orator either?   It
is easy to give a discourse the appearance of depth, or originality, by certain terms and unusualnesses of expression;
or by turning prose into a kind of blank verse.   But this
strikes only the injudicious,—not "the wise in heart."
They easily see, under the garish ornaments, only the mere
common-place which they would not despise, but for its silly
affectation of finery.

I have been asked, whether my happiness was increased
and improved by the change and elevation in life which I
have experienced?   It may not be amiss to offer a few

reflections suited to this inquiry.—"The Lord," says the church, "shall choose our inheritance for us." When Saul's courtiers reproached David as a restless, ambitious young man, who, dissatisfied with a private station, was endeavouring to climb into eminence and publicity, he was able to make this appeal,—"Lord, my heart is not haughty nor mine eyes lofty; neither do I exercise myself in great matters, nor in things too high for me." He well knew that the first notice he excited, and which led to everything else, was, as to himself, purely accidental. He was sent by his father to carry provision to his brethren in the camp, and to learn how they did. He had then no expectation of seeing or engaging Goliath; but it was so; and the Lord brought it to pass; for there was nothing in the event casual as to Him. If smaller things may be compared with greater, I am equally sure, that the revolution in my circumstances was by the providence of God; not a thought of the change—much less a design, was, or could have been, rationally entertained by myself or my friends, till the door was suddenly opened, in an entirely new direction; and I was led by a way I knew not, and in paths which I had not known. In such a case, the will of God is to be supremely regarded; and the dispensation is not to be judged of by what we suffer or enjoy. He has an absolute propriety in us; and may dispose of us as seemeth good in his sight. His work is perfect—his ways are judgment. His purpose also is often comprehensive and extensive, involving references far beyond our present views and circumstances. Men are naturally far from being content with such things as they have; and as to the future, a rising in life seems always to appear very desirable. It would be very ungrateful in me, not to acknowledge the goodness, as well as the agency of God; and especially, considering the results, not to exclaim with David, "What am I, and what is my father's house, that thou hast brought me hitherto?" But I am

not disposed from experience to make men dissatisfied with
their own allotment, and to seek great things for themselves,
by representing all the advantages as to enjoyment, on the
ascending side.   It was not the shepherd of Bethlehem, but
the hero of the age, and the monarch of Israel, that cried,
" Oh that I had wings like a dove, for then would I fly
away and be at rest ! "   If the robe be lengthened, it is not
the less likely to be soiled, or torn, or trampled on.   Pos-
sessions gender fears and cares ; talents increase responsibilities ; where much is given, much will be required.   And
who can be satisfied with his own improvements ?   Many
new sources of usefulness may be opened, and this will
weigh with a pious mind.   But the Lord looketh on the
heart ; and " where there is first a willing mind, it is
accepted according to what a man hath, and not according
to what he hath not."   The Saviour could not have extolled
an apostle, or an angel, more than he did Mary, when he
said, " She hath done what she could."

> " Who does the best his circumstance allows,
>   Does well—acts nobly—angels could no more."

Many new sources of pleasure also may be opened ; but
every comfort has its cross ; sensibility also may be quickened ; but strong feeling may increase anguish as well as
enjoyment.   A man, if destitute of the necessaries of life,
must be wretched ; but if he has a sufficiency with regard to
food, clothing, and habitation, suited to his state, he may be
called poor ; but he is only comparatively so.   Crabbe often
takes his aim too low ; his poor are the abject poor—the
inmates of a parish workhouse, or the contents of the back
streets of a borough, and commonly immoral and vicious.
But take a peasant or a mechanic in a village, sober, moral,
religious ; his wishes bounded by the simplicity of rural life
—his sleep sweet—his meals, though plain, sauced by appetite—his hands sufficient for him—his labour limited and

free from distracting cares—his little garden yielding him
the useful vegetable and the Sunday flower—the Sabbath a
day of pleasing change, and rest, and refreshment of spirits
—the going to the house of God in company—and the
Bible, now more amply read, though not forgotten during
the week—take such an one, and his condition, as to enjoyment, will not shrink from a comparison with the state of
thousands, who never look down upon him but with contempt, or pity, or indifference.

There are those who are not theorists here—they " speak
that they do know, and testify that they have seen." It is
said of Burns, by Dugald Stewart, that as they were walking
together one morning, in the direction of the Braid Hills,
where they commanded a prospect of the adjacent country,
the poet remarked, that the sight of so many smoking cottages gave a pleasure to his mind, which he did not believe
any one could understand, that did not know as he did, how
much of real worth and happiness such humble habitations
might contain. My testimony, perhaps, may be supposed
to be too favourable, and to require some deduction, on two
accounts:—*First:*—That I left village life early, and before I
was grown up, so as to be fully initiated into its good or evil.
There is some little force in this; though I was old enough
to observe, and feel, and judge. *Secondly:*—That in my
boyhood, village life was superior to what it now is. This
deserves notice; for there have been, I fear, many changes
for the worse. I need not describe what it is at present.
But when I left the neighbourhood of my native place,
abject penury, and extreme destitution, and sordid suffering,
were rarely to be seen. Most even of the cottagers had a
swine-sty, and baked their own bread; many of them also
brewed their own beer, or made cider, and, if not for constant use, had a little beverage for festivals and particular
occasions. Those who, during mowing and reaping seasons,
went forth to labour carried their bottle afield with them,

and were generally supplied at meals with cold or warm
meat and vegetables. Now, bread and water, with few
exceptions, is all the provision, all the support, all the comfort, thousands of men, women, and children have amidst
the burning sunshine and exhausting labour of a summer's
day. I was lately walking among a number of hard-working
peasants in time of harvest, with an intelligent and humane
farmer, who said to me, " You see these thin, meagre figures,
with patched and ragged clothing;—they have been toiling
here from early dawn to this scorching noon, and have had,
perhaps, little more than a can of water and a crust of
bread ; and will toil on till evening calls them to a similar
repast at home, and to sleep, their only rest. Oh, sir," said
he, "nothing surprises me so much, as the honesty, and
quiet submission, and unresistingness of these sufferers;—
and we cannot reach and change their state."

> " Let not ambition mock their useful toil,
> Their homely joys and destiny obscure ;
> Nor grandeur hear with a disdainful smile,
> The short and simple annals of the poor."

I am, &c.

LETTER XIII.

MY DEAR CHILDREN,—I feel at a loss to determine what
particulars to communicate concerning myself; but some
things, not generally interesting to others, may be, in a
measure, gratifying, if not useful, to my own relations, and
partial friends.

I would now advert to my reading. As to this I never
pursued any particular plan, but was much determined by
accident, and led by opportune circumstances. I am not
recommending or justifying this course, but stating a fact.
I was never accustomed to write out extracts from authors.
This I lament, as there are many passages I should be glad
to review, but know not where to find them in volumes I
shall probably never have time to look through again.

I was always a devourer of books that came in my way;
and, in order to read the more, and not commanding the
leisure I wished, I have learned to read with great rapidity,
so that I can throw my eye over the pages, and dispatch a
tolerable publication at one or two sittings. My reading
also was very miscellaneous. I seldom refused anything
that came in my way, as I found there was nothing that fell
under the notice of a minister but may be turned to some
account. I, therefore, did not restrict my attention to

works advocating the sentiments of my own denomination.
I was fond of scanning periodicals, few of which, of any
note, escaped me. Though a dissenter, I always read and
admired the "Christian Observer," and took it in from the
beginning. Though a cordial believer in evangelical principles, I never omitted those Cyclopes of literature—the
Edinburgh and Quarterly Reviews. On general subjects—
and how many of these are there!—I have derived profit
from divines whose theological views have differed widely
from my own. In divinity, for unction, illustration, excitement, and effect, I have much preferred the old authors to
most of the moderns. I love not to be singular, but I never
could applaud Baxter *above* his brethren. He was a most
holy and heavenly-minded man; but I am speaking of him
as an author. He was *often* too speculative and metaphysical, and he confessed and lamented it before his death.
He knew his skill, and, therefore, attempted to saw the
beams of cobwebs into planks, and multiplied distinctions
as well as particulars, to the perplexity of the reader. His
more experimental and practical writings are very excellent;
but I never perceived more spirituality, or seriousness, or
earnestness, in them, than in the productions of many of
his cotemporaries. Does he in these qualities surpass
Alleine, or Howe, or others of his brethren?

Leighton and Newton were always, with me, very favourite authors. What men of God were these! What a
Christian spirit, what a Scriptural manner, what an experimental knowledge, what a devotional savour, do we always
find in their writings! When a very young preacher, I was
much struck with Dr. Hunter, and still more with Saurin.
This eloquent author made such an impression upon me,
that I instantly began to learn French, to be able to read
him in the original, and to peruse the remainder of his
untranslated sermons, as well as his other works. By this
acquisition I gained access to the writings of many French

divines, Catholic and Protestant, many of which I continue
to value.

But as we advance towards maturity of taste we shall
relish the natural more than the artificial; and not only
distinguish between finery and elegance, but perceive that
the one is destructive of the other. For disentangling a
subject from confusion, for the power of development, for
genuine simplification, for invention, what writer ever surpassed Robinson of Cambridge ? Yet the sad defection of
this inimitable genius from the truth, and the insinuations
by which, I fear, he aimed to sap the doctrines he did not
openly attack, render familiarity with his works dangerous.
I found it so with regard to myself, and this has kept me
from warmly recommending the perusal to my younger
brethren, who are often in nothing " so much to seek,"
as in simplicity and naturalness.

The composition of Davies's Sermons, of New England, is
too equable and elaborate, and wants relief and shade; but
I must confess, no discourses ever appeared to me so adapted
to awaken the conscience and impress the heart. In reading them, one seems always to feel that they were written
by a man who never looked off from the value of a soul and
the importance of eternity; or sought for anything but to
bring his hearers under " the powers of the world to come."
I could wish the sermons of Flavel were better known,
(especially by some of our ministers,) and more prized
and imitated.   They excel in evangelism and in brevity,
(not the common character of the age in which they were
written,) and in avoiding or rendering needless much ex-
plication; its room being occupied by natural inferences
and striking applications. The late Mr. Hall spoke much
to me in their favour.

Having mentioned the name of this truly great man,
I must judge for myself even in his presence, and express
my dissent from him with regard to Dr. Owen. I think

Mr. Hall must have conceived a prejudice against this eminent theologian, from having read only some unfavourable specimen of his works; for I am persuaded, from his manner when Owen was mentioned in his company, that he was not familiar with his publications at large. However this may be, I cannot but join Newton and Cecil in considering him the prince of divines. We let go some of his controversial works, (though even these display much learning and acumen) ; but it seems not a little strange that the author of the " Exposition of the Epistle to the Hebrews," and " The One Hundred and Thirtieth Psalm," and the treatises on " The Spirit," and on " The Person and Glory of Christ," and on " Spiritual Mindedness," and on " The Mortification of Sin in Believers," &c., should have been called " *a continent of mud*." *

As to commentators, I have always deemed Mr. Scott, upon the whole, the best expositor for the connected meaning of Scripture, and for the consultation of ministers in any difficulties. The very first page I ever wrote that appeared in print was in recommendation of this work. This may seem strange, and be deemed assuming ; but the work was then coming forth in numbers, and (not the author, but) the publishers craved testimonies in its favour from every one who was likely to influence a single subscriber ; and these were printed on the wrappers of the numbers as they came out. Yet I did not write without exercising my judgment, and feeling a conviction which has grown upon me ever since. But for private and pious use I never found anything comparable to Henry, which, as old

* In the Life of the Rev. Robert Hall, by Dr. Gregory, p. 125, this expression is said to have been applied to Dr. Gill's Works. As Mr. Jay does not say that he heard Mr. Hall use the words in reference to Dr. Owen's works, it is very possible that there was a misapplication either by Mr. Jay, or the party from whom he received the anecdote.

John Ryland said, " a person cannot begin to read without wishing he was shut out from all the world, and able to read it through, without stopping."

I always much preferred our own divines to foreign theologians, especially those of the German school—a growing fondness for which I deem no good omen. I have also much prized the French Hugonot divines, who wrote before, and some a little after, the Revocation of the Edict of Nantes. These I consider as deservedly vying with our own theologians, in talent and Scriptural knowledge, and considerably before them in composition, with the exception of Bates. Would God there was a revival of these great and good men in their now infidel, superstitious, irreligious, and distracted country!

As to my *studying*, I never set apart regularly any particular time, thereby reducing the exercise to a kind of mechanism, or compulsion. I endeavoured to think more habitually. As to preaching, I chose my texts and subjects as early in the week as possible. Thus I not only had always something to fill any spare moments ; but, approaching what I had selected for discussion, without constraint and repeatedly, and from different sides and aspects, it opened to my mind more naturally and easily, and with more enlargement and variety.

After a nervous malady, and to avoid sedentariness, I also much accustomed myself to think abroad. The practice was difficult at first, as my attention was often diverted; but I soon by use acquired the power of fixed and regular application ; and the sceneries of nature rather aided than injured my meditations; inspiring also the trains of my reflection with a freshness and feeling underivable from dry and dull porings over books. In these musings in the garden, the meadow, the field, the wood, the leading ideas of my discourse soon fell into their proper places, and a division resulted without much effort; so that when I came

home, I had only to secure what I had already found, and
to write what I had already methodized; and I could, without short-hand, which I lament I never learned, by various
contractions and natural signs, easily remembered, include
much of my subject in a small compass. I, therefore, seldom
or never wrote a sermon at full length, but only a draft or
sketch, (it is commonly, as you know, called a skeleton,)
more or less full, according to its requirements, leaving the
subordinate fillings-up, after meditation and prayer, to the
impressiveness and the excitation of the audience, and in
the delivery, and the assistance authorized to be hoped for
where means have been duly used. Even these notes I
never took with me into the pulpit, till within the past
year, and I am sorry I ever took them. The memory, like
a friend, loves to be trusted, and seldom fails to reward the
confidence reposed in it.

Though I did not usually write my sermons, in order
either to read or mandate them, (according to the Scottish
phrase and practice), yet I rarely neglected my pen. As
I had opportunity, I was constantly committing thoughts
and sentiments to writing. It was one of the advices of
Mrs. Hannah More, at my first acquaintance with her, to
write much. "It matters not, comparatively," said that
extraordinary woman (to whom I early owed much), "on
what a young composer first writes; by the constant use of
his pen, he will soon form a style; and by nothing else can
he attain it." She also recommended writing with as
much *celerity* as possible, regardless of trifling inaccuracies.
"These," she said, "should not be suffered to check and
cool the mind. They may be safely left for correction in
review; while advantage is taken of the heat of composition
to go on to the end; it being better to produce the whole
figure at one fusion, than to cast successively various parts,
and then conjoin them."

I always composed *rapidly*. If I succeeded at all to my

satisfaction, it was commonly at once. What I produced by mere dint of effort seldom pleased me. The mind should, indeed, be excited by love to the subject, or pleasure in the study; but I always found a consciousness of difficulty and elaboration unfavourable to success. The production was wanting in simplicity and naturalness. There is no reaching flowers by ladders and balloons. They do not grow in the air, but on the ground. They are not above our head, but at our feet. We find them in walking. We bend to view them, and stoop to gather them.

I always found one thing very helpful, in the choice and in the study of my *subjects*—for preaching. It was the feeling of a rightness of aim and motive,—*i. e.* a simple regard to usefulness; and a losing sight of advantage, popularity, and applause. This, it may be said, is rather a *moral* than an *intellectual* auxiliary. Be it so. But we know who has said, " If, therefore, thine eye be single, thy whole body shall be full of light." And is not even reputation itself better and more surely acquired when it follows us, than when it is pursued? If we do not lose it, we corrupt it, by making it our aim; instead of leaving it to follow as a consequence in the discharge of duty, and so making it the honour that cometh from God only.

With regard to my *texts*, many from time to time gradually occurred; many also were obtained from the Scriptures read in our family worship; but to avoid the loss of time in searching for others, and to secure a constant sufficiency, I followed the advice and practice of Job Orton. I procured a blank book, and wrote at the top of the page any passage of Scripture that impressed me with the thought that rendered it striking. One part of the book in the same way was separately allotted for texts suited to particular subjects, seasons, and occasions. These were always increasing; and to this store I repaired, if no other passage immediately offered.

I also always had a number of plans of sermons ready for use *beforehand*, in case I should be deprived of opportunity or fitness for my usual preparation; and seldom, if ever, did I take advantage of any one of them from idleness, but only from the want of health, spirits, or leisure.

I am, &c.

LETTER XIV.

My dear Children,—The capabilities of preachers are
not always to be estimated by their performances. This is
the case with those who have numerous claims upon them
for public services. If they are not to neglect their various
other duties, what adequate preparations can they secure for
the many sermons they have to deliver? Dr. Watts
laments, in a letter to a young divine, that he was so soon
after his ordination required to produce two discourses every
week, and rather advises him to make use of published
assistance for one part of the Sabbath. But those among
whom I began my efforts were accustomed to three sermons
every Lord's-day, and one at least in the week, and a
private meeting besides. In addition to this, in their own
places, the ministers frequently preached in the neighbouring villages. To all this I was early inured; and for some
considerable length of time after my settlement in Bath, I
always had to furnish two discourses on the Sabbath, and
one in the week, together with a private admonitory address;
not to mention (by no means infrequent) extra engagements from home.

For nearly fifty years I annually supplied Surrey Chapel.
In this I yielded to the importunity of Mr. Hill, whom I
found it difficult to refuse, as I had rather offended him by

declining his pressing proposal to enter entirely into what he called *his connexion ;* and by which I should have been at his disposal, to divide my labours among a number of places under his influence, if not authority. From taking that wrong step, (for so it would have proved,) I was prevented by the care and wisdom of my friend and father, Mr. Winter, who foresaw consequences of which I was not then aware.

For more than thirty years I supplied for eight Sundays yearly, (a period too long for a pastor to be absent at once from his charge). Then I supplied for six Sundays, afterwards for four, and finally for three only. At last I terminated my annual engagement; and I should have done it sooner, had not many, even of my reverend brethren in London, urged me to continue the service. My reason for gradually shortening, and entirely resigning, the engagement, was not want of respect and attendance in the congregation, to which I was much attached, or want of pleasure in the services; for the cause had become much endeared, and I had often found the place to be none other than the house of God, and the gate of heaven. But, first, my growing disapproval of the system of providing for places by a merely successional supply. This system wants the advantage of a pastoral relation, and robs many churches for too long a time of the labours of their own ministers, while it affects surrounding congregations by tempting hearers, and members, to leave their own places, to follow some one preacher and some another, deservedly or undeservedly popular, with whose novelty and excitement a stated pastor can hardly compete. Secondly, because, in consequence of these engagements, I had less time and liberty to attend to occasional calls for services in other directions ; for these had multiplied, from the various residences of my children, and the amazing increase of new religious interests, and public institutions calling for assistance.

Though, therefore, I curtailed and declined my visits to London, I laboured more in the country, and went oftener abroad preaching on particular occasions, such as ordinations, associations, openings and reopenings of places of worship; and especially for the various benevolent societies that adorn our age and bless our nation. Judging from the results, I was found a tolerably successful beggar, and was made not a little free with, under that mendicant character. Had not David numbered the people, I might perhaps have kept an account of the multitude of collection sermons which I have delivered. But I can truly say nothing has afforded me more pleasure than perceiving that, though I could do but little myself in the way of giving, I had some influence to aid, through others, so many schemes of civil and sacred beneficence.

But in the course of these services my mind has undergone some variation, and, I think, improvement. Though I have not been much at sea I have observed that a kind of side-wind is the best for filling all the sails, and for securing speed. I have, therefore, for some years past, been led to preach very few *direct charity sermons*. Many of the subjects of these appeals are well known, and the common enlargements upon them are become trite and satiating, when a peculiar frame of soul in the audience is necessary; and I regard it as a kind of desecration of the place, and debasement of the glorious Gospel, to deal much in pounds, shillings, and pence. I, therefore, more generally have chosen a very evangelical or experimental subject, the warm discussion of which was more likely to produce in my hearers a favourable state of mind and feeling for every good work; so that at the close of the service their inquiry would be, "Lord, what wilt thou have me to do?" And I have only had to present the case with its nature and claims, all tricks and teasings being unnecessary.

In these occasional services, I have preached as I had

opportunity for *all* parties that invited me. The thing was not *where* I preached, but *what* I preached; and I never felt fetters or embarrassment; such a general agreement is there now in those leading truths which ought on these occasions to be called forth. These interminglings, too, I have always found beneficial. They tend to reduce the strangeness that keeps Christians of different denominations so improperly from each other; and to produce that spirit which will lead us to exclaim, " Behold my mother and my brethren! for whosoever shall do the will of God, the same is my brother, and sister, and mother." " Grace be with all them that love our Lord Jesus Christ in sincerity."

Once I visited Ireland for six weeks, at the invitation of what was then called " The Evangelical Society." This Society consisted of pious individuals of every *Protestant and Evangelical* denomination, who, forgetting their minor differences, were anxious to do something for the spiritual good of their countrymen, especially in Dublin, by employing preachers who were likely to awaken some degree of attention. They professed only to defray the travelling expenses, without any remuneration for their labours. I was one of the invited, but could not have gone at a less favourable season. The rebellion broke out the very day after my arrival; and the alarm and agitation immediately following, together with the fierceness of party rage, were such as for the time to injure, if not destroy, all serious and profitable impressions in the hearers. I was at the house of Alderman Hutton. He took me in his carriage, (which was in our passage several times looked into by the soldiers stationed at the cross-roads,) to preach one week-day afternoon at the Black Rock for the Rev. Mr. Kelly. But this was the only public service in which I could be engaged out of Dublin, being by martial law nearly confined to the city, and almost to the house. Every Sabbath-day morning I preached at Dr. M'Dowall's church. He had a large and

respectable congregation of orthodox presbyterians, but dis-
playing at that time little of the power of godliness. In the
evening I always preached at Plunket-street chapel, where
assembled a few poorer people, but whose hearts God had
touched. I also several times preached at the Baptist
Meeting in St. Mary's Abbey.

It may seem surprising that a temporary missionary
should have gone at *such* a period. The error lay entirely
with the gentleman at whose mansion I was accommodated.
Here (*in England*) we deemed everything lowering and foreboding, and I wrote for leave to resign or postpone my
visit; but he rather ridiculed my apprehension. " He was
upon the spot,"—" He was a magistrate,"—" He well knew
the state of things,"—" There was no more danger in Dublin
than in Bath,"—" Come and fulfil your engagement." I
went, but my preaching was in a sad degree dry and power-
less, and the word, I feared, produced little or no effect.
But in what a state did I find religion, as far as I had opportunity for observation! There were a few grains of salt, but
what were they to save the community from entire corruption? Mr. Walker was then preaching at Bethesda
Chapel and Penitentiary, built by a gentleman at this time
one of my congregation in Bath. Mr. Walker was a man
of erudition, mind, and influence, and distinguished as rather
the leader of the Evangelical party in Dublin, especially
among the Episcopalians. He had an extreme aversion to
everything he deemed Arminian, and he seemed to hate
Mr. Wesley as much as he did Dr. Priestley. He was too
orthodox to be evangelical; *i. e.*, to preach the Gospel to
every creature, and betrayed a disdainful censoriousness
which brought to mind Solomon's aphorism, " Pride goeth
before destruction, and a haughty spirit before a fall." He
soon afterwards fell into one discovery after another, till
" the light that was in him became darkness," and, oh! how
great was that darkness! But there were several most

excellent young men belonging to the university, who then gave promise of what they have since become.   There were also held private meetings in various houses for social prayer, in which persons of all parties zealously engaged ; and, soon after I left Dublin, a considerable revival commenced ; and much has since been done to advance the cause of Christ in that interesting, but always distracted and misgoverned, country.   Had the same exertions been made in former years, what a different state of things might have been now witnessed !

I am, &c.

LETTER XV.

MY DEAR CHILDREN,—In the summer of 18— I visited
Scotland. It was in the service of the London Missionary
Society. I preached my way thither, on public occasions,
at Birmingham, Manchester, Halifax, Hull, and York. At
the latter place I passed a whole Sabbath. A plan was to
have been in readiness to regulate all my public movements
when I arrived at Edinburgh, but it was not well formed.
Hence time was frequently lost, and due notices were not
always forwarded. The neglect was occasioned by the
manner in which the affair of arrangement was settled.
Where a number of persons are engaged, mutual dependence
on each other weakens a sense of individual responsibility,
and often little or nothing is done. Had the ark been
appointed to be built by a committee, it would never have
been finished. In the case to which I am referring, *one*
should have been appointed for the purpose of direction, and
this one a man of business and tact; while here several
individuals were concerned, and I believe all of these were

ministers, who, it is well known, are not always the most apt and punctual men in the world.

Here also I scarcely preached to advantage, and must have fallen short in some degree of the fame that had preceded me, and which was aided by the report of many who had, in a course of years, visited Bath and had heard me in my own pulpit. I was hurried and perplexed, and wanted that freedom from bustle, and that retirement, without which I never could feel or produce much impression. The principal places I preached in were Edinburgh, Falkirk, Stirling, Dumblane, Glasgow, Paisley, Greenock, Largs, and the Isle of Bute. In four of these places, I preached in the Established Kirk, as well as among the Seceders and Congregationalists. From the beginning, the pulpits in the National Church of Scotland had been opened to orthodox divines of other communions; but some little time before my visit the General Assembly had passed a decree to close them.* This seemed to have been done, not only from a dislike of a certain kind of doctrinal preaching, but in a moment of irritation, occasioned, perhaps, in a measure by some indiscreet acts among those who needed only to have preached the testimony of God, as Whitefield did, who knew "nothing

---

* This reference to the closing of the pulpits in the Established Kirk of Scotland but a short time before Mr. Jay's visit, enables us nearly to fix the date which he has left open in the commencement of the present letter. It is well known that the Decree of the General Assembly was attributed to the first visit of the Rev. Rowland Hill, and his itinerant labours in Scotland. That visit took place in the year 1798. The Decree to close the pulpits against ministers of other communions passed the Assembly, May, 1799, for on Mr. Hill's second visit he found it in operation against him. Mr. Jay's visit we may, therefore, suppose from his language, took place within a year or two. So that its date must have been 1800, 1801, or 1802, and could hardly have been later, or he would not have used the words, "some little time before." We possess a letter dated from Dr. Wardlaw's, in Glasgow, July, 1821.

save Jesus Christ and him crucified." It is related that
when he first visited Scotland, the excellent Erskines rather
opposed him, as not sufficiently particular and discriminate
in his zeal; they wished to confine his labours to their own
party, and to forbid his preaching in the Church from which
they had seceded, saying, " God had left it." Then said he,
" It is the more necessary for me to preach in it, to endeavour
to bring him back: I 'll preach Christ wherever they 'll
let me."

It was hoped at this time, by the better members of the
Establishment, that such a decree would not long remain in
their statute-book. Some from the first deemed the decree
more honoured in the breach than in the observance; and it
was pleasing to find how soon, in some actual instances, it
was treated as a dead letter. The last General Assembly,
previous to the Secession which forms the " Free Church,"
nobly abrogated it; but, as it was expected, the Residuary
Church soon re-enacted it. It is the disgrace and the injury
of a Church to *be* exclusive; but it is worse to *become* so,
and to become so when knowledge and liberality prevail,
and the rights of conscience are so much better understood.
In churches just emerging from the bosom of Antichris-
tianism, or rising up when religion was so identified with
superstition, when bigotry and intolerance were the error of
the age, as well as of individuals, some degree of the evil can
hardly be wondered at, and may be for a time tolerated.
But " they that sleep, sleep in the night, and they that are
drunken are drunken in the night; but let them that are of
the day be sober." It is lamentable to think that the
Established Church of England has become more intolerant
than it was formerly. Even in the days of Elizabeth, other
Protestant communities were not unchurched, nor the ordinations of their ministers deemed invalid. It is an historical
fact, that what cannot be done now was more than allowed
then; and that divines both officiated in the Establishment,

and obtained preferments, who had only been set apart by
"the laying on of the hands of the Presbytery." In
Edinburgh I was followed by that good and talented, but
eccentric, or (at least) peculiar character, Dr. Stuart. He
had seceded from the Church of Scotland, but no church
came up quite to his standard of scriptural purity and order;
and, therefore, it is said, he communed with none but his
own servant, in his own house. He always heard more like
a judge than a learner. He weighed everything that
dropped from a preacher's lips in the nicest scales of rigid
orthodoxy, and was never backward to pronounce "Tekel."
I was not, therefore, very likely to escape. Accordingly I
soon found that I had erred in my opinion concerning the
unlikely supreme prevalence of popery, and had shown, with
regard to some parties, a most improper candour. But
when I happened to preach at the Rev. Mr. Innes's meeting,
from the words of John, " Perfect love casteth out fear,"
the sermon so pleased him, that very late the same night he
wrote me a letter much importuning me to give it to the
public, as the best illustration of an important principle he
had ever heard. Here is the letter itself :—

"My dear Sir,—I regret very much that my state of
health, disqualifying me for conversation, has not permitted
me to avail myself of the opportunity of seeing you. I have,
however, been privileged with hearing you three times; and
may I, though without consultation with any one, earnestly
beseech you to let the discourse of to-night appear from the
press? I do not urge this lightly. I do beg it of you from
the conviction that it contained the truth in one of the most
striking representations I ever heard, and is suited to alarm,
rouse, comfort, animate ; but it contains a solution of various
difficulties which will, I know, disentangle many. That it
coincides with *my* sentiments is nothing; in so far I beg
leave to enclose a statement of it. Only meaning to confess

how low it is, compared with the practical, admirable, elevated view of it you delivered.

        "I am, my dear Sir,

            "Your most obedient servant,

                "CHARLES STUART.

"Thursday Night."

I had also once seen him in London, where he frequently heard me; and calling upon me at Surrey Chapel House, he said he had formerly written a review of my sermons, for some part of which he was now sorry, as he had not done justice to the evangelism of my sentiments, of which he was now persuaded from hearing me.

In my long public life and various preachings, I have met with no few of these " tryers," who had, or feigned to have, some scruples as to the stanchness of my *credenda ;* but I never quarrelled with them—never argued with them ; but took care never to flatter them, or *court* their favour. " Thou shalt not bow down to them nor worship them, for I am the Lord thy God." " Call no man master upon earth, for one is your master, even Christ."—In this journey, I always felt an apprehension which had a contracting and depressing influence. It was the thought that my mode of preaching was not congenial with the taste of Scottish audiences. My friend, Mr. Hughes, who had been for education at Aberdeen, contributed to this, by telling me, when I was going to Scotland, that while in the north I must be very careful and guarded, and forbear *freedom,* and especially anecdotes, which would not be relished or endured there. A man always works best when he works in his own way ; and I knew I should do better with my sling and stones than in Saul's armour. My preaching could never dispense with my own manner, and which I am sure was natural to me, and not derived from the schools. Towards the conclusion of my mission, I was preaching in the Isle of Bute ; and near the end of the sermon I mentioned the *caveat* I had received before I left England, adding, that I then felt a strong temptation to break through it. I paused, and then said,—"Well, whatever be the consequence, I will introduce the following anecdote." I saw it told; and the ministers, coming afterwards into the session-house or vestry, said, " You have laboured under a great mistake, we are not averse to anecdotes, but to *some* kinds of them, and to the *manner* of relating and applying *any* of them. When they are well chosen, and properly introduced, they are peculiarly acceptable, as they are more unusual with us, and we want excitement more than information."

One thing struck me much while in Scotland. It was their lecturing, which I believe is invariable on the morning of the Lord's-day, in all their sanctuaries, both in the Establishment and among Seceders. I had only before very rarely employed this mode of instruction, but ever since my return I have frequently introduced it. I once, indeed, had begun an essay on the subject in order to recommend the practice, to which I had intended to annex a volume of such exercises. But I was diverted immediately from my purpose, by the request of my congregation to publish " The Christian Contemplated," which I had just delivered. It is, perhaps, now too late for me to resume the thing; but I here record it as my settled judgment, that nothing would be more profitable to the hearer, and useful to the preacher; and I only wish that our English churches would more encourage it, and our ministers seek to excel in it.

Some difficulty at first arose from my usual method of preaching, which is very textual; and which leads me to notice the several parts, and often even the wording of the text. But in lecturing, many minutenesses must be passed over, and the aim must be to seize and display the spirit or design of the whole passage, and bring it to bear upon the audience in practical application. Preachers differ in their

talents, and all cannot equally succeed in the same department.   But let none decline making an attempt here, or be
discouraged if their efforts be not crowned with immediate
success.   In due time they may reap if they faint not.

I could commonly ascertain before I left the study how I
should succeed in the pulpit.   With me the *tug of war* was
always alone.   If I felt that I had grasped my subject, and
could gain a certain frame of spirit made up of the *solemn*
and the *tender*, I rather longed for the service than dreaded
it; and this was very much the case on all occasions, the
more extraordinary and trying ones not excepted.

I never considered an essay a sermon, or a sermon an
essay; I always loved arrangement and division.   I am
aware that the former may be found without the latter, and
intelligent and reflecting minds may recognize it; but as to
the mass of hearers, concealed method is much the same as
none.   And why should it ever be concealed?   The lower
orders peculiarly need it; it relieves and quickens their
attention; it aids their apprehension and understanding.
It also enables them the better to retain and carry away
what they hear; and how limited is the efficiency of what
pleases and interests *in the act of hearing only!*   And how
desirable is it, that our people should keep in memory what
is preached unto them, that they may not believe in vain!

Hence it is much to be wished that the divisions should
be short, simple and easy; the language everywhere plain,
and the exemplifications natural and familiar.   Few can
imagine how much I have always made this my aim and
effort; nor have I less wished and endeavoured to be, in
some measure, not only intelligible but impressive.   This is
no easy thing; and some of the means that would conduce
to it, especially among the vulgar, are by many too much
overlooked or despised.   But is it not strange that men of
God, who profess to be ministers in a kingdom not of this
world, and who are sent to seek that which is lost, should,

while sitting in judgment upon their mode of preaching, inquire not what kind of address and illustration is most likely to be useful to the bulk of an audience, but what agrees best with the most admired modes of composition! Longinus, or Quintilian, or Cicero, has more authority with them, even in the things of the Spirit, than the manner of the sacred writers. The Jews had no schools for dialectics and rhetoric; their orators spoke only the eloquence of nature. Rules were originally derived from the excellency of works, and not works from the excellency of rules. Criticism is useful in its degree and place; but it is not a standard of *absolute* authority, especially with him that like Paul would "become all things to all men, if by all means he might save some."

I early preached in villages, and never discontinued the practice, as long as I was able and had opportunity. I ought, therefore, to know from much experience what is required in such services. I never went to them unprepared. It appeared to me strange that any should suppose, that less care and labour are necessary in preparation as those we address are less disciplined and qualified to receive instruction. I always peculiarly studied for these occasions, only my study was how to be intelligible and interesting. The minds of the rustics are not inaccessible, but you must take the trouble to find the avenues to them. There are modes of making them look eagerly, and hang upon the preacher's lips; and the preacher who secures *their* attention, whatever some think, has the honour of resembling Him of whom it was said, "the common people heard him gladly."

Persons of education may be approached through mere intellect, but the poor generally are like women, whose heads are in their hearts. They are like poets, who feel before they think. Application with them is an effect rather than a cause. They attend not to feel, but must be made to feel in order to attend. When will preachers remember the observation of Rollin,—viz., that "the eloquence of the Scripture is the eloquence of things, and not of words ; and therefore it is, that so much of the spirit and mode of the original shows itself even in the plainness of the translation."

I seem disposed to continue a little longer in the same strain. I shall, therefore, venture a few more remarks freely with regard to preaching.

Upon the principle before mentioned, the *ex re nata* of extemporaneous speaking will always be more effective than what is read from composed documents, or doled forth from mere recollection. Animation is desirable, and with ordinary minds no other quality will fully supply the want of it ; but then it must *appear* to be the result of feeling. Whenever this is really the case, the animation will glow and rise with the subject. What is *continuous* and *invariable* must be mechanical and assumed. This is a sad secret let out by the uniform and constant bawlers or strainers. I have heard a whole sermon from the beginning to the end, whatever inequalities there were in the importance of the parts, delivered precisely in the same degree of tone and forced vehemency. But how can the fire precede the friction ? And how can all the picture be light without shade ?

Nothing that requires a lengthened connexion of argumentation will succeed with ordinary hearers. They are not accustomed to unbroken trains of thought or discussion. For them, if the preacher be wise, he will find out acceptable *words ;* for the *words* of the wise are as goads and as nails. The masses are not mathematical ; they are not logical. The deep and the subtle in reasoning will commonly escape them. Yet there is often in them largely—the principle of common sense ; and they are capable of taking in even a profound proof or argument, if it be despatched with brevity and plainness. It is also very advantageous, if not necessary, in their case, to attach to the proof or argument some fact or image, not in evidence, (for metaphors prove nothing,) but in illustration. Thus a kind of handle is given to the subject, by which they are enabled to lay hold of and carry away what would otherwise be too large, or unfit for their grasp.

I have always thought the regular Dissenters were to blame at the origin of Methodism. They did not indeed oppose, as the Church generally did, on the ground of doctrine; for in this they essentially acquiesced, but as to the mode of preaching. The Dissenters were educated ministers themselves, (for at that time there was scarcely a lay-preacher among them,) and their sermons were not only orthodox but studied, grammatically correct, and methodical; but, with a very few exceptions, pointless, cold, and drawled off from notes. On the other hand, many of the new preachers had not been trained for the ministry; and delivered themselves in a way very unacceptable, in many respects, to cultivated minds. They were often boisterous, rude, coarse, incoherent. Yet they were powerful and efficient; and noise and novelty will not account for all the effect they produced. Reflecting men might have perceived this. Our ministers saw that the Meeting was thinly attended, and that crowds were drawn to the Tabernacle. Instead of listening to reports, which always magnified the mistakes of these men, and dwelling so much upon their deficiencies, they should have owned that God honoured them and did much good by them; they should have heard and judged for themselves; they should have examined whether there were not some things in which these labourers, (for such *indeed* they were,) deserved not only to be tolerated, but even imitated. And there were a few who nobly differed from the many of the general body. They were candid and judicious enough to own these men, without approving everything in them. They perceived, that, with all their supposed or real faults, they had an earnestness in their

manner, with strokes of fancy, touches of passion, striking
metaphors, plain anecdotes, bold addresses and characteristic applications to the conscience, which might be detached
from their accompanying improprieties, and adopted in an
improved state, in combination with elements of their own.
Accordingly, these ministers soon displayed, in addition to
their own superior learning, accuracy, and order, an ease
and a liveliness which they knew not before.

And it is this union, so to speak, of the Dissenter and
Methodist, that has produced the better style of preaching
than either of them had separately attained. They have
corrected and improved each other; and introduced freedom
without irregularity, arrangement without stiffness, animation without violence, soberness without dulness, solemnity
without sanctimoniousness, readiness without rapidity, and
plainness without vulgarity.

With regard to *subjects* :—what I have always deemed the
best kind of preaching is neither highly doctrinal nor drily
practical; but distinguished by what I should call *experimentality*, or a constant blending of the doctrine and practice
of the gospel strongly with the affections and feelings. Many
of our northern divines have been sadly deficient here.
Their sermons have had theology enough in them, and were
well methodized; but there was little in them to rend or to
melt.   How much of "The Scotch Preacher" (not the last)
might be read through without the troublesomeness of a
single emotion!   There was an extreme among the "Marrow
Divines," and a mode of evangelical composition which for
a good while obtained there, best denominated, perhaps, by
the term "luscious."   In many instances, preaching is now
getting towards the right medium in Scotland; and our
brethren there, with the talents and learning which distinguish them, are likely to become, generally, able
ministers of the New Testament, not of the head only but
also of the heart.

There is nothing against which a preacher should be more guarded than length. "Nothing," says Lamont, "can justify a long sermon. If it be a good one it need not be long; and if it be a bad one it ought not to be long." Luther, in the enumeration of nine qualities of a good preacher, gives as the sixth,—"That he should know when to stop." Boyle has an essay on patience under long preaching. This was never more wanted since the Commonwealth than now, in our own day, especially among our young divines and academics, who seem to think their performances can never be too much attended to. I never err this way myself but my conviction always laments it; and for many years after I began preaching I *never* offended in this way. I never exceeded three-quarters of an hour at *most*. I saw one excellency was within my reach—it was brevity, and I determined to attain it.

I am, &c.

LETTER XVI.

CRITICISMS ON HIS SERMONS :—DEFENCE OF HIS METHOD :—AMERICAN
REVIVAL PREACHING : — SCRIPTURAL LANGUAGE : — OBJECTORS :—
PASTORAL VISITING :—COMPLAINTS :—HIS EXPLANATION.

My dear Children,—I cannot be ignorant that, besides
frequent references to my sermons on public occasions, my
preaching has been more expressly criticised in different
publications. Six of these have come under my view. A
man would not be allowed to be a judge in his own case, or
otherwise I could say, that neither the commendations that
have been graciously given me, nor the defects which have
been noticed, have appeared to myself very appropriate or
discriminative; nor has the secret of the degree of impression which I have produced, and which has been rather
extensive as well as durable, been very justly explained. If
I considered myself competent to supply the deficiency, it
would be indelicate to attempt it; though, when this is read,
I shall be beyond the reach of human praise or censure.

One thing I cannot help remarking. I never saw any
allusion to my preaching as abounding more with images,
and facts, and instances of things, than what commonly
prevails. If I have not succeeded in this, my practice has
not always accorded with my conviction, and aim, and endeavour. Bunyan's motto, borrowed from Hosea, could
never be adopted by some preachers—" I have used simili-
tudes." But such a usage is sanctioned by the constitution
of human nature, and recommended by the example of Him
who " spake as never man spake." Dr. Carey is reported

to have said to a young minister who had preached before him, "My young friend, I have much approved of your sermon, but it had one deficiency, it had no '*likes*' in it." And when asked for an explanation, he added, "Why, when you read our Lord's discourses, you constantly meet with the expression, 'The kingdom of heaven is like unto leaven,' 'like unto mustard-seed,' 'like unto a net,' 'like unto a marriage,' and so on.   Now never preach again, my young friend, without some '*likes*' in your addresses."

God, the only wise God, who, having made us, knows what is in man, and what is necessary to him, has given us the largest proportion of the Old and New Testament in the form of history and biography.   Is it not, therefore, strange that public instructors should lose sight of God's method, and be always getting into the commonness of declamation, or the dryness of speculative discussion?   "A story," says Cecil, "will hold a child by the ear for an hour together," and "men are but children of a larger growth."

Nearly allied to this is another thing, in which the sacred writers, (did we deem them worthy our imitation,) would usefully guide us.   Instead of defining, they describe ; and instead of describing, they exemplify.   They hold forth all things, not in the nakedness of abstraction, but clothed with their attributes, and palpable in their effects.   To show us what the power of religion is, they tell us what it does.   The believer *comes* to Christ.   The penitent *looks* on him whom he has pierced, and *mourns*.   We have not the rules and tactics of the war, but we see the warrior from his arming till he has triumphed.   We have not the representation of the pilgrimage, but we have the pilgrim, and follow him step by step from the city of destruction up to the celestial abode.

If I mention some things which have been noticed in my style of preaching, not censoriously, yet rather in a way of complaint, it will not be for the purpose of defence, but explanation. It will then be seen, if I have erred, that it has been more by rule than by thoughtlessness ; and the reader will be left at full liberty to judge for himself. I am aware of what has been said of the importance of unity of design in a discourse, especially by Mr. Fuller, who so well exemplified his own advice. With this mode I have not been wanting sometimes to comply ; and I have occasionally found great advantage in selecting a single sentiment, and pursuing it through the whole discourse. But I have much more generally followed the textual treatment, deriving the contents of the sermon from the parts and even the terms of the passage, and this unavoidably rather trenches on unity. But may not the want of unity in the subject be compensated, and more than compensated, by variety ? In the Drama, much has been written of the unities by the French, who also always boasted of their maintaining them. But has one of their authors anything equal to the mixed productions of Shakspeare, who often violates all the unities ? But in preaching it should be remembered, what diversities of persons and cases there are before us at every service, and how unlikely these diversities are to be reached by the very same thing. We are rightly to divide the word, and give to each a portion of meat in due season. The *Day of Judgment* admits of many separate views. It may be considered as a day of aggregation—a day of separation—a day of manifestation—a day of retribution. And Bourdaloue or Massillon would confine himself to one of these exclusively. But would this method be likely to be so useful, or to strike various and different minds as efficiently as a few bold strokes on all of them ?

An American divine was one day endeavouring to account to me for the effect of their revival-preaching. He ascribed much of it to its restriction to one thing, observing, for instance, that though repentance may be considered as including conviction, contrition, confession, conversion, and,

as necessary to the whole, looking on Him whom we have
pierced—they should not notice these together, but give
each a separate and distinct discourse.   But the same individuals may not hear all these distinct discourses; and if
other persons drop in and hear only one of them, how defective may their information be!   I could not divide in the
same sermon the cause and the effect.   I could not preach
repentance without preaching the Cross.   How is the one
to be effectively presented without the other?   Let us read
the Acts and the Epistles.

Some have complained of my sermons being filled with
too much Scripture.   If this be an error, it is surely on the
right side; and, as Dr. Geddes* says, "I love to give God's
children plenty of their own bread."   I am sure of this,
that I never used quotations from the Scripture merely to
fill up or to lengthen out a discourse; and I trust I have
never introduced any fancifully, or regardlessly of the mind
of the Spirit; yet I own there is here occasionally some
excess; and it has probably resulted from my familiarity
with the language of the Bible, having, before many other
books came in my way, read it much, and committed much
to memory.

Am I to allow the charge of too much amplification and
diffuseness in my preaching?   When Mr. Pitt once received
an intimation of this kind with regard to his speeches, his
episcopal biographer tells us, that he made this reply: "A
man who addresses a popular assembly must either use
repetition or diffusion; and I prefer the latter."   If *he*
deemed this needful in *such* an assembly as he addressed,
can it be unnecessary in ministers when speaking to a
mixed multitude, many of whom have little education or
talent, and were never accustomed to any fixed application
of mind?   We should consider that what, either in con-

* An esteemed correspondent suggests that there is probably a
mistake in the name; and that Mr. Jay meant Dr. Gillies.

firmation or illustration, is superfluous for one hearer, is
even insufficient for another.   We often see as we go on in
our discourse, from the straining attention of some in the
crowd, that we have not yet succeeded in what we have
spoken.   Are we then to go forward without making
another attempt with some change of address, or variation
of imagery?   The eloquent Isaiah would say, " Precept
must be upon precept, precept upon precept; line upon
line, line upon line; here a little and there a little."

Who has entirely escaped the reflection that freedoms
degenerate into vulgarity and coarseness?   Certainly not a
Shakspeare, a Burke, a Hopkins, or a South.   Certainly not
many of our most forcible writers; and they incurred the
accusation *because* of their *force*.   In aiming at great impression and effect there is always some danger.   There is
none in tame correctness.

> " They who crawl
> Can never fall."

But they who rise and they who run may.   Yet is not
occasional failure in attempt better than perpetual deficiency
and indifference?   Have not a thousand beauties been
snatched from the very verge of impropriety?   May not a
man deserve the rebuke of Quintilian, who, speaking of a
certain author, says, "His greatest excellence was that he
had no fault, and his greatest defect that he had no excellence?"

Give me an impressiveness and an excitement that will
not allow a hearer to perceive a fault, or, if he does, leaves
him no mind to *regard* it.   And is there nothing, if not to
applaud, yet to extenuate, in even a mistake, in endeavouring to do good to those who are destitute of a thousand
advantages, and whose condition is such, that they must be
sought after?   We do not admire their low and grovelling
taste, yea, we wish to raise and improve it; but how is this
to be done if we never *approach* them?   Can you take up a

child from the ground without bending? And when *kind-ness* makes you stoop, honour crowns condescension.

I have found it difficult, if not impossible, to give satis-faction to a certain class of hearers, while wishing to do justice to the Scriptures at large. *Some* of these objectors (for I could not think so of *all*,) have been good men, but of contracted views. I admired their love of the truth as it is in Jesus, and their peculiarly relishing it when brought forward in a discourse. I acknowledge also that a minister should frequently and largely dwell upon it, and treat everything in connexion with it. But this connexion ex-tends much further than they seem to suppose. It does not follow that, because one point is to be made more prominent in a discourse, all others are to be disregarded. We are no more to abridge than to mangle the Gospel. We must keep back nothing that is profitable, but declare the whole counsel of God. It will be better to be able at last to make the appeal, "I am free from the blood of *all* men," than to find that we have succeeded in gratifying the taste of a few, whose preference is of little value in the pos-session, and commonly a snare in the obtaining.

The apostles are our models; in their Epistles we find doctrine and practice, duty and privilege, always blended together. They knew that everything in the Evangelical scheme was not equally important; but they regarded nothing as useless. They took great care to lay the founda-tion firmly and broadly; but then they omitted nothing in the superstructure that was needful or ornamental. They preached only a crucified Saviour; but "warning every man and teaching every man in all wisdom, that they might present every man *perfect* in Christ Jesus." They con-tended that the grace of God alone brings salvation; but showed that it teaches us to "deny ungodliness and worldly lusts, and to live soberly, righteously, and godly, in this present world."

Yet I could never have felt at liberty to preach a series

of sermons on a number of evil characters, such as the apostle mentions as abounding in the last days: "Lovers of their own selves; covetous; boasters; proud; blasphemers; disobedient to parents; unthankful; unholy; without natural affection; truce-breakers; false accusers; incontinent; fierce; despisers of those that are good; traitors; heady; high-minded; lovers of pleasure more than lovers of God; having a form of godliness, but denying the power thereof;" yet I knew a pastor who edified his people for nineteen Sabbaths following, with a separate discourse on each of these. I also knew another, not green in age, who was three years in going through the ten commandments. I could hardly consider myself justified in preaching a whole sermon before a multitude of perishing sinners from the words of Solomon, "He that hateth suretyship is sure." Not that such intimations and cautions are to be overlooked; but it is better to strike at the thing with a remark or two as we go on. It should also be remembered, that we may often *insinuate moral* hints, while we are illustrating some Christian principle. By teaching the children of God what they ought to be, I teach other children their obligations; and by holding forth the character of God as a Father, I instruct and admonish other fathers in the duties which lie upon them.

It should, however, never be forgotten that "we are the servants of the Most High God, who show unto men the way of salvation;" that the Gospel is good news for perishing sinners; and that this is to be preached to every creature; and "there are some doctrines," says Mr. Venn, "that should not only be always implied and referred to in our sermons, but should be distinctly and fully treated, several times in the course of every year."

A few observations may here be made on Pastoral Visitation. You probably have heard more than myself, of the complaints which have been made of your father, with regard to the article of visiting.

I can truly say, it affords me no satisfaction to find

similar complaints very prevalent wherever I have gone.
Nor do I, in this case, wish to attempt *wholly* to justify myself—far from it. I might have done more, especially in
some cases, than I have done, by more decision, arrangement, and diligence. Who can look back on any department of duty and usefulness, and not have reason to exclaim, "If thou, Lord, shouldest mark iniquities, O Lord,
who shall stand ?" Yet I would remark a few things, by
way, at least, of explanation, rather than of excuse.

No little of this censured neglect was *voluntary* with me,
and, therefore, it did not aggrieve my mind. I saw that
much of what was commonly expected was *unreasonable;*
and that it was *consequence* rather than *improvement* that
was affected by disappointment.

I saw several kinds of visitants whom I did not think I
was called to follow.

First : The smokers, furnished with a pretty pipe, and
its usual concomitant, at every house of call :

Secondly : The listless and self-indulgent, who found that
diligent study was much less inviting than lounging from
one company to another, and hearing the news of the
neighbourhood :

Thirdly : The truly pious, who are really concerned to
do good, but were often less useful than they meant or
imagined. Many of these have not the oily slang of religious phrases ; they are not apt at free and appropriate
address, or turning all incidents to profitable account ; yet
they might preach to advantage, had they time and leisure
for reading and meditation.

I saw also that their calls were not always acceptable or
convenient. This was the case with mechanics and men in
business ; and still more so with females in ordinary life, who
were commonly taken up with their domestic cares.

I saw also that the whole congregation must be visited ;
in which case, if it were a large one, the whole of a

preacher's time would be occupied, or the minister would be deemed a respecter of persons, giving as much pain as pleasure; flattering the pride of one, and gendering the envy of another, by supposed partiality.

I also could not but see how little profit resulted from more *set* visits, of longer continuance, and including table and tea-entertainments. In these meetings, how nearly impossible is it to commence or maintain discourse by which you can either gain or do good!

I am aware that there must be interviews and intercourses, when they are of no particular character or utility. They contribute to good neighbourhood and social pleasure; but I am now speaking of things in reference to their ecclesiastical relation, and the importance of their bearing on ministerial duty and excellence.

If familiarity does not breed contempt, it reduces reverence; and too much intimacy has often lowered the impression and influence of many a minister; for there are but few who have the same presence and address in the parlour as in the pulpit.

I have no opinion of a pastor that is not very studious. But study demands leisure and retirement; and "through desire, a man, having separated himself, seeketh and intermeddleth with all wisdom." He should, therefore, as much as possible, avoid publicity, and be covetous and niggardly of every fragment of time. A man who has some degree of talent, especially an easiness and fluency of speech, may do for an itinerant or an occasional preacher, by his brisk superficialities; but let him become stationary, and have to preach three or four times a week to the same people, and he will soon abound with sameness, and become sapless and unedifying; the young will feel little attraction; the intelligent will be tempted to withdraw; the dull will become drowsy; and the ignorant that remain will be ignorant still.

People for their own sakes should do all they can to promote a habit of mental application in their ministers; and be concerned to allow them every opportunity within their reach for exerting it, especially their mornings and evenings. Of course, if they love their pastors, they will feel pleasure in their company, nor will that company be unreasonably refused; but let them, as much as possible, choose the time of intercourse, and not accuse them of indolence, or self-indulgence, if it be not so frequent as they could wish. Perhaps at the very moment of their hearer's complaint they are in their retirement praying for them, or studying to comfort or profit them, if not with the sweat of the brow, with the sweat of the brain; for "much study is a weariness of the flesh."

I, therefore, never felt anything like self-reproach when conscious of being fully employed; and I am persuaded that I was better subserving, not only my own welfare, but that of my people and of the public, in my study, than in gadding about without an aim, wasting time in idle interviews and nursery talk.

I mention not this, however, to make those easy who rise not before seven in the morning; hang loose from strenuous improvement all the day; are drawn aside by every trifling excitement; and apply the time they affect to husband *from* visiting to no equal purpose, or no purpose at all; but for the sake of upright and conscientious men, who are anxious to make full proof of their ministry, but grieve because they cannot do the things that they would.

But is not a minister a pastor, and is not a shepherd to mind and manage the state of all his sheep? He is; and he must peculiarly regard cases of urgency and distress: he is to bind up that which is broken; to bring back that which has wandered, &c.; but he can only feed, and lead, and fold the flock *together* or *collectively*.

Cases of affliction have special claims on pastoral attention; and in these, consolation and spiritual profit may be

administered by a word in season.   But here ministers
have sometimes been blamed for remissness, when they
have not been made acquainted with the distress.   The
rule is, "Is any sick among you, let him *call* for the elders
of the church;" thus at once informing them of his case,
and expressing his desire to be visited.

I observe also, that much in this supposed delinquency
was with me *unavoidable*. I began my course under many
early disadvantages; for I began young, and nearly from
the beginning was thrown into situations and circumstances
which had many and exciting demands upon me, without
assistance.   Though physically incapable of enduring so
much confinement and engagement as some of my brethren,
I had four services *per* week at home, besides frequent calls
abroad.

. Bath, the place of my residence, exposed me to many
interruptions; and my own people little knew how much
I was *necessarily* engaged in visiting strangers who came
there for health, and were away from their usual, pious
helps.   I might also mention that I was early uninten-
tionally led to become an author; and God giving me much
acceptance, I regarded the press as well as the pulpit,—the
one indeed, as to extensiveness and continuance, superior
to the other.   This also required time and attention, and
much more than justice to my subject demanded.

As congregations have grown larger and more respectable; as more preparation for the pulpit is needful now
than formerly; as institutions have so much multiplied, and
pastors must often be engaged in services added to their
home-routine of duty; new and serious difficulties arise in
the present discharge of the ministerial function.   How are
they to be met?   It seems now hardly possible to combine
equally in the same man the excellences of the pastor and
the eminence of the preacher.   I have seldom seen an
instance of both.   Dr. Mason of New York, in his farewell

address to his church, says, "If you would have us not only to preach Christ publicly, but from house to house, you must put your hands into your pockets, and support a dozen more pastors."

If pastors and pastoral assistants cannot be multiplied, may not something be done by an increase of good and efficient deacons and elders? Could not they relieve their ministers from some of their exertions, and allow them the more freedom to give themselves to the word of God and prayer? Is there nothing they can do but serve tables? Could not females be usefully and properly employed? Were they not in the first churches officially engaged, (not indeed in preaching, this was expressly forbidden—and inspiration is only common sense here,) but in cases that did not compromise the duties and decencies of their peculiar sphere and character? Paul says to the Philippians, "Help those women that laboured with me in the gospel." To Timothy he speaks of a "widow well reported of for good works, if she have brought up children, if she have lodged strangers, if she have washed the saints' feet, if she have relieved the afflicted, if she have diligently followed every good work." "I commend unto you," says he to the Romans, "Phœbe our sister, who is a servant of the church which is at Cenchrea. For she has been a succourer of many, and of myself also. Greet Mary, who bestowed much labour on us."

I flatter not, but speak the words of truth and soberness when I say, our churches and ministers suffer no inconsiderable loss by the non-official engagement of the sex, whose taste and talent, piety and goodness and zeal, are now so useful, but which may be rendered much more so than they are.

One thing I did to remedy, in a degree, my deficiency in visiting. For the sake more expressly of the busy, the poor, and the aged, I had a meeting in the vestry on the Monday evening, in which I always sat, and, for near an hour, spoke in a more free and familiar manner than it became me to use in my pulpit. I considered this like meeting the party in a room for conversation, only I had all the talk to myself. But while I spoke to the whole company, each could hear as well as if I spoke to him only and alone; yet some have grudged that others should partake of the benefit; and would have had it more expressly and distinctively appropriated to *themselves* alone. What evil often veils itself under religious pretension! What to some is usefulness, compared with selfish gratification! "Look not every man on his own things, but every man also on the things of others. Let this mind be in you which was also in Christ Jesus."

I am, &c.

LETTER XVII.

MY DEAR CHILDREN,—While musing with my pen in
hand, and hardly knowing what to write next, it struck me
that you may be ready to ask, how my life appears in
review?

It is commonly said to appear short, and to some even in
advanced years it may so appear; but they have been persons whose condition has been distinguished by much sameness, whose progress has seemed to consist of one journey,
whose passage has been always smooth, and who have not
many things to strike and, as it were, detain the mind, in
looking back. But life to others in retrospect seems to be
like a succession of stages, each having its beginning and
ending, and a variety of separate, intermediate residences;
from one of which to another the memory can hardly pass,
without re-entering and enjoying or suffering these scenes
and events again. And this gives the notion of length.
Now in my case, life has not only run through infancy, and
childhood, and youth, and manhood, and in a great measure
through age itself; but has been made up of such diverse
states, and has been attended with so many new (as to my-

self) and interesting occurrences, that I cannot go over it quickly; and my first consciousnesses, feelings, and actings, seem a long way back.

But, you may ask, should I be willing, such as I have found it, to go over life again? I have heard many express the sentiment, though not in the poetry of Cowper,—

> " Worlds should not bribe me back to tread
>   Again life's dreary waste,
>   To see the future overspread
>   With all the gloomy past."

But such language is not for me. I should not shrink from the proposal of repetition. "Goodness and mercy have followed me all the days of my life." My duties have not been burdening and irksome. My trials have been few compared with my comforts. My pleasures have been cheap and simple, and therefore very numerous. I have enjoyed without satiety the seasons and the sceneries of nature. I have relished the bounties of Providence, using them with moderation and thankfulness. I have delighted in the means of grace. Unutterable have been my delights in studying and perusing the Scripture. How have I verified the words of Young :—

> " Retire and read thy Bible to be gay !"

Preaching has been the element of my heart and my head. My labours have met with much acceptance—nor have I laboured in vain. I have seldom been without hearing of some instances of usefulness from the pulpit or the press. God has honoured me to call by my labours not a few individuals, even into the ministry. The seat of my residence was, of all others, the place of my preference. My condition has been the happy medium of neither poverty nor riches. I had a most convenient habitation, with a large and lovely garden—a constant source of attraction, exercise, and improvement. I had a sufficient collection of books of all kinds. My wife was a gentle-woman, a saint, and a domestic goddess. My children were fair, and healthy, and dutiful. My friends were many, and cordial, and steady. Where shall I end ?

> " Call not earth a barren spot,
>   Pass it not unheeded by :
>   'Tis to man a lovely spot,
>   Though a lovelier waits on high."

I do not believe that in this earth misery preponderates over good. I have a better opinion of mankind than I had when I began my public life. I cannot, therefore, ask, what is the cause that the former days were better than these ? I do not believe in the fact itself. God has not been throwing away duration upon the human race. The state of the world *has* been improved and *is* improving. Who justifies slavery now ? What noble efforts have been made to break every yoke, and to let the oppressed go free ! How is the tendency to war, on every slight pretence, giving way to reference and negotiation ! How delightful is it to think of what is doing abroad among the heathen; and of the exertions that are put forth by all denominations of Christians to make the Saviour's way known upon earth, and his saving health among all nations !

We also rejoice in *hope*. We have many and express assurances in the Scriptures, which cannot be broken, of the general, the universal spread and reign of Christianity, which are not yet accomplished. Nothing has yet taken place in the history of Divine grace, wide enough in extent, durable enough in continuance, powerful enough in energy, blessed enough in enjoyment, magnificent enough in glory, to do anything like justice to these predictions and promises. Better days, therefore, are before us, notwithstanding the forebodings of many. " Every valley shall be exalted, and every mountain and hill shall be made low;

the crooked shall be made straight, and the rough places plain, and the glory of the Lord shall be revealed; and all flesh shall see it together; for the mouth of the Lord hath spoken it."

As so many distinctions and divisions prevail in the Christian world, you may require from me a few words concerning our religious denominations and parties.

I never viewed these so aversely and fearfully as some have done. Several things pertaining to them I would remark.

First: I do not consider them as incompatible with Christian unity. God promised to give his people one heart and one way; and our Saviour prayed that all his followers may be one. Can we suppose the promise and the prayer have never *yet* been accomplished? But if they have been fulfilled, we may reason back from that fulfilment, and see what was the oneness intended. We perceive that it was not a oneness of opinion, or a ritual oneness; but a oneness of principle, and affection, and dependence, and pursuit, and co-operation. For this *has* taken place among the real followers of the Lamb, and among them only.

Secondly: They are not inconsistent with the support and spread of the Christian cause; yea, I consider them, by the excitements they favour, and the mutual zeal they kindle, and the tempers they require and exercise, as far more useful than would be the stagnancy of cold and dull uniformity, the idol of every bigot; and which *must* always be not so much real as professed, and held in hypocrisy where there are numbers; and where persons with so many sources of diversity in their structure, their education, and opportunities, think for themselves.

Thirdly: I do not, therefore, conclude that prophecy authorizes us to look for their entire suppression, but for their correction and improvement only. In what is called "the latter-day glory," they will indeed see eye to eye, but this will regard the clearer and closer perceptions of the great objects of vision, and not the minuter appendages; and they will perfectly accord, and see eye to eye in *one* sentiment, viz., "Let every one be fully persuaded in his own mind." Judah and Ephraim shall remain, so to speak, distinct tribes; but "Ephraim shall not envy Judah, and Judah shall not vex Ephraim."

The creatures figuratively mentioned by the prophet Isaiah will not be transformed into each other, but "the wolf also shall *dwell* with the lamb, and the leopard shall lie down with the.kid; and the calf and the young lion and the fatling *together;* and a little child shall lead them. And the cow and the bear shall feed; their young ones shall lie down together: and the lion shall eat straw like the ox. And the sucking child shall play on the hole of the asp, and the weaned child shall put his hand on the cockatrice' den. They shall not hurt nor destroy in all my holy mountain: for the earth shall be full of the knowledge of the Lord, as the waters cover the sea."

Fourthly: We may view denominations as we do individual Christians. None of them are absolutely perfect; and none of them are entirely defective. Neither is possessed, and neither is destitute, of every truth and every excellency. All the members of the body have not the same quality, or the same office, yet they are alike parts; and though they may be compared, they are not to be opposed; and though one may be more admired, another is not to be depreciated. One denomination may excel in diligence and zeal; another in discipline and simplicity of worship; another in contention for purity of doctrine; another for intelligence and liberality; and thus they not only stand in the same relation to Christ, but are members one of another;—checking each other's extremes, and supplying each other's defects, and sharing each other's advantages; and so by mutuality producing a comparative perfection in the whole.

Fifthly: In consequence of this, I could never regard the differences of the truly godly as essential; and though I have had my convictions and preferences, they were never anathematizing or exclusive. And I could have communed with any of their churches, and should not have been sorry if circumstances had enabled me to say I had done so.

I know religious parties are too free in censuring other bodies as less liberal than themselves; but in this respect I have not seen, (and my opportunities have been favourable for observation and comparison,) much difference between them. There are bigots in them all, both as churches, members, and teachers; and there are men of real candour who can say from the heart, " *Whosoever* shall do the will of my Father which is in heaven, the same is my brother, and sister, and mother." And if one party were by constitution or accident more rigid and narrow than another, the more commendation is due to the noble minds among them that rise above their fellows and their trammels; and let us never try or wish to detach them from their own communities, but rejoice in the influence they may exert in bettering and liberalizing them.

In accordance with these views and reflections, I have commonly lamented, when persons holding the Head, and differing only in minor matters, pass from their own fellowship into another, especially in country towns and villages. It often excites suspicions that unfair means have been used to proselyte such individuals; and grudgings are felt by the losers, to whom one member was perhaps of considerable importance. I have known ministers and members becoming, by such changes, shy of each other; while the individual who has changed his communion has been more noticed by his new party for a particular tenet than for his general excellence; and been in danger of attaching too much

importance to it himself. I have often observed the zeal of
proselytes subsiding into little things; and I never remember to have seen an individual improved in religious character and excellence, by passing from one Christian church to
another, unless it was called for by something more than a
non-essential difference. If our present connexion requires
of us anything we deem sinful, our duty is clear, and we
must follow our convictions, regardless of consequences;
but I am taking the matter on lower ground, that is, where
there may be imperfections with which we may bear, and
which we may endeavour to correct, rather than withdraw.
And surely, some regard is due to the providence of God
which orders our situations, and to the solemn act by which
we gave ourselves to the Church, in which we have taken
sweet counsel together, and " our fellowship has been with
the Father, and with his Son Jesus Christ."

A question may be now asked, concerning the ecclesiastical community to which I belong. If a man be not a
party-man, he can hardly avoid being of a party; neither
is it safe or useful, (though he may occasionally do some
execution,) for a soldier to be isolated and rove about alone,
impatient, perhaps, of authority and direction, rather than
acting with some regiment or company. I was always a
friend to order and regularity—not tyrannical order, or
enslaving regularity—but that which will oppose the whims
and vagaries of self-willed and self-conceited individuality;
so that zeal may not rush and spread like flood-water, but
be a river guided and restrained, flowing between its proper banks.

I do not think, as I have expressed myself in one of my
lectures, any very particular form of government is absolutely laid down in the New Testament. I am not ignorant
that this will surprise and offend several classes of advocates, all of whom appeal to the Scriptures, and all of
whom find their peculiar and opposite systems laid down

there clearly and definitely—that is, to themselves. Yet
there are not wanting in the New Testament general principles of church-government, which will admit, without sub-
verting them, of considerable modifyings, in their application, according to times, places, and circumstances. *All*
our present religious communities, perhaps, really deviate
in some degree from these model-maxims ; though some
diverge more than others. I could never be reconciled to
Prelacy ; but I have thought differently of Episcopacy,
where the bishop, as Usher says, is only a *primus inter
pares*, and is chosen, by his *brethren*, for his age, talents, and
piety; having no secular function, or not being em-
powered to lord it over God's heritage. This is now
pleaded for by many churchmen themselves, and is much
defended in the United States, where the connexion between
Church and State is as much censured by Episcopalians as
by Congregationalists. Perhaps, had I been left to choose,
instead of being led by circumstances, I should have preferred Presbyterianism, as to church order and regimen.
But the truth is, I never deeply studied the theories of
ecclesiastical government. I had neither inclination nor
leisure ; and other things of greater moment always seemed
to press upon my immediate attention. Nor was my mind
upon this subject made up so entirely and exclusively and
stiffly, as that I could only have moved in one direction.
By the providence of God, I was trained among the Independents, and with them I remained. I agreed not in
every iota of their system, but I approved of it in the
main ; and felt nothing in it that violated my conscience,
or abridged my liberty. I found also in it many advantages and efficiencies. It allowed the people the privilege
of choice, and the minister a sufficiency of authority. It
secured church-purity, and maintained due discipline. It
promoted Christian communion and edification. It befriended, urged, and employed means and exertions for the

conversion of sinners; and presented a ready and unfettered medium for the extension of the Redeemer's cause, abroad and at home. But could it not be relieved of a little of its democracy, and of its great dependence on individual suffrage? Or would a change here, in its working, (it is possible,) introduce an agency, more exceptionable and liable to abuse? Could there not be established some power of appeal, so that its ministers, in cases of accusation or complaint, should be heard and judged by their peers, and not be left to interested, prejudiced, and ignorant arbiters? Could nothing be done to render a number of churches, of the same faith and order, within such a distance, constituent parts of a *whole*, with some delegated power for this purpose, without invading their independence? Cannot the Table of the Lord be preserved from profanation, unless a lion be placed at the door of entrance; and conditions be exacted of candidates, which will drive back many who ought to be encouraged; but which are unlikely to check few, if any, of those who ought to be restrained?

This feature of the old discipline I softened in my own case; and I believe many of my brethren have had influence to do the same, while others lament the continued and unconditional requisition of oral or written experiences, delivered before the church. But bodies of men are not easily moved; and the mistakes of pious men, being conscientious, are with difficulty rectified.*

* We must request the reader to pause at this statement, while we offer a brief comment. Our venerated friend seems to take credit to himself, in the above sentences, for a commendable innovation upon an ancient and common practice. But the practice was certainly never so strict nor so common as he intimates; nor was he the only one, nor the first, that had broken through it, at the period when he wrote. Moreover, we are rather inclined to think it crept into the Independent churches from the Methodists, who dwelt much more upon the consciousness and palpable evidences of conversion, than the Independents had been accustomed to do. Some of Mr. Jay's

My doctrinal views, both as to their truth and importance, have undergone very little variation from the beginning, though of course, on the subjects they contain, I have read and thought much. I have felt indeed less disposed to inculcate them " in the words which man's wisdom teaches," or in dry and straitened systematic arrangement. Divinity cannot be taught at the college without system; but, in preaching, it is better that many things should be assumed than technically discussed. It is better for the preacher to give way to his holy and fervent feelings, than to be chilled and checked by the apprehension of some supposed inconsistency. It is better to let the text speak its own language, naturally and glowingly, than to use coercive measures, and torture out the meaning, or bombard it into submission.

There is a magnificence and a vastness in the Scriptures, which no human attempts can comprehend, or limit, or define; and it will be our highest wisdom, at present, to endeavour to understand and improve the interesting *parts* of a *whole*, which all our creed-mongers have found and will find too wonderful for them.

In my considerable acquaintance with the religious world, some of the most exemplary individuals I have met with have been Calvinists. Of this persuasion were the two most extraordinary Christian characters I ever knew—John Newton, and Cornelius Winter. They held its leading sentiments with firmness ; but their Calvinism, like that of Bunyan, was rendered, by their temper, milder than that

first connexions were Calvinistic Methodists, and from them, probably, he received the impression of the prevalence of the custom which he here condemns. The enforcement of such a rule of admission was, at any time, far from general or rigid. It may possibly have prevailed more among Baptist churches than among Independents. But it certainly went into general disuse about the time when Mr. Jay renounced it. There is, we conceive, not a single case in which it is now *enforced;* so that, if it ever was, it certainly is no longer, the "lion" Mr. Jay represents it, guarding the door of access to the Table of the Lord. (Let. viii.)

of some of their brethren; and they were candid towards those who differed from them; and esteemed and loved them as fellow-heirs together of the grace of life.

With this scheme of divinity my principles accorded generally more than with any other; but certain parts of it I could never admit. If it be said that the inclusive and the exclusive parts are inseparable, and that we cannot hold the one without the other, I hesitate.—We know not enough to determine, in hardly any case, what is impossible. A difficulty, apparently inexplicable, may not be a contradiction, but be solved by an extended view of the subject. Things which appear quite inconsistent to the apprehension of a *child*, and which, for want of capacity, it *cannot* harmonize at present, jar not in the mind of a *man*. But what a difference must there be between the perceptions of a finite and an infinite understanding! and in the Scriptures we have "the deep things of God," as well as the plain.

Two grand truths have always seemed to me to pervade the whole Bible, and not to be confined to a few particular phrases, viz., that if we are saved, it is entirely of God's grace; and if we are lost, it will be entirely from ourselves. I know full well, a man may easily force me into a corner with things seemingly or really related to the truth of either of these affirmations; but he will not shake my confidence in either, while I can read, "O Israel, *thou* hast destroyed thyself: but in *me* is thy help." The connexion is like a chain across the river; I can see the two ends, but not the middle; not because there is no real union, but because it is under water. Lower the water, or raise the links, and I shall see the centre as well as the extremes.

Paley observes, that we should never suffer what we know, to be disturbed by what we know not. And Butler remarks nearly the same, when he says, "If a *truth* be established, *objections* are nothing. The one is founded on our *knowledge*, and the other in our *ignorance*."

You may here remember what you have so often seen, and which I early prefixed to my *Study* Bible.

In reading this Book, let me guard against four things—

1. The contractedness of the Systematic:
2. The mysticism of the Allegorizer:
3. The dogmatism of the Bigot:
4. The presumption of the Rationalist.

Let me tremble at God's word, and let me, in reading it, keep three purposes in view:

1. To collect facts rather than form opinions:
2. To regulate practice rather than encourage speculation:
3. To aid devotion rather than dispute.

I am, &c.

LETTER XVIII.

MY DEAR CHILDREN,—You have expressed a wish to have my opinion *comparatively* of the state of things when I commenced my public labours, and now I am withdrawing from them.

I am fully persuaded that, by the good providence of God, we have experienced a thousand beneficial changes. Our Code of Judicial Law has been revised, and many of its sanguinary penalties repealed. Our Civil Legislation, and our political arrangements, have been much improved. Various wrongs have been rectified, and rights have been equalized. Freedom has largely gained. Trade and Commerce have exceedingly multiplied; while the amazing advancement in Science and Arts has added much, not only to our fame, but also to our accommodation and comfort—philosophy has rendered every element subservient to our use.

It is needless to attempt to enumerate or specify *these* advantages. *My* way lies in another direction; and I would only glance briefly at the bearing of things used *morally*, *religiously*, and *evangelically;* and I cannot look at various progressions without exclaiming, " What has God wrought!" And here I must censure some good persons whose forebodings and complainings, with regard to the times, appear unjust, improper, and ungrateful. When we consider that our "whole world lieth in wickedness;" and that, as a country, we have been "a sinful people, a seed of evil doers, children that are corrupters;" the wonder is that *He* has not long ago abandoned us; and surely we ought to notice thankfully every token for good with which we are favoured. Is it meet to be silent towards a benefactor on whom we have no claims; or to say, by our manner, Is this all thou hast done for us?   Surely the way to obtain more of his gracious influence and operation, i� to praise him for the favour he has already done us; and *thus* ask for more. We are, therefore, directed "in every thing by prayer and supplication, with *thanksgiving*, to make our requests known unto God." How offensive and grievous, then, must it be to his Holy Spirit, to deny, or speak meanly, or lightly, of his goodness, when he has done so great things for us, whereof we should be glad!

Though the day far exceeds the dawn, the dawn will not be unnoticed or undervalued by those who have seen and felt the darkness of the night. Some are not old enough to look back upon the past, and form comparisons which must prove no less than contrasts with the present. Though not a prodigy of age, I have had an opportunity to see some blessed fulfilments of the promise, "The wilderness and the solitary place shall be made glad; and the desert shall rejoice and blossom as the rose. Instead of the thorn shall come up the fir-tree, and instead of the briar shall come up the myrtle-tree; and it shall be to the Lord for a name, for an everlasting sign that shall not be cut off."

And can we believe this, and see this, and be ungladdened and ungrateful?   Or shall we suffer a few private or public burdens and trials to keep us repining and murmuring, when in Judah things go well, and the walls of the temple rise, though in troublous times?   The evils of which some seem almost exclusively sensible, are the more easily seen, and the more deeply felt, because of the presence and prevalence of so much good.   And what good !

When I first went to London there were no Missionary Societies, except those of our Moravian and Wesleyan brethren; but now we have the Baptist, the London, the Episcopalian, Missionary Institutions; all sending forth the truth as it is in Jesus; and all depending for success upon the Spirit of the living God; and, therefore, all carrying on their operations with prayer, and all crowned with encouragement and success, proportioned to their means and endeavours.

Then, too, we had not the noblest of all institutions since the apostolic era, the Bible Society; nor the Tract Society; nor the Jewish Society; nor the Hibernian Society; nor the Irish Evangelical Society; nor the Home, nor the Colonial, Missionary Society; all of which have for years been in full operation.

Here we have not mentioned the Anti-Slavery Society, nor the Peace Society; but though these are not formally and immediately religious institutions, they indirectly aid them; they are congenial with them, and are sanctioned by all their provisions and commands; yea, they have been derived from their spirit.

We also pass over the numerous local and private Societies attached to our several congregations;—and what congregation is there among us without some of them?   Most of which, besides a charitable aim, have also a religious :— for instance, societies for visiting the sick, not only affording temporal succour, but furnishing also spiritual instruction and prayer, when the mind is prepared by affliction to receive it, or peculiarly needing it.   Sunday Schools also not only teach poor children to read their Bible, but inform their minds in the leading truths of the Gospel; and I have never met with a religious interest without a Sunday

School, while many of these Schools now are formed in the
villages where, at present, there is no religious interest; and
which are attended to by persons who go from our churches
on the Lord's day, and consecrate a good portion of the
Sabbath to this work and labour of love; and find the
reward of their journeyings and toil in the pleasure of doing
good.

Think of the spread of the Gospel in the Establishment,
and compare Mr. Romaine's total of fifty Gospel clergymen
with the number in the same church now! Think what an
amazing multiplication of Dissenters there has also been!
And if there has not been such an increase in their *light*,
as in that of some other connexions, (and which was less
needed,) there has been a glorious one in their liberty,
liberality, and life, and usefulness. What a diminution
have I known of heterodox congregations; and what additions to those who know nothing, save Jesus Christ and him
crucified! The number of new places, at the opening of
which I have preached, and the number of enlarged places,
at the reopening of which I have preached, would appear
hard of belief. Yet others of my brethren have been employed in the same work, in *their* respective neighbourhoods
and connexions, all through the land. Several new schools,
also, or to modernize—"colleges," for the sons of the prophets, have been established; and ampler provision made
for those completer preparations for the ministry which the
day demands.

And what a change has there been in public-spiritedness
and generous contributions! How would some of the good
men, who lived eighty or ninety years ago, have been astonished, could they have been told of the sums obtained at
one anniversary meeting; or what is now raised by a single
congregation annually! Where one collection was formerly
made at the doors of the sanctuary, twenty are now made.

The same proportion would hold in the number of applications made personally to individuals, and seldom made entirely in vain.

Love also has abounded more and more, in knowledge and in all judgment. How much less stress is laid on minor and circumstantial things in religion than once! And how much more disposed are the various parties to unite and hold intercourse with each other! I remember how it was wondered at, when Mr. Eyre of Homerton, of Calvinistical sentiments, was asked to preach at Mr. Wesley's chapel, in Moorfields, and preached, without giving offence, from Gal. i. 8,—"Though we, or an angel from heaven, preach any other gospel unto you than that which we have preached unto you, let him be accursed!" Now, without abolishing our distinctions, we have learned to hail, and bless, and help each other. We have agreement without compromise. Our regiments retain their own colours and officers, but fight against a common foe, and for the same King of Glory.

I am aware that some will say, "all is not gold that glitters," and there is much more hearing, and talking, and show, and profession. In a degree this is as true as it is lamentable. There have been also abuses and excesses. These will always grow out of awakenings, while human nature remains as it is. But that there has been a remarkable revival and extension of *genuine* religion, since the rise of what is called Methodism, notwithstanding the imperfections attending it, what can induce us to deny? The dead have been enlivened; the sleeping have been aroused; the form of godliness has not been without the power, though, in some instances, the power has had too little of the form. Faith has not been a cold assent of the understanding to certain dogmas, but a vital principle in the heart and life. The professors of it have denied themselves, and taken up their cross, and followed the Redeemer in the

regeneration. We proclaim not perfection ; but this reno-
vated religion has been essentially and eminently of the
right kind—evangelical in doctrine, practical in operation,
lively in experience, and noble in effects.

But there are persons who, though they allow of some
reality in this statement, yet think that modern Christians
are much inferior to those who lived in the times of our
forefathers. Instead of speaking disparagingly of these
men, we would have inscribed on their tombs, "Of whom
the world was not worthy!" They were martyrs for conscience; the word of God dwelt in them richly; they had
much to do with their own hearts; and were distinguished
by their domestic and private devotions. But they would
not, and could not, have abounded so much in some even of
their own excellences had they lived in a later day. The
stream, then rendered deeper by confinement, has since
widened; and the water flows over more surface. They had
not so many openings and calls for action abroad; and
their spirit partook something of their state. The churches
then seemed to feel little or nothing of the missionary
character; and to some it may seem surprising, how little
is found in the letters, diaries, and sermons of that period,
but what almost exclusively regards the defeats, or prosperity, of their own souls, or immediate communities. And
how little even they who made mention of the Lord obeyed
the injunction, "Keep not silence, and give him no rest till
he establish, and till he make Jerusalem a praise in the
earth." The time, the set time to favour her, was not yet
come. Zion was not in labour to bring forth. She had
hardly conceived. But now—

> "All the promises do travail
> With a glorious day of grace."

And, to drop metaphor;—of late years, persons are not
allowed to look only on their own things, but constrained

also to look on the things of others; and especially the
things that are Jesus Christ's. And they are to be judged
of by the manner in which they do the work of their own
day, and not by their conformity to others who lived under
a different order of things.

But were not Christians who lived at the commencement
of this new and evangelical era, superior in experience to
those who have followed them? I am not entirely unprepared to answer this question. A number of the original
converts of Wesley and Whitefield, were yet living when I
began to appear in public, and some of them I knew intimately; and they made too deep an impression upon me to
be forgotten. They were certainly better acquainted with,
and more endeared to, each other, than the larger proportion of professors now are: but two reasons may be assigned
for this, without making the dead, even by implication, to
depreciate the living.

It was, *first*, in some degree, owing to the persecution and
reproach of the world, that they were drawn together for
intercourse and comfort. It also, *secondly*, arose from the
paucity of their numbers. When religious parties are
smaller, they partake more of a family character; and the
members know, and are known of each other. But this
cannot be equally the case in large societies, and where
multitude prevents intimacy. But then these larger societies have other advantages. They are more public, more
known; they are more firm, independent, and active; they
attract more attendants, are capable of more enterprise,
and can raise more for the cause of God at large, in the
support of charities, schools, missionaries, and evangelists.
It is in vain to expect every recommendation united in any
species of excellency, or department of agency.

But to return to these earlier converts. There was something rather peculiar and specific about them. They seemed
to feel that they were fast and tried disciples, and had a

right to be heard. They were fond of going back, and referring to their first love, and first enjoyments and exercises.
They talked rather too frequently of their own experience,
and made it too much a standard for others; and were too
positive and unyielding, in some little and indifferent points,
to which they attached undue importance. But who could
help admiring their deadness to the world?—their heavenly
mindedness?—the readiness and zest with which they
entered into religious conversation?—the manner in which
they invariably spoke of the Lord Jesus, as all their salvation and all their desire; and with whom they had to do
immediately in all the concerns of the spiritual life?—their
forwardness to relieve the poor, and visit the afflicted, and
to be content with such things as they had?—and their
patience and cheerfulness in tribulation?

I was also much struck with their general freedom from
the fear of death. They never seemed unwilling to be
reminded of its approach. They spoke of it with pleasure; and in conversing with their dying friends, they
appeared concerned to reconcile them to the thought of
recovery, (should this be the event,) rather than to their
dissolution. They rejoiced with them in the prospect of
their speedy release from a wicked world, and an evil heart;
and of their going so soon home, and seeing the Saviour,
and being for ever with the Lord. And when they followed
them to the grave, they sorrowed more for themselves, that
had sustained the loss, than for their connexions, whose
death they knew was gain. And does not even Paley allow,
that in all this they much resembled the first Christians?
Their attachment also to the means of grace was intense;
nor would they suffer distance, or weather, or slight indispositions to detain them. The Sabbath was their delight,
and they numbered the days till its arrival. And as to the
poorer of them—

> "Though pinch'd with poverty at home,
>   With sharp afflictions daily fed ;
> It made amends, if they could come
>   To God's own house for heavenly bread."

Nor were these services only pleasing to them in the performance. They were remembered and talked over for days and weeks after. For the sermons they heard, if not highly polished, left effects which were as goads, and as nails fastened in a sure place, by the hand of the Master of assemblies.

They also seemed to have more veneration for the Scriptures ; and to peruse them with more directness, simplicity, and docility,—for the Bible, as yet, had not been turned into a work of science, rather than of faith ; and of everlasting criticism, rather than of devotion ; nor were thousands of tutors and multitudes of volumes, found necessary to explain a simple book, designed for "the poor" and "the common people," by the only wise God himself.

What is the simple and grand design of revelation? "These things are written, that ye might believe that Jesus is the Christ, the Son of God ; and that believing ye might have life through his name." What care is needful to keep the reader from being diverted, by a thousand subordinate notices, from the inquiry—"What must I do to be saved?"

Excuse the freedom of this letter, and the preference I have given, (but not in *all* things,) to a body of Christians, with whose modified descendants I have been more called to mix and co-operate. And let us serve our own generation, by the will of God ; seizing its advantages, and endeavouring, instead of quarrelling with a few comparative evils, to rejoice that so much has been done ; and that "blessed are our eyes for what they see, and our ears for what they hear."

I am, &c.

PART II.

SUPPLEMENT TO THE AUTOBIOGRAPHY

OF

THE REV. WILLIAM JAY.

PART II.

SUPPLEMENT TO THE AUTOBIOGRAPHY.

In attempting to supply some facts additional to the very few relating to the latter part of Mr. Jay's life, recorded in the Autobiography, we must be permitted to state, that it is impossible now to recover an accurate account, of many events and circumstances of interest connected with his public life. Time is frequently revealing the usefulness of his labours, both as a preacher and an author; but it is more than probable that many remarkable instances of his success will remain untold upon earth. We have reason to believe he knew of many more than he has anywhere recorded. Some of the more remarkable circumstances of his life and ministry, he has scarcely, if at all, noticed. It is our intention to record as many of these, as we have been able clearly to ascertain. But some have been published which are unsupported by sufficient evidence, and others which are certainly false. The chronological order we shall endeavour to observe, as far as possible. The dates, which we have gathered with some difficulty from a variety of sources, will enable the reader to form in his own mind, after reading the Autobiography with the following additions, a tolerably correct as well as orderly conception of the events of Mr. Jay's life.

His own account of his birth and education, is more full and satisfactory than many other parts of the history. It appears that, immediately upon completing his term of

study under Mr. Winter, he was engaged by the Rev.
Rowland Hill to supply his pulpit at Surrey Chapel. This
event, as he himself states, was of great importance, as it
brought him into acquaintance with Miss Davies, who became Mrs. Jay; and also introduced him to the friendship
of Mr. Newton, Mr. Ryland, and others. The continuance
of these annual visits drew him also into connexion with
some of the eminent and excellent men who, shortly after,
formed the plan of the London Missionary Society. It was
in the year 1788, that Mr. Jay fulfilled his first engagement
at Surrey Chapel. The Missionary Society was planned
and founded in 1794; its first May meetings were held in
1795; and at its first anniversary in May, 1796, Mr. Jay
was called to preach, though then only twenty-seven years
of age. His sermon from Psalm lxxii. 19, "And let the
whole earth be filled with his glory, Amen and Amen," &c.,
was published at the time, and is included in the uniform
edition of his works. This sermon was the means of the
conversion of an eminent and distinguished individual, John
Poynder, Esq., as may be seen in the "Reminiscences" of
that gentleman. Speaking of him in a letter to Mrs.
Bolton, many years after, he says, "Yesterday I was informed dear Mr. Poynder had left us. His death will lead
to another 'Reminiscence,' which I began last evening.
I know as yet no particulars of his departure. He was
one of the most noble and useful converts God ever favoured me with."

Some years after preaching at the first Anniversary of
the London Missionary Society, Mr. Jay took a journey on
its behalf into Scotland. An interesting memento of this
visit he has preserved in the Autobiography. These facts
sufficiently attest his great popularity, in the early years of
his ministry. But his intimate connexion with the London
Missionary Society, and his deep interest in its progress,
as well as the honour which its successive directors have

awarded to him, will be shown by the facts we have now to state.

In the year 1826, he was called to preach, at the anniversary of that Society at the Poultry Chapel, to its juvenile friends. In 1834, he preached a third time at its May meeting. His fourth sermon, before the same Institution, was preached at its Jubilee in November, 1844; and again a fifth time he preached at the annual meeting of 1851, in Surrey Chapel. The honour of preaching five times at the meetings of this Society in the metropolis has, we believe, fallen to the lot of no other individual. Although we have singled out his services rendered to this Society, yet there are many others among our public Institutions, the interests of which he has ably and successfully pleaded, both in London and the country, though generally from the pulpit.

In the year 1810 the College of New Jersey in North America, conferred upon Mr. Jay the degree of Doctor in Divinity. Though he did not assume the title, yet he acknowledged the honour done him. But that which gave him the highest satisfaction, was the extensive circulation and usefulness of his writings in that country, among all evangelical denominations.

In the course of the year 1820 he experienced a deep affliction, referred to pretty fully in his Autobiography, Letter IX.; on which occasion he addressed the following characteristic note to the deacons of his church:—

To the Deacons of Argyle Chapel, Bath.

My dear Friends,—This comes to you from the house of mourning and from a bleeding heart. I mourn much: but I pray that I may not murmur. I have sympathized with you in your respective trials; and I know I shall not ask in vain for a share in your tenderness and prayers. But now that God has taken away my darling child, this is to say with Abraham, " *Give me a place where I may bury my dead.*" Having passed the best part of my life among you, it is my wish to die in your service. I wish to have a tomb that

would contain my own remains, whenever it shall please God to
reunite me to my child, and also my dear wife's, and perhaps those
of some of the other branches of the family.   I much desire, if you
have no objection, to have it under the burying-ground house, and
would thank one of you to come over with whom I have communicated upon the subject, either this evening or to-morrow morning
early, as no time can be lost.   Excuse brevity.   I cannot write, but
mine eye poureth out tears unto God.   Believe me, my dear friends,
as respects the whole Church,

Your affectionate and devoted Pastor,

WILLIAM JAY.

This refers to the death of his daughter Statira, who was
seized with fever while he was on a journey in Devonshire,
and from which he was recalled, and only reached his home
in time to see her die, without an opportunity of communication.   Her death occurred August 31, 1820, in her nine-
teenth year.   Being the first inroad made by death in the
happy circle of his family, it was deeply felt by him, as
appears by the lines written on the occasion, which have
already appeared in several publications.

The year 1831, witnessed the arrival of the fortieth anniversary of his pastorate.   The following documents will
attest the deep interest his congregation felt in that event,
and show how he improved it :—

At a Meeting of several of the Members of the Church and Congregation held in the Vestry of Argyle Chapel, on Friday the 28th
January, 1831,

Mr. Griffiths in the Chair,

It was unanimously resolved,

That this Meeting desire to express their gratitude to Almighty
God, for the continuance of a faithful and acceptable Gospel
ministry, under the pastoral care of the Rev. William Jay ; and
for the uninterrupted harmony which has subsisted between their
beloved Pastor and this church and Congregation, for a period of
Forty Years.   And that we, being desirous of presenting to Mr.
Jay some lasting memorial of affection and esteem, do unite, with

such other persons as are willing to contribute, in raising such a sum as may be necessary for the purpose; and that a Committee be appointed to decide upon the most desirable mode of carrying this object into effect, in a manner the most congenial to the feelings of our Minister.

That a copy of the foregoing Resolution be transmitted by the Chairman to Mr. Jay.

HENRY GRIFFITHS, Chairman.

In pursuance of this proposal, a handsome landaulet, accompanied with a silver inkstand, bearing the following inscription, was presented to him:—

" This Inkstand, together with a Landaulet, was presented by the Church and Congregation assembling in Argyle Chapel, to their beloved Pastor, in commemoration of Forty Years' faithful labour among them.

" *Bath, January* 30, 1831."

The following acknowledgment was subsequently addressed by Mr. Jay to the contributors, through the hands of Thomas Kingsbury, Esq., who had acted as chairman of the committee :—

Bath, January 29*th*, 1831.

MY DEAR SIR,—I beg to express my very sincere and hearty thanks to all friends, for the kindness they have shown, in contributing to the handsome compliment you have presented me; and also to the Committee for the trouble they have taken, and the taste they have displayed, in the management of the design.

As a token of regard from my Church and Congregation I shall highly value the Inkstand and the Carriage. The larger portion of my ministry has now of course terminated. It yields me great satisfaction, (among a thousand causes of humiliation,) that it has continued for forty years to meet with the approbation and acceptance of those I have *endeavoured faithfully to serve;* and I pray that my remaining labours, whether they may be of longer or shorter duration, may be equally favoured by them, and far more blessed to them. The present has reached the Receiver in a state of great affliction and anxiousness, during which nothing can afford him the pleasure it would produce, could the entirely loved wife of his youth and riper years be capable of appreciating and enjoying it along with him. Should she be able to employ the vehicle in her infirmity, and derive benefit from the use of it, nothing could lead him so much to prize it, as he can never discharge the obligations he is under to *one* who has so sedulously watched over his life, health, and comfort; and by keeping his mind disengaged from all other things, and free to follow his important and delightful work, has so much aided him, in any little usefulness he has rendered his hearers and his readers, from the pulpit and the press.

Let him importunately beg, in addition to the favours thus acknowledged, that *you* and *all* the friends in whose name you have made the communication will not in your prayers forget,

My dear Sir,

Your grateful, but tried Friend and Pastor,

WILLIAM JAY.

This anniversary was also celebrated by a sermon preached in the morning of Lord's Day, January, 30, 1831, to a crowded and deeply-affected audience. As this was a discourse of great excellence, and productive of a deep impression, and as it is not included in his collected works, we shall insert so much as related to Mr. Jay and his congregation.

Let us imagine a *Member of this Christian Community* reviewing these years. It is not easy to satisfy the benevolence and the zeal of a truly pious mind. Such an individual always laments that more is not done, and that it is not done better; and yet I think that a person attached to this social body—a person who has been led to pray, "Peace be within these walls, and prosperity within this palace; for my brethren and companions' sake, I will now say, Peace be within thee,"—must see something that is pleasing and grateful in the review. He must have seen how "the little one has become a thousand;" how many have been "added to the church of such as should be saved;" and how few comparatively have been excommunicated, or rebuked for immoral conduct. He must have seen the unity and the harmony that have prevailed from the beginning within our church, without discord; and yet the times we have lived in have been troublous. In what a state of danger and fermentation has society been! And there has been enough of the latter among some of our neighbours; but we have enjoyed tranquillity. Yet we have not all thought alike doctrinally. There have been shades of difference with respect to church government; some have not been Independent in their views; some have preferred Presbyterianism or Episcopalianism; yet there have been no discords. We have not all thought alike with respect to the ordinances of religion, but "here," as Cowper said, "the dipped and sprinkled have lived in peace." I have always treated those who, in this matter, conscientiously differed from me, with Christian candour; and I must say they have abundantly repaid it. As it has been with sentiment, so it has been with liberality. We have had institutions of our own: the Sick Man's Friend Society, and others of the same description. We have aided other institutions of the Gospel; the London Missionary Society; the Home and Irish Societies; besides admitting occasionally other collections, which have always been such as to do honour to the minister and the congregation.

The cause, also, must be considered here as having been a candle-stick holding out the light to others. Bath is a place of peculiar resort and intercourse. Many have, therefore, dropped in here who have received conviction, and carried it away with them. How often have I been delighted, when called to preach in various parts of the country, to meet many individuals who have acknowledged that their first impressions of religion were received from the preaching of the word within these walls. Several dissenting ministers, and no fewer than three episcopal clergymen, whose names I might mention, have acknowledged to me that here they first received the knowledge of the truth as it is in Jesus.

Once more, the *preacher* must be allowed to review these years. I know there are many strangers in this congregation, and I really feel for them this morning. It is hardly to be supposed that they will feel interested in a great deal of what I deliver on this occasion. But I must depend upon their candour and good sense, to excuse a recapitulation in which the preacher and the hearer must be considered as feeling a concern, after an interesting connexion of so many years. It is impossible also now to go on without some reference to myself. Whether I have credit enough with the audience to prevent the imputation of egotism and vanity, I cannot determine; I must be content to lie under the suspicion—a suspicion which, I can appeal to God, is undeserved—the design of the reference being, not to set off myself, but being, in fact, altogether inevitable. It is impossible, then, for the minister, in a review of these forty years, not to feel both gratified and solemnized, yea, to feel a number of emotions so mingled in his bosom, that he cannot express them separately. In general, I can say, that these years have been years of pleasure; and I should have no objection to go through them again. Goodness and mercy, intermingled with some trying dispensations, have followed me all the days of these years. But I have a livelier idea of the kindness of Providence than when I began them —a better opinion of my fellow-creatures, and more confidence in them. My views of some religious subjects have been rendered more liberal, and encouraging, and satisfactory. My life, too, has been preserved, while so many of my brethren, and many of them much younger, have been hurried off in the midst of their days. And then, for some time, my own life, I believe, was deemed precarious by my medical friends; of this I am sure, my life was deemed precarious by myself; I had the sentence of death within myself, and never did I expect to reach anything like this anniversary. But God was pleased to raise me up, to renew and establish me. Some of my own order, these forty years, have fallen by temptation; some who having put their hands to the Gospel plough, have looked back; some have been drawn off by dangerous errors, injuring their character and destroying their usefulness; while "by the grace of God, I am what I am." Many years have passed, many changes have occurred, yet have I been upheld till now. Who could hold me up but Thou, O God? During these years I have become a father, and I have lived to see my children's children. I have also become a pretty extensive author; and, on this latter account, I feel peculiarly grateful, having received so many testimonies, both at home and from abroad; and because, by my writing, I may be doing good in many places, and to many individuals, at the same time;—because I may be useful through these means, when I myself am here no more; and because by these my own people may have in remembrance, after my decease, many of my religious sentiments, and I may be aiding them in the closet, and at the family-altar, when the clods of the valley are round about me. Of these numerous works, unless indeed it be their imperfections, were I dying, I should not wish to blot out a single line; and I hope there is not a single sentence of them that can give offence to Christians of any denomination. I desire to bless God for having continued my acceptance, and I trust, my usefulness also, so long. The charm of novelty must long ago have been worn off; and you will bear me witness, that I never attempted to strike into any new paths. I have never tried to get into any new wind of popularity; and if any such wind has aided me, it has fallen in with my own steady course. It sought me; I never sought it. But I have other feelings on this occasion. How is it possible that I should not be affected with the loss I have sustained in hearers and members? What family is there here that has not bled during these forty years? What pew that has not been stripped of some of its occupiers? What think you, of those who signed my call when I came here, there are only three individuals now alive! Oh, how much precious and endeared dust have I interred in our burying-ground! Who has not something there now which he calls his own? Blessed be God, I see others rising up: and instead of the fathers the children; but "my soul desireth the first-ripe fruit." Can I be otherwise than affected with the preservation of my own life? When I was ordained here, this almond tree had not then flourished. But, blessed be God, not one of the hairs have grown grey in the service of the world and of sin; yet the greatest part of my life is gone, and by far the greatest part of it has been spent in your service. The evening of life has now set in, gently and mildly indeed; but, to alter the metaphor, you had part of the spring; you have had the whole of the summer; and if there be any ripeness in the winter, this is before us. But the winter has come, and how can I help being affected with my awful responsibility? How many services during these forty years have I engaged in! How many individuals must I meet at a righteous tribunal! But a merciful Saviour—here is my consolation—I serve a Master who knows our frame, and remembers that we are dust. I have a consciousness that I never perverted my office to secular purposes; that I never shunned to declare what I thought to be the whole counsel of God; that I have never concealed the truth, nor mangled it, at the expense of my own convictions.

Though I do not consider kindness shown to ministers as elee-mosynary, yet I cannot but publicly express my thanks to those who have all along shown me so much of their esteem and regard. As for others, they will feel easy. I never burdened any one, in any in-stance, or degree; and at the end of forty years, I have no obliga-tion, in reference to them, to acknowledge—a boast which perhaps few ministers of my standing or acceptance, in the kingdom, can make.

But I have already encroached too much upon your time. If the great apostle of the Gentiles entreated of those to whom he wrote, an interest in their prayers at the throne of grace, how much more have I reason to say, "Brethren, pray for us," "and for me, that utterance may be given unto me, that I may speak boldly as I ought to speak;" that I may be supported and sustained in my afflictions; that the arms of my hands may be made strong by the hands of the mighty God of Jacob: that I may be long spared to preach to you the unsearchable riches of Jesus Christ; and that at last, as an un-profitable servant, I may be enabled to look for the mercy of our

Lord Jesus Christ unto eternal life ! "The Lord bless you and keep you; the Lord make his face to shine upon you, and be gracious unto you; the Lord lift up the light of his countenance upon you, and give you peace !"

With this benediction I was about to conclude; but how can I conclude without reminding some, whom, long as I have addressed them in this place, I have yet addressed in vain ! How many hundred, how many thousand, affecting invitations, and solemn warnings, and urgent admonitions, have you heard from my voice ! With that voice, like birds in the belfry, you have grown familiar ; and the peal which once alarmed you, now passes by and leaves you unaffected. You are just what you were twenty, thirty years ago, and some of you even forty years ago. Ah no ! you are not the same ; you cannot be the same ; if you are not the better, you must be the worse ; if the preaching of the word has not proved, in your experience, "the savour of life unto life," it must prove "the savour of death unto death." Under what a condemnation will some of you perish ! You cannot now dissolve the connexion which you have had so many years with the means of grace, even if you *would* now detach yourselves. And the image of this place, the figure of the preacher, the tones of his voice, and the messages of grace which he has delivered, will be remembered hereafter, and will be as fuel to that fire that shall never be quenched, and food to that worm that shall never die. O that I could this morning bring you to consider ! O that God would awaken your consciences ! And when this voice which, for these forty years, has filled this house, is silent, and when another shall occupy this sacred desk, may "the beauty of the Lord our God be upon you, establishing the work of our hands—yea, the work of our hands, may God establish it upon you ! Amen."

SIR WILLIAM KNIGHTON AT BATH.

In the year 1833, an eminent and distinguished individual, who might not have been expected to feel any curiosity to hear the Dissenting minister of Bath, was present in Argyle Chapel on two successive Sundays, and on both parts of the day. The following extracts from the "Memoirs of Sir William Knighton, Bart., Physician to King George IV., and Keeper of the Privy Purse," written by Lady Knighton, will be interesting to the readers of Mr. Jay's Life:—

"June 9, 1833. We this morning attended Mr. J.'s chapel. He had been visited, as he stated, with domestic affliction during the previous night. It was supposed to be the illness of Mrs. J. He preached from the 119th Psalm, 32nd verse,—'I will run in the way of thy commandments, when thou shalt enlarge my heart.'

"He said, this saying by David comprehended three things—a complaint—a dependence—and a resolution. He propounded in a very beautiful manner the usefulness of knowledge in Divine things, and stated that this was a qualification not sufficiently preached—but without which we could do nothing—we could not even make a beginning. 'Faith in Christ.'—His illustrations were beautiful. I wish I could remember them sufficiently to write them down. He praised the Liturgy of the church, and said it was to be lamented that the doctrines of the reading desk were not always preached in the pulpit: and observed that they (meaning himself and congregation) did not deserve to be called Dissenters, for they did not dissent from the doctrines of the beautiful Litany ; but that they were called Methodists, fanatics, and enthusiasts, for preaching them.

"The chapel was quite full, and seemingly with well-dressed people. We went in the evening again to hear Mr. J., and were disappointed to find he was not to officiate ; but Mr. —, who preached, completely satisfied us. I never heard a more delightful discourse. His text was from the fourth chapter of the Hebrews, 9th verse : 'There remaineth, therefore, a rest to the people of God.' He drew a most affecting picture of the miseries of this probationary life, and the joys that await the true and holy Christian—for in heaven there is a day of rest. There was no sorrow, no calamity, no adversity, no deep affliction in this life that he did not bring home to one's understanding and feelings. He brought many of them before us with a heart-rending eloquence, as if the sources were drawn from his own bosom. The loss of a child—perhaps an only child—here he paused, and I fancied I saw his lip quiver as the tongue gave utterance to the sentence. When he called upon his Christian hearers to look to that day of rest when corruption would cease, and the joys of heaven supersede all the woes connected with our present earthly tabernacle, his manner of conducting the subject was delightful. He said that he had no doubt, deducing his authority from Scripture, that saints and Christians do know each other in a future state; that the child taken from the disconsolate parent in early life would welcome the pious and holy Christian parent to heaven. This earthly separation, therefore, as being only for a season, bears marks of Divine love; and not the dispensation which, in our sorrow, we feel as an overwhelming calamity. I underwent great emotion as he proceeded, and so did Mr. D., and never felt my heart more under the holy influence of religion. I am sure poor Mr. Jay must have felt the prayer, and the able discourse. I fancy he was in the chapel. Mrs. Jay is alive, but she was struck with paralysis the preceding night. This has been a very interesting day, and I shall not readily forget it."—Vol. ii. p. 307—311.

"Sunday, 16th June, 1833. We hailed this morning with great pleasure, because we had the satisfactory prospect of again hearing Mr. Jay, and we were not disappointed. He preached from 119th Psalm, 18th verse: 'Open thou mine eyes, that I may behold wondrous things out of thy law.' He began by explaining what was meant by the law. It was nothing more nor less than the commands of God. David saw the Gospel in the law. It is in vain to go to this book with any opinions of your own. You must take it as it is—the law of God cannot be changed. If your conscience when awakened under the terrors of the law has found comfort under the Gospel, you may hope that you are in the right road. But let me tell you, he said, that religion and the knowledge of this book are not of sudden growth. This I would not only address to the infidel and unbeliever, but also to the fanatic and enthusiast. The one adapts every thing to his own presumptuous notions and opinions; the other mystifies and confuses revelation from heaven with things not yet revealed. That such states are both dangerous may be well understood, when David, who knew so much, calls out, not in the self-sufficient language of our times, but in the words of the text, 'Open thou mine eyes,' &c.

"Mr. Jay adverted to the wonders of the universe. He referred to the chapter he had read before the sermon, in which the miracle is related of our Lord's restoring the blind to sight, and stated that spiritual blindness was quite as perceptible as corporeal blindness. The man corporeally blind could not indeed deceive you—the loss of

the sense was apparent—but the spiritual blindness was also evident
to the true Christian. The soul must receive a Divine influence, not
miraculous, (for there is no such thing now-a-days,) but a sense of
its own unworthiness ; then follow penitence and prayer ;—an earnest
desire for the Saviour's image to be implanted in the heart; a life in
the ways of godliness according to the law and the Gospel. Cicero,
the greatest philosopher, and the wisest among those of his day, was
accustomed to say, that we lived by the power of the gods—but that
to live well, and not wickedly, was in our own power. Seneca said,
that those men who lived in the rules of virtue were in merit above
the gods, because the very nature of their existence did not admit of
their being otherwise. Here you have the reasoning of the wisdom
of this world. Truly, when you come to contemplate the establishment of Christianity, it strikes you with awe and wonder that a few
unlettered fishermen, without learning, or what we call education,
should be sent forth to preach the redemption of mankind to the
uttermost corners of the earth.

"In the evening, Mr. Jay's discourse was from Job ix. 4. 'He is
wise in heart, and mighty in strength : who hath hardened himself
against him, and hath prospered ?' He began by giving the character
of God most beautifully, and then he drew the picture of the
hardened sinner. I wish that every sinner could have heard him.
In giving the catalogue of sins that belong to sinful man, he said, it
was wonderful with what a degree of complacency words were found
to palliate all the vile passions of wickedness. Covetousness was a
sense of prudence to one's self and family ; revenge, a just sense of
what was due to one's self on the score of honour ; a departure from
truth, a necessary observance of the ways of the world ; and so on.
He mentioned that Lord Bacon had said, that ' Knowledge is power ; '
and this saying had been put forth as Lord Bacon's, but Solomon had
said long before Lord Bacon was cradled, that ' Wisdom is a defence,'
and so it is. It gives a power that wealth cannot often give, although
Solomon says that ' Wealth buyeth all things.' There seemed no
end to the beautiful and appropriate truths put forth in this discourse ! "—Vol. ii. p. 328—332.

This will, no doubt, be interesting to the reader, as evincing the deep impression which Mr. Jay's preaching was
calculated to make upon persons of cultivated minds, and
moving in the highest walks of life. Many such took the
opportunity of hearing him when in Bath, and, in numerous
instances like the present, have been known to express both
the great pleasure and spiritual profit they had experienced.

THE JUBILEE OF MR. JAY'S PASTORATE.

The next important event in Mr. Jay's history which it becomes us to record, was the completion of the fiftieth year of his ministry in Argyle Chapel. The commemoration of this event was looked forward to, with no little interest, by a very wide circle of friends. Those in particular who formed his church and congregation resolved to celebrate the day, in a manner honourable to all parties. Of this memorable occasion, we now proceed to give an abridged account, from the little volume which was afterwards published—observing, at the same time, that, since we could not and did not deem it needful or proper to transfer the whole to these pages, we have limited our extracts to the speeches of Mr. Jay and the Chairman, with those portions of Mr. Jay's sermon which were specially appropriate to the occasion.

The first meeting was one for devotion, held on the morning of Lord's day, January 31, 1841, in Argyle Chapel, at seven o'clock; when fervent thanksgivings and prayers were offered.

At nine o'clock the scholars in the Sunday Schools belonging to the chapel were assembled, and received presents of books, bearing appropriate inscriptions, commemorative of the day. A suitable address was delivered to them by the Rev. Samuel Nichols, of Darwen, Lancashire.

At eleven o'clock the public service was held in the chapel. The introductory devotional service was conducted by the Rev. S. Nichols, after which Mr. Jay preached from 1 Thess. ii. 19:—" What is our hope, or joy, or crown of rejoicing? Are not even ye in the presence of our Lord Jesus Christ at his coming?"

The sermon contains highly interesting instruction, addressed to the disciples of the Gospel—under the different classes of those who *encourage*, those who *solace*, and those who *dignify* ministers. After the general discussion of the text, the author enters into a detail of the circumstances which led to his settlement at Bath, and a review of his lengthened ministry, the substance of which being contained in the Autobiography now published, we pass over, for the sake of introducing a few of the solemn and affecting paragraphs which close the sermon.

"Such are the reflections derivable from the subject of our text, and the occasion of the day. And now, what can I add more? As I ascended this desk, and looked down upon this vast audience, I said to myself, Ah! where will all this assembly be by the return of this Jubilee? Some of you will remain, and perhaps you will then be talking over what is now passing here : but where, oh where, will the majority of you be found then?

"As to many of us, a much shorter period will have removed us, and the places that now know us will know us no more for ever. Other occupiers will fill these pews ; other singers will lead the psalmody, when the voices of those who now charm us will be silent in the grave ; and another voice will be heard in this pulpit than that which has filled it for fifty years past.

"To how many of you is my ordination a matter of history! You have been born since that day, which many of your fathers and mothers attended. How many of you have I taken in these hands, and offered to God in holy baptism! How many of you have I hailed at your coming to the table of the Lord! And how many of your connexions have I followed to our burial-ground! 'Ah!' says one, 'there lies my cherub-child!' 'And,' says another, 'there lies the desire of mine eyes, taken away with a stroke!' 'And there,' says another, 'lies the guide of my youth!'

"I am glad, therefore, when every church has a place of interment of their own : it seems keeping up still a kind of connexion with the departed. Our dead lie not among strangers. 'There I buried Abraham, and Sarah his wife ; there I buried Isaac, and Rebecca his wife ; and there I buried Leah!' We have all our precious dust in yonder ground. Where is the person belonging to us who does not go to the grave to weep there? I am sometimes ready to be jealous lest our burying-place should become richer than our church. But no ; instead of the fathers are their children. Our sons are as plants grown up in their youth ; our daughters are as corner-stones polished after the similitude of palaces : and we have a noble band of the young and middle-aged, who have covenanted with God, and who are saying, WE will not forsake the house of our God. Oh, how does old age, while it leaves life, peel off continually its connexions, till we seem left even as a beacon upon the top of a mountain, or as an ensign upon the hill ! Oh, how many of the various relations of life, during such a varied and extensive acquaintance as mine, have gone down to the dust, and have seen corruption ! How many ministers have been taken away ! 'The fathers, where are they ? and the prophets, do they live for ever ?' Of all the ministers that belonged to the Wiltshire Association when I entered it, I am the only survivor ; and of all those who signed my call when I came here, only one remains, whose venerable head you would have seen here this day, but for indisposition. And, Oh ! what a curtailment are fifty years in a brief duration like ours ! Your preacher, therefore, feels this ; and though, in some measure, he can talk like Caleb, who said, ' As yet I am as strong this day as I was in the day that Moses sent me : as my strength was then, even so is my strength now, for war, both to go out, and to come in,' yet he does not forget that the days of our years are threescore years and ten. Yes ; therefore a period cannot be far remote when, as he hopes he shall never stand in the way of usefulness, he will either entirely resign his labours, or share them with another : and, though he knows the extreme difficulty attached to a concern where three parties are so deeply interested, the Lord can provide. Now I seem to be taking a farewell of the fifty years which I have passed within these happy walls ! What a difference between the day of which I am reminded, and this day ! *Then*, I was rapidly entering life : I am now gradually withdrawing from it. Then, I was commencing my voyage across an untried ocean : now, with the glass in my hand, I am looking for the fair havens. Then, I was a mere youth : now, surrounded with children and grandchildren. What was then anxiety is now repose ; what was then hope, is now accomplishment ; what was then prayer is now praise. What a season of humiliation, you will naturally conclude, must this have been ! We are hardly aware of our deficiencies and imperfections till something occurs which drives us to retire, and reflect, and review. But who can look back upon fifty years, and not exclaim, 'Enter not into judgment with thy servant, O Lord ; for in thy sight shall no flesh living be justified.' ' O Lord, if thou shouldest mark iniquity, O Lord, who can stand !' Yet what a source of thanksgiving ought it to be ! How has my life been indulged ! How few have been so satisfied with favour, and filled with the blessing of the Lord ! Yet I have had trials enough to remind me that

'Full bliss is bliss divine.'

"Though I have not drunk deep of the cup, I have tasted the bitterness of affliction. One trial has pressed upon me with peculiar force ; and concerning which I should have been ready to say, Lord, afflict me in any other point—but his ways are judgment.

"But what deliverances have I experienced during this period ! Serious attacks of indisposition formerly prepared me to expect an abbreviated ministry ; and perhaps you looked for it too ; but, having obtained help of God, I continue to this day ; and, after all the Ebenezers I have reared along ·the road, I now rear the largest of them all. And

> ' Here in thy house I leave my vows,
> And thy rich grace record ;
> Witness, ye saints, who hear me now,
> If I forsake the Lord.' "

On the evening of the same day the Rev. Timothy East, then of Birmingham, preached from Daniel xii. 3 : "They that turn many to righteousness (*shall shine*) as the stars for ever and ever."

On the Tuesday morning following, (Feb. 2,) a public breakfast took place at the Assembly Rooms. The number of persons present at the breakfast was eight hundred and twenty. The ministers attending, both from the city and neighbourhood, were about forty. Henry Godwin, Esq., was called to the chair.

In his introductory observations, Mr. Godwin particularly alluded to the friendship of Mr. Wilberforce for Mr. Jay. He said,—

"There is one witness whom I could almost wish were here this morning, to bear his testimony to the worth of our beloved pastor. Believe me, sir, I am not going to indulge in the language of adulation : it would be as repugnant to me as it would be offensive to you ; and as contrary to the canons of good taste as to the canons of Scripture. I wish the sainted Wilberforce were here to testify his esteem for you : and we know not but that he may be looking down with pleasure upon us now ; for if angels rejoice over a repentant sinner, why should not glorified saints look with ecstasy upon such a scene as this? But I can give you the testimony of Wilberforce himself; and I give it you on the veracity of a man who feels, I trust, that he stands in the sight of God.

"Though not intimately acquainted with that good man, I had the pleasure of having three interviews with him, in one of which Mr. Jay was the subject of conversation; speaking of whom he said, 'There is one thing in Jay, (for he spoke familiarly, and I will speak familiarly too,) there is one thing in Jay, dear Jay, that I love: it is his uniform consistency, his uniform humility. I remember, when he was a very young man; and I know that the popular applause which followed him was enough to turn a young head; but he always kept his steady course: I never saw him in the least inflated by it. I never saw the least indication of his being so: he seemed to shake it off as the lion shakes the dew from his mane. Dear Jay, I love Jay!' Such was the testimony of Wilberforce; but his sons appear to have forgotten that love; at all events they have not shown it in the Biography of their Father."

After some further observations appropriate to the occasion, the chairman read the following address from the church and congregation :—

" TO THE REV. WILLIAM JAY.

"Reverend and dear Sir,—Fifty years have rolled away since a gracious God was pleased to direct the Church and Congregation assembling in Argyle Chapel to choose you as their pastor. Solemn is the thought, that of those who then crowded to hear you profess 'a good profession before many witnesses,' few—very few—remain to welcome this day; and of those who then invited you to accept the ministerial charge, one, only one honoured individual survives. But God has preserved you,—and we are now assembled to commemorate the lapse of half a century, spent in holy duty and affectionate intercourse between yourself and the people of your charge.

"We come not to praise you. It would not be acceptable to you, and we regard the occasion as too hallowed for any such purpose. We desire to unite with you in fervent gratitude to the Great Head of the Church for the signal blessings He has bestowed on you, in fitting you for the high, and sacred, and distinguished course of ministerial usefulness He has enabled you to fulfil; and on us, as a Church and Congregation, in providing for us so rich and edifying an exhibition of the Gospel of the grace of God.

"But while we bow in gratitude before the Most High, and would devoutly adore Him for his goodness, we cannot be insensible that under Him, 'from whom cometh every good and perfect gift,' we owe you much. To the great Apostle of the Gentiles, Philemon owed his 'own self.' To you some of us are under similar obligations; and it is our prayer, that, with those of our predecessors and fellow-worshippers, who have departed in the faith, we may unitedly rejoice in the day of Christ, that you have neither run nor laboured in vain.

"Receive from us, very dear sir, the assurance of our strong affection and unabated regard; and with it, as a token of our attachment to your person, of our veneration for your character, and of our gratitude for your labours as a faithful minister of Christ, we request your acceptance of the accompanying tribute of esteem.

"Finally, we pray for your prosperity, and commend you to the love of the Saviour. May the evening of life, which is now come upon you, and upon one who has tenderly and long augmented your joys, and alleviated your anxieties, ever be irradiated by the Divine presence; and when it shall please Him, whom you serve, to call you to the temple above, may these glorious words break upon your ear, 'Well done, good and faithful servant; enter thou into the joy of thy Lord.'

"Signed, on behalf of the Church and Congregation, Bath, January 30th, 1841 :—

HENRY GRIFFITH.

WILLIAM NEWALL.	ISAAC TITLEY.
JAMES BRYANT.	JACOB TITLEY.
R. H. GRIFFITH.	SAMUEL FISHER.

Deacons of the Church.

H. GODWIN, Chairman of the Committee.
RICE HOPKINS, Secretary of the Committee.

JOHN MATTHEWS.	WILLIAM GEORGE.
GEORGE KING.	JOHN BARNARD.
RICHARD PARKER LEMON.	EDWARD SAUNDERS.
WILLIAM PRICE.	CHARLES GODWIN.
RICHARD FINIGAN.	GEORGE NORTHMORE.
WILLIAM JAMES.	THOMAS BARTER.
JOHN GRIFFITHS MANSFORD.	JAMES GRIFFITHS.
J. C. SPENDER.	WILLIAM GIBBONS.
S. KING.	HENRY EDMUND GOODRIDGE.
HENRY MORGAN.	

"Being the Committee appointed at a General Meeting of the Church and Congregation, held 13th October, 1840.

"With this Address, sir, which so fully expresses my own sentiments, I have to present you also with this salver, and purse, which contains £650, as a token of our united esteem, affection, and gratitude."

The salver was of silver, with a shell pattern border, containing in the centre the following inscription, surrounded with an engraved wreath of flowers:—

Presented,
Together with the Sum of Six Hundred and Fifty Pounds,
to the

REV. WILLIAM JAY,

By the Members of the Church and Congregation
Assembled in Argyle Chapel, Bath,
And by other Friends,
On the
Completion of the Fiftieth Year of his happy and useful Pastorate,
As a Tribute of
Christian Esteem, Affection, and Gratitude,
January 30, 1841.

The Rev. William Jay then addressed the assembly as follows:—

"Mr. Chairman, and my Christian friends,—Of late years you have not often heard me speak publicly, unless in my own appropriate sphere. It was not without reflection and conviction that, believing every man is best in his own order, considering the limitation of human powers, and knowing how liable I was to importunities, and feeling the pressure of various important engagements, I was induced to lay down a rule—and which I rendered general, in order to avoid giving particular offence—that I would decline all platform engagements, and confine myself more exclusively to the press and the pulpit.

"With regard to the former, I hope I have not erred, because I have not failed, God having given large acceptance and circulation to my various and numerous publications; in consequence of which I have the pleasure to think that, after my decease, there are many who may derive some pleasure and profit from the labours of my pen; and especially that my own church and congregation will be able to have in remembrance many of the things they heard from the living voice.

"Nor do I think I have been mistaken with regard to the latter, when I was led to view my principal duty as lying in Argyle Chapel, since, after having preached there for more than half a century, I have had no diminution in attendance or attention; and I now survey this large and voluntary assembly convened together to exhibit tokens of their regard.

"Without any intimation or promise from myself I fear an expectation has been raised, that, on this occasion, I should take rather a large review of a ministry, the fiftieth anniversary of whose ordination, so many of my friends have agreed to celebrate in this flattering manner. But, in the first place, in the usual course of nature, you will soon, from what I may leave behind me, learn some of the circumstances of my earlier history, if they may be worth inquiring after; and you will see the peculiar, the very peculiar manner, in which the providence of God, without any design or effort of my own, or of my humble friends, led me into a work to which I have consecrated so large a portion of my life happily, and I hope not unprofitably. And, in the next place, on Sabbath-day morning last, (as our Chairman has mentioned,) I took a pretty large review of things, especially as they led to the formation of my connexion with those who have so long been 'my hope, and joy, and crown of rejoicing;' together with some other circumstances connected with the Church and with the Pastor.

"I seem, therefore, now only called to do what would be a very pleasing duty, were it not for the load of emotion under which I am called to discharge it: for, unless I were made up of insensibility and stupidity, you must suppose that I could not receive such an address, such a token, such a testimonial, without feelings which would be too oppressive and embarrassing to allow of a full, or perhaps even proper, utterance. I will not, therefore, attempt what I feel to be impracticable; but will briefly and simply, and in a manner the most respectful and grateful, acknowledge my obligations to you, Mr. Chairman, for your disinterested, zealous, and judicious agency—to the gentlemen of the Committee who have been connected with you; and to all those who have contributed on this occasion, as if mentioned by name. Many of them are present; they can receive my thanks from my own lips immediately; and I hope that, in some way or other, they will reach all those contributors also who are absent; for I find that I have had friends not only at home but abroad; and also to that distinguished and truly Christian Poet who has deigned to employ his Muse on this occasion.

"But what do I owe to those Ladies who darted into this business, and who have shown (they are always combined in *them*) so much earnestness and taste in the arrangement of this festival? I never, indeed, despair of anything being done, and being done well, when it once gets into the heads, and the hearts, and the hands of females. My fair sisters, I am not indulging in the language of flattery. My conscience bears me witness that I have always had a concern in private and in public to plead the cause of your sex; and you may take it, if you please, as a kind of testamentary avowal, that, in a long and not unobserving life, I have always found females—like the dear afflicted one at my right hand—worthy of peculiar confidence, esteem, and praise.

"I hope I have character enough to obtain for me a belief, when I affirm, that all, with regard to this Jubilee—excepting the sacred part of it—originated with, and has been carried on by, others; and, therefore, all the guilt must rest upon the heads of a numerous body of friends, who have been, perhaps, too partial and too warm in their friendship.

"I should be sorry if any have been led to imagine, because I have generally been successful in life, that I had now well feathered a nest for myself, or for one dearer to me than myself. But I can glory in saying this is not the case. While, therefore, with regard to the pecuniary part of this oblation, I am not at a loss to employ it, especially relatively and prospectively, yet it is not with this that I am principally impressed. 'How long have I to live that I should go up with the King to Jerusalem?' I hope Providence and grace have taught me, in whatsoever state I have been, therewith to be content. Nor can I expect to derive any immediate comfort from this present; but, as a testimony of respect and approbation, I exceedingly prize it: and there are few things which could have afforded me more pleasure, considering the principle from which the gift has sprung, and the various expressions of esteem and regard with which it has been accompanied.

"I feel also the unsectarian nature of this boon, as it has come from churchmen and dissenters, and from the various religious parties for whom I have often preached, and for whom I have always prayed, saying, 'Grace be with all them that love our Lord Jesus Christ in sincerity;' for, 'whosoever shall do the will of my Father which is in heaven, the same is my mother, and sister, and brother.'

"From the rank and office of some of the contributors, in Church and State, perhaps it may be expected, that there should be a more distinct acknowledgment. I am very willing to render to them the praise which is their due; but you will allow me to say, I have been most affected with the poor of my flock; and nothing will so long remain written on the fleshly table of my heart as the generosity of one individual who presented sixpence to one of my deacons, adding, ' I only wish it were a hundred pounds.'

" I have only one thing more to add. I take this purse, and I present it to you, madam, (*addressing Mrs. Jay, in whose hands he placed the purse amidst the warm applause of the company,*)—I present it to you, madam, who have always kept my purse, and, therefore, it has been so well kept. Consider it as entirely sacred to your pleasure, your use, your service, your comfort. I know this has been perfectly unexpected by you, but it is also perfectly deserved by you.

" Mr. Chairman, and my Christian friends,—There is not one here this morning but would acquiesce in this appropriation, if they knew the value of this female as a wife for more than fifty years; and if they knew also the obligation the public is under to her, if I have been enabled, in any measure and degree, to serve my generation; and how much her sex owe to one who always raised and confirmed my estimation of them; and especially how much my own church and congregation owe to one who has watched over their preacher's health, who has cheered him under all his trials, who has reminded him continually of.his duty, who has animated him in the prosecution of it, and who has freed him, when in her power, from every interruption and embarrassment, that he might be free in his work; and how much my family owe to her for aiding in training up a number of children, who will always call her blessed; and being the mother of another mother, who now resides in America, shining at the head of a lovely train of thirteen children, all walking with her in the way everlasting."

After the delivery of Mr. Jay's speech the following gentlemen addressed the meeting,—the Rev. R. Elliott of Devizes, the oldest of Mr. Jay's contemporaries then present; the Rev. J. G. Bedford of Winchester, a minister of the Established Church; the Rev. T. Haynes of Bristol, the Rev. T. East of Birmingham, W. T. Blair, Esq., the Rev. S. Martin of Cheltenham (since of London), and Edward Smith, Esq., of London.

The Rev. J. Jackson, of Taunton, then gave out one of the hymns composed for the occasion by James Montgomery,

Esq.; after which he pronounced the usual benediction, and dismissed the assembly.

EVENING MEETING.

At the evening meeting, in Argyle Chapel, Henry Godwin, Esq., was again called to the chair.   On one side of the pulpit was placed a handsome stone pillar commemorative of Mr. Jay's predecessor, the Rev. Thomas Tuppen, and of the erection of the chapel; and, on the other side of the pulpit, a corresponding pillar commemorating the fifty years' pastorate of the Rev. W. Jay.   The pillars are of Scotch granite, beautifully polished, and surmounted by a bronze lamp.   Prayer was offered by the Rev. John Glanville of Kingswood, and one of the hymns composed by Mr. Montgomery was sung by the congregation.   The chairman then addressed the assembly as follows :—

"I believe the present meeting is assembled to praise God, and that praise will constitute the greater part of our employment this evening.   We are also assembled for an object which must be familiar to most of our friends who are at all conversant with profane history. We know that the setting up of pillars and obelisks was very common in ancient times; and so early did the practice obtain in the world, that the period when the pyramids of Egypt and others were set up, has been the subject of dispute among historians; and, to the present day, there is a difficulty, if not an impossibility, of ascertaining how early the setting up of pillars might have begun in the profane world.   We see them also in use in our own time.   We have our Wellington pillars and our Nelson pillars, and our obelisks, and the crosses which we see at the roadside; and votive altars which are discovered in digging foundations for buildings in this neighbourhood, show us that the custom is ancient, and perhaps laudable.

"But these trophies, these obelisks, these pillars, were raised for mortal heroes, to perpetuate the fame of those whose glory was in the field of battle, who carried carnage, with garments rolled in blood, through the world.   They have been crowned indeed with the emblems of victory; but the victory has been attended with the sighs, the mourning, and the tears of widows and orphans.   We are, however, assembled this evening to set up other pillars.   We have a higher and a brighter object.   We have to-night to set up peaceful emblems,—to follow examples recorded in the Scriptures as our authority for what we are about to do.   I am sure that most of those who hear me now are familiar with some of the first pillars which were set up, such as that erected by Jacob on his journey to Padan-aram.   The pillar which he there set up produced an awful impression upon his mind, which constrained him to say, (and may we now and at all times, when we enter this sacred house, entertain similar feelings,)—'How awful is this place !   This is none other but the house of God, and the gate of heaven.'   A little of this feeling to-night, amidst all our joy and all our praise, will not be either inconvenient or inconsistent.

"There are other accounts in the Scriptures recording similar occurrences, such as the setting up of the twelve pillars by Moses in the wilderness.   But there is a pillar spoken of in the Apocalypse which we all should think of; that is the pillar which is to be in heaven; the pillar that is to bear the temple there; the pillar that is to bear the inscription of the Christian's name, and be placed in that city whence they shall no more go out.   Oh ! let us be more emulous than ever, that we may become the pillar that St. John saw in the temple, and that our names may be written upon it."

Resolutions were then passed recording the events celebrated, and expressing the gratitude of the assembly for the successful and happy pastorate of the Rev. W. Jay through fifty years.

The speakers were the Rev. T. East of Birmingham, the Rev. W. Bunting of Manchester, the Rev. T. Haynes of Bristol, the Rev. S. Nichols, &c.

The younger members of the congregation having determined to take part in the celebration, presented their minister with a handsome gold medal and a silver salver.   On one side the medal presents a likeness of Mr. Jay, with the following inscription :—

"The Rev. WILLIAM JAY completed a Pastorate of Fifty Years, January 30, 1841."

The reverse shows the front elevation of Argyle Chapel, with the inscription :—

" Argyle Chapel, Bath, Erected 1789.
First Enlargement, 1804.
Second Enlargement, 1821."

The salver bears the following inscription :—

"The Juvenile members of the church and congregation of Argyle
Chapel present this salver, bearing a gold medal, commemorative of
the event, as a tribute of affection to their highly-esteemed pastor,
the Rev. William Jay, on the completion of the Jubilee of his ministerial labours, with the sincere hope that he may long be spared to
them as their shepherd.—Bath, 30th Jan., 1841."

This testimonial was presented by a deputation of the
young people, headed by Mr. King and Mr. Finigan. Mr.
Jay then ascended the pulpit, and addressed his young
friends as follows :—

"I feel more at home *here*, though not entirely so, amidst these
peculiarities. Mr. Chairman, and my dear young friends,—I little
imagined I should have been called upon for a second address on
this occasion. I feel entirely exhausted, not by exertion, but by
emotion : for who ever endured such a persecution of kindness,
and friendship, and honour, as I have endured this morning and
evening ?

"And yet I cannot complain of being called to this service. Yea,
I ought to feel gratified and grateful in no ordinary degree. The
token I have now received is enhanced and endeared by the very
quarter from whence it comes. For the young are the hopes of our
families, and of our churches, and of our country. On them we
depend to fill all the sacred and civil departments in the community;
for one generation passeth away, and another cometh, and none is
suffered to continue by reason of death. But, Oh, could we see a
larger number of the rising race coming forward as a seed to serve
the Redeemer, who shall be accounted to him for a generation ;—
how would this gently loosen the cords of life, and enable us to say,
'Lord, now lettest thou thy servant depart in peace, according to
thy word ; for mine eyes have seen thy salvation.' My dear young
friends,—what a privilege—for I will not refer to it as a *duty* now—
what a *privilege* is early piety ! Hence the language of Solomon which
we so often quote, 'I love them that love me, and they that seek me
early shall find me ;' and which has so frequently adorned an early
tomb. All that seek shall find. The force of this promise, therefore,

must be considered comparatively. All alike find, but all do not find alike. Is there no difference between your finding Him now in the beginning of your journey, to guide you safely forward, and finding Him after wandering in wrong roads, and after being robbed and wounded by thieves, and having your strength worn out, and the shadows of the evening falling upon you? Is there no difference, my young friends, between finding Him in the loveliness and cheerfulness of life, and finding Him 'when the days and the years draw near wherein ye will say, We have no pleasure in them?' No difference between your finding Him in the health of your countenance and the vigour of your strength, and finding Him only when your bones will be filled with the sins of your youth, which lie down with you in the grave? No, none find Him like those that seek Him early. None find such peculiar acceptance with Him, none derive such distinguished privileges from Him. A thousand satisfactions and advantages are wanting in a late conversion which adorn and bless an earlier one. Take an old man; his conversion is of importance to himself; but what is it to others? His conversion secures him for eternity, but it is attended with no usefulness in life. He runs no race; he accomplishes no warfare; he gains no laurels; glorifies not God in his body and spirit; nor serves his generation according to the will of God.

"There is a proverb which you, perhaps, may have met with, which says, 'Young saints prove old devils.' I would rather reverse this, and say, that *young saints often prove old angels.* Read through the Scriptures; notice the history of Joseph, and Samuel, and David, and Daniel, and John, and Timothy. Read through the history of our godly ancestors. Remember the language of Beza in his will: 'Lord,' says he, 'I thank thee, that at the early age of sixteen, I was enabled to dedicate myself to thy service.' Here the speaker could refer to his own experience, and perhaps it would not be improper on this occasion. My young friends, if he had been the victim of youthful vices, and had not been cut off in the midst of his days, what a different figure would he have made at this time! And I am persuaded that there is not a Christian here who is not, next to the salvation of his soul, most grateful for an early consecration to the service and glory of God.

"Now I presume that many of our young friends, who have joined in the testimony of respect, are already walking in the truth, and I can have no greater joy than to see this. But I hope this will be the case with all who have joined in this token of respect. Oh, my young friends, it would be sad, it would be dreadful, for any of you, after having come forward thus to honour your minister now, to constrain him hereafter, on a more public occasion, to condemn you—to say, Lord, they are guilty : Lord, they have destroyed themselves. I instructed them ; I warned them ; I invited them ; I besought them with tears to come unto Thee. But they turned away from Him that speaketh from heaven ; they neglected so great salvation ; they rejected the counsel of God against themselves. But I hope better things of you, and things that accompany salvation, though I thus speak. And, O my young friends, who have thus favoured me, could I take many of you by the hand and lead you to the table of the Lord, it would afford me much more delight than the reception of this medal. And yet I do not undervalue this present ; yea, I prize it, not only for the exquisite beauty of the workmanship, but for the sake of those who have presented it. It will remind me of you, my young friends, and lead me to remember you, too, for good.

"This medal, you are aware, cannot long remain in my possession ; but it will, as our Chairman has remarked, serve as an heir-loom in my family ; so that my children and my children's children, when they look upon it, may prize it, and remember how long their father laboured within these walls, and how God smiled upon him, and was pleased to favour him to the last.

"Here are two pillars erected. Delicacy and my feelings will not allow me to refer to them. Indeed, the allusion would be unnecessary after the remarks which have been made by our Chairman. But remember they are *memorials*. One of them is a memorial of my predecessor ; the other, after a while, will be a memorial of myself. Oh, then, may I be enjoying Him above, while you are zealously serving Him below, and at last may we all unite in that blessed world where *adieus* and *farewells* will be a sound unknown ! ' O God, let thy work appear unto thy servants, and thy glory unto their children ; and let the beauty of the Lord our God be upon us, and establish Thou the work of our hands upon us ; yea, the work of our hands establish Thou it.' Amen."

The Rev. D. Wassell of Bath then gave out one of Mr. Montgomery's hymns, and the Rev. W. Lucy of Bristol pronounced the usual benediction. The Chairman then dismissed the assembly.

We subjoin the hymns composed for this interesting occasion by James Montgomery, Esq.

HYMN I.

A blessing on our Pastor's head,
Lord God, we fervently implore;
On him, this day, a blessing shed,
For life, for death, for evermore.

For all that Thou in him hast wrought,
For all that Thou by him hast done,
Our warmest, purest thanks be brought,
Through Jesus Christ, our Lord, thy Son.

To Thee he gave his flower of youth,
To Theé his manhood's fruit he gave;
The herald of life-giving truth,
Dead souls from deathless death to save.

Forsake him not in his old age,
But while his Master's cross he bears,
Faith be his staff on pilgrimage,
A crown of glory his grey hairs.

With holier zeal his heart enlarge,
Though strength decay, and sight grow dim,
While we, the people of his charge,
Still glorify thy grace in him.

So, when his warfare here shall cease,
By suffering perfected in love,
His ransomed soul shall join in peace
The Church of the First-born above.

HYMN II.

Hallelujah! heart and voice,
Yielding all the praise to Thee,
Lord, the flock would now rejoice
In the Pastor's Jubilee.

Hallelujah! heart and voice,
When the day of God they see,
All Christ's sheep will thus rejoice,
On his own grand Jubilee.

Hallelujah! heart and voice,
Then in heaven one fold shall be,
And one Shepherd,—to rejoice
In eternal Jubilee.

The following letter from Mr. Montgomery, addressed to the chairman of the committee, H. Godwin, Esq., will appropriately conclude this account of the Jubilee celebration :—

"The Mount, Sheffield, Feb. 9th, 1841.

"DEAR FRIEND,—Accept my best thanks for your packet and the accompanying newspaper, which duly arrived on Saturday. I do heartily congratulate you and your brethren, as well as your venerable pastor *and his partner*, on the happy celebration of his Jubilee Anniversary in Bath. I have read the proceedings both of the Sabbath and the Tuesday following with great delight; for yet, amidst all the strife, envy and uncharitableness *in* churches, and *between* churches, so flagrant at this time, you have shown that there are occasions when, and there may be found professors, of whom, even an ungodly world can say, (reverence touching their hearts, and softening their tongues, while they utter the words,)— 'See how these Christians love one another !' Alas ! how seldom is this exemplified ! The record of your festival, however, will be hailed throughout the country, and perhaps through all Christendom, as a blessed evidence of a Philadelphian spirit yet living and breathing in a Laodicean age, when the suspended animation of lukewarmness is only disturbed by the hallucinations of that vain-boasting which says, 'I am rich, and increased with goods, and have need of nothing,' when—you know where to look for the sequel, and what *that* is. 'For the divisions of Reuben there were great *thoughts* of heart,' says Deborah in her song, and she doubles the burden of her lamentations, by adding, 'For the divisions of Reuben there were *searchings* of heart.' In the multitude of *our* thoughts within us, on our unhappy divisions, personal, domestic, and denominational, as Christians, may there be great searchings of our hearts, and trying of our ways, that we may turn again to the Lord, and to our *first* love, if we ever loved at all ; for assuredly there is an awful apostasy from this, *among* and *between* every section of the catholic church in this land,—and the plague has extended its baleful influence even into the fields of missionary labours. But I must forbear,—the digression has not been wilful, but I was drawn into it insensibly, from feeling that the scene of holy harmony at Bath ought not to have been one of rare occurrence, but, more or less, of every-day felicity among our Saviour's disciples, when and wherever they meet in His name and He is in the midst.

"I thought much of you on the two days, especially on the Tuesday, when the meetings—the love-feasts I ought to call them

—were held, because with us the weather was tempestuous, and I feared that with you, if the visitation reached so far, many of your friends might be disappointed of 'the hope deferred' which they were already cherishing when I was at Bath, fourteen months ago, of being partakers and helpers of the joy of their brethren and companions, on the expected Jubilee of their venerated pastor's ministry among their fathers already called to glory, and themselves, I trust, on their way thither, under the staff and rod of the Great Shepherd's ministry to the flock of God in your neighbourhood, over which he has been so long a watchful and faithful overseer. It appears, however, that whatever storms might rage without, there was peace within, and as many to enjoy it as the rooms would contain.

" I am greatly indebted to Mrs. Godwin for the Jubilee-medallion —the workmanship of which seems to me admirable, the likeness of your good pastor excellent, and the simple register of dates, on either side, the most appropriate of inscriptions in such a case. It was a beautiful and affecting sequel to the solemnities of the Sabbath, and the festivities of the breakfast on Tuesday, that the children and the youth were allowed to bring their offerings of gratitude and love to the father in the gospel of both old and young in your church and congregation. I have only to add my heart's desire and prayer to God for you all, that every one of the number of those who participated in the privileges of those two memorable days, may be finally associated in that place where, a thousand and ten thousand ages hence, each may remember, with adoring gratitude, the blessedness of those meetings on earth, which many of you, no doubt, felt to be an earnest and foretaste of the glory and felicities of that house of God eternal in the heavens,

' Where congregations ne'er break up,
And Sabbaths have no end.'

*   *   *   *   *   *

" I am, your obliged friend and servant,
" J. MONTGOMERY."

A few days after this commemorative service the committee of the Bath Auxiliary Bible Society passed the following resolution, at a very full meeting, by a unanimous vote :—

"That this Committee, participating in the prevalent disposition of the Christian public to glorify God in the long course of consistent piety and extensive usefulness, maintained for half a century in this city by the Rev. W. Jay, and fully appreciating the value of his unwavering attachment to the British and Foreign Bible Society, from its earliest formation—do appoint a deputation to wait upon him, and request his acceptance of the office of a Vice-president of the Bath Auxiliary."

The deputation consisted of the Rev. John East, the mover of the resolution, W. T. Blair, R. Perfect, and W. Sutcliffe, Esqrs. The interview was of the most cordial and pleasing description. Mr. Jay accepted the honour, and his name henceforward was placed on the list of Vice-presidents of the Bath Auxiliary.

———

In the year 1845 Mr. Jay experienced a severe trial in the death of Mrs. Jay. She expired, Oct. 14 of this year, in the 79th of her age. From the time of her first seizure, which Mr. Jay has sufficiently described in his Autobiography, and which took place in the year 1830, she never recovered the full use of her faculties; and, as age produced greater weakness, she gradually sank under the power of disease, so that at length it became impossible to hold intelligent conversation with her. She continued, however, to attend the house of God through a great part of her affliction, but it was doubtful whether she understood anything. Even as early as the year 1834, Mr. Jay said, in a letter to Mrs. Bolton, that her mother was often very low on her account, and adds, " You will suppose I have no little engagement in attending to her in her advancing infirmities, and her almost total absence of employment and amusement." Again, in a letter written in 1837 to Mr. and Mrs. Bolton, then in America, he says, " Your dear mother grows feebler with years. I think also she gets blunter in apprehension, and more perplexed in speech." In April, 1840, speaking of other members of his family, he says, " They have more leisure and opportunity than I have, with so many things pressing upon me alone, which your precious mother formerly divided with me, or rather, entirely took from me." In October, 1841, he says, " Your invaluable mother gets very feeble, and a short walk soon fatigues her, and she is no stranger to lowness, especially in thinking of death. This is, I believe, a frequent case with those who are best prepared for it: But she does not and cannot complain of any want of esteem, and love, and attention, even to devotedness, from all that are about her; and, with regard to myself, she seems to get dearer every day."

A funeral sermon for Mrs. Jay was preached at Mr. Jay's request, by the Rev. George Rogers, now of Camberwell, who has obligingly furnished a copy of the characteristic letter which he received from Mr. Jay on the occasion.

"Bradford, October 24, 1845.

" MY DEAR SIR,—When, in compliance with my desire (especially in reference to my present affliction), you consented to spend another Sabbath of your acceptable labours in Argyle Chapel, I more than once mentioned that I neither *expected* nor *wished* for what is called a Funeral Sermon, on the behalf of my loving and entirely loved wife. First : because you knew her not, and, therefore, could only speak of her from report; and, secondly : because I feel less and less attached to discourses of this kind, and wish to show this in a case which may keep many from complaining, if any of their friends and relations should not be *nominally* and *expressly* noticed in the pulpit, *unless as furnishing instances of mortality, which always admit and deserve improvement.* In *personal* characterising, on most occasions, preachers are greatly perplexed and tried between their convictions and a desire to please ; and, at such times, no little often *will* please. Many individuals, too, however amiable and pious, afford no striking points of observation ; their path resembling the course of the sun, always useful, but every day the same. The best likenesses of persons are taken before they are dead. Their best eulogies are their lives. Their best witnesses are their inmates, who see them without restraint or disguise. A woman's best sphere is her own house. A wife's best honours are derived from the poor, from her servants, from her children, and her husband. 'Her children rise up and call her blessed ; her husband also, he praiseth her. The heart of her husband doth safely trust in her; she does him good, not evil, all the days of his life.'

"Those who most deserve public notice commonly shrink most from it. I would not, therefore, violate the known wish of the departed, by any attempt to display her worth, her excellences, and her claims; and which would be deemed less proper as coming from one so nearly related, although best acquainted with her. Hence, I must say nothing of her early *piety*, her *consistent conduct*, her Christian and lovely temper, her evangelical principles, her love to the Gospel, her intuitive readiness of perception, her warmth of friendship, her benevolence of disposition, her entire freedom from selfishness, her delight in doing good; and her patience, resignation, and cheerfulness under her peculiar and long-continued affliction. I have always expressed a great, and am not afraid to say, a preferable regard for female character; and this has been in no small degree derived from her *example and influence*. We naturally judge of the whole by parts, and of course by those parts which fall most under our own inspection. They who degrade or speak lightly of women are always those who have only had converse with depraved or imperfect specimens of the sex; but there are females who not only *endear*, but *adorn* and *dignify* their order, 'and put to silence the ignorance of foolish men.' 'A gracious woman retaineth honour: give her of the fruit of her hands, and let her works praise her in the gates.'

"I only add, that if I have benefited the public by my writing, and my people by my preaching, and if I have, in any good degree, been able to exemplify what I have taught, I wish it to be *known* and *acknowledged* how much of this I have owed to the agency of this now glorified saint; in her ceaseless care of my health and peace of mind—in her rendering my home the abode of love and happiness—in her securing me from interruptions and anxieties, so that I might be free to devote my powers to my work; and, *not less*, by her counsels and cautions, her encouragements and admonitions, in which I never found her mistaken; so that I can truly adopt the eulogium of Mr. Newton when speaking of *his* wife—'I never followed her advice but I was thankful; and I never deviated from it but I had reason to repent.'

"I need not ask my beloved church and congregation to sympathize with me under a breach which has broken up so indulged a connexion of fifty-five years' standing, and at a time when life has passed its average era, and the days are coming whose 'strength is labour and sorrow.' May their sympathy lead them to pray that I may not faint in the day of adversity, but be better prepared to rejoice with them that do rejoice, and weep with them that weep. 'I know, O Lord, that thy judgments are right, and that thou in faithfulness hast afflicted me. Let thy merciful kindness be for my comfort, according to thy word unto thy servant.'

"Use this as you please, and believe me to be,

"My dear Sir,

"Your most obliged and affectionate brother,

"WM. JAY.

"To the Rev. G. Rogers."

Some months after Mrs. Jay's decease he expressed himself thus: "There is not a day, nor hardly an hour, in which I do not think of your inestimable mother; and though she was getting increasingly helpless, yet still I had her, and delighted to attend her. I now feel very solitary, and often sad, from my social disposition and long experience of such a companion, and as privations and infirmities are likely to increase."

To have watched and attended her so many years under this painful affliction, and with so much tenderness and constancy, under his own advancing years, must have been a heavy burden, and a severe discipline for his heart. But his Christian excellency shone the brighter through this dark domestic cloud. At length it passed away, when her sorrowful spirit was emancipated from the bonds of mortality, and preceded her beloved and faithful companion to the realms of perfect and unending bliss.

In the following year he wrote thus to Mrs. and Mr. Bolton: "You blame me for not writing, but did you know what I have felt (yet how strange!) at the thought of writing since, as it would necessarily turn much upon my great affliction, you would perhaps blame me less. I have yet answered no one. I physically felt the more as other afflictions preceded it; and I was nearly five weeks confined from air and exercise by my accident; so that my strength was lowered, and my spirits broken, when I was called to surrender one who had been my honour, my comfort, my happiness, for fifty-five years. I need not enlarge upon her worth to you. You know I could not say too much of her as a daughter, a wife, a mother, a woman, a Christian.

"What a mild season! My garden already begins to bud forth. How many rose-trees do you imagine I have? Between four and five hundred. How fond I get of flowers! I lately heard of a pious female who, dying, said, 'I am going to a land of peace and flowers.' Yes—

'There everlasting spring abides,
And never-withering flowers.'

"Well! in that happy region is now ———, and soon we shall follow. Oh for grace while we live, to live unto the Lord, and when we die, 'to die unto the Lord.' "

Referring to the same topic in another letter, he says, "We rejoice to find that you are so improved in health, and are looking forward, with glowing hope and pleasure, to an interview in the spring—lamenting only that time will turn the visit into a vision. One mighty loss you will feel and deplore, though on her account we ought to be more than resigned—freed as she is from the burden of the flesh and growing infirmities. There is not a day but I have her variously in remembrance."

Early in the year 1846 Mr. Jay received a deeply interesting testimony of affectionate respect and gratitude from one class of his congregation, whose welfare, both for this life and that to come, he had often laboured to promote: these were the female servants. They united their humble offering together, and presented to him a silver sugar-basin, stating simply, that it came from many attached female servants in connexion with the church and congregation.

Mr. Jay's reply is as follows:—

"Mr. Jay will thank Mary Rogers to communicate to the kind domestics, who with herself have testified their regard by presenting him with a piece of plate:—First, that he is much pleased with the utensil itself, and admires its form and simple elegance. Secondly, that he much values it as to the quarter from which it comes. From no class of his hearers would it have been so welcome. He has, as is well known, always avowed the obligations we are under to good servants, and has always pleaded for their rights. Thirdly, that he is peculiarly thankful, that, while they afford him this token of their esteem, they also acknowledge their having derived spiritual benefit from his labours, and that he has not preached among them in vain.

"He prays and hopes that his services may continue to be acceptable and profitable; and that they who have contributed to this 'work and labour of love,' may unceasingly 'serve the Lord Christ;' and at last hear from our *one* Master in heaven, 'Well done, good and faithful *servant*, enter thou into the joy of thy Lord.'

> "'Honour and shame from no condition rise:
>   Act well your part,—*there* all the honour lies.'

"He now desires each of the servants to accept one of his publications, inscribed with their names and with his own. This will aid their remembrance of him, when the lips upon which they now hang will be silent in the grave; and by this, he 'being dead,' may yet be speaking.

"He gladly subscribes himself their grateful and affectionate Pastor,   WILLIAM JAY.

"Bath, Jan. 7, 1846."

Mary Rogers is still living, and mourning the loss of her beloved master and pastor. She was an ancient and most valuable servant in his family.

Mr. Jay some years since preached a funeral sermon for a female servant; upon which occasion he observed, that there were two things which caused religious servants to be too generally disliked. The *first* was their fondness for religious gossiping, or *cronyism*, which made them regardless of their time, &c. And, *secondly*, their aptness to carry their equality as Christians into their secular stations, and to use an unbecoming familiarity, instead of a dutiful respect, to their masters and mistresses.

In the year 1846, Mr. Jay having been for some time a widower, and having all his children removed to a distance from him, deemed it desirable to change his state. He chose as his future partner Miss Head, an excellent and pious lady, with whose parents he had early become acquainted through the introduction of his friend and tutor, Mr. Winter, who was much attached to them on account of their Christian zeal and liberality. Mr. Jay preached and published the funeral sermon for Mrs. Head. Miss Head was the last surviving member of this family, and the marriage which took place was not only with the entire approbation of all Mr. Jay's family, but appeared to them, as well as to himself, kindly ordered in Providence to promote the comfort of his latter days. He always referred to it with the liveliest gratitude to God. The ceremony was performed September 2, 1846, at the Congregational Chapel, Worthing, Sussex.

———

In the year 1847, Mr. Jay proposed to obtain permanent assistance in his ministerial labours; and, with a view to such an arrangement, Mr. R. A. Vaughan preached for a period of three months with much acceptance. At the expiration of that period he received a unanimous invitation to become assistant-minister at Argyle Chapel. He accepted the invitation, and entered upon his stated duties in April, 1848, and continued to discharge them till March, 1850, when he resigned, and removed to Birmingham. In the autumn of this year Mr. Jay wrote thus:—

"I cannot do things so quickly and easily as I once could, and feel a growing reluctance to exertion. I must, therefore, be judged of, not by my former, but present self, at going on for eighty-two, and feeling, in a degree, Solomon's description,—'the grasshopper is a burden,' and desire fails. Yet I do what I can in my own old work; and, I assure you, friends are not disposed to spare me. We are yet at sea with regard to an assistant; but I hope the Lord will provide, as I want to effect a settlement and retire."

Towards the end of the year 1851 he expressed his sense of growing infirmity and anticipation of the coming trial in his own peculiar manner, thus:—

"As to myself, I am as well as I can expect to be during the remnant of my advanced life. God has two kinds of duty for us—the *active* and the *passive*—'for they also serve that wait;' and I expect to find the latter more trying than the former : but his grace is sufficient for us."

In the spring of 1852 the Rev. Dr. Johns, Rector of Christ Church, Baltimore, paid a visit to this country, and through his acquaintance with the Rev. R. Bolton, obtained an introduction to Mr. Jay, and a temporary sojourn in his house. In a letter to Mr. Bolton he gives the following interesting account of that visit:—

"We arrived in Bath on Saturday, June 26, 1852, and were kindly welcomed by your aged relative, then, I believe, in his eighty-third year. I can never forget the sentiments with which his form and face, his dignified and easy manner, filled me. He was not entirely well, however ; and having to preach on the ensuing day, excused himself at an early hour, saying, 'I must retire into the wilderness. I must pump awhile. You, in travelling, need not do so, but I must.'

"I asked him if he was in the habit of preaching from notes ? 'From catch words, on a slip of paper,' he answered; 'but I wish I had never used even these, for the memory is like a true friend, it loves to be trusted.' This remark made a deep impression on me at the time, and I resolved to treasure it for the benefit of others. He informed me that he endeavoured to select his text on Monday morning, stating that by so doing he could meditate upon it all the week. 'But,' said he, 'no clergyman ought to study on Saturday, but should allow his mind perfect rest at that time. He approved of formal divisions in sermons, and said his rule was to have about five. His opinion was that they aided the memory of the hearer, and made the subject of the sermon more open and clear. Referring to the Calvinistic system, he said it was a thing to be held, not formally preached. His idea seemed to be, that it should leaven the whole character of the pastor and preacher, but not be urged dogmatically.

"In a subsequent conversation, he alluded to the Rev. John

Newton, with whom he had been intimately acquainted, and spoke of him with all the warmth of an early friendship, and observed that he surpassed all the ministers of the gospel he had ever known, in the variety and solidity of his qualifications for the sacred office. Alluding to the Rev. Mr. Romaine, he observed that he was a good man, but a high churchman.   Mr. Romaine, he went on to say, once remarked to him, that at the beginning of his ministry he could only count fifty evangelical clergy in the Establishment, but that he could then name five hundred.

" Referring to the present prospects of the English church, he freely gave it as his opinion that the evangelical clergy would carry the day, as they were not only increasing more rapidly than the opposite class, but were more active and enterprising.   He said that when he first came to Bath, sixty years ago, there was scarcely a clergyman in the Established Church there who preached the gospel. ' Now,' says he, ' there are few here who do not preach it.'   He alluded, in terms of deep regret, to the disposition evinced by many of the evangelical clergy to withdraw from the free and affectionate associations which they formerly cultivated with the dissenting ministers.   He said, he thought he noticed a change in this matter, and noticed it with sorrow, and appeared to think both would be losers by it.   I informed him the same thing was true of the United States, and that we mourned over it.

" On Sunday, June 27th, I heard Mr. Jay preach in the morning in Argyle Chapel.   His text was, Psalm cxix. v. 17, ' Hold thou me up, and I shall be safe.'   The passage had been sent to him by a friend, with a request that he would preach from it.   He made it the basis of an examination of the question,—When may the Christian be said to be in a safe state ? or rather, What may be considered a safe state ?   His heads of discourse were something like the following :—

" 1. When the person is under the influence of a deep concern for his spiritual welfare.

" 2. A sound conviction of the exposure to which the soul is ever subjected in its journey through this world.

" 3. An abiding conviction of our liability to spiritual injury arising from our weakness.

" 4. An unfailing confidence in the faithfulness and ability of God our Saviour to make and keep us safe.

" 5. A spirit of earnest prayer, and a devout reliance through it upon God.

" Mr. Jay's manner was calm, and his voice clear and distinct. His object seemed to be to show the sinner's weakness on the one hand, and his safety on the other ; and these points, sustained from Scripture, were also illustrated by one or two quaint but very forcible anecdotes. No one but a person of his age could have used them with advantage ; but with his peculiar manner they told with great effect upon the audience, reminding me of Bishop Latimer's favourite style. I have never heard more of the gospel in a single sermon ; and in reply to the inquiries of American friends, as to whose preaching I liked best of all I heard while in England and Scotland, my answer has uniformly been, 'The old preacher at Bath, whom you all know as the author of the "Morning and Evening Exercises." ' His sermon was full of Christ, discriminating and searching, while in point of style I did not notice a sentence 'out of joint,' from the beginning to the end, and it was an hour in delivery.

" On the ensuing Monday morning, as we were gathered around the breakfast table in the library-room, good kind Mrs. Jay presiding, and by her gentle hospitality making the stranger feel as if he were at home instead of 3000 miles from it, an incident occurred which I noticed with pleasure. He inquired of his grand-daughter, Miss Jay, if she recollected the text of a sermon she had heard at Ventnor the previous week, and he continued to inquire until the young lady gave it to him. I suspect it was his custom with the young, and was designed to show his desire that they should retain what they had heard. Few opportunities of doing good to souls around him were allowed to pass unimproved ; and yet so cheerful, and at times even playful, was his manner, that there was nothing morose or forbidding about him, or calculated to do other than attract even the youngest.

"I cannot omit speaking of his remarkable solemnity in conducting family worship. He read the Scriptures with an emphasis, and expounded as he passed on ; whilst in the prayer he seemed to carry all along with him. I do not think there were any with us who could have been much troubled with wandering thoughts. He seemed to chain each heart to his own, and to draw the whole to the Saviour's feet. His accents appear, even now, almost to sound in my ears, as I revert to those sweet and blessed moments.

" Conversing with Mr. Jay seemed like speaking with a past age. He had seen and known and heard nearly all the distinguished men in both Church and State, for more than sixty years ; and as his memory was fresh, in reference to early incidents, he described Whitfield and his contemporaries, with the leaders in parliament, and in all the important movements of benevolence, with a minuteness and graphic power that no studied writer could well give to them. How few have lived so long, and lived through an age so abundant in events so deeply interesting to the Christian! As I gazed upon this venerable man, and thought of his long-extended labours both in the pulpit and through the press, and then anticipated what has since occurred, his entrance to our Master's presence above, I could scarcely contain my emotions. God be praised for such a life; yet when removed from earth, what a blank is left! Be it ours, my dear brother, to follow him as he followed Christ, and to strive to imitate his meekness and fidelity, his love of souls, and his enlarged interest in the cause of Christ.

"Truly and affectionately, your friend and brother,

"To the Rev. R. Bolton.   HENRY V. D. JOHNS."

On Lord's-day morning, July 25, 1852, Mr. Jay preached what proved to be, though unexpected at the time, his last sermon, in Argyle Chapel, from the text, Ps. lxiii. 1, 2: "O God, thou art my God; early will I seek thee: my soul thirsteth for thee, my flesh longeth for thee in a dry and thirsty land, where no water is; to see thy power and thy glory, so as I have seen thee in the sanctuary." The preacher was in his usual health, and none who heard him supposed they were listening to his last address from that pulpit. A few of the closing sentences we insert as a beautiful specimen of the interesting and impressive manner in which he terminated his faithful testimony among his people.

"But I dare say you think it is time for me to conclude, and my age and weakness tell me the same. I therefore hasten to a close, by observing one thing only; that is, experience is both *alarming and encouraging*. It is very alarming to those of you who are strangers to it. And this is the case with many who are very familiar with the means of grace. 'You come as God's people come;' that is, if you do come to God's house—but no further. You come from curiosity or custom, or to comply with the desires of your connexions, or to appease conscience; not to please God, and to hold communion with Him. You have never come—you *know* you have not—to see His power and His glory. You never prayed for it before you came; you never examine yourselves when you go there, whether you have enjoyed Him. Oh! it is awful to think what a length of time this has been the case with

some of you. Five, ten, fifteen, or twenty years, without one effectual religious movement ! Dear hearers, what will these means of
grace do for you? You will never hear to purpose till you *so hear
that your souls may live*. You, *singers*, if you do not sing with
melody in your hearts to the Lord here, you will not be found
among the blissful number of those who shall celebrate His praises
in the courts above. And you, *hearers of the gospel*, if you are
hearers only, you are deceiving your own souls ; and this word of
life will only be to you ' a savour of death unto death.' You *worshippers*, if you ' draw nigh to God with your lips, and honour Him
with your mouth, while your heart is far from Him,' and you do not
worship Him who is a Spirit in spirit and in truth, you will pass on
from possessing a name and a place among the people of God here,
to that place reserved for hypocrites and unbelievers. May you
' seek the Lord while He may be found, and call upon Him while
He is near ! '

" But some of you can say with the Psalmist,—

> " ' I 've seen Thy glory and Thy power
> Through all Thy temple shine ;
> My God, repeat that heavenly hour,
> That vision so divine ! '

Let the pleasure of former experience increase your expectation.
May you ever repair to His temple, humbly believing that you shall
be satisfied with the goodness of God's house, ' and made to drink
of the water of life.' And then you shall soon see God in the sanctuary above ! And, oh, what a sight will that be ! how satisfying !
how beatifying ! how eternal !—

> " ' If such the sweetness of the streams,
> What will the fountain be,
> Where saints and angels draw their bliss
> Immediately from Thee ! '

Then, with all the redeemed, you shall be before the throne of God,
and serve Him day and night in His temple ; and He that sitteth on
the throne shall dwell among them. ' They shall hunger no more,
nor thirst any more, neither shall the sun light on them, nor any
heat. For the Lamb which is in the midst of the throne shall feed
them, and shall lead them unto living fountains of water ; and God
shall wipe away all tears from their eyes.' ' Ah ! ' said Philip
Henry, ' if this be heaven, oh ! that I were there ! ' "

HIS ILLNESS AND RESIGNATION OF THE PASTORATE.

After this service he went to Worthing to enjoy his usual relaxation, but was seized with alarming illness. His friend and physician, Dr. Bowie, hastened to attend him, and he was removed to his own house with as much speed and care as possible. To his attendants he then said, "*I am going home, to go home.*" After a few weeks, his sufferings were alleviated, and he then resolved to resign his pastorate. He accordingly addressed the following brief but pathetic letter to his people.

"*Bath, October 5, 1852.*

"To the Church of Christ assembling in Argyle Chapel.
"To the deacons and all the members of the church.

"My most dearly beloved,—

"I had fully intended to send from Worthing an official intimation of the resignation of my pastorate, January next; a measure to which my mind has been brought by various considerations and proprieties of things; but a dreadful and painful assault of disorder prevented my doing anything. As soon as possible, I now thus announce officially what I then intended, and had mentioned to my deacons before. Had I my usual ability I should do this in a very different manner; but you must now excuse a want of enlargement, dictated by extreme depression and weakness.

"The Lord bless and direct you, and enable you to preserve the union, and harmony, and prosperity, and reputation of a church which has been exemplary in the world, endeared by the affectionate and happy connexion of more than sixty-three years to your now resigning pastor,

"WILLIAM JAY."

Upon this a meeting was held on October 30th, at which the following resolution was passed:—

"That this church, in receiving the intended resignation, on the 30th of January next, (the day of his ordination,) of its revered and beloved Pastor, devoutly acknowledges the goodness of God in permitting it the distinguished privilege of enjoying a ministry so faithful, valued, and eminently useful for a lengthened period of sixty-three years; and while it deeply sympathizes with him in his present affliction, prays with submission he may be restored, occasionally to preach the 'gospel of the grace of God;' and that, when his labours shall close, an entrance may be ministered unto him abundantly into the everlasting kingdom of our Lord and Saviour. That it also traces with gratitude to the same Divine source, the unanimity and peace which have hitherto marked its history; and while it would seek to maintain the unity of the Spirit in the bond of peace, prays that the great Head of the Church may afford it wisdom and guidance in the appointment of a successor to the venerable William Jay."

CHOICE OF A SUCCESSOR.

Early in the year 1853, among other persons who came to supply the pulpit at Argyle Chapel, was the Rev. William Henry Dyer, of West Bromwich, Staffordshire. After a suitable season of probation, the choice of the majority of the church fell upon Mr. Dyer; and although there was a respectable minority, who dissented from the choice, yet the majority asserted its right of election, and determined to give Mr. Dyer an invitation to the pastorate. This occurred in the month of April, and shortly after Mr. Dyer accepted the invitation, and took upon him the oversight of the church and congregation. A division ensued, and a separate church has been since formed, under the ministry of the Rev. Richard Brindley, for whom a new chapel has been erected. This event was the occasion, at the time, of considerable uneasiness and even pain to Mr. Jay; but in this, as in many other instances, the Great Head of the church has overruled the infirmities and differences of his servants for the trial of their faith in Him, and for the furtherance of his own gracious designs to the world and the church.

It was, in one respect, painful, that a church which had been so long distinguished by its harmony, should be divided; and especially so that its venerable pastor should be called to witness the division. But, in another view, it was time for so large and flourishing a body to colonize. The storm often bears precious seed to new fields; and both persecutions and disagreements have been among the means of scattering the good seed of the kingdom more widely. Two ministers of the Gospel are now labouring in the place of one, and it is to be hoped that both will gather fruit unto eternal life; and that, while intent upon the one object which filled the mind and inspired the heart of their venerable predecessor, their people will respectively forget their differences, and strive, if not together, yet separately, for the furtherance of the Gospel in the populous city where their lot is cast.

Immediately before the separation of the community took place, the following Resolution was unanimously passed by the church and congregation:—

"That an annuity of £200 be paid out of the funds of the chapel, by quarterly payments, to our beloved pastor, the Rev. William Jay, during his life, and to commence from the day of his resignation of the pastorate."

The last payment was made December 26th, the day before his death.

LAST ILLNESS AND DEATH.

As early as the year 1844 the complaint which proved fatal to Mr. Jay had begun to manifest itself, but for some time it did not materially interrupt his labours either from the pulpit or the press. He continued to bear up calmly and energetically, notwithstanding occasional seasons of weakness and attacks of pain. But about a year previous to his last sickness, came on the severe attack at Worthing, already noticed. From this his recovery was only partial and temporary. Yet, in the spring and summer of the following year, (1853,) he was enabled to take short journeys, and enjoy a little of the society of his friends. During this period he visited Bradford, and preached several times

there and at Bratton, between April and the end of August.
Early in September he visited Mr. and Mrs. Bolton, and
preached at the opening of Lord Ducie's new chapel at
Tortworth, from John xx. 16: "Jesus saith unto her,
Mary. She turned herself, and saith unto him, Rabboni;
which is to say, Master!" Again: the following Sunday,
Sept. 11, he preached at Tortworth, from Ps. cxxxvii. 4.

"In the next week," says Mr. Rice Hopkins, "he came
to spend a few days at the house of his old friend, Mr. Long
(my father-in-law), at Kingswood, near Wotton-under-Edge,
and I was there to meet him. Although frequently suffering much pain, he was remarkably cheerful, and every day
rode or walked out, and visited several friends in the neighbourhood. On the following Sabbath (Sept. 18) he preached
in Kingswood meeting-house, and that was the last time he
ever preached. The sermon occupied fifty minutes, and
was delivered with great pathos. You will be able to form
some idea of its contents from the following brief heads.
The text was taken from the fortieth chapter of Job and
part of the fourth verse, 'Behold, I am vile.'"

In his introduction he remarked that self-knowledge is
of inestimable importance. Even the heathens used to say
that the adage, "*Know thyself*," was descended from heaven.
Truly has Mr. Pope said, that "the proper study of mankind is man." Having briefly enlarged upon this topic,
and pointed out the importance of every man being fully
acquainted with his own character and prospects, he proceeded to consider the subject of the text, and noticed,

I. The nature of the self-accusation—"I am vile."

1. What it included. *Vile* signifies base, mean, des-
picable, worthless; and it can only be applied to that which
is sinful.

2. The person by whom it was uttered. It was not by
a notorious sinner, nor by a penitent brought for the first

time to a conviction of his sin; nor by a backslider returning to God; but by Job, an eminently pious man.

3. The time when it was uttered. It was after he had had manifestations of the glory of God.

II. The way in which this perception of vileness is obtained.

1. The Spirit of God operating upon the mind.

2. The medium is the Word of God, convincing of sin, and showing the spirituality of the Law of God.

3. The manner is sometimes instantaneous, but more commonly gradual.

III. The effects of this perception.

1. Conviction of sin.

2. A sense of our own inability to save ourselves.

3. A conviction of the necessity of salvation by Jesus Christ.

4. A persuasion of the importance of regeneration by the Holy Spirit.

5. Candour and tenderness in judging of the faults of others.

6. Hatred to sin, and an increasing desire of holiness.

IV. The way to endure this perception.

1. Are you vile? This vileness is not peculiar to yourself.

2. Are you vile? If a Christian, you are only vile considered in yourself, but not in Christ Jesus.

3. The time will soon come when this vileness will be done away.

> "Yet a season, and you know
>   Happy entrance will be given;
> All your sorrows left below,
>   And earth exchanged for heaven."

Christians, is not this worth dying for ?

These were the last words of the last sermon preached by

the venerated deceased, he being then in his eighty-fifth year.

Upon his return to Bath, after the visit to his children and friends, he wrote thus to Mr. Ashton :—

"We arrived here in safety about two hours before your and dear Garfit's letters came to hand. You are mistaken in supposing I am returned so much better than I went. I behaved as well as I could; but I felt exceedingly weak, and suffered more than usual from my complaint, and do suffer. But I valued and enjoyed the visit. How could it be otherwise, when every attention was exquisitely paid me, as if I had been a prince royal; and I was in the midst of such a family as I never witnessed. I was often, from indisposition and suffering, in a mood to find fault, but not one thing could I censure, —yea, I kept applauding.

"As well as weakness and pain would allow, I preached with freedom and pleasure in the new chapel, and was much pleased with my visit to the new Earl and his Lady. I daily rode out, drawn by the ponies, and was much amused in feeding them. Mr. Long and Mr. and Mrs. Hopkins were unusually kind and attentive, as if they thought (not an unreasonable conclusion) that this might be my last visit.

"Bath, Sept. 19, 1853."

From the date of this letter till about Christmas, he suffered much anguish of body, but was occasionally able to read and write a little. As his sufferings permitted, he attended to the printing and publishing of his last work, entitled, "Female Scripture Biography," the last sheet of which was corrected and sent to the press only on Friday, December 23rd, 1853; and on Tuesday, the 27th, at half-past six in the evening, he calmly slept in Jesus.

He had never laid much stress upon death-bed experiences, and used to say, "Tell me not how he died, but how he lived." Without entering, therefore, into a lengthened detail of his last days and hours, we may yet put on record a few of his memorable and emphatic words, which will enable his numerous friends to realize, in some measure, the character of the last scenes. The acuteness of his sufferings sometimes gave a tinge of melancholy to his utterances; but these were the groanings of the creature waiting to "be delivered from the bondage of corruption into the glorious liberty of the children of God."

In his various conversations, particularly with Mrs. Jay, he said, "Will he plead against me with his great power? No; but he will put strength in me." "He hideth himself on the right hand, that I cannot see him; but he knoweth the way that I take: when he hath tried me, I shall come forth as gold." "And now, Lord, what wait I for? My hope is in Thee. I know, O Lord, that all thy judgments are right."

"The sharpest sufferings I endure flow from his faithful care."

"What are all my sufferings here when once compared with His?"

"'Surely he hath borne our griefs and carried our sorrows,' &c. Oh, blessed prediction, and how gloriously fulfilled! 'His sweat was as it were great drops of blood falling down to the ground.'"

> "Were the whole realm of nature mine,
> That were a present far too small;
> Love so amazing, so divine,
> Demands my soul, my life, my all."

"'Yea, doubtless, and I count all things but loss for the excellency of the knowledge of Christ Jesus my Lord.'"

> "Jesus, thy perfect righteousness
> My beauty is, my glorious dress;
> 'Midst flaming worlds, in this array'd,
> With joy shall I lift up my head."

> "Nothing in my hands I bring,
> Simply to thyself I cling."

On another occasion he expressed his feelings thus:—
"But I am poor and needy, yet the Lord thinketh upon

me." " O my God, give me patience, forsake me not, a
poor sinner. O God, Thou hast taught me from my youth,
and hitherto I have declared thy wondrous works. Now,
also, when I am old and gray-headed, O God, forsake me
not." Adding, in the words of the hymn,

"Even down to old age my people shall prove
My sovereign, eternal, unchangeable love;
And when hoary hairs their temples adorn,
Like lambs they shall still in my bosom be borne.
The soul that on Jesus hath lean'd for repose,
I will not, I will not desert to his foes;
That soul, though all hell shall endeavour to shake,
I'll never, no never, no never forsake."

Afterwards he exclaimed, " Exceeding great and precious
promises!

" ' Sooner all nature shall change,
Than one of his promises fail.' "

On another occasion, while one of his attendants was
reading to him, as was the constant practice, mention was
made of a certain speculative work on theology, which was
then occasioning much controversy, when he said, " Don't
puzzle yourselves with such subjects. View God as He is,
infinitely holy, wise, true, merciful, gracious, amiable. View
him not as a tyrant, but as he is, God of all grace. Look
entirely to him at all times, and under all circumstances.
He is ever waiting to be gracious. He changeth not. He
is 'the same yesterday, to-day, and for ever.' "

One day, while suffering under great bodily distress, he
said, " I fear God has forsaken me. Let me not be impatient; let me repose in his love. I fear I am impatient."
Mrs. Jay replied, " Think of the feelings of your precious
Saviour: like you, he said, 'My God, my God, why hast
thou forsaken me?' He has promised never to forsake you.
His grace is sufficient for you." He then replied, " I
mourn, I do not murmur. 'It is the Lord; let him do

what seemeth him good.' I desire to lie passive, and know
no will but his. 'In patience possess ye your souls.' Lay
no more upon me than thou wilt enable me to bear; and I
will glorify thee in my sore affliction."

> " ' Dear Lord! though bitter is the cup
> Thy gracious hand deals out to me,
> I cheerfully would drink it up;
> That cannot hurt that comes from Thee.
>
> Dash it with thy unchanging love,
> Let not a drop of wrath be there;
> The saints for ever blest above
> Were often most afflicted here.
>
> From Jesus, thy incarnate Son,
> I learn obedience to thy will;
> And humbly kiss thy chastening rod,
> When its severest strokes I feel.'

"The language of the publican," he said, " did, does, and
ever will, befit me; and even down to death must be my
cry, ' God, be merciful to me a sinner.'

> " ' Mercy, good Lord, mercy I ask,
> This is the total sum;
> Mercy through Christ is all my suit;
> Lord, let thy mercy come.'

" I do not murmur—allow me to groan. It seems to ease
my pain. Objects most dear and attractive now fail to
interest. Oh for a grateful heart! I have made some little
stir in life, but now I am nothing. God seems to be
saying, 'I can do without you.' An official character is
not to be judged of by his ministerial work. He is compelled often to administer comfort to others when he is,
perhaps, not enjoying it himself. You see the sail, but not
the ballast."

On Christmas-day his sufferings were very severe, and he
said to Dr. Bowie, " O Doctor, what a Christmas-day! but
I can say, 'Thanks be unto God for his unspeakable gift;' "

and then he quoted 1 Pet. i. 3, 4, 5 : " Blessed be the God and Father of our Lord Jesus Christ, which according to his abundant mercy hath begotten us again unto a lively hope, by the resurrection of Jesus Christ from the dead, to an inheritance incorruptible, and undefiled, and that fadeth not away, reserved in heaven for you, who are kept by the power of God through faith unto salvation ready to be revealed in the last time !" He was particularly partial to the hymn, " Guide me, O thou great Jehovah !" often repeated it, and especially the last verse—

> " ' When I tread the verge of Jordan,
>   Bid my anxious fears subside ;
> Death of death, and hell's destruction,
>   Land me safe on Canaan's side :
>   Songs of praises
>   I will ever give to Thee.' "

He was most intensely alive to every attention paid to him by any one, and grateful for it. With peculiar pathos, never to be forgotten, he one day said to his faithful servant who sat up with him, along with his affectionate wife, who never left him,—"Thank you, Ellen ; be very tender and kind to your precious mistress. May the Lord bless you !"

On the morning of Tuesday, Dec. 27th, the day of his death, he said, " Oh, none of you know what it is to die." From this time he spoke little, but sank gradually into the arms of death, becoming so still and calm that the precise period of his departure could not be perceived Though he uttered but few words on the bed of death, yet there was the silent testimony of a settled peace ; while his long life and entire labours had afforded a faithful and consistent witness for God and Truth.

THE FUNERAL SERVICE AND INTERMENT.

In accordance with the wishes of Mr. Jay's widow and

the other members of his family, it was determined that the funeral should be as private as possible.*

The interment took place on the 3rd of January, 1854, in the vault which had been prepared many years before for members of his family previously deceased, in the cemetery at Snow Hill, belonging to Argyle Chapel.

The service was conducted by the Rev. John Owen, minister of the Vineyard Chapel, in the connexion of the late Countess of Huntingdon. In the course of the funeral oration Mr. Owen paid the following tribute of affectionate respect to the memory of Mr. Jay :—

* Mr. Ashton, as Mr. Jay's son-in-law, legal adviser, and executor, attended and directed the obsequies of his venerable relative. On the very day following his return to his residence at Cambridge, after the affecting and exciting scenes at Bath, he was smitten by an alarming attack of paralysis; from the severity and peril of which he was somewhat recovered, when he was suddenly overtaken by the most afflictive bereavement which a husband can be called to endure. On Sunday afternoon, Feb. 19th, 1854, Mrs. Ashton, while walking in those beautiful grounds which she had herself planned, and every tree and shrub of which was planted by her own hand, or under her direction, was taken suddenly ill. She hastened into the house, and medical aid was instantly sent for, but before it arrived the vital spark was extinct. She expired in the room and before the eyes of her suffering husband. Thus abruptly was this superior and excellent woman snatched from an earthly paradise which she had embellished by her taste, and animated by her presence. Along those walks, and amidst those shrubberies, she had often led her beloved father, under whose smiles and in whose presence they appeared still more interesting and lovely. Both have now disappeared from the fairy-land, to meet and unite, we trust, in a fairer, happier Eden.

The bereaved, afflicted husband still remains in this lovely spot to converse with the reminiscences of "joys departed never to return" *here*, but to be renewed and surpassed in the society of those loved ones where neither death nor sin can enter. May the Divine Comforter grant him, in his solitary and mournful hours, many bright hopes and blissful anticipations of a happy union in the celestial paradise with all that was most dear to him here.

"In referring to our departed friend, whether we regard him as a believer in Christ, as a minister of the everlasting Gospel, as a pastor of a Christian church for so long a period, as a philanthropist, as an author, as a citizen, or as a friend, we cannot but sorrow,—but most of all that we shall see his face no more on earth. There are circumstances, we admit, my dear friends, which greatly soothe our pain under the loss we have sustained, and which tend to moderate our regret, and to chasten our grief on this occasion, when we call to mind the early commencement and lengthened period of his religious course,—the remarkable and increasing acceptableness and usefulness of his ministrations,—the variety and unique excellence of his published works;—when we look at the unsullied purity of his moral character, when we reflect on his peaceful end, and think of his present blessedness in the presence of Jehovah,—there is much, my brethren, to soothe our griefs. We mourn, but not on his account. No! He has fought the good fight, he has finished his course, he has kept the faith, and has now joined the general assembly and church of the First-born which are written in heaven; he is with the spirits of just men made perfect. He is with the Saviour he loved, the Saviour he proclaimed, and will be with Him for ever.

"And yet we cannot but mourn on our own account. We suffer a loss—a great loss—by his removal from our midst. We lose his wise counsels, his instructive example, his ready co-operation, his tender sympathy, and his fervent intercessions, and therefore we mourn. Jesus wept at the grave of Lazarus, and we may weep at the grave of the venerated Jay. His name will for ever be imprinted on my memory. For fifty years I have known it: for forty in connexion with religion, for thirty-five as a fellow-minister of the Gospel, and especially during the last twenty-five have I regarded him as a son would regard connexion with his father. From my first taking up my residence in this city to the last day of his life, there was never a mis-thought or a mis-word between us, and therefore I cannot but mourn his loss on my own account. But how can we best express the sincerity of our grief, and manifest our tender regard for his memory? Why, by embracing the blessed truths which he so long proclaimed, by following the course he pointed out from the pulpit, and recommended through the press,—by devoting ourselves to the service of the Lord,—by imitating his excellence,—and by seeking, through faith in Christ and dependence on the Holy Spirit, to attain that rest into which he has entered, and to be with him for ever in the presence of God and of the Lamb. In order to this we must have an interest in God our Saviour and Sanctifier:

and then, while we stand mourning at the tomb of our departed friend and father, we may yet, in the triumphant language of the Apostle, say, 'O death, where is thy sting? O grave, where is thy victory? The sting of death is sin, and the strength of sin is the law; but thanks be unto God which giveth us the victory through our Lord Jesus Christ.'

"I shall not attempt to refer to the loss sustained by the bereaved relations who are present, and those who are absent, because of the near approach of the solemn service in which our revered friend from Birmingham, (the Rev. J. A. James,) who is with us this morning, will take part; and, when aided by the Spirit of God, he will offer such instruction and consolation as may render the removal of our beloved friend of advantage to our souls."

The day of interment was one of the most inclement in a winter of extraordinary severity, yet a train of mourning friends, members of his own church, with many from other denominations, joined of their own accord in the sable procession, to pay this last tribute of affectionate respect and esteem to the memory of the aged pastor; and, regardless of the drifting snow and piercing wind, to drop a silent tear at his grave, while many a sorrowful heart devoutly exclaimed, "My father! my father! The chariots of Israel and the horsemen thereof!" But for the wishes of the family to make the obsequies as unostentatious as possible, a large number of ministers, both from the city of Bath and the neighbouring towns, would gladly have been present on the mournful occasion, to do honour to the memory of the deceased. Many of the houses and shops in the line of the procession gave evidence to the sympathy of the inhabitants by their closed windows; while, within the cemetery, a large concourse, despite the severity of the weather, had assembled to witness the interment.

The Rev. John Owen, after the address from which we have given an extract, offered an impressive prayer, and having pronounced the apostolic benediction, the funeral procession was formed again, and the mourners left the ground. Then the hundreds, who had congregated to behold the mortal remains of William Jay consigned to their last resting-place, flocked into the little building to gaze upon his coffin, and slowly and sorrowfully the assembled multitude dispersed.

The inscription on the coffin was as follows:—

REV. WILLIAM JAY,
DIED
27TH DECEMBER, 1853,
AGED 84 YEARS.

On the following Thursday, Jan. 5th, the funeral sermon was preached in the Vineyard Chapel by the Rev. John Angell James, from 2 Kings ii. 14 : " Where is the Lord God of Elijah ?"

Funeral sermons were also preached on the occasion, in Argyle Chapel on the following Lord's-day, by the Rev. James Sherman of London, and the Rev. W. H. Dyer ; also by the Rev. Richard Brindley, to the separate congregation worshipping *pro tempore* in the Assembly-room.

Thus closed the lengthened earthly career of this eminent servant of Christ, who, through the period of *sixty-three* years, faithfully discharged his ministerial commission, and diligently served his generation, in a city distinguished indeed by its fashion and gaiety, but yet not wholly insensible to the attractions of his eloquent and evangelic labours.

Whatever may be the monument which shall be raised to perpetuate the memory of so good, so great, and so useful a man ; and whatever may be the terms of just eulogy which the hand of affection may inscribe upon it, this volume, mainly from his own pen, as well as his other published works, will constitute his best and most durable memorial. The characters engraved by the chisel of the sculptor will be obliterated by " Time's effacing fingers," and the marble that shall bear them will resolve itself into dust; but the truths he has embalmed in his writings, or by his eloquent tongue written upon living hearts, will retain their interest and influence undiminished amidst all material ruin and desolation; and the writings of William Jay will continue to shed light upon the pathway of many a traveller Zionward, and to train many of the heirs of immortality for their mansion in the skies.*

When William Jay died, the city in which he had so long laboured lost one of its most honourable patriarchs, one of its richest ornaments and holiest attractions. *There*, under his ministry, senators, wearied with the cares of state, had listened gratefully to the Saviour's invitation: "Come unto me, all ye that labour and are heavy laden, and I will give you rest;" and found that repose which only faith and hope can impart. *There* many of the slaves of dissipation and vice were emancipated, by the gracious words which proceeded out of his mouth, from the fetters of their fatal

---

* Since the above was written, a suitable tablet, bearing the following inscription, has been erected in Argyle Chapel:

Sacred to the Memory of
THE REV. WILLIAM JAY,
For more than Sixty-two Years
The faithful and beloved Pastor
Of the Church and Congregation
Assembling in this Place of Worship.
His distinguished Gifts, his holy Life,
And his unwearied Labours were crowned,
By the Divine Blessing, with extensive usefulness;
And he left a conviction of his inestimable worth
Which this TABLET,
Erected as a Tribute of Affection,
Is designed to commemorate.
He was born May 8, 1769,—Ordained Jan. 30, 1791,
Died December 27, 1853, in the 85th year of his age.
'He was a good man, and full of the Holy Ghost, and of Faith.'
Acts xi. 24.

enchantment, and were brought into the glorious liberty of the children of God. *There* the eager votaries of fashion, thirsting for the pleasures of sense, and proving the emptiness of the wells from which they had hoped to draw them, were allured by his mellifluous tones to taste the fountain of living water, and found the bliss which they had in vain sought from worldly sources. There, too, the victims of fell diseases, who had tried many remedies and were nothing bettered, were directed by him to the Divine Physician of their souls, and received that healing which made their bodily afflictions light, by teaching them to triumph over death.

But this ministry is now closed. He that granted it for so long a space, and made it so rich a blessing, has seen fit to withdraw it. The city that possessed his pulpit, around which such distinguished assemblies crowded, now exhibits his sepulchre. From the one they heard his living voice, from the other they will learn the silent but eloquent lesson of his death. No saintly shrine will be erected to court and stimulate the incense of superstitious and idolatrous worship; though he was a saint in the church below, and is now a glorified one in the church above; yet to his tomb a pathway will be worn by the feet of many pilgrims of affection, from various parts of the earth, who will inquire for the spot—not where rest the ashes of the great dramatist, poet, philosopher, or statesman, but where, till the morning of the resurrection, repose the mortal remains of the wise, and good, and holy William Jay, the great and useful preacher of the Gospel of our salvation.

We shall here subjoin some Miscellaneous Recollections and Sketches of his life and manners, which will, no doubt, interest the reader, by giving him a pleasing sight of Mr.

Jay in the heart of his family, and among his familiar friends.

DOMESTIC SKETCHES.

"It was the practice of my dear father," writes one of his daughters, " to throw off all study on the Saturday, that he and his subject might be fresh for the Sabbath. On that day (and oh, what a joyous afternoon that was to us children!) we were indulged in rambling with him in a country walk, choosing the side of some running brook, which he delighted to follow, or sending us scrambling into field or hedge-row for wild flowers; and, when each brought their little nosegay, to receive the prize held out to them for the best flowers, or best arranged.

" How full of hope and happiness was he, and how free to make others the partakers of his joys ! How many will remember the pleasure in his later years it gave him to fill his pockets with apples, books, and pence; and then either from the carriage-box, or in walking, he would throw them so dextrously to a too ready group of boys and girls, who were fleet enough, or had skill enough, to carry away the prize; and how he always gave his throw in favour of the girls.

" Our dear father was strongly excited by music, of the pleasure of which he was susceptible in the highest degree. He had an ear formed to enjoy the simplest melody, and, though little cultivated, he relished its highest charms; and a simple air would transport his feelings to the utmost pitch. In his last visit to Stone, how did he delight to lie on the sofa, and hear his granddaughters sing, and often said,—' How delightful now to enter heaven !'

" Another little trait of his character was his sweet thought of giving pleasure to others. It was almost always his habit to go into his garden before service, and pick each of the servants a good handful of flowers, arranged by himself, which they were desired on no account to bring home, but give to some of the poor people, who would value them doubly sent from such a garden.

FAMILY PRAYER, SIMPLICITY OF MANNER, ETC.

Mr. Bolton says, "My father-in-law came in to breakfast with us, as our early hour suited him best. In family worship I was struck with his prayer for us:—

"'Peace be to this house! May thy servants at the head of it enjoy much of this peace—that peace which the world cannot give by its good things, nor by its evil things take away—that peace which passeth all understanding. Let all their dear children live before Thee, be the care of thy tender providence, and the early subjects of thy grace. We are now going forth into the engagements of the day: let thy presence go with us. Whether alone or in company, may we sanctify Thee in all our thoughts, and all our words —concerned to improve all our opportunities of gaining good, and doing good, and the more so as we see the day approaching which will deprive us of both.'"

A near witness testifies, that "his simplicity seemed innate and natural; for he was as free from affectation as from guile. The gentleness, ingenuousness, and unsuspiciousness of a little child were ever displayed by him. Thinking no evil himself, he believed every one open and sincere as himself, and his heart was pained when he met with deceivers."

"Nothing could satisfy him in his preaching but bringing forth the whole story of Matthew Henry's three R's, Ruin, Redemption, and Regeneration—Jesus Christ and him crucified, to meet the condition of poor sinners—to try to save souls; and if, in any part of his sermon, he considered that he had been deficient, his heart felt deeply, and he longed for the next opportunity of preaching more fully, more pathetically and practically. Such seasons were most prayerfully and tearfully implored in private previously, and he would then bless God for the enjoyment, and entreat that it might not be different with him in public. Sometimes he seemed under such a happy Divine influence, that a blessing was felt to rest in an indescribable manner upon his conversation. His heart was all alive to participate in the woes of those around him, and his expressions were so balmy that they soothed the deepest wounds even when they could not heal. The piety and copiousness of his prayers were very remarkable. You felt that they were poured forth from a heart which seemed the very sanctuary of devotion. He lived, as it were, in the precincts of heaven, and was ever ready to present petitions to God. He was especially observant of devotion when he had public services in prospect. He always took a *prayerful* review of his subject, and often was a tearful, wrestling season of communion with God in private, the prelude to the holiest and happiest seasons in public. His practice uniformly was to go from the closet to the pulpit. Nothing was allowed to intervene." In this, doubtless, may be found one of the elements of his efficiency and success. He came as from the Divine Presence with a message from God to men. Devotion had given greater strength to his arm, and keener edge to his weapon. Hence he spake "not as pleasing men, but God, who trieth our hearts." Happy would it be for the church of Christ if all its ministers conscientiously followed this example! How would it contribute both to their happiness and success!

DR. BOWIE'S RECOLLECTIONS OF MR. JAY, AND ACCOUNT OF HIS LAST DAYS.

" I had the great privilege of affording him my medical assistance to the close of his honoured life (*a period of more*

than thirty years), and am happy to say, of receiving to the
last, and at the last, the same proofs of esteem, affection,
and regard, which he had for so many years bestowed on
me, and for which blessing I indeed give God thanks. You
ask me—if I have any recollections of our dear departed
friend ? I answer, *none in writing*, but many in mind. It
would be perfectly impossible for any one to have had the
privilege I possessed for more than thirty years, of having
him as my pastor and friend, without having numerous recollections of one I ever considered a shining star, and one
of the most extraordinary individuals this country, or indeed any other, ever saw. I will here say, that I allude
now to him as a preacher of the Gospel of Christ. Here,
in my opinion, he was *quite unique*, and unlike every other
preacher I ever heard. If you will allow me to say, it was
not, in my opinion, that Mr. Jay possessed any *one* peculiar
point of mental character which made him the highly-
finished preacher ; but he appears to me to have combined
in himself a number of faculties arising from his organiza-
tion, which in the highest degree fitted him to excel as
a preacher. He possessed very great powers of imagery,
pathos, and irony, all of which were occasionally brought
out in the pulpit ; and when to these powers are added Mr.
Jay's great knowledge of the Holy Scriptures, which enabled
him to *dovetail*, as it were, all his statements with texts
suitable to his subject ; his general information, derived
from his extensive and laborious readings, which, having a
most retentive memory, he could use at all times ; and his
great knowledge of the human heart—I need not say that,
with his vigorous and powerful mind brought under the influence of the operation of the Holy Spirit, these points and
advantages enabled him well to fill the office of a minister
and teacher. I must not forget, in this my catalogue of
excellences for the pulpit, that Mr. Jay was the simplest
preacher possible to be conceived ; his sermons were all de-

livered without the least effort and difficulty, and so simple
that any one might have said—nay, indeed, I often did say
—I could do all this myself.   In this simplicity of dear Mr.
Jay's preaching, I consider, lay one of its chief excellences;
and certainly it may be said, that by Mr. Jay the poor had
the Gospel preached unto them.   He was, at the same
time, a most sententious preacher, and could, by a few
words, said in a pithy and sometimes quaint manner, produce
a wonderful effect.   This I have often seen and felt, and
some such sayings have never been obliterated from my
mind, even after a distance of many years.   Although this
was often the case to a remarkable degree, yet all his sermons were from first to last most interesting and powerful;
and no individual ever kept up the continued attention of
his hearers more than our beloved friend.   He was emphatically a textual preacher, never wandering from his
subject; and in this point he so much excelled, that, in
endeavouring to give what he considered to be the true
meaning of the Scripture he had in hand, he might appear
at different times to preach against many of the precon-
ceived views of some of his Christian hearers; so anxious
always was he to give every text its true interpretation,
without reference to any system of divinity, however good
and admired.   This it was, combined with the great variety
of subjects chosen by him for the pulpit, which made it
necessary to hear Mr. Jay again and again, previous to any
one being enabled to come to a proper and sound opinion
as to the nature and exact character of his preaching.   One
thing more I only will add to the list of qualities possessed
by Mr. Jay for a preacher, and that is, his most melodious
and well-modulated voice, by which he indeed gave the
grand truths of the Gospel through a silver trumpet; and
he was, in my opinion, from the combination of all the
powers I have now mentioned, the most fascinating preacher
this country has seen for many a day; and so interesting

was his preaching, at least to myself—and I hope I may add useful—that all preaching appeared tame after hearing him. This may, perhaps, have arisen from his peculiar style, so unlike any other, and from the fact that, during about thirty-four years, when I had the privilege of hearing him generally twice a week, and occasionally three times, I had been so deeply identified with his mode of preaching, that I could hear no one else so well, nor, I think, so profitably. It was not only preaching but teaching, and that, too, in the most beautiful and winning manner. The simple and clear way in which Mr. Jay divided and explained all his sermons, added to the attractive style of delivery, made all he said easily remembered; and, indeed, *so attractive* was his mode of preaching, that numerous individuals whom I have met with during my lifetime who have heard him only once, have been at the end of years able to give the substance, if not the division, of the only sermon they ever heard from his lips. One of many such instances I will now relate. A few years ago a clergyman of the Church of England, now dead, called on me for medical advice. On seeing in my room a print of Mr. Jay, he at once recognized it, and inquired kindly after him. I asked him if he was acquainted with Mr. Jay; he replied, 'No; but I have heard him preach once, and I shall now give you his sermon.' He arose from his chair, and gave the text, Psalm xvi., verse 3. He then began, and at once I saw he had indeed heard him preach, as I recognized the well-known manner of treating his subject. I inquired when it was that he had heard this sermon, which had so deeply impressed him. He replied, 'Thirty-five years ago. I was then a student at Oxford, and passing through London, I understood that the far-famed Mr. Jay of Bath was to preach in Surrey Chapel. I went, and I have now given you the outlines of his sermon, which I shall never forget.'

" One other instance of the simplicity and attractivenes

of his preaching, so as to awaken a spirit of inquiry in a child, I shall relate. Travelling in a railway carriage some little time ago, an elderly gentleman sat opposite to me. Finding I came from Bath, he asked me how Mr. Jay was. I told him, and he informed me that, at the early age of eight years, he was deeply interested with a sermon which he heard preached by Mr. Jay at Argyle Chapel; and filled by it with a spirit of inquiry. His mother had taken him to chapel, and the preacher took for his text Acts ix. 16: 'Come over into Macedonia and help us.' When he went home he eagerly asked his mother many questions regarding what he had heard, as, 'Where was Macedonia? what help was wanting? and who was to go over?' Although young, it made him desirous and anxious to know more on the subject which had so engrossed his attention, and the recollection of the sermon was even then most vivid. I have already said, that Mr. Jay did, in his preaching, often make a wonderful impression by a single sentence delivered in a powerful manner. One of these I shall mention, as pressing most strongly at this moment on my mind, although heard by me many years ago. He had been preaching on the repentance of Judas, and took occasion in the discourse to attack the love of money, as one sin, if not the principal sin, of the Church of God; and at the close of one of the divisions of his subject, he burst forth in his own peculiar and emphatic manner with the following awful sentence; 'Avarice, avarice, is the monsoon, the devil's trade-wind, from the church into hell.' Another instance presses itself forcibly on my memory, and although, perhaps, by the very fastidious it may be deemed not well fitted for the pulpit, yet at the time of delivery it made a wonderful impression, and now is so clear before me that I must give it. Mr. Jay was speaking of the glaring inconsistency of many professors of the Gospel, and endeavouring to show how impossible it was to expect the Divine blessing to rest on half-

and-half, undecided professors of religion. He rested much on the necessity there was for decision for God, and the clear manifestation before the church and the world, in the believer's walk and character, so as to leave no doubt who indeed was his Master; and, in the midst of a powerful appeal, pronounced the following:—' Some of you, my dear brethren, are so inconsistent and undecided, that if at this moment I saw the devil running away with some of you, I could not call out, Stop thief!—he would but carry off his own property.'

" Mr. Jay I would call, in his views, a moderate Calvinist; but he never was shackled by any system of divinity, and never feared to give from the pulpit what he conceived to be the whole counsel of God. If he apparently met with difficulties in the subject he was at the time treating, he would mention the circumstances, and leave them, without an attempt to combine what was, in his opinion, far beyond man's finite powers.—Thus, one day speaking of Judas, he said he was foreordained of God to betray the Saviour, and yet he betrayed Him willingly, and is damned for the deed:—having said so, he, in his own peculiar and well-known manner, leaned over the pulpit, and exclaimed, 'Now, do not look at me for an explanation of this subject—both statements are true—the foreknowledge of God, and the free agency of man; and when we reach heaven, and not till then, shall we be able to understand all, which in our present imperfect condition is quite beyond the grasp of our finite minds.'

" I may here allude to Mr. Jay's great faithfulness in the pulpit, and most fearlessly giving reproof to any of his hearers, if by him deemed necessary. One instance of this is now most vivid before me, although it happened many years ago, and that to myself. The valuable and most interesting course of lectures, now forming one of his published volumes, under the title of ' The Christian Contem-

plated,' was delivered in Argyle Chapel, and occupied the
Sabbath morning of each week till completed. At the time
of delivery I was much younger than I am now; and from
God's peculiar dealings with me, added to my natural
character, I had embraced, more than was agreeable to my
beloved pastor of what are usually called the high doctrines
of the Gospel; and I fear I had more than once been led
to declare, that I considered the lectures from their practical nature to be Christless. At the close of the delivery
of the last lecture, he said,—' My brethren, I have done
with the course of lectures which I had announced, but I
have not done with those of you who have denounced them
to be Christless.' Having said this, he began an admonition of a wise and useful character, in the following
striking and forcible manner: ' You mushroom-Christians—
you men of one idea—you who would have a minister go
round a few of your favourite texts, just like a blind horse
in a mill—am I to be taught preaching by you?'—I may
add, that the next day I called to visit Mrs. Jay professionally: I met Mr. Jay in the room, who actually was
looking for a leaf of the lecture preached on the previous
day, which he had mislaid, and in his own quick way he
addressed me by saying, ' How are you, doctor? Did you
take part of my sermon yesterday?' I answered, ' Yes, I
did.' He replied, holding out his hand, ' Then give it to
me, for I have lost a leaf; and if I am to publish these
lectures, I must find it.' I said, ' No, dear sir, I have no
leaf of your lecture, but I did take part of it notwithstanding.' He instantly replied, ' Doctor, if the cap fits
you, wear it,'—and left the room. I do hope and believe this
quiet and just reproof tended, under God's blessing, to
make me more prudent and cautious for the future.

"It is well known that, occasionally, Mr. Jay would
engage the attention of his hearers most powerfully, by the
introduction of an anecdote into his sermon, which was

always much to the point, and told with much effect. This
habit, however, for several years previous to his retirement
from the pulpit was much given up, and seldom or never
indulged in.

"From my long and intimate acquaintance with Mr. Jay,
it may be expected that something ought to be said by me,
with regard to his social habits and character. Here, however, little need, or, indeed, can be related. He lived in
such a primitive manner,—so as to put it very much out of
the power of any individual like myself, engaged in active
employment, to see much of him. He rose at five—break-
fasted at seven—dined at one—drank tea at five—supped
at nine—went to bed at ten—and this I may say was a
general rule without any exception. He was most regular
in his daily exercise; and one of the many reasons which,
under God, tended to give him such a fine constitution, was
his choosing the early part of the day for his pulpit and
press studies. He, from breakfast till dinner-time, devoted
himself to this work—and after that period, he, I have
reason to believe, seldom or never did so—and I have heard
him more than once say, that he never was found in his
study after nine o'clock at night. The after part of the day
was usually spent in exercise and general reading. His
mind was so well stored with information, and his memory
so retentive, that it was quite a treat to pass a short time
in his society. You never could be with him for any time
without discovering the depth of his information, the
strength of his mind, and the easy and simple manner of
his conversation, which was at all times so interesting and
attractive, that you had much difficulty in leaving his company; and never did so without admiration and instruction.
My usual time for seeing him was when I knew he was at
tea, and at which hour I often contrived to be professionally
in his neighbourhood, that I might have the pleasure of a
little conversation with him. Mr. Jay was all his life so

completely accustomed to be listened to, and not much to listen, that, perhaps, for some years after I knew him, he might occasionally appear impatient of being interrupted or contradicted; but that indeed was seldom attempted by any one, as all were generally too glad to hear the good and great man, whose words flowing from him were like the dew which watereth the earth. Mr. Jay was a man with whom no one felt he could ever take a liberty; and of all men I ever knew, he was the only one in whose presence I always, in a manner, felt a kind of reserve, fearing in any way to give him the smallest offence; in fact, I had an exalted opinion of him, and gave him reverence."

"Like all on earth Mr. Jay had many trials, and none greater than the long and severe illness of his first wife; and I may, I trust, be allowed to say, without any fear of misconception in the mind of any one, that he grew much in grace under his trials; and when I add, that he was at times thankful *even to me* for a word of admonition or encouragement, it will, I think, be evident, that his fine mind and understanding were much brought into subjection to the grace of that blessed Redeemer whom he had so long preached, not only as the atoning Saviour, but the bright Example.

"During his long and most painful illness, for nearly eighteen months, he never murmured, but gave a noble testimony to the truth of the Gospel, and its being able to sustain the believer under every trying dispensation—he became, in fact, like a little child;—and in the midst of great sufferings and sleepless nights, over which medicine had little or no control, he was enabled to glorify God in the fires, and to leave a powerful and lasting evidence of the truth and efficacy of that Gospel which he had so many years so truthfully preached to others. Mr. Jay through life had always a natural fear of death—that is, of the agonies of the dying struggle—but even all this he was at last quite freed from; and he died so peacefully and quietly that, for a short time after the spirit had taken its flight to mansions in the skies, it was not known to his sorrowing relations that he had gone home to Jesus. 'Mark the perfect man, and behold the upright, for the end of that man is peace.'"

MR. JAY'S FAMILIAR EXPOSITIONS AT THE PRAYER MEETINGS.

Those who knew Mr. Jay at home, in the weekly round of his duties, would scarcely deem our work complete, if we failed to exhibit him, as for a very long period he had appeared, in his vestry on a Monday evening, like a father in the midst of his family, explaining to them and enforcing upon them some portion of God's Word, in the most simple and familiar manner.

It is believed that he rarely, if ever, made any written preparation for these services; but having fixed upon a portion of Scripture before he left his home, he turned it over in his mind as he walked to his chapel, a distance of nearly a mile. When he entered his vestry, he took his seat in his arm-chair at a table, and gave out a hymn in his own peculiarly feeling and devotional way. When this had been sung, he would call upon one of his deacons to engage in prayer. He then opened the Bible, read a text or a few verses, and, in a style more like serious and engaging conversation than preaching, spoke upon the words or subject in an easy and colloquial manner, often with striking originality, point, or pathos, as the text might require. The hearer felt, and could hardly fail to feel, as much at ease as the speaker, who sat all the time as if in your parlour, conversing with you on your spiritual interests, and the great things of God's salvation. A specimen or two of these

familiar services we shall here insert.   They have been furnished by friends who were accustomed to take notes, and
of course do but imperfectly represent the original :—

Psalm xci. ver. 14 : "I will set him on high, because he hath
known my name."

This psalm has sometimes been called the charter of the believer's
privileges ; and in this sense I wish you were all chartists, and in no
other ; for I do not approve of the other charter at all. A great man
once said : "The whole of this psalm has been fulfilled in my experience, except the last clause of the last verse ; and that will be
fulfilled, I am fully persuaded, within an hour."   Now what is that
verse ?   "With long life will I satisfy him, and show him my salvation."   The former part had been fulfilled, for he died at the age of
ninety-five.   He had lived long enough, I should suppose, to have
seen all that was worth seeing, to hear all that was worth hearing,
and to enjoy all that was to be enjoyed ; and he must surely have
known the vanity of all things here below.   But what is meant by
the last clause, which yet remained to be accomplished ?   "And show
him my salvation."   This is future.   How can that be ?   The believer is saved *now ;* that is, he is in a state of salvation, in a state of
safety—

"More *happy*, but not more secure,
    The glorified spirits in heaven."

But the believer's salvation will be more fully shown, when Christ
shall say to all his redeemed, "Come, ye blessed of my Father,
inherit the kingdom prepared for you, from the foundation of the
world."   But only think of this good man's saying,—that he was fully
persuaded that this would be accomplished *within an hour !*   Oh,
what a solemn thought !   How would many of you feel if you *knew*
that you were but one hour out of eternity !—but one hour from a
world of spirits !—that in *one* hour you would be in the presence
of your Redeemer !   Beyond the reach of every care.   There is
but a step between me and death !   Perhaps there is but a step
between you and—*hell !*   But oh, what an overwhelming thought,
if there is but a step between you and *heaven !*   I remember good
Ambrose, sitting in his chair, feeling the pains of death coming over
him, he raised his eyes, and exclaimed : "Come, good angels,
and do your office, and gently waft me into Abraham's bosom."
But you will say, what has all this to do with the subject ?   Why,
it is a part of the loaf that I wish to divide among you to-night :
and I do not think it much signifies where I begin to cut first.

Now,—" I will set him on high because he hath known my name."
The Name of the Lord is often put for the Lord himself. Many
texts might be brought forward to prove this. I will mention only
one : Prov. xviii. 10, "The name of the Lord is a strong tower, the
righteous runneth into it, and is safe." Not into a word, but into
Jehovah himself. Now, what is it to know the Lord? People
sometimes speak of head-knowledge. But it is a singular expression ; as if there were such a thing as *arm-knowledge* or *leg-knowledge.*
Where should knowledge be but in the head? At the same time, it
is very expressive, as marking the difference between a mere speculative knowledge of the great truths of Christianity, and that knowledge and conviction of the heart which is here implied. Ah, what
pleasure does it give you to say—" I know such and such a distinguished person." What an honour would you feel it to be able to
say, "I know the king and am intimate with him." Or, if he were
living, to be able to say, "I know Milton, and am intimate with
him." But the Christian can say far more : "I know the Lord, the
King of kings, and am intimate with Him. He is my Father and
my Friend."

Now, here is the promise,—" I will set him on high, *because* he hath
known my name." We must not look on this word *because*—as a
condition. Our dear brother used this term last night, and I began
to fear lest he should be misunderstood. But he afterwards explained
himself very clearly. Yet why should we use a word of doubtful
meaning, when there are others that would answer the purpose quite
as well, if not better? It is true that some of the old writers use
this term, but it is in a different sense to that in which it is employed
now-a-days. *Now* it is employed to signify a sort of claim that one
has upon another for a reward ; but they used it to express a sort
of connexion, that God would do one thing *because* He had done
another : thus, *because* God had given faith, He had also given salvation, and in that sense it is used here.

Now, what is meant by this promise—" I will set him on high"?
Is not Christ risen from the dead? Has he not ascended above the
skies? And are not all his believing followers ascended with him?
Is not this to ascend on high? Cannot the believer look forward to
heaven as his inheritance, his kingdom, his everlasting portion?
Call you not this *high?* The king is the highest civil officer, the
priest the highest ecclesiastical; and God will make all his people
kings and priests unto himself, and their kingdom shall be an everlasting kingdom, and their priesthood one that endureth for ever.

But notice not only the promise, but the Agent by whom it is performed, that is, God himself. There are many kinds of promises.

There are the devil's promises, they are false and deluding.   Oh! beware of them!   There are the world's promises.   They seem all bright and fair; but what are they?   Only vanity; yea, lighter than vanity itself.   Then there are men's promises.   Oh, trust not in them, for they are uncertain—often deceptive.   But there are God's promises.   They are all yea and amen in Christ Jesus.   Lean on THEM, trust in THEM, and you shall never be confounded.

> " O for a strong, a lasting faith,
>   To credit what the Almighty saith,
>   T' embrace the message of his Son,
>   And call the joys of heaven *our own*."

Another Monday evening Exercise was as follows: having read the words, "O Lord, forgive; O Lord, hearken and do," Daniel ix. 19, he observed,—

This is one of Daniel's prayers.   The Scripture is full of prayers, and I love them much.   Now let us speak of Daniel.   He was a temperate man.   This will account for his haleness and vigour, at least in some measure.   But he was rich in grace.   He had been raised from one stage to another, till he became prime minister over twenty-seven provinces; yet he found time to pray thrice every day. Many people who have not half the business to attend to that he had, say they have scarcely time to pray *once* a day.—Daniel was highly favoured.   Three miracles were performed *by him;* one was interpreting the king's dream; the second, recalling Nebuchadnezzar; a third, interpreting the handwriting on the wall.   But one miracle was performed *for him;* that was, his safety in the den of lions. Twice the angel Gabriel came to him with the words, "O Daniel, man greatly beloved!"   Some will say, "I would not have told him that to his face, lest it should make him proud."   But Gabriel knew better.   The proud are always the most backward to praise. The reason is, they judge from themselves; because when they are praised *they* are so *puffed up*, they think others must be the same. The celebrated Dr. Robinson* having preached three times on one Sunday, at a chapel in London, after the evening service a man came into the vestry and said to him,—"This morning, sir, it was a very dry opportunity; in the afternoon I got no food for my soul; but this evening you have preached a most blessed sermon, and I hope to live in the enjoyment of it for some time to come.   But I hope

---

* Mr. Jay most probably meant Robert Robinson of Cambridge.

you will not be proud at my telling you so." "No, no," said the doctor, " for I have no opinion of your judgment."

Let us notice this prayer before us. How importunate it is ! It is not one of the sleepy prayers. If a person were to come and ask a favour of you, and were to fall asleep in doing it, you would spurn him from your presence. Yet how often do we act so with the blessed God !—The first thing here is *forgiveness*,— O Lord, *forgive !* The second thing to pray for is *attention*,—" Hearken and do." Do what? He does not say what, and I am glad he does not. If a beggar were to call out to a king as he was passing, " *Hearken and do*," he would be repulsed for his impertinence. But how different it is with this King ! He says, " Call upon me, and I will answer:" " Ask, and ye shall receive." He can change the hardest heart; can renew and sanctify the vilest passions ; and can make those whom we imagine to be beyond the reach of mercy, " pillars in the house of our God." He will do this for you, if you apply to him. He did not turn a deaf ear to the cry of Daniel. Nor will He to your cry. Let your sins be what they may, He can and will wash them all away in the blood of His dear Son. Blessed be His name.

One Monday evening, he had been addressing his people on the importance and blessedness of humility, and closed his remarks by observing,—

" How beautifully Bunyan has represented the shepherd's boy in the valley of humiliation, cheerful and happy, while singing,—' He that is down need fear no fall,' &c. But you all know his song, and we will now unite in singing it, for it will do for us as well as for him.

> " ' He that is down need fear no fall,
>   He that is low no pride ;
> He that is humble ever shall
>   Have God to be his guide.
>
> I am content with what I have,
>   Little be it, or much ;
> And, Lord, contentment still I crave,
>   Because thou savest such.
>
> Fulness to such a burden is
>   That go on pilgrimage :
> Here little, and hereafter bliss,
>   Is best from age to age.' "

He then proceeded with the following verses, which were sung in succession, as if they had formed one hymn:—

> " Turn, pilgrim, turn—thy cares forego ;
>   All earthborn cares are wrong :
> Man wants but little here below,
>   Nor wants that little long.
>
> There shall we sit, and sing, and tell
>   The wonders of his grace,
> Till heavenly rapture fire our hearts,
>   And smile in every face.
>
> For ever His dear sacred name
>   Shall dwell upon our tongue,
> And Jesus and salvation be
>   The close of every song."

The impression produced by the mixture of verses, as well as by the climax, was felt to be highly profitable and elevating. Those who witnessed that scene will never forget it.

It was at one of these week-evening meetings he finished his labours at Argyle Chapel, observing at the close, " I shall never enter this place again ;" adding some remarks of great tenderness and solemnity to his friends, who stood round him.

On the 21st of March, 1853, he went to the vestry, intending to give only a short address ; but the congregation assembled was so large that they were obliged to adjourn to the chapel. He selected for his subject the appropriate words of the 116th Psalm, verses 1 and 2 : " I love the Lord, because he hath heard my voice and my supplications. Because he hath inclined his ear unto me, therefore will I call upon him as long as I live." The testimony of so venerable, so faithful a man of God, labouring under much weakness and pain of body, yet with all the devotedness and zeal of his youthful days, pointing all to the throne of grace, and expressing, with touching sensibility, his own gratitude for the help he had thence derived, was felt to be most deeply impressive and affecting.

The following Monday evening, March 28th, Easter Monday, was the occasion when he made the remark above noticed, that he should enter that place of worship no more. On this last occasion he spoke again in the chapel, but on neither of these occasions from the pulpit. The subject was taken from Isaiah liv. 17: " This is the heritage of the servants of the Lord, and their righteousness is of me, saith the Lord." This is described by those who were present as a most interesting, solemn, and edifying address.

Thus ended his public ministry in Bath.

The following testimony of respect and expression of friendship for Mr. Jay from so excellent a nobleman as the Earl of Gainsborough, will doubtless be gratifying to the reader, and suitably terminate this section of the work:—

In a letter to Mrs. Edward Jay, written since the solemn event took place, the Earl of Gainsborough says,—

"Although at his good old age the great change has been a glorious one, for your excellent father, yet I cannot hear of the departure of my long-loved and revered friend without much sorrow and emotion, and deep concern for all those who have sustained so truly irreparable a bereavement. I hope his last hours were free from much suffering.

"It is painful for me to have been out of England; for it would have been a real gratification to me to have followed the dear and honoured remains of my beloved friend to the grave.

"It will give me much pleasure to hear from you, and that Mrs. Jay and all of you are well.

"It grieves me that I have not seen dear Mr. Jay lately; and should I live to return to England, it was one of my pleasant anticipations that I should have seen him once more. I trust, through the mercy of that blessed Saviour he so long and so ardently served, to meet him again where friends will no more be separated.

"Believe me, my dear Mrs. Jay, sincerely and affectionately yours,

"GAINSBOROUGH.

"Naples, Feb. 4, 1854."

PART III.

PRACTICAL ILLUSTRATIONS OF CHARACTER,

IN

A SERIES OF REMINISCENCES,

BY

WILLIAM JAY.

" Clothed in sanctity and grace,
   How sweet it is to see
Those who love thee as they pass,
   Or when they wait on thee."—COWPER.

" Mark the perfect man."—DAVID.

PREFACE.

My residence in Bath gave me many opportunities of multiplying connexions, or at least acquaintances; and, in a long course of years, I have become more or less intimate with many interesting individuals from Wales, Ireland, Scotland, and various parts of England.

Not long after my settlement in this city, I found a coterie of rather singular characters: it included Loutherbourg the celebrated landscape-painter, Sir James and Lady Wright,* Miss Lee, the natural daughter of Lord le Despencer,† Rev. Bryan Hill,‡ Miss Wesley, &c.

All these occasionally attended my preaching, and I was

---

* Both these lie in our burying-ground, and their escutcheons were sent into the vestry. Lady Wright was the sister of Moore, Archbishop of Canterbury. None of the family attended the death or the funeral.

† She was a woman of great talent and much learning; yet I fear from her neglect of public worship, and a prayer (which she showed me) written for her daily use, on the principles of pure deism, that she was at least sceptical as to the truth and importance of Christianity.—After some injuries which the tomb of Sir James and Lady Wright had sustained, she repaired it, and had her name engraved as the repairer in the corner of the panel. Some may remember her strange flight with a gentleman, as if carried off unwillingly; also her throwing away a camphor-bag from her bosom.

‡ Author of a Poem on Italy, and brother to Sir Richard and Rowland Hill.

personally acquainted with them all. They *seemed* alive to eternal things, and to be in a state of serious inquiry. They had their own private and social meetings (it would seem for various purposes), but I could never learn how they conducted them; and they held some occult sentiment, which they were neither ready to explain nor to recommend. Many supposed they had some leanings towards the continental *Illuminati*.

In a long ministry, and in a varied and extensive intercourse with the religious world, I have met with not a few *curious* characters, mental and moral nondescripts; owning no party, and owned by no party; signalized and observable by uncommon, strange, preposterous opinions, usages, pretensions. With very little that is romantic in my frame, I have never been able to pass by such anomalies without notice and reflection; and if I had a descriptive humour, by a little enlargement and colouring, I could produce reminiscences enough to excite wonder and ridicule, laughter and sadness.

But, oh, how many have I seen and admired in the various denominations of Christians, who have been Israelites indeed, in whom there has been no guile; enlightened in their principles, walking in the truth, consistent and uniform in their conduct, devoted to the cause of the Gospel, and ready to every good work; and, though not free from infirmities, "adorning the doctrine of our Saviour in all things."

These are worthy of observation, and remembrance, and a record; and we are commanded to "*mark* the perfect man, and *behold* the upright, for the end of that man is peace."

As I have not found many of these among the very rich, so I have found none of them among the *abject* poor. Whatever *they* were originally, converting grace made them temperate and diligent; gained for them the countenance and help of their fellow-Christians, and secured for them the favour of Providence, so that not only their "bread was given, and their water was sure," but it "blessed their bread and their water," and made "the little that a righteous man had, better than the riches of many wicked."

Lo this! we have proved it—so it is—"I have been young, and now am old, yet have I never seen the righteous forsaken, nor his seed begging bread."

I here, then, notice some of these individuals in various conditions and circumstances of life; especially those I was acquainted with in the earlier parts of my ministry; and who had some considerable influence on what I have *been*, and what I have *done*, and what I have *written*.

While I thus, in a measure, gratify allowable curiosity, I desire and hope to do something more. Facts are better than definitions, and exemplifications than descriptions; and as we cannot form an idea of love or hope, pride or avarice, in the abstract—virtues and vices, excellences and defects, are best shown in their subjects and actings. And is not *this* the method of the sacred writers?

Almost every memento of celebrated personages is desired and welcomed, and readers are anxious and eager to catch at every trifling anecdote that helps to form a conception of their individuality, or to connect their private history with their public fame. I have, therefore, rather largely brought forward several more public and distinguished characters; but my design extended beyond them.

There are other beings who deserve attention, and who may be, as examples, more within common reach. Johnson has said, that "there is hardly a life of which some useful narrative may not be furnished." Yes; there are many who never see a college nor enter a pulpit, nor publish a book, who can serve their generation by the will of God. They embody and fulfil religion in their private stations; and though they make no figure in the annals of worldly renown, are great in the sight of the Lord. "Their day is coming, called "the manifestation of the sons of God," when, however shaded here, they will shine forth as stars in the kingdom of their Father."

Some of these I have selected, and would gladly have noticed by name many more; but I have been obliged to restrain my inclination, and confine myself to a few; and, had I chosen much humbler individuals than any I have selected, the Scriptures would have justified my choice; for while they leave in oblivion philosophers, statesmen, and conquerors, they furnish to all ages the very name of "Rhoda," the poor damsel who announced with so much ecstasy the presence of Peter. Inspiration says nothing of the builders of the Egyptian pyramids, but it records the names of the "midwives, Shiprah and Puah, who feared God, and for whom God built houses." An oak was consecrated to memorialize Deborah, Rebekah's nurse.

> " Laurels may flourish round the conqueror's tomb,
> But happiest they who win the world to come :
> Believers have a silent field to fight,
> And their exploits are veil'd from human sight.
> They, in some nook, where little known they dwell,
> Kneel, pray in faith, and rout the hosts of Hell :
> Eternal triumphs crown their toils divine,
> And all those triumphs, Mary, now are thine."
>
> *Cowper's Epitaph on Mary Higgins.*

Will my readers just notice what follows, not as apologetical, but explanatory?

First: As I profess to give only brief sketches, let none look for anything more.

Secondly: I have not endeavoured to observe the precise order of time in which intercourse with the characters noticed was carried on;—as I write from the present promptings of remembrance; and I know of no cases in which dates would have contributed to the proof or importance of the events and circumstances recorded.

Thirdly : In some of these Reminiscences, I fear instances of a similarity of remark and reflection may be found repeated. But I was not able to compare them for the purpose of such detections; and the recurrences may not be useless, being found in different connexions, and applied to different purposes.

Fourthly : I hoped, but in vain, to have had time and leisure to transcribe and correct the whole of these hasty and free sketches. In that case, I might have reduced some parts, and added others; but I should have *altered* little, as I always wrote according to my knowledge and conviction, and only spake the truth in love.

Finally : Some will probably censure the egotisms which seem so much to abound. But, in a work of this kind, references to myself were unavoidable; and, in such narratives, personal circumstances are often inseparable from things introduced *solely* to illustrate somewhat pertaining to the character itself under review.

And here the writer must be satisfied with the consciousness of his own motives. When his work itself is read, he will be out of the reach of human censure or applause.

REV. JOHN NEWTON.

Mr. NEWTON, once the vicar of Olney, and afterward the rector of St. Mary Woolnoth, is well known by his remarkable conversion, his various writings, and his usefulness to the church of God at large.

During my first visit to London to supply Mr. Hill's chapel, one Friday morning, after hearing me, he came into the vestry. I did not then know his person; but he introduced himself, and, to my surprise, intimated a wish to retire into the house with me. I led him into the study; and I have never forgotten the condescension and kindness with which he addressed me. Taking me by the hand, he said, "Some of us are going off the stage, but we rejoice to see others rising up, and coming forward. But, my young friend, you are in a very trying situation, and I am concerned for your safety and welfare. I have been so many years in the ministry, and so many years a minister in London; and if you will allow me to mention some of the snares and dangers to which you are exposed, I shall be happy to do it." How could I help feeling, not only willing to receive, but grateful for, such a seasonable warning? And how useful might the aged servants of God be to the younger, if they would privately and freely communicate of their experiences and observations! Some of the things he mentioned seemed for the moment rather strange and needless; but I confided in his wisdom, and time has fully shown me that they were all words in season.

Contrasts strike us; and it is curious and useful to observe the different qualities and manners of good men themselves. A week after this interview, one of his very attached followers (a Mr. B——y) wished to introduce me to Mr. Romaine. I can truly say I shrunk back from modest timidity; but he urged me and prevailed; and one Tuesday morning, after the service at Blackfriars Church, he took me into the vestry, and, with a few words, mentioned my name. But Mr. Romaine noticed me in no other way than, as immediately leaving the room, he said very audibly, "There *was* a Sir Harry Trelawney." I inferred that some faithful caution was intended, but, a mere youth from the country, and little acquainted with the religious world, I had never heard of the person by whose errors or fall I was to be warned, until I inquired. I have no doubt of the aim of both these admonishers, and I ought to have been thankful to the latter as well as to the former; but severity does not actuate like affection; and "he that *winneth* souls is wise."

Mr. Newton also invited me to call upon him, and to his kind of open breakfast I soon repaired; and for years afterward, whenever I was in town, I availed myself as often as it was in my power of this invaluable privilege. On these occasions one met with ministers and Christians of all denominations; for he loved all who loved the Saviour, and all, while they were with him, felt themselves to be "one in Christ Jesus."

In the family worship, after reading a chapter, he would add a few remarks on some verse or sentence, very brief, but weighty and striking, and affording a sentiment for the day. Whoever was present, he always prayed himself; the prayer was never long, but remarkably suitable and simple. After the service and the breakfast, he withdrew to his study with any of his male friends who could remain for a while, and there, with his pipe (the only pipe I ever liked, except Robert Hall's), he would converse in a manner the most easy, and free, and varied, and delightful, and edifying.

Much has been published concerning this excellent man, and it is possible, that some of the few things I would gratify my readers with, may have been reported by others who witnessed them; but I shall mention nothing underived from my own personal knowledge and observation.

There was nothing about him dull, or gloomy, or puritanical, according to the common meaning of the term.   As he had much good-nature, so he had much pleasantry, and frequently emitted sparks of lively wit, or rather humour ; yet they never affected the comfort or reputation of any one, but were perfectly innocent and harmless.   Sometimes he had the strangest fetches of drollery.   Thus, one day, by a strong sneeze, he shook off a fly which had perched upon his gnomon, and immediately said, " Now, if this fly keeps a diary, he 'll write, ' To-day a terrible earthquake !' "   At another time, when I asked him how he slept, he instantly replied, " I 'm like a beef-steak — once turned, and I 'm done."

" Some people," said he, " believe much better than they reason.   I once heard a good old woman arguing in favour of eternal election.   ' Sir,' said she, ' I am sure if God had not chosen me before I was born, he would never have chosen me after.' "

At another time he mentioned facetiously, and with his peculiar smile, the language of a poor good woman when dying :—" I believe His word, and am persuaded, notwithstanding my unworthiness and guilt, that my Lord Jesus will save me from all my sins and sorrows, and bring me home to Himself ; and if He does, He will never hear the last of it !"

He one day told of a countryman who said to his minister, " You often speak of our FORE-fathers ; now, I know only of three—Abraham, Isaac, and Jacob.   Pray, sir, who is the *fourth ?*"

He also more than once mentioned, that he knew a good man and woman, who read the Scriptures morning and evening in their daily worship, to whom a gentleman gave a folio commentary to aid them.   But after they had tried it for some time, the husband said to the wife, " I think we did better before we had this great book.   When we read the Bible itself only, it was like a glass of pure wine; but now it is like a glass of wine in a pail of water."

One day, speaking of the various effects of affliction, he said, " I lately visited a good woman who had just had her house and goods destroyed by fire.   I said to her, ' Madam, I am come to congratulate you.'   'What!' she replied, ' upon the destruction of my property ?'   'No, but to hail you on your possessing property which nothing can destroy.'   This awakened a surprise and a smile in her tears, like a sunshine in the showers of April.   ' What enabled the Hebrew believers to take joyfully the spoiling of their goods, but knowing in themselves that in heaven they had a better and an enduring substance ?' "

When I one day called upon him, he said, " I am glad to see you, for I have just received a letter from Bath, and you may know something of the writer," mentioning his name.   I told him I did, and that he had been for years a hearer of mine, but he was a most awful character, and " almost in all evil."   "But," says he, " he writes now like a penitent."   I said, " He may be such ; but, if he be, I shall never despair of the conversion of any one again."   " Oh," says he, " I never did, since God saved me."

I recollect a little sailor-boy calling upon him, with his father.   Mr. Newton soon noticed him, and, taking him between his knees, he told him he had been much at sea himself, and then sang part of a naval song.   Was this

beneath him? Would not the lad always favourably remember him?

One morning in the family worship he read 2 Pet. iii.
1—9, the last words being, "but is long-suffering to
us-ward, not willing that any should perish, but that all
should come to repentance." He began his exposition
thus: "These words, I suppose, are a hard bone for a Calvinist to pick." He was aware that one in the company
required some moderating. This person, a little too forward, as well as too high, afterwards, as we were at breakfast, rather abruptly said, "Pray, Mr. Newton, are you a
Calvinist?" He replied, "Why, sir, I am not fond of
calling myself by any particular name in religion. But
why do you ask me the question?" "Because," he
replied, "sometimes when I read you, and sometimes when
I hear you, I think you are a Calvinist; and then, again, I
think you are not." "Why, sir," said Mr. Newton, "I am
more of a Calvinist than anything else; but I use my Calvinism in my writings and my preaching as I use this
sugar"—taking a lump, and putting it into his tea-cup, and
stirring it, adding, "I do not give it alone, and whole; but
mixed, and diluted."

Another morning a forward young man said, "Pray, Mr.
Newton, what do you think of the entrance of sin into our
world?" "Sir," said he, "I never think of it. I know
there is such a thing as moral evil, and I know there is a
remedy for it; and there my knowledge begins, and there
it ends."

Another morning there was, with several other preachers,
sitting in his study, a Baptist minister, a very good man,
who had appeared to some disproportionately zealous in
making converts to his own opinion. The conversation
was turning upon the choice of texts. "Ah," said Mr.
Newton, "Brother S——n, there is one text *I* can preach
from, and which *you* cannot." "Sir," said he, "what can

that be?"—Mr. Newton replied, "Christ sent me not to baptize, but to preach the Gospel." Mr. S——n took the hint without the least offence, and no one laughed more heartily.

As my brother-in-law was vicar of Olney, I sometimes visited that hallowed spot; and as, of course, I could not minister in the church, I always went, when I was going to engage in the meeting, and studied my sermon in the pew where Cowper heard, and in sight of the pulpit where Newton preached. "Superstition!" say some. But I found it good to be there. And how was I struck, when at the parsonage-house I went up into the attic, which was the study of this man of God, and saw, over his desk, on the wall, in very large letters, "REMEMBER THAT THOU WAST A BONDMAN IN THE LAND OF EGYPT, AND THE LORD THY GOD REDEEMED THEE;" and "SINCE THOU HAST BEEN PRECIOUS IN MY SIGHT THOU HAST BEEN HONOURABLE, AND I HAVE LOVED THEE;" and—"UNUS PRO OMNIBUS!"

While residing at Olney, Mr. Newton did much to liberalize and harmonize the religious parties; and one of his candid arrangements, I know, continued years after, and I hope does continue still. It was this:—At the beginning of the year, the Episcopalians, Independents, and Baptists blended their congregations three days following, and each minister preached in his own place a sermon to the young. I suggested the propriety of a little alteration, viz., for one sermon to be addressed to the young, and one to the middle-aged, and one to the old. As another proof and instance of his liberality and candour, though a beneficed clergyman of the Established Church, he drew up the plan for the Dissenting Academy at Newport Pagnell, which was placed under the superintendence of the Rev. Thomas Bull, and supported by that great philanthropist, John Thornton, Esq.

In those days pious and evangelical clergymen of the

Establishment were very few; and, owing to their sentiments and zeal, were often less regarded in their own communion than among many of the orthodox dissenters; and,
therefore, when invited by them, they scrupled not to visit
them, and even to make a considerable stay at their houses.
Mr. Newton for many years visited Portswood, near Southampton, a place from which many of his printed letters
were directed. Here lived Walter Taylor, Esq., a dissenter
in affl:ent circumstances, and blockmaker to the navy.
Under his hospitable roof Mr. Newton commonly spent five
or six weeks annually, and while there he sometimes heard
the Rev. Mr. Kingsbury, Mr. Taylor's brother-in-law, and
pastor of the Independent Church, and preached also frequently in his host's laundry to his family and workmen,
and the neighbouring villagers.

Thus he speaks in one of his letters to Mr. Campbell:
"Here are five churches, but no pulpit open for me. But
Mr. Taylor has opened his house, and made room for about
300 hearers. I preach three evenings in the week while I
stay. We are often full. My hearers are chiefly from the
neighbouring villages, and seem willing to hear the Gospel,
if they had any one to preach it to them. But, alas! in
these parts, and in many parts of the kingdom, 'the hungry
sheep look up and are not fed.'

Mr. Romaine also for many years annually visited Mr.
Taylor for the same length of time; but he would never
enter the meeting at Southampton with the family, nor
speak in their unconsecrated premises to the poor, and
ignorant, and perishing, who would have hung upon his lips.
But high-churchism had no scruples to accept the accommodations about the house, and table, and carriage, and
horses, for these were not schismatics, though their owner
was. A Puseyite would have been more consistent. He
would not have gone in with the uncircumcised and the
unclean, nor had fellowship with them—"no, not to eat."

I remember another instance of Mr. Newton's candour and liberality. When Dr. Buchanan, who had been much befriended by him, went out to India, holding a valuable ecclesiastical appointment, he seemed at first to have been shy of the Baptist missionaries. Upon hearing this, Mr. Newton wrote him a kind but faithful letter, in which he said, (I had this from his own mouth,) "It is easy for you (little as yet tried in character, and from your superior and patronized station), to look down upon men who have given themselves to the Lord, and are bearing the burden and heat of the day. I do not look for miracles; but if God were to work one in our day, I should not wonder if it were in favour of Dr. Carey." The admonition was well received, and this great and good man became kind and friendly.

The first year I went to London I heard two popular clergymen, who were going through the same epistle—the Epistle to the Ephesians. Both went on leisurely, and from verse to verse, till they came to the practical parts and relative duties of husbands and wives, parents and children, masters and servants, when one of them intimated he could not enlarge here, for the grace of God would teach them all this ;* the other endeavoured to do as much justice to the preceptive, as to the doctrinal demands. I need not say this was Mr. Newton.

Moderate and candid men are the most firm and unyielding with regard to their principles. Mr. Newton exemplified this. In his letters to persons from whom he differed, we find him avowing his own convictions without the least hesitation or reserve; and not even sparing reproof when necessary, and without respect of persons. Dining one day with Mr. Henry Thornton, I remember his speaking of Mr. Newton's curate, Mr. G——nn. He said, " I

* How came the apostle not to know this? why took he the needless trouble of enforcing these duties?

went to hear him, and was much dissatisfied with the lowness of his address, and the manner in which he spiritualized
his subject, which was, 'I will make you fishers of men;' in
the discussion of which everything, with regard to fishing
and fish, was quaintly and facetiously explained and applied.
Deeming it very objectionable, and likely to cause reproach,
I wrote my complaint to Mr. Newton; in reply to which
here is his answer: ' My dear Sir,—I fear you did not go to
hear my good man with a spiritual appetite, or you would
have found food, as well as the many who hung on his
lips,' " &c. Nor did the able and enlightened statesman
(Mr. Thornton), though not convinced, take it amiss, but
admired his rebuker.

Mr. Newton's intimate connexion with Cowper is well
known. Some have thought the divine was hurtful to the
poet. How mistaken were they! He was the very man,
of all others, I should have chosen for him. He was not
rigid in his creed. His views of the Gospel were most free
and encouraging. He had the tenderest disposition; and
always judiciously regarded his friend's depression and
despondency as a physical effect, for the removal of which
he prayed, but never reasoned or argued with him concerning it. Hence, also, on the other hand, when his niece,
Miss C., was for a season in the public institution for mental disorders, in visiting her, he found two individuals there
whose cases, he was persuaded, had been mistaken. He
considered them merely as subjects of spiritual distress;
and he not only conversed but corresponded with them;
and I remember his reading some of their letters, and remarking that here the preacher, rather than the physician,
was wanted; adding, that he " thought God sometimes
placed persons there to keep them out of this mad world."

I can testify to a case in some measure confirmatory of
this. I knew a female whose irreligious friends, misunderstanding the nature and cause of her complaint, had sent

her to this place of confinement. Her distress and despair arose from a deep conviction of her state as a sinner, and an utter ignorance of the way of salvation. One day, therefore, seeing a gentleman passing by her ward, whom she had known at her father's house, she most earnestly pressed him to obtain her release for a few days, during which he could judge concerning her state, when he would find it was not derangement. He did so. The gentleman was Mr. Wathen, the celebrated oculist. At his desire I immediately met her. After she had heard me at Surrey Chapel, on the narrative of the Syro-Phœnician woman, she retired to pass the remainder of the day in weeping, not tears of sorrow, but of joy; for now she had found the consolation of Israel, the balm in Gilead, the Physician there. She returned no more to her confinement, but some time after married, and I believe is now living, an excellent wife and mother. There are cases in which, in this respect, it is extremely difficult, yet very important, to distinguish things that differ, both as to ourselves and others.

Mr. Newton's attachment to his wife, I was going to say, was extreme. Some have wondered at this, as she seemed to them to have few, if any, attractions. But neither strangers nor friends could have known her like himself; and we may be assured love and esteem so deep and durable were not expended on little worth. Besides, God had in many ways remarkably employed her, both as his preserver and benefactress. He has told the public what supports and frames the Lord gave him at her decease; and how he inferred from them, that it was the will of God he should not lie by from his official duties, but perform them as at other times, regardless of the opinion or censure of the world. Accordingly, the Reminiscent heard him preach, while she lay unburied, from "He hath done all things well;" a text which not every divine could safely have taken on such a trying occasion. He also, the following Sunday, preached her funeral sermon, from Habakkuk iii. 17, 18, "Although the fig-tree shall not blossom, neither shall fruit be in the vine; the labour of the olive shall fail, and the fields shall yield no meat; the flock shall be cut off from the fold, and there shall be no herd in the stalls; yet I will rejoice in the Lord, I will joy in the God of my salvation."

This text, he said, he had never taken before, keeping it in reserve for his greatest affliction, should he be exercised with it. And here a curious thing was observed. When he came to speak of Mrs. Newton, (which he did with a voice rather tremulous at first,) he said, it might seem strange for him to speak of the excellences of his wife, but he hoped he might be permitted to mention candidly a few of her faults or failings. He then spoke of her excessive attachment to himself—of her judging and estimating others by their regard to himself, &c., which had the effect, (though in the simplicity of his character he meant not so,) of leading his hearers to think and ask,—"If these were her chief faults, what were her excellences?"

He always seemed to have a present and lively feeling of his obligation to Divine grace, in saving him from his former state. He often, therefore, adverted to it in his conversation. Perhaps, with regard to his *profligacy* in that state, from the subsequent spirituality of his mind, like Bunyan, and some other good men, he spake too strongly. Yet he must have gone great lengths in *guilt* to justify what I have more than once heard him say,—that he had so sinned away the advantages of a good education, and resisted and stifled all his convictions, that for a time he had no more conscience than a brute; that, do what he would, he felt no moral reproof; and that, when a disease had brought him apparently near to death, he had no terror, and would have died like a lamb.

Though, at his first awakening, owing to his being then engaged in it, and the force of habit, he was not struck with the evil of the accursed slave-trade—yet, when led to just reflection upon that subject, no one could think worse of its enormity, or bewail himself more for the share he had had in it.   To this, also, he often referred; and one day, as a person told him that the Americans had dubbed him D.D., he said, " I always resolved I would accept of no diploma, unless it came from the poor blacks."

Not long before his death, a minister I well knew visited him, to whom he said, as he shook hands with him, " I suppose you will expect some sentence at parting ?   Well, let it be this,—

> " Beware of Peter's word,
>   Nor confidently say,
>   ' I never will deny Thee, Lord ; '
>   But, Grant I never may ! "

Alas ! that this kind of dying, oracular admonition was lost upon this person, for he fell under the power of temptation!

I saw Mr. Newton near the closing scene. He was hardly able to talk; and all I find I had noted down upon my leaving him is this,—" My memory is nearly gone ; but I remember two things: That I am a great sinner, and that Christ is a great Saviour."   And, " Did you not, when I saw you at your house in Bath, desire me to pray for you? Well, then, now you must pray for me."

Mr. Southey says, and says truly, that " Mr. Newton was a strong-minded man."   He did not, indeed, *always* show this in his preaching; for, owing to his ease of address, and illustration, and enlargement, and on which he could lean, and the numerous claims upon his time from the poor and afflicted, and visitors, and correspondents, he often entered the pulpit with little preparation; and frequently, as Mr. Cecil in his Life remarks and laments, (and which he himself owned,) got the substance of his discourse between his house and his church.   Some of his published sermons are exquisitely natural, and simple, and intelligible, and easily remembered; and would be much better models for young ministers than such as abound with abstruseness, and elaboration, and pomp, and finery.

I always admired, not only Mr. Newton's theology, which moulded doctrine, and experience, and practice so finely into each other, but also his composition. Not a few of my younger brethren were formerly surprised at my calling it elegant; but they now have a much better authority than mine. Cowper has expressed his preference of his style to that of either Gibbon, or Robertson, or Hume. His volume on ecclesiastical history is above all praise, and makes every reader lament that he was not enabled or encouraged to continue that work to our own times. But he is most known by his admirable " Letters."

I heard him one day mention the sovereignty of God, not only in the choice of his instruments, but even in the mode in which he used them, and which often did not correspond with their own wishes, or the expectations of others. "Hervey," said he, " who was so blessed as a writer, was hardly able to mention a single instance of conversion by his preaching, and nothing could exceed the lifelessness of his audience; and I rather reckoned upon doing more good by some of my other works than by my ' Letters,' which I wrote without study, or any public design; but the Lord said, ' You shall be most useful by *them*;' and I learned to say, ' Thy will be done! use me as Thou pleasest, only *make* me useful.' "—What thousands have derived repeated profit and pleasure from the perusal of these utterances of the heart! Nor ever will they cease to be found means of grace, whilst God has a church on earth. With regard to myself, I commonly had one of these letters read to me on every Sabbath evening, after the labours of the day; and what refreshment and profit have I derived from them!

As numbers of his letters are continually issuing in collections, and also appearing separately in periodicals, evincing how acceptable, and even called for, they still are, perhaps the Reminiscent will be more than excused, if he here introduces the two following, as they are very characteristic of the man and his manner.

The first was addressed to, and given me by, Mrs. Wathen, wife of the celebrated oculist to King George III., and dated from Portswood Green, near Southampton, July 26th, 1799. It was as follows:—

"MY DEAR MADAM,—As you kindly engaged my promise to write, I need make no apologies; you will receive my letter in good part, and I am sure I shall write it with a hearty good will.

"But what shall be the subject? Indeed, properly speaking, I have, or ought to have, but *one*. This, however, is very comprehensive; I mean Jesus Christ and him crucified. It will at least help to fill up the paper, if I give you some account how I have in general managed it, as minister.

"When the Lord, after he had mercifully given me some experimental knowledge of the Gospel for myself, was pleased to honour me with a commission to preach to others, I found myself possessed of an infallible medicine for the cure of all diseases, and I was surrounded with multitudes whom I saw were sick of a mortal disease, and, as we say, at death's door. I thought at first to do great things with my catholicon. But I soon observed the fatal disorder I wished to relieve was attended with one very discouraging symptom. Most of the sick people, though I could read death in their countenances, thought themselves well; they insisted on it that nothing ailed them, and were angry with me because I would not believe them. Some of them could scarcely hear with patience what I said of the power and skill of the Physician who gave me the medicine. Others thought they might apply to him when they were really ill, but at present they had no need of him. Oh, how I laboured with some, but all in vain, to convince them of their danger! Now and then I did prevail with one, who then thankfully took the medicine, and presently recovered.

"And as I and my fellow practitioners were daily praising the virtues and efficacy of our medicine, some of our patients learned to talk after us; they did not *take* the medicine, but they praised it. They would allow they had been sick once; but now, to be sure, they must be well, for they could say as much in favour of the medicine as we could ourselves. I fear many died under this mistake. They would not make such a mistake in common life. Many go to see the table spread at a Lord Mayor's feast, but the sight of the delicacies, which they must not taste, will not satisfy the appetite like a plain dinner at home. But, alas! our patients were not hungry.

"Some felt themselves unwell, but would not own it; they tried to look as cheerful as they could. These depended on medicines of their own contrivance; and, though they suffered many things, and grew worse and worse daily, they refused to try mine. It was judged by one too *simple;* like Naaman, who for a time, though he would have done some hard thing, disdained such an easy remedy as —'only wash, and be clean.' Others refused unless I could clearly explain to them all the ingredients belonging to my medicine, which I had neither ability to do, nor they capacity to comprehend. They said, likewise, that the regimen which I prescribed was too strict; for I told them honestly that, if they did not abstain from some things of which they were very fond, my medicine would do them no good. I was often grieved, though not so much as I ought, to see so many determined to die, rather than take the only medicine that could preserve their lives.

"There were more than a few who deceived both themselves and me, by pretending to take my medicine, and yet did not. None grieved me more than these; but they could not deceive me long. For, as the medicine was infallible, I knew that whoever took it, and observed the regimen, would soon show signs of convalescence, and that they were getting better, though they were not perfectly well; and, therefore, when these signs were wanting, I was sure the medicine had not been taken.

"I have not time to enumerate all the signs that accompany salvation, but I shall mention a few. First, a broken and contrite spirit. This is indispensably necessary, for by nature we are full of pride; and God resisteth the proud, but giveth his grace only to the humble. Secondly, a simple and upright spirit, free from artifice and disguise. It is said of the blessed man, whose sins are forgiven, in his spirit there is no guile. He is open and undisguised. Thirdly, gentle, gracious tempers. If a man like a lion takes my medicine, he presently becomes a lamb. He is not easily offended. He is very easily reconciled; he indulges no anger; he harbours no resentment; he lives upon forgiveness himself, and is therefore ready to forgive, if he has aught against any. Fourthly, benevolence, kindness, and an endeavour to please, in opposition to that selfishness which is our natural character. Fifthly, a spiritual mind, which is the beginning of life and peace; a weanedness from the world and its poor toys, and a thirst for communion with God through Christ.

"I could go on, but let this suffice. These signs are at first weak, for a Christian is a child before he is a man; but grace grows by exercise, by experience, and by a diligent use of the appointed means. My medicine enlightens the understanding, softens the heart, and gives a realizing of what the Scriptures declare of the glorious person, the wonderful love, the bitter sufferings of the Saviour, and the necessity and efficacy of his death and agonies upon the Cross. When these things are understood by the teachings of the Holy Spirit (whose influence is always afforded to those that take the medicine), the cure is already begun; all the rest will follow, and the patient recovers apace; though there are sometimes transient relapses, and a spice of the old disorder will hang about them, until they are removed to the purer air of a better world.

"I hope, my dear madam, this medicine is your food, that you live upon it, and feel the salutary effects of it every day. Oh, what love! that such a Saviour should die for such sinners as we are; and what a marvellous mercy to me, that I should be brought from the horrid wilds of Africa to proclaim his goodness! That I, who was an infidel, a blasphemer, and a profligate, should be spared to stand as a proof that Jesus Christ came into the world to save the chief of sinners! You and I are far advanced in years; we know not what a day may bring forth. Perhaps we may never meet upon earth; but, oh, may we meet above, to praise Him who loved us, and washed us from our sins in his own blood! to partake of that fulness of joy, and to drink of those rivers of pleasure, which are at His right hand for evermore!

"JOHN NEWTON.

"Portswood Green, July 26th, 1799."

The second was addressed to a sister of my wife, Mrs. H——ll, on a domestic bereavement; the date worn off. The following is a copy:—

"MY DEAR MADAM,—Upon returning home last night I found your favour, dated the 10th. I must begin to write immediately, as I am very busy; but other business must wait till you are answered. I have thought of you and yours almost continually since Monday evening, when I first heard the affecting news. I have felt for you, and your family, and Mr. H——ll. I called on him on Tuesday, and dropped my tear with his. I had proposed going on to G—— Street, but he told me you were gone to S——. And now, what shall I say? *I also* have seen affliction; I have been wounded where my feelings were most sensible; and I have found, as you now find, that the Lord is all-sufficient, and can bear us up under the severest trials. I congratulate you on the comfortable words she spoke before she went home. I longed to hear such language from my dear Mary. I thought it would be a great alleviation to the stroke, but it pleased the Lord to show me he could support me without it. I bless his name I have good reason to hope and believe she is now before the throne; but during the latter part of her illness her mind was overwhelmed with a black cloud of dark and dreadful temptations. They were mercifully removed before her departure, but not till she was brought too low to be able to speak. She could only wave her hand as a token that the bitterness of death was past. I often think how our Queen's parents felt when our King sent to demand her in marriage. I suppose when she left them they did not expect to see her again; in this sense she was dead to them. Yet it was not considered a subject of condolence; neither they nor their court went into mourning for her; on the contrary, there was much rejoicing; they thought she was going to be Queen of Great Britain, and the hope of hearing of her welfare and prosperity made amends for the loss of her company, and they gave their full and cheerful consent to her coming hither.—But if a woman were raised even from a dunghill to be a queen, it would be a small thing compared with the change Mrs. W—— has experienced. Far superior to all the queens of the earth, she is now equal to the angels; yea, much more, nearly related to Him whom all the angels worship. We cannot hear directly *from* her, but we may hear *of* her as often as we please; the good Word of God tells us *where* she is, and *how* she is; we know not the local spot, but she is with her Saviour; the Lamb that was slain has brought her home to himself, to see his glory; she has done with sin, sorrow, and pain for ever; she feeds upon the fruit of the tree of life, and drinks at the fountain-head of happiness; the glory of the Lord which she continually beholds has transformed her fully into the same image; she sees Him as He is, and by that sight she is become like Him, to the utmost measure of creature capacity. Is, then, her removal to be bewailed as a calamity? I know that as a mother you must feel; may all your painful feelings be sanctified! but I rather call upon you to rejoice; your daughter is daughter to the great King; she is now clothed with light and glory; it is but a short separation; you will follow

her soon, and I trust that all your daughters will in due time follow
you. May I meet you all there! Miss C—— unites with me in
cordial love to you, to them, and to Mrs. P——, if with you.

"I am,

" Your very affectionate, and much obliged,

" JOHN NEWTON."

Besides two or three volumes of his letters which he published himself, or left selected and arranged for publication
after his death, there are before the public his letters to
Cowper the poet, to Mr. Wilberforce, and Mrs. More (inserted in their Lives) ; his letters to the Rev. Samuel Palmer ;
his letters to the Rev. John Campbell ; his letters to the Rev.
Mr. Coffin ; his letters to Mr. Jones, a deacon of an Independent church; a volume of letters called "The Aged
Pilgrim ;" and his letters to the Rev. Wm. Bull. To all
these we may add those that have appeared singly in the
Christian Observer, the *Guardian*, the *Evangelical Magazine*,
the *Congregational Magazine*, &c.; and yet the letters in
print are nothing to the number he wrote!

One star differs from another star in glory. True religion exists in various degrees. Nehemiah not only feared
God, but feared God above many ; and the good ground
yielded thirty, sixty, and a hundred fold. I deem Mr.
Newton the most perfect instance of the spirit and temper of
Christianity I ever knew—shall I say—with the *exception ?*
—no, but with the addition of—*Cornelius Winter !*

REV. JOHN RYLAND, Senior, M.A.

Mr. Ryland had resided at Northampton as the pastor of the Baptist church, where also, for many years, he had kept a large and flourishing school. He had, when I became acquainted with him, no pastorate, but preached occasionally for any of his brethren. His residence was then at Enfield, where he had a seminary; but he passed his vacations at the house of one of his sons, who carried on trade in Blackfriars Road. There he was all the time of my first and second engagements at Surrey Chapel; and, as the chapel was near, he frequently heard me, and I gained his approbation and attachment.

He was a peculiar character, and had many things about him *outré* and *bizarre,* as the French would call them; but those who have heard him represented as made up only of these are grossly imposed upon. We are far from justifying all his bold sayings, and occasional sallies of temperament; but, as those who knew him can testify, he was commonly grave, and habitually sustained a dignified deportment; and he had excellences which more than balanced his defects. His apprehension, imagination, and memory, to use an expression of his own, rendered his brains like fish-hooks, which seized and retained everything within their reach. His preaching was probably unique, occasionally overstepping the proprieties of the pulpit, but grappling much with conscience, and dealing out the most tremendous blows at error, sin, and the mere forms of godliness.

Mr. Hall has said in print, "He was a most extraordinary man, and rarely, if ever, has full justice been done to his character." The Rev. James Hervey, rector of Weston Favell, often entertained him at his parsonage, and kept up a frequent correspondence with him, as may be seen in seventy of his letters inserted in his Life by Mr. Ryland. These letters show, not only the value he attached to Mr. Ryland's friendship, but the confidence he placed even in his judgment, consulting him with regard to his own several publications, as well as desiring his opinion of the works of others.

The first time I ever met Mr. Ryland was at the house of a wholesale linendraper in Cheapside. This gentleman, Mr. B——h, told him one day, as he called upon him, that I was in the parlour, and desired him to go in, and he would soon follow. At this moment I did not personally know him. He was singular in his appearance: his shoes were square-toed; his wig was five-storied behind; the sleeves of his coat were profusely large and open; and the flaps of his waistcoat encroaching upon his knees. I was struck and awed with his figure; but what could I think when, walking towards me, he laid hold of me by the collar, and, shaking his fist in my face, he roared out, "Young man, if you let the people of Surrey Chapel make you proud, I'll smite you to the ground!" But then, instantly dropping his voice, and taking me by the hand, he made me sit down by his side, and said,—"Sir, nothing can equal the folly of some hearers; they are like apes that hug their young ones to death." He then mentioned two promising young ministers who had come to town, and been injured and spoiled by popular caressings; adding other seasonable and useful remarks.

From this strange commencement a peculiar intimacy

ensued.   We were seldom a day apart during my eight weeks' continuance in town, and the intercourse was renewed the following year, when we were both in town again at the same time.   As the chapel was very near, and spacious, he obtained leave from the managers to deliver in it a course of philosophical lectures, Mr. Adams, the celebrated optician, aiding him in the experimental parts.   The lectures were on Friday mornings, at the end of which there was always a short sermon at the reading-desk; and the lecturer would say to his attendants, " You have been seeing the works of the God of Nature; now go yonder, and hear a *Jay* talk of the works of the God of Grace."

As I was then single, and had the chapel-house to myself, he soon found its roominess and quiet more agreeable than the noise of grandchildren; and, as he did not dissent much from Mr. Berridge's notion, that prudence is a rascally virtue, he quartered himself too much upon me, often bringing over his friends with him; regardless of the fact that I was not the owner, but only the occupier of the dwelling.   As I was near, and rose early, (as he also did,) he soon turned me also to some account.   He was often publishing, and was fonder of *dictating* than of writing.   I was, therefore, gradually and increasingly drawn in to be his amanuensis; and at different times I wrote from his lips his " Qualifications of an able Expositor," for Scott's Bible; " The Corner Stone of the British Constitution;" "Address to the Youth of England and France;" and a large proportion of the " Life of James Hervey."   His publications were very numerous; too numerous for the contents to be distinct and finished; yet all abounding with strong and striking passages.

As he was eccentric, and eccentricity often appears like a degree of derangement, and with some always passes for it, this, perhaps, considerably affected the circulation and influence of his various works.   I was struck with him as an original, and only viewed him as eccentric. His conversation, and illustrations, and expressions, were frequently very uncommon and impressive. His mind was never quiescent. He always seemed labouring to throw off something fresh and forcible, not only in his public discourses, but in his ordinary conversation. He sometimes failed, and you had (yet rarely) only extravagance; but he sometimes succeeded, and persons of some mind must have been surprised at his fine touches and strokes of genius. As to myself, I derived no little advantage from him. He was full of information, and ready to communicate. He seized my mind, and was always leading me to think. By his commendations he cheered and encouraged me; and several of his counsels and admonitions guided my youth, and have not been forgotten through life. One of them he often repeated: it was against sitting up late to study. He dwelt on the baneful consequences of this practice, and ran over several instances in which good and useful men had been sufferers by it, losing their health, and shortening their days.

He never seemed so much in his element as when he had those around him, who were not only willing to receive, but eager to draw forth from his ample stores. The young could never leave his company unaffected and uninstructed. I once passed a day at his house. It was the fifth of November. He took advantage of the season with his pupils. There was an effigy of Guy Fawkes. A court of justice was established for his trial. The indictment was read; witnesses were examined; counsel was heard. But he was clearly and fully convicted; when Mr. R. himself, being the judge, summed up the case; and, putting on his black cap, pronounced the awful sentence—that he should be carried forth and burned at the stake; which sentence was executed amidst shouts of joy from his pupils. Of this, I confess, my feelings did not entirely approve.

Speaking of him one day to Mr. Hall, he related the following occurrence :—" When I was quite a lad, my father took me to Mr. Ryland's school at Northampton. That afternoon I drank tea along with him in the parlour. Mr. Ryland was then violently against the American war ; and, the subject happening to be mentioned, he rose, and said, with a fierce countenance and loud voice,—' If I was General Washington, I would summon all my officers around me, and make them bleed from their arms into a basin, and dip their swords into its contents, and swear they would not sheath them till America had gained her independence.' I was perfectly terrified. ' What a master,' thought I, ' am I to be left under !' and when I went to bed, I could not for some time go to sleep."

Once a young minister was spending the evening with him, and when the family were called together for worship, he said, " Mr. ——, you must pray." " Sir," said he, " I cannot." He urged him again, but in vain. " Then, Sir," said he, " I declare, if you will not, I'll call in the watchman." At this time a watchman on his round was going by, whom he knew to be a very pious man ; (I knew him too ;) he opened the door, and calling him, said, " Duke, Duke, come in ; you are wanted here. Here," said he, " is a young pastor that can't pray ; so you must pray for him."

At this time, the first opposition was made to the Slave Trade, and he threw all his impassioned energies into the condemnation of the accursed traffic. One morning I was reading to him some of the reported miseries and cruelties of the middle passage ; among others, of a captain who had a fine female slave in his cabin, but, when her infant cried, he snatched him up, and flung him out into the sea ; still requiring the wretched creature to remain, as the gratifier of his vile passions. At the recital of this Mr. Ryland seemed frantic, and to lose his usual self-control. He was agitated, and paced up and down the room, " O God, preserve me ! O God, preserve me !" and then, unable to contain any longer, burst forth into a dreadful imprecation, which I dare not repeat. It shocked me, and I am far from justifying it; and yet, had the reader been present to witness the excitement and the struggle, he would hardly have been severe in condemning him. Is there not a feeling of justice, as well as of mercy? And what is mercy, compared with justice? The one is confined to our economy of imperfection and of evil; the other pervades all worlds, and reigns for ever. " Justice and judgment are the habitation of *His*throne," who is *holy* in *all* his ways, and *righteous* in *all* his works.

One afternoon we went together to drink tea with Mrs. ——, and she prevailed upon us to spend the evening. His supper was always spinach and an egg on a slice of toasted bread, and a glass of pure water. At the domestic worship he said, " You, Eusebius," (so he commonly called me, I know not wherefore,) " you shall pray, and I will for a few minutes expound." (He was never tedious.) He took the story of the woman of Canaan. After commenting on her affliction, and application for relief, he came to her trial and her success;—reading the words—*"And he answered her not a word;"* he said, " Is this the benefactor of whom I have heard so much before I came? He seems to have the dead palsy in his tongue."—*" And the disciples came, and besought him, saying, Send her away, for she crieth after us;"*—" And why should we be troubled with a stranger? We know not whence she is, and she seems determined to hang on till she is heard." *" But he said, I am not sent but to the lost sheep of the house of Israel:"*—" and you know *you* are not one of them; and what right have *you* to clamour thus?"— *" Then came she, falling at his feet, and cried, Lord, help me! But he said, It is not meet to take the children's bread, and to cast it to dogs; and she said, Truth, Lord, yet the dogs eat of the crumbs that fall from their master's table.* What I want is no more to thee than a crumb, compared with the immense provisions of Thy board; and I come only for a crumb, and a crumb I must have; and, if Thou refuse me a seat at Thy table with Thy family, wilt Thou refuse me a crawl and a crumb underneath?   The family will lose nothing by my gaining all I want." . . . . Omnipotence can withstand this attack no longer; but He yields the victory,—not to her humility, and importunity, and perseverance,—but to her *faith*, that produced and employed all these; for "all things are possible to him that believeth." —" *O woman, great is thy faith; be it unto thee even as thou wilt.*"   "Lord, what was that you said?"   "Why, be it unto thee even as thou wilt."   "Why, then, I will have my dear child instantly healed."   "Be it unto thee even as thou wilt."   "Why, then, I will have my poor soul saved." "Be it unto thee even as thou wilt."   "Why, then, I will have all my sins pardoned and destroyed."   "Be it unto thee even as thou wilt."   "Why, then, I'll have all my wants supplied from thy riches in glory."   "Be it unto thee even as thou wilt.   Here, take the key, and go, and be not afraid to rifle all my treasures."

"Now, Mrs. ——, this woman was a dog, a sad dog, a sinful dog, and, if she had had her desert, she would have been driven out of doors; and yet there is not a woman in this house comparable to her.—Let us pray."

N.B.—I relate as characteristic, what I did not wholly admire as proper. I repeat the same with regard to another instance :—

He took my place one Tuesday-evening at Surrey Chapel, and preached a most striking sermon from Daniel's words to Belshazzar,—" But the God in whose hands thy breath is, and whose are all thy ways, hast thou not glorified." After an introduction, giving some account of Belshazzar, he impatiently and abruptly broke off by saying,—" But you cannot suppose that I am going to preach a whole sermon on such a rascal as this,"—and then stated, that he should bring home the charge in the text against every individual in the place, in *four* grand instances.

Mr. Ryland was exceedingly full of striking, and useful, and entertaining anecdotes; and (which is everything in anecdotes) he told them with admirable clearness, and brevity, and ease. I heard him repeat, more than once, many of those which Dr. Newman has published in his account of him; some of which, for want of his stating the circumstances, which introduced or followed them, appear less credible than they otherwise would do. For instance, when, during the execrable badness of the singing after sermon, he said, " I wonder the angels of God do not wrench your necks off," --he had been preaching on the presence of the angels in our assemblies. The thing itself was very exceptionable, but this circumstance rendered it less unnatural and improbable.

Though he was rather high in his doctrinal sentiments, and not entirely friendly to some of Mr. Fuller's views, he was not sour and malignant towards others.

He was intimate with Mr. Whitfield and Mr. Rowland Hill, and much attached to many other preachers less systematically orthodox than himself; and laboured, as opportunity offered, with them. He was, indeed, a lover of all good men ; and, while many talked of candour, he exercised it. Though he was a firm Baptist, he was no friend to bigotry or exclusiveness. He warmly advocated the cause of mixed communion, and republished Bunyan's reasons for the practice, with the addition of some of his own. And this brings to my mind the following occurrence:—I was one day to dine with him at a friend's house: the company was large: and, while waiting for the dinner, a minister asked him his opinion concerning strict communion, and excluding pious men from the Lord's table. He replied thus,—" You *decide* the thing by calling it *the Lord's table.* Suppose, sir, when I entered this room, I had taken upon

me to say,—'Mr. Such-an-one,' (naming him,) 'you shall
not sit down at this table; and Mrs. Such-an-one,' (naming
her,) 'you shall not sit down at this table:'—what would
Mr. D——, the master of the house, say? Why, John
Ryland, you have forgotten yourself. *You* are not the
owner of this table, but the *master* is. The table is mine,
and I have a *right* to invite them; and I *have* invited them;
and is it for *you* to forbid them? So in the church. The
table is *the Lord's;* and all who are called by his grace
are *his* guests, and he has *bidden* them."

I cannot but think some of his own brethren, and of
his own denomination, bore too hard upon him for some
difficulty in his pecuniary circumstances. They did not,
indeed, charge him with dishonesty and injustice, but they
seemed to forget that a brother may be overtaken in a
fault, and that the fault in this case was in reality the effect
of an excellence, or virtue. In his ardour for learning and
science, he was too free in the purchase of books for his
own use, and to give to poor ministers who had few intellectual helps; and also in the exercise of beneficence to
the poor and needy, he was drawn beyond his means. I
was told by a person who attended the examination of his
affairs, that, when something rather reflecting on his integrity had escaped from one of the party, he instantly rose
up, and turned his face to the wall, and, looking up to
heaven, said, " Lord, thou knowest I am not wicked! Oh,
give me grace to preserve my temper and tongue, while I
endeavour to answer and rectify the mistake of my brother."
This instantly softened and melted the party, and Mr. R.
soon gave them full satisfaction. If God had not called Lot
"*just* Lot," we should probably never have registered him
in our calendar of saints. Dr. Rippon, one of his permanently attached friends and advisers, preached his funeral
sermon: and, as they were letting down the deceased into
the grave, he pointed to the coffin, and said, with admirable
impression,—

" Defects through Nature's best productions run,—
    Our friend had spots,—and spots are in the sun!"

The Rev. Mr. Bell, of Cheshunt, who attended him, informed me of the blessed state of his mind in his dying
hours; reporting, among other things which he addressed
to himself:—" Oh, Bell, I charge you, I charge you to love
and preach Christ! Oh, how good has he always been to
me, and how good is he now! My body is as full of ease,
and my soul is as full of joy, as it can hold!"

Dr. Newman, the late tutor of the Baptist Academy at
Stepney, who has published affectionate Memoirs of him,
was originally a youth whom Mr. Ryland took up, and
entirely educated gratis.

I need not say that the late Dr. Ryland, of Bristol, was
his son, who had the ability, and learning, and excellence of
his father without any of his *errata*. Dr. R.'s praise is in all
the churches. His character, consistency, and integrity,
were proverbial; so that Mr. Hall, who preached his funeral
sermon once said, " I would as soon have Dr. Ryland's word
as Gabriel's oath." John Ryland, the father, was a devourer
of books, and an excessive praiser of some of them. Thus
I remember his saying,—" If the dipping my pen in my
very blood would recommend ' Witsius's Economy of the
Covenants,' I would not forbear doing it for a moment."
Of Henry's Exposition he said,—" It is impossible for a
person of piety and taste to read this work, without wishing
to be shut out from the whole world, and to read it through
without one moment's interruption." Dr. Owen, also, was
an extreme favourite with him. His Latin treatise on
" Divine Justice," he translated and published. He gloried
in Bunyan; and I recollect his speaking with warmth
against Mr. Booth, who, in his defence of strict communion, had said,—" Let him (Bunyan) *dream*, but not lay
down rules for gospel-worship."

He had a great number of manuscripts, some of which I

saw from time to time. He used to say, "These I shall bequeath to twelve ministers, each having a key to the box containing them; and, if you are a good boy, you shall be one of them." What became of them?

Though so many years have elapsed since, I feel it pleasant, and useful, to recall the opportunities I had of being in company with him; and of leading him about from place to place, when leaning on my arm; and I retain many impressions he made upon me, when I was most susceptible of impressions.

If sometimes he seemed severe, it was really more in the force of his expressions than in the feeling of his heart. No one was more capable of tenderness; and I remember his saying,—"My mother died when I was five years of age; and I have ten thousand times wished that she were alive, that I might wait upon her."

I wish I had written down more of his sayings and remarks. These are a few of them:—"My dunghill heart." —"The promises are the saints' legacies."—"When a Christian is matured for heaven, he leaves the present world as the acorn leaves its cup."—"Work for the world is done *best*, when work for God is done *first*."—"It is perilous to read any impure book; you will never get it out of your faculties till you are dead. My imagination was tainted young, and I shall never get rid of it till I get into heaven."

He used facetiously to mention that, when he resided in Warwick, he lived in the Parsonage House, which he rented of the Rector, Dr. Tate; who, when he was reflected upon by some high ecclesiastic for letting it to a Dissenter, replied,—"What would you have me do? I have brought the man as near the Church as I can, but I cannot force him into it."

WILLIAM WILBERFORCE, ESQ.

It was very soon after my settlement in Bath, that I had the honour and advantage of commencing an acquaintance with this inestimable man, and which led to an intimacy which continued for his life.

He was then lodging in Queen's Square Terrace, his relation, Mr. Henry Thornton, member for the Borough, being with him. It was by a note of invitation I called upon him. As I had not been before in the company of any distinguished personage, I felt exceedingly as I approached the door, and held the knocker some seconds in my hand before I could use it. But unlike his excellent kinsman, whose manner was as cold as his disposition was generous; and with whom, instead of advancing, you had always to begin your friendship, and never could be free; he instantly loosened me from my fears and embarrassment; and, without lowering my respect, inspired me with confidence and attachment.

Was there ever a being who possessed such a power of endearing himself, making all hearts his own, as soon as they approached him; and not only preserving but increasing affection, by every additional opportunity of intercourse! Perhaps, if one sentence could more fully describe him than another, it would be *an incomparable readiness to give pleasure, and to be pleased.*

I had several other interviews with him, during that visit

to Bath. They were all delightful and useful. One Sabbath morning, after hearing me on a subject which had reference to the Doctrine of the Trinity, he mildly asked me, whether something I had advanced did not carry the distinctions in the Divine Nature too far; and whether it might not be made to countenance Tritheism? He was correct; I saw my mistake; and was thankful for such an early proof of his attention and kindness.

He asked me if I had Quintilian, and finding I had never seen the work, he promised, on his return, to send it to me ; but, for what reason I know not, instead of this, he sent me the works of Dr. Witherspoon. To the Treatise of this Author on "Regeneration," he was much attached; and some years after he wrote an Essay to be prefixed to it, in a series of Publications issued by Chalmers and Collins of Glasgow. Concerning this admirable Essay, I remember his complaining, that he wrote it only to prefix to Witherspoon's "Treatise on *Regeneration;*" but the publishers connected with it the work on *Justification*, "with which," said he, " I was less acquainted, and might not have so highly and entirely approved. This was not fair."

His preferences in religion were not censorious or exclusive. He had a real and large liberality towards those who differed from him, in some of the more external and subordinate parts of Christianity; or rather its administrations ; and, therefore, he made no scruple to attend occasionally in places which at that time ignorance, and not *law*, called *conventicles;* and in two instances, at least, he partook of the Lord's Supper in Nonconformist Churches; for which he is *now* doubtless ashamed and grieved, in the presence of Him who said, " Whosoever shall do the will of my Father who is in heaven, the *same* is my *Brother* and *Sister* and *Mother*." Could his Biographers be unacquainted with this ? Are all those dead who have heard him more than once say,—" Though I am an Episcopalian by education and conviction, I yet feel such a oneness and sympathy with the cause of God at large, that nothing would be more delightful than my communing, once every year, with *every* Church that holds the Head, even Christ." And did this render him a worse Churchman? What must we have thought of such a Church if it had?

While I was preaching in London, and he was visiting in Bath, I received from him the following letter:—

Near Bath, Sept. 22nd, 1803.

MY DEAR SIR,—I commence my letter with unaffected doubts whether I should apologize for delaying it so long, or for even now writing it. I have for a fortnight past been on the point of taking up my pen, and knowing, on the one hand, that I am addressing a man of whose candour and liberality of spirit I would rather speak to any other than to himself; and, on the other, my conscience bearing me witness, that I am actuated by motives of pure benevolence, and love without dissimulation; I will proceed to fulfil the most valuable duty of friendship. Yet, when I go on to state, that it is to observe on your mode of preaching that I have resolved to address you, I am aware that I may, not without reason, appear guilty of somewhat of the same presumption, as the philosopher who undertook to lecture Hannibal on the Art of War; for you must, it can be no compliment to say it, have studied vastly more than myself the way of addressing your hearers, and have balanced opposite considerations, &c. &c. Yet it may be of use to a minister, that a friend should tell him what the hearers say; not to control but to inform his judgment; that, having all before him, he may at length decide for himself.

I have then, (to come to the point,) been told from various quarters, that your general strain of preaching has been of late not sufficiently Evangelical; and, though the few opportunities I have myself had of hearing you, (opportunities which I always prize as the greatest of my Bath pleasures,) scarcely qualify me to judge for myself on this question; yet I should not be honest, were I not to confess, that they have rather confirmed the report which had reached me from others. It has been ascribed to your having witnessed the sad consequences of an unwarranted application of the promises and blessings of the Gospel; and I have myself also ascribed it to a cause connected with the former; I mean, to your observing that the bulk of professors were shamefully uninstructed in the Christian system, and ignorant of the very Scriptures in which they say they have eternal life.

I hope I need not assure you, that no man is more vehement against that way of preaching which indolence, I fear, more than any other consideration, has rendered so general, of following so little the example of the sacred writers, as to be always insisting on one single topic. I cannot want you to leave your *fatness*,* with which your talents and knowledge enable you to honour God and serve man. I cannot wish you to give up the various melodies, with which a bountiful Creator hath endowed you, for the unvaried strain of one cuckoo-note; but there is a mode, (and no man knows it better,) of preaching evangelical truth practically, and applying evangelically the rich and full variety of the doctrines and precepts of the Word of God. I am aware, too, that there may be no danger of your being misunderstood by your own stated congregation. But, indeed, my dear sir, you are " a debtor to the Greeks and barbarians." Consider the situation in which you stand. Not another minister in Bath, whom any of the poor wretched upper classes are likely to hear, who preaches the Gospel. They come, perhaps, to your chapel; they never heard the word of life before; they never may have another opportunity. Pity them, my dear sir, as I know you do. They, above all others, deserve to be pitied. I have, alas! been more conversant with them than you; and am, therefore, the more impressed with a sense of their wretched ignorance in spiritual things.

And now, my dear sir, I have only to express my hopes that you will do justice to the motives of esteem and regard which have dictated this letter; and it may be as well to add, that no human being, not even Mrs. W. herself, knows of its being written. It appears to me, that all friendly offices of this kind are likely to be more pure from all improper mixture, when they are known by the two individuals alone, from whom and to whom the representation is made. And besides this motive for secrecy, I must add, that it requires a very different degree of evidence and conviction to warrant the *private* communication of a hint to a friend, and the mention of it, if it is to become ever so little more public; for, if anything be *at all* divulged, who shall say, " thus far, and no farther ?"

I cannot pass this occasion of expressing the sincere pleasure, and I hope I may say, improvement, with which I have read your first, and a great part of your second, volume of Sermons; the publication of which may, I trust, be beneficial in various ways; and I must advise your sending forth an addition to their number.

I remain, my dear Sir, yours very sincerely,

W. WILBERFORCE.

* Alluding, no doubt, to Judges ix. 9.

"Let the righteous smite me, and it shall be a kindness; and let him reprove me, it shall be an excellent oil which shall not break my head; and even my prayer also shall be for him in his calamity." This letter was most gratefully received. Nothing also could have been more seasonable. It was really needed. There was ground, at least in a considerable degree, for the pious apprehension. From the motives mentioned by him, I had insensibly been led too far, and enlarged too much on what some have called, "the guarding side." Perhaps also, with regard to some, from a little vain wish to avoid the offence of the Cross. As I found this friendly admonition useful to myself, I hope it will be serviceable, especially to some of my younger brethren, who may be in danger from a similar mistake. The truth is, we are not to preach the *less* the doctrines which some pervert or abuse; but to preach them the *more*, only in a better manner, holding them forth, not only in all their richness, but also in all their connexions, proportions, influences, and effects. I trust I was enabled to act upon the counsel so timely and delicately given; and many of my friends noticed, forthwith, the advantage in my general strain of preaching. But little were they aware of the cause to which, under God, it was owing.

And what a view does it give us of the mind of this preeminent man, that, amidst all his public engagements, he could turn his attention to a humble individual, who had no secular distinction, and who was labouring in a different religious community from his own! But he considered the importance of his *situation*, and his opportunities of doing some good there; and especially, *that* good which was spiritual and eternal, and which was the first and last wish of his heart, by *whomsoever* it might be accomplished.

I have said in another place, and I repeat it, that some are too Orthodox to be Evangelical. Because Mr. Wilberforce held not the exclusive part of Calvinism, suspicions have prevailed that he was not quite sound in doctrine. But let any who question even the degree of his evangelism, read not only his own invaluable book,* but even this letter, and see what kind of preaching that was for which he was so zealous, and to which he was persuaded God only gave testimony, as to the word of his grace.

And may I not ask, and does not even a regard to Truth itself allow me to ask, whether this Letter does not breathe a regard which his " Memoirs " seemed designed to deny or to diminish?

I need not quote the—*only*—kind of references to the reminiscent which appear in that work; but I leave the reader to inquire, for what purpose such insignificant notices were inserted. And let a thousand instances of kindness, and the following correspondence, assist them to answer.

I prefix a note from Mrs. Wilberforce :—

Bath, Sunday Night.

DEAR SIR,—Permit me to offer a *trifle* towards the good work which I heard of to-day,—the enlarging your Chapel. May the undertaking lead to as much good as your heart can desire.

With every good wish to yourself, Mrs. Jay, and family,

I am, my dear Sir, your obliged and faithful, B. A. WILBERFORCE.

No. 7, South Parade, Thursday Evening, 14th Oct. 1830.

MY DEAR SIR,—Though I trust you know the cordial esteem and regard which I feel, and have long felt for you, too well, not to be *sure* that I must sympathize with you in your present season of affliction ; (and let me say the same, and with no less truth, for my dear Mrs. Wilberforce also ;) yet I must intrude on you for a few moments, to assure you of the sincerity of my condolence. May it please God to support and comfort you under this trying dispensation.†

I remain, my dear Sir, ever sincerely and affectionately yours,

W. WILBERFORCE.

P.S.—I beg you will not trouble yourself to return me any answer.

---

* " A practical View of the prevailing religious Systems of Professed Christians in the higher and middle classes contrasted with real Christianity."

† It was the first seizure of Mrs. Jay, noticed fully in Letter X.

No. 5, Queen's Square,
Friday.

MY DEAR SIR,—I am just now requested to introduce to you some young people, who are truly worthy of the privilege of your acquaintance, and, I hope, friendship.

The ladies are the daughters of a widow recently become such, Mrs. Wolf. The gentleman, an officer in the navy, a son of Dr. Hall, Dean of Durham, and late head of Christ Church, Oxford. It has pleased God to touch his heart to true piety, which is more attractive by the singularly pleasing form in which it is presented. He is about to be united with Miss Amelia Wolf, and she also, I am assured, is truly religious.

I could not refuse their desire, that I would recommend them to your friendly attention; though I tell them how little time you can spare even to your oldest friends.

I am ever, my dear Sir, yours sincerely,

W. WILBERFORCE.

N.B.—I ought to mention that Mr. Hall's wish to know you arose first from a sermon he heard you preach last night.

No. 5, Queen's Square,
26th May, 1826.

MY DEAR SIR,—It would have given both Mrs. Wilberforce and myself pleasure to call again on Mrs. Jay and you, before our departure to-morrow; but I fear we cannot; and therefore I trouble you by the pen with a question or two, which I should otherwise put orally.

It occurs to me that you can probably inform me who and what Mr. Campbell is. He writes to me occasionally from Edinburgh upon religious subjects, and I have now occasion to answer a recent letter of his, concerning the Apocryphal dispute. I know not whether to call him *Rev.* or *Esq.*; and he may think it strange that I do not know his proper description; I probably did know it, but I have forgot it.

We may probably be able to go to Mr. Hall's chapel on Sunday. Can you inform me where it is situated, and at what hour service begins?

I take the pen in my *own* hand to add, that I cannot but sincerely regret my not having had the profit and pleasure of hearing you, and joining with you in worship, during this visit to Bath. Both you and I, I believe, and indeed I cannot doubt it, are much more closely bound to each other by the substance of Christian principles, (besides a personal friendship which has long been, and will continue, I trust, during our lives, to be a subject of mutual pleasure to both of us,) than we are separated by any differences as to the outward form and mechanism of religion.   I had rather wished for a few minutes' private conversation with you, but I fear I shall not be able to call (or Mrs. W. on Mrs. Jay) before my departure to-morrow about 12 o'clock.   If you should be walking this way, I should be happy to see you; and if not, let me thus take my leave for the present, assuring you of the cordial esteem and regard with which I am, with our best respects to Mrs. Jay,

My dear Sir, yours very sincerely,

W. WILBERFORCE.

No. 9, North Parade,
Wednesday, 17th Oct. 1831.

MY DEAR SIR,—We cannot but remember with pleasure the visits you kindly paid us last year, and Mrs. Wilberforce and I much wish to renew the enjoyment.   Mrs. W. reminds me that you used sometimes to take your tea while we took our dinner.

Would you favour us with your company at a quarter before five o'clock to-morrow?

I can truly say that the hope of seeing you is always one of the most gratifying objects in my prospect, when I look forward to the renewal of my visits to Bath; and that I am, with cordial esteem and regard,

Ever sincerely yours,

W. WILBERFORCE.

Near Uxbridge, 7th Jan.

MY DEAR SIR,—I enclose you a £5-note, to reimburse you for the sum you were so kind as to lay down for me; and I return you thanks for so kindly inquiring into the case; perhaps it would be for the poor young man's own benefit, to caution him against relying on future aid from me.   I have sometimes found a little pecuniary assistance practically injurious for the want of this warning.

I thank you for naming the Eclectic, and will procure the number; I used to take in that publication, but discontinued it, partly because the increasing numbers of such periodical works compelled me to select; and still more, because it became so much more of a party work; otherwise my knowing that occasionally R. Hall and Foster wrote in it, was a strong inducement to take it in.   Were not my eyes very indifferent, and my stock of leisure *very* small, I would enter for a few minutes into the Roman Catholic Question.

I have not seen "Cobbett" for some time. My chief reason for ever taking in his paper was, that I could not otherwise see it; and I thought it right to know what were the lessons of a very able and influential political teacher on the passing events of the day. But when I heard his paper circulation had much declined, I declined also.

My motives for supporting what is very ill-entitled Catholic emancipation, were, not that I thought that when granted the Roman Catholics would desire no more; still less, because I did not entertain a very strong repugnance to the Roman Catholic religion of the present day; (and this last I thought it right in fairness to declare to the two Roman Catholic deputies, who called on me as a friend a few years ago, Drs. Everett and Murray); but because I really believe the actual state of the laws tends to maintain, nay, probably to extend, certainly to exasperate and embitter, the influence of the Roman Catholic tenets. The Roman Catholics can and now do vote for Members of Parliament, though they cannot become such. The consequence is, that they choose Members, who, though Protestant by profession, (commonly, perhaps, neutrals at heart,) are full as subservient to Roman Catholic interests as avowed Roman Catholics could be, while they may speak a language which, uttered by Roman Catholics, would call forth a spirit in the Protestants to at least an equal amount; but to which, when held by Protestants, no objection could be made without a man's being considered guilty of a personal affront. Put the question arithmetically. The influence exerted on the side of the Roman Catholics is now the sum of their own and that of Protestants whom they elect or favour. When Roman Catholics should be eligible, it would be only the difference. The existing state of the laws keeps the Roman Catholics in a continual state of irritation, reminded of their incapacities; for they are brought forward to vote, but not to be elected. I also lay much stress on the effect of Roman Catholic gentlemen mixing in Parliament with Protestants, and thus habitually learning to disrelish, as galling and humiliating, the subjection to the priests, in which, after all, consists much of the strength and evil of their religion. But I must lay down my pen, only remarking, that I cannot be afraid of Popery in this country, but that I should not be greatly surprised to see the Roman Catholic oriflamb waving in Ireland, the Roman Catholic mass being supported by the military regulars of some continental Roman Catholic power. However, be this as it may, I cannot but trust all will end well, both for Ireland herself, and much more for England, when I witness the continually increasing flood of light which she (England) is the instrument of diffusing through the Pagan world.   India is likely, I hope, ere long, to become the glory of this country.

My dear Sir, you seduce me, you see, even on paper, into too long a *tête-à-tête*, and I have scarcely left myself room to request you to present Mrs. W.'s and my own best remembrances to Mrs. Jay, and to assure you of her cordial good wishes as well as my own, for the temporal, and still more for the spiritual, well-being of you and yours.

Ever, my dear Sir, your sincere and affectionate friend,

W. WILBERFORCE.

When I published my "Evening Exercises," I dedicated them to my Illustrious Friend. As the preface was long, and animadverted on various, and some of them disputed, topics, I sent it to him in manuscript, begging he would strike out whatever he disapproved of; but he returned it without a single erasure; and when the volumes came out, as soon as he received the copy I presented to him, he wrote me the following letter :—

Elmdon House, near Birmingham, 30th Dec. 1831.

MY DEAR SIR,—Though I will not withhold from Mrs. Wilberforce the pleasure of answering your friendly letter, I cannot be satisfied without assuring you, with my own pen, that I feel honoured as well as gratified by the proof of your esteem and regard for me, which you gave by desiring to place my name at the head of your publication.   It gives me unaffected pleasure to reflect that my name will thus be permanently associated with yours; and may this, my dear Sir, with all your other labours of love, be abundantly blessed. May the Gracious Giver of all good, who has already rendered you an instrument of such extensive usefulness, continue to prosper your endeavour to promote the temporal, and still more the eternal, benefit of your fellow-creatures; and after a long protracted sphere of usefulness and honour, may you at length hear addressed to you those blessed words—"Well done, good and faithful servant," &c.

Suffer me also to add my humble prayer, and let me hope that it will be yours also, that I may one day welcome you into that better world; and that, though by somewhat different paths, yet tending to the same point, and graduating, if I may use the expression, to the same centre, we may at length meet where holiness and happiness, where love and peace, and gratitude and joy, will be unalloyed and everlasting. Such, my dear Sir, is my sincere wish, and sometimes shall be the prayer for you, and for all that are dear to you, of

Yours, with cordial esteem and attachment,

W. W.

As a *beautiful* contrast to this, I insert a few sentences from a little work its author sent by post to *Mr.* William Jay, Bath, a few years ago.

They were all pencil-marked to render them the more *emphatic.*

" . . . and this is the reason why church people, and especially clergymen, may not keep company with, and make friends of, any of those who call themselves Dissenting ministers.

"Every Dissenting teacher is plainly making a division; every churchman, therefore, is commanded to *avoid him.* Be his gentleness and mildness what they may, in comparison with the miserable bitterness of most modern Dissenters; be his personal holiness, his mind and intellectual qualifications, what they may; be his friendship however dear to me, how can I continue it, when God has commanded me to avoid him? To pray for him as an erring brother, —to desire his present and future welfare,—to cherish towards him all kindly and brotherly feeling,—to assist him, if need be, with my counsel or my purse;—these things would be a duty and a pleasure; but to make him any longer a friend or an intimate would be a *sin.*

"Therefore he feels (*i. e.* a true churchman) that it would be sin to attend their places of worship or preaching, to acknowledge them in public meetings, or elsewhere, as fellow-ministers of the Word of God, or choose them as the friendly companions of his leisure hours.

"If this tract has done the readers any good, it will influence their conduct, and make them resolve never to make themselves partakers of other men's sins, by going to a Dissenting meeting even *once;* whether on Sunday or week-day, in the morning or afternoon or evening; whether because they hope to get good or for curiosity; or to be friendly and neighbourly. It is quite plain that all Dissent is sin; now, how very shocking it is that many good sort of people think really of coming to church on the Sunday morning, and then going to meeting in the evening! But people, I am afraid, will have to answer, not only for their own sin in going sometimes, but for the sin of those who go always, and whom, by their example, they have encouraged to do so."

" CHRISTIAN UNITY," *
BY HENRY WILLIAM WILBERFORCE, M.A.,
INCUMBENT OF WALMER, KENT.

What wonder such sentiments led to Rome! They spring from it. "A corrupt tree cannot bring forth good fruit." "By their fruits ye shall know them. Men do not gather grapes of thorns, or figs of thistles."

Mr. Wilberforce sent me, as soon as they were published, inscribed with his own hand, his "Practical Piety;" and his work on "Slavery," addressed "to Prince Talleyrand."

I remember, owing to some occurrence, Mr. Wilberforce gave me an admonition never to notice *any* thing concerning one's-self in the public prints. "If you do," said he, "you must notice *every* thing; or what passes unnoticed will pass for truth which cannot be refuted;" adding, "our character and conduct must be both our defenders and advocates."

He then mentioned the following imputation concerning himself:—"Some time ago, in Benjamin Flower's 'Cambridge Journal,' it was said, 'Behold an instance of the Pharisaism of St. Wilberforce! He was lately seen walking up and down in the Bath Pump Room, reading his prayers, like his predecessors of old, who prayed in the corners of the streets, to be seen of men.'

* Referring to this uncharitable pamphlet in a letter dated Bath, Oct. 17, 1837, Mr. Jay observes,—"Mr. Wilberforce's Life is forthcoming, but I expect it will be a very partial representation of him, especially on the score of his *liberality*. It is written by his two clerical sons, who are now so high, that one of them has published a tract in condemnation of Mr. Baptist Noel's candour; and calls upon the members of *the* church, to have 'no *social* or *friendly* intercourse with any Dissenters, and to visit them only as subjects of poverty and affliction to relieve them.' Yet their honoured father used to say,—'Though I am an Episcopalian, I should like to commune once every year with every Christian church that holds the Head.'"

"As there is generally some slight circumstance which perverseness turns into a charge or reproach, I began to reflect ; and I soon found the occasion of the calumny; and it was this :—I was walking in the Pump Room in conversation with General ———— ; a passage was quoted from Horace, the accuracy of which was questioned; and, as I had a Horace in my pocket, I sought, and found, and read the words. This was the plain *bit of wire* which factious malignity sharpened into a pin to pierce my reputation; yet I never thought it worth while to attempt to refute or rectify what I could so easily have done."

When there was some thought of abridging the privileges enjoyed by Dissenters under the Toleration Act, Mr. Wilberforce wrote to the Reminiscent. I am sorry I have either lost or mislaid this letter; but I well remember its contents. He expressed himself as exceedingly averse to the design, and wishing and hoping that all interference by government might be avoided. But he would just ask, whether the Dissenters and Methodists, in the licensing of preachers, would object to the requisition of a certificate or testimony from the *churches to which they belonged*. I answered, that, as far as I knew them, their apprehensions were too much excited to acquiesce even in such an *apparently* safe measure. At that season, however, and for want of some reflection, I confess I was *rather* disposed to differ from them; and the more so, as it had been till then the wise and good usage among them, before any of their members went forth officiating, to receive a sanction from the united approval, benediction, and prayers of the minister and people in whose communion they lived. And what has been often the result of persons becoming preachers without consulting with, and unrecommended by, any one but themselves?

Here I remember a case rather curious and instructive. A young man thought he was called to leave common and civil life, and to enter the ministry; neither his own pastor nor father knew anything of this. The persuasion of his sacred destiny originated solely with *himself.* Though fully satisfied in his own mind, yet from a kind of respect for a family friend, and to save appearances, he wished to converse with me upon the subject. By no means like-minded with himself, and fearful of giving offence, (a sad infirmity in such a case,) I begged him to consult an older authority, and one who I knew had a firmer, bolder manner. An interview soon taking place, the young man told him he had been for some time persuaded he was called to the ministry; and asked his aged adviser what he deemed the best sign or evidence of a Divine call to the work. " Sir," said the sage, " what I should deem the best sign or evidence would be a man's not thinking of it, but considering himself the last person in the world God would select for this purpose; and who, if God came for him, would be found like Saul, 'hid among the stuff,' and requiring an effort to draw him out."

I remember his relating a remarkable circumstance concerning Carlile the Infidel. " The wretched creature," said he, " was then in prison at Dorchester, having been prosecuted for his vile and infamous publications. As I was then visiting at the house of a magistrate in the neighbourhood, I thought I should like to see the prisoner and converse with him, perfectly *incog.* After some general conversation, I learned from him something of his former life, and found that he had formerly been among the Wesleyan Methodists, and even a class-leader. I then began to speak on the subject of religion. He said he did not wish to enter on that topic; for he had long ago made up his mind, and did not wish to have it disturbed; and, seeing me take out my little Bible, he said, 'I wish to have nothing to do with that book; and you cannot wonder at this, for if that book be true, I am damned for ever!' I was shocked, and said,

'No, no, Mr. Carlile: according to that book, there is hope for all who will seek for mercy and forgiveness; for it assures us that God hath no pleasure in the death of him that dieth.' I also said more, but it seemed to have no effect at the time, and I knew not that it had any afterwards. But," added Mr. W., "we see, (as we are needing hope) how desirable and necessary it is that there should always be an obvious and powerful ground for it; that despair hardens even more than presumption; and that men live so as to make the Bible their enemy, and then hate it because it does not prophesy good concerning them, but evil."

I cannot help adding a circumstance not irrelevant to this occurrence. Preaching one Tuesday evening at Surrey Chapel, after his (Mr. Carlile's) release from prison, I mentioned in my sermon the above anecdote. When I came down from the pulpit, some one told me that Carlile had been hearing me, and insisted upon seeing me. I said, "By all means, desire him to come into the vestry." He entered; I arose and received him courteously, and gave him my hand, remembering that "the servant of the Lord must not strive, but be patient towards all men, in meekness instructing those that oppose themselves, if haply God might give them repentance to the acknowledging of the truth." I asked him for what purpose he wished to see me. He said, "I do not charge you with intentional misrepresentation, but I have heard you say this evening what is not true." Then stating what I had related, I said, "Are you sure this is not true?" "I am: I am certain Mr. Wilberforce never conversed with me, nor saw me in prison." "Do you know Mr. Wilberforce personally?" "I do not. I look upon him as a bigoted, but very good and benevolent man; but I am sure I never saw him." "Well, as you never saw him, how are you sure that, among others who visited you, he never saw you in your confinement; especially as his design was to keep himself unknown?

Do you think," said I, "Wilberforce would forge a letter, or utter a serious falsehood?" "No, I think he would not." "And as for myself," I said, "I am sure I have accurately reported his relation, for I received it in writing at the time." This rather softened and silenced him, and he only murmured, "Well, I remember nothing of it."

I desired him to be seated, and said, "I should be glad, Mr. Carlile, to have a little further conversation,"—to which he seemed disposed; but some of his disciples, who had followed him into the vestry, rudely urged him to come away; saying,—" These gospel-preachers will say anything that serves their purpose."

As he had not behaved improperly, and as such characters are often too harshly treated, I felt a disposition to pray for him, and determined I would call upon him. This I did the next day, but he was not at home, and as I had to leave London immediately, I had no opportunity to repeat the call. I regret I did not write to him.

In their periodical, the week after, there was a tolerably fair account of the thing, unaccompanied with any reflections on myself.

I may add, that Mr. Wilberforce, after relating the above occurrence, said, " It is a very difficult and perplexing subject, but I begin to question whether such prosecutions are not more injurious than beneficial, as they awaken attention to their works, and frequently enlist feeling on behalf of the writers;"—remarking that Carlile probably did more mischief while in prison than before his trial and condemnation;—alluding to several tracts he issued while there, composed entirely of Scripture, quoting *only* passages which would represent the Bible as filled exclusively with what seemed indelicate and impure; and excusing, if not countenancing, immorality!

" It was," says Lord Brougham, "the constant maxim of my revered friend, Mr. Wilberforce, that no man should be prosecuted for his attacks on religion. He gave this opinion in Parliament; and he was wont to say, that the ground of it was his belief in the truth of religion. If religion be, as I believe it to be, true, it has nothing to fear from such assaults; but it may be injured by the secular arm interposing."

I cannot omit noticing my last interview with him. Having received a note from Mrs. Wilberforce, stating that they should leave Bath in two days; and mentioning the increased indisposition of her beloved husband, and the possibility of my not seeing him again,—by her desire I called. I was introduced to him alone, as he was lying upon the sofa. Though it was obvious that the outward man was fast declining, all his pious and friendly principles and feelings evinced their full vigour. Propriety required the interview to be short; there could be, therefore, no lengthened conversation. The following, however, I have found, which I wrote down as soon as I returned, precluding any mistake concerning it.

Something had led him to mention that noblest of all Institutions—the Bible Society; and as the Trinitarian Bible Society was about that time making a noise in our city, and assailing and seeking to divide and injure the old Institution, he eagerly inquired whether there were many defections. I told him I believed the defections were almost entirely confined to his own community; for I did not know, in the circle of my acquaintance, one minister or member among all the Dissenters and Methodists who had revolted. "Well," he said, "I am thankful for this; and hope the good cause will continue to flourish."

He also said, "I see what is the best way to reduce an undue attachment to the subordinate things in religion;— it is to keep up a supreme regard to the more important ones; for we shall then have little time and less inclination to engage in the strivings and strifes of bigots."

He also observed, " I see much in the state of the world and church which I deplore; yet I am not among the croakers. I think real religion is spreading; and, I am persuaded, will increasingly spread, till the earth is filled with the knowledge of the Lord, as the waters cover the sea."

Taking my hand at parting, he pressed it to his bosom, and said, " I am glad you have not turned aside after any of the '*Lo! heres*' and '*lo! theres*,' many of which you must have witnessed; but have kept to the common, plain, and important truths, in which all Christians are nearly agreed; and I hope you will never leave the good old way:—God bless you!"—What an interview! what a parting! what a benediction!

I leave others to speak of him as a politician. I know some of the liberals were much dissatisfied with him; but he would not be a gagged party man. He preserved his independence by accepting nothing from Government; and always gave his vote according to his conviction. I remember after the French Revolution, and for some time during the war, when the rage of opinion ran so high, he more than once desired me to say among my connexions, (he knew that some whom he valued were puzzled and grieved with his seeming devotedness to the prime minister,) that they were not to suppose he entirely approved of *all* Mr. Pitt's measures; but the times were peculiarly perilous, and it was necessary to support the Government generally, when there were so many tendencies to anarchy and confusion.

I well remember how Mrs. More herself, and others of his friends and advisers, wondered and grieved at his favouring the Catholic Emancipation Bill. No one could dislike popery more than he did: but he thought it reasonable that all its adherents should realize their civil rights and immunities; and that, with regard to religious parties, all restraints and oppositions excited and strengthened their zeal the more; and resembled the dams in a river that caused the water to rise higher, and spread wider.—(See a preceding letter to the Reminiscent on this subject.)

But time and language would fail me to speak of this man as a benefactor, and especially as the poor negro's friend. His disinterested, self-denying, laborious, undeclining efforts in this cause of justice and humanity are too well known to need enlargement; and will call down the blessings of millions; and ages yet to come will glory in his memory.

Whose very soul has not melted, not only at the poetry, but the praise of the sonnet, by the author of the "Task?"—

> Thy country, Wilberforce, with just disdain,
> Hears thee by cruel men and impious call'd
> Fanatic, for thy zeal to loose the enthrall'd
> From exile, public sale, and slavery's chain.
> Friend of the poor, the wrong'd, the fetter-gall'd,
> Fear not lest labour such as thine be vain.
> Thou hast achieved a part: hast gained the ear
> Of Britain's senate to thy glorious cause;
> Hope smiles, Joy springs; and though cold Caution pause,
> And weave delay, the better hour is near
> That shall remunerate thy toils severe,
> By peace for Afric, fenced with British laws.
> Enjoy what thou hast won, esteem and love
> From all the Just on earth, and all the Blest above.

But who or what can do justice to such a character? Every notice of him is necessarily an eulogy. Here was a man not only great among the good, but good among the great. The most popular man (according to Madame de Staël) in this country; and yet an example of " whatsoever things are true, whatsoever things are honest, whatsoever things are just, whatsoever things are pure, whatsoever things are lovely, whatsoever things are of good report," whatsoever things have any virtue or any praise in them.

But what, amidst so much and such varied intercourse with company and scenes so little favourable to religious decision and improvement, enabled him to maintain such spirituality and fervour, and to be always ready to engage so easily and naturally in pious conversation and exercises?

First:—The firmness of his convictions. Religious sentiments in him were firm,—were not opinions, but principles. That is,—sentiments which had attached to them both certainty and importance.

Secondly:—His inviolable sanctification of the Lord's-day. With him how truly was the Sabbath a delight, and the holy of the Lord, honourable! When did he not "turn away his foot from the Sabbath from polluting it, not doing his own ways, not finding his own pleasure, not speaking his own words?"

I was once dining with him on the Sabbath: it was before his marriage. We were quite alone; no servant was in attendance; we had only a dumb-waiter. The conversation turned upon the subject of my discourse that morning,—"The harvest is past, the summer is ended, and we are not saved,"—of which he begged the outline. "I just now," he said, "met Mr. Bushe on the North Parade; he told me there was very bad news; but I did not ask concerning it, and I dare not open a paper on the Lord's-day."

Thirdly:—His always attending, when in his power, the House of God and the preaching of the Word, and that word which was found to be the savour of life unto life.

Fourthly:—His family worship. Here I refer not only to its existence and regularity, but to the manner in which he discharged it. What a solemn importance seemed always attached to it! What a freedom from formality! What a simplicity in the performance! What a seriousness and degree of impression, and of effect!

Fifthly:—And, perhaps, above all, his determination to secure time for private devotion. This befriended the effect two ways—first, by the natural influence of these exercises themselves; secondly, by the supply of the Spirit of Jesus Christ, which prayer, and especially such prayer, is accredited to obtain. "Draw nigh to God, and he will draw nigh to you." "But when thou prayest, enter into thy closet, and when thou hast shut thy door, pray to thy Father who is in secret; and thy Father who seeth in secret shall reward thee openly."

It would not only be needless but presumptuous in me to speak of his senatorial rank and claims. It is undisputed what an eminent place in oratory he occupied and maintained, when eloquence in the House of Commons rivalled that of Athens and Rome. His voice was fine, deep, clear, distinct, and flexible; his animation was often great; and the impression of many of his speeches, especially of those he delivered on the Abolition of the Slave Trade, peculiarly powerful.

"I never," says Mackintosh, "saw any one who touched life at so many points; and this is the more remarkable in a man who is supposed to live absolutely in the contemplation of a future state. When he was in the House of Commons, he seemed to have the freshest mind of any of those there. There was all the charm of youth about him, and he is quite as remarkable in this bright evening of his day, as when I saw him in his glory many years ago."

"I never," says Southey, "saw any other man who seemed to enjoy such a perpetual serenity and sunshine of spirit. In conversing with him, you feel assured that there is no guile in him; that if ever there was a good man and a happy man on earth, he was one." Again, "There is such a constant hilarity in every look and motion, such a sweetness in all his tones, such a benignity in all his thoughts, words, and actions—that you can feel nothing but love and admiration for a creature of so happy and blessed a nature."

APPENDIX BY THE EDITORS.

The following additional letters of Mr. and Mrs. Wilberforce to Mr. Jay, we venture to insert as further proofs of their friendly and confidential intercourse. Before we do so, however, we beg to make a few observations.

If any of the readers of this article should also have been readers of Mr. Wilberforce's Life by his sons, the disclosures here made will create surprise, and be, in some respects, painful. It will be no matter of surprise that two such men, residing in Bath at the close of the last century, when Evangelical preaching was rare in the Church, should have become friends ; and that the friendship of two such souls should have become permanent, and ripened into mutual cordiality and confidence. But the matter of surprise and pain will be to observe, that a Life of Wilberforce could possibly be written, and a voluminous Life too, in which it could be made to appear, that there existed between them nothing but a mere cold, slight, and, on Mr. Wilberforce's side, not very respectful or polite, acquaintance.

For the purpose of enabling the readers of Mr. Jay's Reminiscence of Wilberforce, to judge of the representation of this matter, by the two Reverend sons, who have taken upon them virtually to ignore the friendly intimacy of their Father with the Dissenting Minister of Bath, we shall extract from their Work all the notices of Mr. Jay we have been able to find ; and then an opinion may be formed of the spirit which dictated this meagre, and not very delicate, exhibition of facts for public perusal from Mr. Wilberforce's Diary.

Vol. II. p. 234, under date 1797 :—

" Sunday. Randolph's, morning—Evening, Jay's—comfortable, happy Sunday."

Vol. II. p. 240. Same year :—

"Asked to subscribe to Jay's velvet cushion, but refused."

Vol. II. p. 313—date 1798 :—

" Sir George Beaumont, Creykes, &c., with us. Jay told us his origin and story very simply—a bricklayer employed on Beckford's house—began to preach at 16—humble and not democratical."

Vol. II. p. 351—date 1799 :—

"I found that so much use was made of my going to Jay's that I have kept away."

Vol. II. p. 361. Date 1800. (Referring to a projected Bill to restrict Dissenting preachers, and stating that he had explained to Mr. Pitt the only limitation of the Toleration Act to which he would consent, viz., that no one should exercise the office of a Teacher without a testimonial from the Sect to which he belonged, he says :)

" This would put a stop to the practice which I am told prevails at Salisbury, and (as I heard from Mr. Jay, the Dissenting Minister) at Bath, of a number of raw, ignorant lads, going out on preaching parties every Sunday."

Vol. V. p. 258—date 1825 :—

"——— at Jay's, where I greatly wished to go, but thought it wrong."

This sentence seems ambiguous through the omission of a name. It evidently refers to some person in Mr. Wilberforce's family, less scrupulous than himself, who went to hear Mr. Jay (possibly Mrs. W.). We are at a loss to conceive for what purpose the extract was made, unless to give publicity to Mr. Wilberforce's opinion, that it was wrong for him to go to the Dissenting Chapel to hear the Dissenting Minister with whom he had been on terms of the strictest friendship for nearly thirty years; whom he had frequently entertained at his table, introduced to his selectest friends, corresponded with familiarly and confidentially, and allowed his name to appear in the dedication of one of his works ; expressing his sense of the honour, and his gratification at the request ; and adding, " it gives me unaffected pleasure to reflect that my name will thus be permanently associated with yours." Thus wrote Mr. Wilberforce, Dec. 30, 1831—six years later than when he thought it *wrong* to hear him preach.

After this, as appears from the foregoing Reminiscence, Mr. Jay visited Mr. Wilberforce during his illness at Bath, at the special request conveyed to him by Mrs. W., when other esteemed friends were not allowed access to him. From these facts it appears, that there had been no suspension of intercourse or decay of friendship, either between 1799 and 1825, or from 1825 to the end of the year 1831, when he so kindly and gracefully accepted the *dedication* of " The Evening Exercises." Even the entry made in the Diary in the year 1799, respecting his " keeping away from Jay's Chapel, because so much use was made of it," is certainly not intended to intimate that, after that period, he never attended again ; for it is well known that he did go after that date.

In the Correspondence now published, there is a note dated a year after any notice of Mr. Jay given in the Life of Wilberforce,—" Queen's Square, May 26, 1826," in which Mr. Wilberforce requests directions of Mr. Jay where in Bristol he might find Mr. Hall's Chapel, saying, " We may probably be able to go to Mr. Hall's Chapel, on Sunday." If Mr. Wilberforce had relinquished so early as 1799 the pleasure and profit of attending upon Mr. Jay's ministry, and in 1825 thought that it was " *wrong*," that is, morally sinful, though he wished for it greatly, would he have asked the way to another Dissenting Chapel in 1826, and would he, or could he have said, in the same note of inquiry, " *I cannot but sincerely regret my not having had the profit and pleasure of hearing you, and joining with you in worship, during this visit to Bath ?*"

It is certainly not *impossible* that the same pen should have written the two notices in the Diary, respecting attendance at Mr. Jay's Chapel, and those other sentences we have quoted from the Letter of May 26, 1826, to Mr. Jay. But if it did, then something unmentioned would, if known, reconcile them with honour and integrity; or some intentional concealment gives them the appearance of contradiction. If no explanation can be given of this matter, Mr. Wilberforce's memory will have to bear the suspicion of hollow profession and faithless friendship; or the monument his reverend sons have reared to his memory will convey a most unjust, as well as false, impression.

These two good and great men, while living, appear to have had no misunderstanding and no alienation, through a friendship of thirty-five years; and they have now met in a happier world, and united in purer worship than they ever joined in here. But the Biography of the one was undoubtedly made the means of deeply wounding the heart of the other; because he was conscious that it gave to the world a most inadequate and unjust view of the long friendship which had existed between himself and Mr. Wilberforce. It had been kinder and wiser, as it now appears, not to have let the world know that Mr. Wilberforce had any acquaintance with the Dissenting Minister of Bath, or had ever delighted to hear and to honor him; than to have published the few slighting and ambiguous extracts we have cited from the Diary.

The following are the additional letters, which still further show the kind of friendship subsisting between them.

Mr. Wilberforce to Mr. Jay.

Near London, May 7th, 1805.

My dear Sir,—I will not quite take you at your word and return no answer at all; but I will so far avail myself of your friendly allowance for me, as merely to thank you for your kind communication.

Archbishop Usher's, and Bishop Bedell's Life, have long been in my library, and have been favourites with me.—I have often quoted them to some of our Irish Rulers ; and had their examples been followed, Ireland would have been in a far better state.

I am, dear Sir, yours faithfully,
W. Wilberforce.

P.S.—The memorandum I hope to get to-morrow when I go to town. I am detained here to-day by indisposition.

Mr. Wilberforce to Mr. Jay.

Pulteney St., Wednesday.

My dear Sir,—Will you and Mrs. Jay dine with us on Friday next, at half-past four or a quarter before five, to meet my friends, Mr. and Mrs. Noel, with whom I wish to bring you well acquainted? And may I beg you to bring your son-in-law, Mr. Bolton, also, on whom I meant to call in order to entitle myself to ask him ; but I trust he will excuse the breach of ceremony. I hope his lady and little one are doing well.

With cordial esteem and regard,
My dear Sir,
Ever sincerely yours,
W. Wilberforce.

Mr. Wilberforce to Mr. Jay.

Maidenhead Bridge,
28th August, 1817.

My dear Sir,—One word merely to satisfy you that your letter has reached my hands. I thank you for pointing out to me how I may fulfil my intention of begging Dr. Kollock's acceptance of a pledge of my friendly esteem : though, unless, on my return home, I find Mr. V——k's address, or unless you can favour me with it, I shall still be at a loss. If I find the former not to be the case, I will——

(Here the letter breaks off and is taken up again.)

Near London, December 26, 1817.

Such was actually a letter I meant to send to you four months ago ; and I now send it chiefly to do myself justice both with you and other gentlemen concerned, by preventing its being supposed that I had neglected the business. I found Mr. V——k's address after a time (I think at the Northumberland Coffee-house) but he was gone from it.

What, however, has now prompted me to despatch this long retained letter, is my wishing to request from you in confidence any intelligence you can send me concerning ——. A more intemperate, or, in all respects, unadvised publication I scarcely ever read. Who is Mr. ——? What his connexions? What his talents and acquirements? *　　*　　*

Let me assure you, with best remembrances to Mrs. Jay, that I am, with cordial esteem and regard,

My dear Sir,
Yours sincerely,
W. WILBERFORCE.

Excuse the effects of great and necessary haste.

Mr. Wilberforce to Mr. Jay.

No. 8, North Parade,
Saturday, 19th September, 1829.

MY DEAR SIR,—When we arrived at Bath we were told you were absent, but soon after we heard you had returned, and ever since I have been wishing, and Mrs. W. not less, though she knew of Mrs. Jay's absence, to pay our respects to you. But the weather has been so variable, as to render it quite unsafe for any one who, like myself, may probably suffer greatly from the slightest exposure to rain, to venture far from shelter, or from a Sedan chair. Our time, however, is hasting away, and it would really grieve me to have visited Bath without seeing an old friend whom I so sincerely esteem and love. Will you give us the pleasure of your company in the way in which we enjoyed it formerly—you taking your tea while we are at dinner? Do name a day on which we may hope to enjoy this pleasure at half-past four o'clock.

Believe me, with cordial attachment,
Ever sincerely yours,

The Rev. Wm. Jay. 　　　　　　　W. WILBERFORCE.

P.S.—We have heard with unfeigned concern of Mrs. Jay's indisposition, and hope she is mending.

If the *same to you*, I had rather see you any other day than Monday next; but if that day suit you better, I will make it convenient to us also.

Mrs. Wilberforce to Mr. Jay.

Elmdon House, Birmingham,
December 29th, 1831.

MY DEAR SIR,—Allow me to offer you many thanks for your most kind and acceptable present in addition to the most valuable " Morning Thoughts." May we only all of us profit by them as we ought. I am very sorry I have not been able to write sooner, as you wished to hear from me before you take measures respecting the stereotyping. It gave us much satisfaction to hear of the former volumes having been thus fixed, and that these latter ones are to share their fate; and America to profit by them as well as England. We cannot offer any alterations. I should have said that my husband gladly accepts the undivided moiety which you offer him in these volumes. But I hope *he* will add a few words for himself, though you know his eyes forbid much writing, and I am sorry to say that we have much business of an uncomfortable nature demanding time and writing, which has been one of the results of our losses; until we are a little freer from these demands, more falls to Mr. W.'s share to dictate and write than is good for him; added to all which, we have now much anxiety about our dear daughter's health. Her brother found her far from well—and she has a cough, which I fear began before her confinement, and still hangs on her, though till very lately little noticed by her medical man; we know not yet what to expect respecting her. Her brother Robert has hitherto remained with her, hoping to send us better accounts, but as yet they are not mended, and we are very uneasy about her. You, my dear Sir, who have now above a twelvemonth been suffering from much anxiety and daily sorrow, will know how to sympathize with us.

I write to-day in much haste—therefore will not enter on this sad Bible Society question; but with best regards, and every good wish to yourself, Mrs. Jay, and all your family, subscribe myself,

My dear Sir,
Your much obliged and sincere,
B. A. WILBERFORCE.

Since writing the above I am thankful to be able to say, we have heard a much better account of our daughter. The cough seems yielding, and we are encouraged to hope there is no cause for alarm; and that we shall soon hear she is better.

The readers of Mr. Jay's Reminiscence of Mr. Wilberforce are now in a situation to judge how far the half-dozen trivial and, several of them, scarcely respectful, notices of Mr. Jay, which we have given from the Life of Wilberforce, do honour or even justice to that long and tender friendship which, as it was unvarying and constant, appears to have been no less sincere and unaffected. If Mr. Wilberforce has preserved no other memorials of his friendship for Mr. Jay than those his sons have published, happily for the memory of the latter *he* has left no one to doubt his sincerity, but has supplied ample proof of his generous and affectionate regard for Mr. Wilberforce.

MRS. HANNAH MORE.

SOME time after the publication of the Life of Mrs. More in four volumes, and which (with a few exceptions) I much approved, I received, being then in London, the following note :—

141, Strand, Monday, March 9.

REVEREND SIR,—In consequence of the communication made here this day by your son, respecting a new Memoir of my late excellent friend Mrs. H. More, I write to say, it will afford me much pleasure in having a conference with you upon the subject.—Will it suit your convenience to call upon me to-morrow between twelve and four? Or shall I call upon you between twelve and three?

Your obedient Servant,

THOS. CADELL.

The interview explained the design. Many persons, he said, had expressed a wish for a memoir of his admired friend, more select and compendious, &c.; and he asked if, knowing her as I did, I would undertake it? I immediately declined, saying, I wanted leisure, and did not deem myself fully adequate to the work; that, with whatever candour I wrote, a tinge of my own principles as a Dissenter would hardly be avoidable; that Mrs. More was an Episcopalian, and a very large majority of her connexions belonged to the Established Church; and that an author of her own community had better be employed, especially for his own profit as the publisher. He said, in reply, that the objection did not weigh with him; but, if I declined, he had an offer from a clergyman, which, as yet, was unanswered, &c. I also intimated that it was probable I should leave behind me a reminiscence of her, along with some others.

The intimation is here imperfectly realized.

With this eminent and excellent woman I was, by the kind providence of God, early and intimately acquainted. When I took up my residence in Bath she had a house in Pulteney-street, in which she passed the winter-half of the year. To this I had a free and welcome access, which was the more inviting, as it afforded an opportunity of frequently meeting with very interesting company, though none was so attractive and engaging as her own.

Mr. Pope has said, "Most women have no character at all." If this be intended to satirize, it fails of its purpose; for, as it is ordained that, in their complete state, light should be without colour, and air without odour, and water without taste, so it is actually the perfection of woman to be characterless. Mrs. More had the proof of true greatness, to be distinguished by nothing extraordinary on ordinary occasions. In her habits she had no little peculiarities, or solecisms, or *wonderfulnesses*. When, therefore, Mr. Hall, returning one day from a visit to her house, was asked by an eager inquirer what he found in Mrs. More remarkable, he answered, "Nothing, ma'am."

She was perfectly free from all direct and indirect attempts at display, so that no one in the company was terrified into silence by a profusion of talent, but each was rather encouraged to speak. Nor, though entitled to take the lead in conversation, did she engross a disproportionate share of the discourse. Yet she spoke with great ease and elegance, and what she delivered was always seasonable, and pertinent, and tending to usefulness. No one could be freer from the common fault of tale-bearing and scandal, or more heedful of the admonition, "Speak evil of no man."

At the period after the French Revolution, when there

was such fierceness of party spirit, both political and ecclesiastical, it was surprising with what address she contrived
to manage and harmonize the different parts of her company;
so that, if they met as foes, they separated as friends.

On one side Mrs. More's parentage was descended from
Nonconformists, but she herself preferred the Establishment; not, however, to the unchurching of other churches,
or the invalidating of the orders of their pastors. For many
years after my settlement in Bath, I never heard of any
clergyman of a decidedly evangelical character officiating in
any of the Established pulpits; so that when Newton, Scott,
Cecil, Foster, and others visited our city, they had access
only to my father-in-law's church at Bath Easton, who held
the same sentiments with themselves. As, therefore, Mrs.
More had begun increasingly to appreciate and relish a certain kind of preaching, as to *doctrine*, she made no scruple
to sacrifice a little of the Episcopalian, and attended *frequently* and *commonly* in Argyle Chapel.

I think I have elsewhere mentioned some hints, which I
received from her as to delivery and composition; but here
I remark one thing only, with regard to preaching. Even
in this more early stage of her religious experience, and
notwithstanding her talents, if she peculiarly noticed a sermon, it was sure to be, not one that betrayed a little ingenuity or originality in the preacher, but one that bore
upon the conscience of the hearer, and was most likely to
awaken and convert the sinner; observing, that preaching
was an instrument, and that the best instrument was that
which answered its end best; adding, "a knife is valued
for its edge, and not for its ebon handle." Thus, even her
praise, like everything else about her, was moral, instructive,
and edifying.

From hence may not some preachers derive a lesson?
When they preach before an individual or two of greater
learning and talent than others, in order to suit and please

them, how often are they tempted to overlook the body of the congregation; and to drop familiar illustrations and striking applications, which would be useful to the common people and the poor! But, first,—are hearers, merely on account of literary or intellectual endowments, deserving of such exclusive, or at least peculiar, reference and regard? And, secondly,—are even such personages always, or commonly, pleased with such (shall I call it?) flattery, or partiality? If they have anything like piety and benevolence, as well as personal distinction, they will always commend a discourse, which is best adapted to benefit the people at large. Such an aim, therefore, has frequently failed of its purpose; and the mistaken preacher has been unprofitable to the many, and not acceptable to the select few. What case is there in which "he who walketh uprightly does *not* walk surely?" And in what does not God honour those that honour him? Perhaps a personal allusion here may hardly be allowable; otherwise I would say that, as I have had more opportunities of addressing such peculiar individuals than some of my brethren, so I was never induced by their presence to alter the manner of my preaching, which I had been led from conviction to adopt; and I never found that I had cause to repent of my consistency.

Besides Mrs. More's attendance on my ministry, she did (oh! tell it not in Gath, publish it not in the streets of Askelon!) she did, one Sabbath (oh! let that day be darkness! let not God regard it from above!) she did—affected by the discourse she had been hearing on the love of Christ, and feeling powerfully inclined to remain, and join with those who were just going to commemorate the death of their common Saviour—she actually did stay, and partake with them.

The offence, it would seem, was not repeated. She, therefore, years after, applied to me, by Mr. H——, for a kind of certificate that she had only received the communion

in Argyle Chapel *once;* saying, that it was not with her for
a moment a question of *right* or *wrong*, but of *truth* or *falsehood;* for the Anti-Jacobin Review and other enemies had
charged her with the thing as her *common* practice; whilst
she, whenever asked, had said it was a *single* deed.

The affair itself excited much animadversion and censure
at the time, and also since. There was also some misrepresentation of the fact itself.   Dr. Valpy, in particular, in his
Reminiscences, has related the account of this *awful* transaction, given him, he says, by Mrs. More herself.   I am
far, very far indeed, from accusing such a man of wilful
mis-statement; but, could I believe in the exactness of the
relation, I should despise, as much as I now respect, the
memory of Mrs. More, whose veracity and honour were un-
impeachable.   The inaccuracy of the *circumstances*, therefore, was doubtless casual; and probably arose, after a
distance of time, from indistinctness in remembering a conversation too trifling, in such an article, to have made a very
deep impression upon so occupied and candid a mind as that
of Dr. Valpy.

The late Rev. J. Owen, Secretary to the British and Foreign
Bible Society, assured me he was once present at the table
of Bishop Porteus, when this affair was mentioned in a way
not very friendly to Mrs. More.   The narrator had enlarged
the thing, and several clergymen present had much censured it; but his Lordship, stripping off the additions, and
stating the case precisely as it took place, and which he
could do, from his intimacy with Mrs. More, said, with a
smile, " This is the front of the offending; but it had been
better, especially for the sake of her friends, not to have
done it."

This, from such a quarter, was rather candid; but he
might have said, as the late Rev. Richard Cecil did, when
hearing of a similar accusation against a good churchman,—
" Have ye not read what David did, when he was an hun-

gred, and they that were with him; how he entered into the
house of God, and did eat the shew-bread, which was not
lawful for him to eat, neither for them which were with him,
but only for the priests?"

And now, what do the spread of such clamours and the
need of such denials and apologies imply? Is it a state of
things which a mind imbued with the spirit of the New
Testament can approve? Are we not only to have our own
convictions, but to forbid everyone else to be fully persuaded in his own mind? Are we not only to *prefer*, but
to *exclude?* While our general practice shows our choice,
are we by no single act to evince our charity? Are we to
behave towards those we believe to be born of God, as if
they were strangers and foreigners, and not our fellow-
citizens, because they live in another street? Or, as not
being of the household of faith, because, as children, they
are not of the same growth; or, as servants, they are not
in the same employment? Shall we resemble John, or
Jesus? John, who said,—"Master, we saw one casting
out devils in thy name; and we forbad him, because he fol-
loweth not with us?" Or Jesus, who said,—"Forbid him
not: for there is no man who shall do a miracle in my name
that can lightly speak evil of me. For he that is not
against us is on our part?"

Two other questions may be asked:—*First;* As all the
present distinctions and differences among Christians will
be done away with hereafter, is an approach to the spirit
and manners of that heavenly state, to be considered an
excellence or a disparagement *now?*

Secondly; If the Lord's Supper were designed, as it obviously was, to unite the followers of Christ, reminding
them, by the participation of the *same* bread and the *same*
cup, that they are all equally partakers of the same symbol-
ized benefits; is it not as strange as it is lamentable, that
this ordinance should ever become the means or occasion of

dividing them; and making them think and feel that they are not one in Christ Jesus? And whence is it that Christians can join in all other acts and exercises of religion, and turn from, and turn against, each other, when required to sit at the same table, and eat and drink in remembrance of Him who died for them and rose again? Oh, let the same mind be in us which was also in Him, who stretched forth his hand towards his disciples, and said, "Behold my mother and my brethren; for *whosoever* shall do the will of my Father, which is in heaven, the *same* is my *brother*, and *sister*, and *mother!*" And must we always be ashamed, and blush to own all that love our Lord Jesus Christ in sincerity, unless we meet them in a particular place, or wearing a particular dress?

Some feel and display a better disposition, and form a noble contrast to many miserably contracted beings. Archbishop Usher having expressed his sense of, what he apprehended, the deficiency of certain churches abroad, in being without *Episcopacy*, adds,—" Yet, for the testifying of my communion with these churches, which I do love and honour as true members of the church universal, I do confess that, with like affection, I could receive the blessed Sacrament at the hand of the Dutch ministers, if I were in Holland, and at the hands of the French ministers, if I were at Charenton."

And the Rev. Baptist Noel, more honourable by his spirit than by his rank, though a clergyman of the church, even pleads for the possibility and propriety of an occasional exchange of services, between the Episcopalians and Dissenters. And would this tend to destroy anything, but what is better abolished than maintained, in our respective departments? This was formerly allowed in the Kirk of Scotland; and was it this that injured or endangered its institutions? The Free Church safely and nobly tolerates and promotes the same practice now; and "as many as walk by this rule, peace be on them, and mercy, and upon the Israel of God."

It is marvellous, but it seems there are those who profess to believe not only the truth, but the importance of evangelical principles, who can wish that Mrs. More, whose talents were to have such an extensive influence over others, should, at the formation of her spiritual character, rather never have heard those evangelical doctrines, than have heard them where she did hear them!

To return from this unintentional digression, which, yet, I found it almost impossible to avoid;—I never knew a person in whom the words of our Lord were more exemplified:—"To him that hath shall be given;" or the promise by the prophet:—"Then shall we know, if we follow on to know the Lord." She always lived up to the light she possessed; and a constant advancement was made in her acquaintance with "the truth as it is in Jesus." Her spiritual progress is perceptible in her successive publications; and this *progressiveness*, rather than more instant maturity, was attended with advantage ; as many of those who were disposed to read *her* works, could not bear everything in the Evangelical system at once. They required "milk, and not strong meat." She, therefore, laid hold of them in this degree of their knowledge, and led them on gradually by her side to the more perfect day. And in *this* view, I have met with some of more sudden and profound attainments in "the deep things of God," who have much underrated the amazing good she certainly accomplished; for her works were bought and read almost without measure.

I communicated by request, as may be seen in the last volume of her Life, a few anecdotes concerning her, to which it would be easy to add more.—Though she did not believe in absolute predestination, and loved the doctrine of universal redemption, she was peculiarly fond of perusing the works of the old Puritan and Nonconformist divines, whose sentiments, in these articles, differed from her own : and when asked how this was, she replied, "I find nothing so good as the lean of their fat." One day, as her letters came in, I saw she broke off the seals and put them into a jar. I was anxious to know why she preserved them. "Ah," said she, "see the ingenuity of poverty; there are those who get a trifle towards their support by melting these into a second-ary kind of wax." Was not this gathering up the fragments, that nothing be lost? She one day wished to inform me of some very improper returns she had met with from an afflicted pauper I had recommended to her beneficence; but she called me away from the company, lest they should hear, saying, "You know we must not speak of these things before persons, for they will make them excuses for their illiberality;" adding, "it is well, perhaps, for us to meet with such instances as these, to let us into a discovery of our motives in giving, and to remind us of our own vileness with regard to God; for what is the ingratitude of the worst of our fellow-creatures towards *us*, compared with our ingratitude towards him?"

I cannot, in fairness to Mrs. More and to myself, but notice what seems a remarkable circumstance. Towards the close of her Memoirs it is said—"Mrs. More's regard for Mr. Jay is well known, and that she frequently attended his ministry, for reasons which she has assigned in her address to her Diocesan, in a former volume." If a person should think it worth while to turn back to this document, they will find *no* reason assigned; or even the name of the preacher mentioned, but only a statement or defence of her true Churchism. What was inserted was correct, but the *explanation* is not found. Is this omission the effect of design? And did it result from a presump-tion that no inquiry would be made; or from an appre-hension that anything she had favourably said to justify or excuse her attendance, might induce others also to offend? I hope, and would believe, that her *reasons* were left out

by mistake and oversight.   However this may be, the whole
of the address to his Lordship, with the addition of some
extenuations of her supposed crime, furnished by her sister,
may be now seen in her Life by the Rev. Mr. Thompson.
This biographer, who has written with ability, knew not
Mrs. More personally, and only came to the church at
Wrington, as she was leaving the neighbourhood, owing to
the conduct of her servants and tradesmen, to reside at
Clifton; and much of his information appears to have been
derived from persons who could have known little of her
earlier connexions and habitudes.   Yet, even with these
partial accounts, Mr. Thompson finds no little difficulty in
bringing her off a spotless *church-woman;* that is, in his
meaning of the term.   There is, therefore, as to many
particulars, much mis-statement.

This was the case also as to the "Blagdon Controversy."
The clergyman of the parish, provoked to become her enemy,
(and the less from any other cause than her evangelism and
zeal, and her not exerting herself to get him preferment,)
endeavoured himself, and prevailed upon others to co-operate
with him, to run her down for irregularity as a member of
the Church, and encouraging sectarian practices.   The case
was this:—Though at length, very much by her influence,
a number of evangelical clergymen surrounded her, and
gladly acted with her, (they were called contemptuously
by her adversaries "*Hannah More's nine-pins,*" in allusion
to their number,) yet it was not so when she began her
efforts in the neighbouring villages; and I have often heard
her confess that what she did *then*, was not only without
clerical countenance and aid, but was opposed by them.
Yet she established schools, and placed over them pious
masters and mistresses, who not only taught the children
to read, but to understand the simple truths of the Gospel.*

---

* She more than once applied to me to recommend such as, she
said, would be called Methodists; adding, "I find none seem to do
my poor children good beside."

They were also accustomed to pray with these children, and to address them occasionally, in plain and familiar language, concerning their souls and their duties. Sometimes, also, a hymn from Watts or Wesley was sung. During these exercises, some of the ignorant rustics would now and then drop in, and listen, and feel a religious concern. When her parochial accuser published these things, with his colourings and enlargements, void of the circumstances of explanation or excuse, some took great alarm, and, eager for her defence, plunged incautiously into the dispute; and, judging only by what they knew of her *then*, they denied things which many living could not but own had been substantially true. She could not come forward to contradict her injudicious friends, and she disdained entering into a conflict with her unworthy foes. In this dilemma her suffering and perplexity were great. Some of the results of this vile persecution led her to change, not her principles, but some of her movements and proceedings. She gave up her residence in Bath, and resigned her *worshipping intercourse* with some of her former connexions; endeavouring by her change of conduct, if possible, to cut off occasion of offence from many who were not only dear to her, but had contributed, and contributed still, largely in furtherance of her charities.

Here persons will differ in their opinions, and not a few have censured her. But she has always stood clear in my own mind. I am fully persuaded she acted conscientiously. She is to be viewed as a very extraordinary character, in a very peculiar situation, as one whose duties must be judged of by circumstances. *She* only perfectly understood her own position; and, after reflection and comparison, she could not but act according to her own convictions. I well remember her saying,—"I throw myself upon the candour of that part of the religious public I as much esteem as ever, to exercise some spiritual self-denial, and which I find to be the most trying of all self-denials." She, therefore, never withdrew her friendship; sent me, as usual, her books when they were published; and at last remembered me in her will.

My own testimony concerning her is,—and I speak advisedly, and from no little acquaintance and observation,—that her piety was equal to her talent, and that her talent was superior even to her fame. Genius is not commonly combined with a strong and hale constitution. Mrs. More often suffered from indisposition; and often composed under aches and pains which would have entirely deterred others from the use of the pen.

Her poetical productions are few compared with her prose, and her renown as a writer will be more derived from the latter than the former. Coleridge has remarked that, though the force of female genius might be supposed to lie chiefly in imagination, yet, into the long standard list of English poets, no female author has been thought worthy of admission, while so many of them have been distinguished as novelists and dramatists ; and he asks—whether this does not prove that other qualities are as necessary to good poetry as what is called imagination? But may we not venture to ask, whether this non-admission of females has in no degree arisen from the empire and jealousy of the Lords of the Creation? Surely, some one of our females deserves a place among the canonized bards, equal to that of *some* of the poetical, privileged males?

By nothing, perhaps, did Mrs. More do more good, or display her talents to more advantage, than by throwing herself into the social feelings and habits of the common people, in the series of tracts she published for their use. I remember being present when she started the proposal. It was at her own house, and at a breakfast-party. The company was large and select.* They were asked by her

* It was on this occasion I first met with the famous John Foster. He was silent all the morning. (The Editors think it not improbable

their opinion of the probable circulation and usefulness of a number of cheap, short, and familiar publications; especially as they might become a substitute for the poor, licentious, and injurious trash found on stalls, and vended by hawkers. When all naturally approved of the scheme, and doubted not of its success, Mrs. More, as a specimen of the sort and quality of the articles intended, produced "The Shepherd of Salisbury Plain," which she had composed for the purpose. I was called upon to read it. This I did, not without difficulty, being affected to tears with some of its exquisite touches. This probably was not unpleasant to the writer; but all were delighted with the simple and beautiful, fictitious tale. I say "fictitious," for it was not, as often supposed, founded in fact.* A multitude of these tracts soon followed.

that it was to this meeting Mr. Foster alluded in one of his letters to Dr. Fawcett, dated Bristol, Oct. 15, 1791. " Life and Correspondence of John Foster."—Vol. i. p. 16.) "A few days since, in company with Mr. Hughes, I spent a day with Miss Hannah More. She, with four other sisters, all unmarried, resides at the distance of about ten miles from the city. They are all very sensible and agreeable, but she is quite interesting. She was familiarly acquainted with *Johnson*, and many other distinguished persons who are dead, and is equally well known to most of the geniuses of the present day. Perhaps her poetical abilities, though acknowledged very great, form one of the least of her excellences. If piety and beneficence can give lustre to a character, hers is transcendant. She lives in a kind of retirement, little noticed, except by her distant friends; and, in conjunction with her sisters, whose minds are congenial with her own, employs most of her time in benevolent undertakings, in visiting the poor, furnishing them with necessaries, and procuring instruction for their ignorant children, at the very time that she could figure among poetesses and peeresses. Some of her undertakings, in the design, conduct, difficulties, and success, are so very remarkable, and discover such evident interpositions of Divine Providence, that they almost assume the air of romance. If I ever saw the spirit of the Redeemer and his religion realized, it is in her conversation and character. I expect the pleasure of visiting her to be pretty often repeated."

* There is good reason to doubt the correctness of this statement.

I need not mention that many of them were not of *her* composition. Several of them were written by her sisters, Sally and Patty, and more by other friendly helpers; and though none of them can compete with her own, they were all valuable and useful.*

Did this lead, by example and reflection, to the establishment, in London, of "The Tract Society," which has become so vast and useful an institution?

Mr. Jay was probably not aware, or had forgotten, that several authorities had stated in print, that the tract in question was founded on fact; and that the original had been clearly traced in the history of David Saunders, of West Lavington, Wilts. In the Evangelical Magazine for 1805 (Supplement), it is said,—"David Saunders, the Shepherd of Salisbury Plain, being the undoubted subject of the beautiful tract which, some years since, issued from the ingenious pen of Miss Hannah More, under this title."

* * * *

"Miss More's admirable tract, before referred to, contains a just delineation of this extraordinary person; and though for many of the incidents we are doubtless indebted to her elegant and inventive pen, the reader will peruse it with new interest, when he finds the outlines to be faithful, and the conversations recited in perfect harmony with the real character of the man; for though 'simple and unlearned,' as the world would call him, he possessed uncommon natural abilities; and what is far better, was endued with a large portion of that 'wisdom which is from above, pure and peaceable.'"

There is also an admirable letter in the same magazine for the year 1803, p. 475, from the pen of the Shepherd himself; and also an extract from a London newspaper of September 15, 1796, as follows:—"Last week died at Wyke, between Bath and Bristol, in the seventieth year of his age, David Saunders, of West Lavington, Wilts, whose distinguished piety and moral excellence furnished Miss H. More with materials for her much admired story of 'The Shepherd of Salisbury Plain.'"

See also "Letters from the Rev. Job Orton and Sir J. Stonhouse to the Rev. T. Steadman."—Vol. i. p. 22.

* Among the private papers of Mrs. More, was found an interesting record which she made on the completion of this series of useful publications:—"Bless the Lord, O my soul, that I have been spared to accomplish this work! Do thou, O Lord, bless and prosper it to

In these compositions, and some larger publications of a similar kind, Mrs. More has been charged with partiality; and there is some ground for it. In her sketches of good and evil characters, the excellences are almost always exemplified in members of her own Church, while defects and improprieties are found in the adherents to Methodism and Dissent. Her reading, her personal acquaintances, her judgment, her candour, should have prevented this. There is no perfection on this side heaven.

Mr. Hill, in his " Village Dialogues," is thought by some to have erred in the other extreme, especially in his clerical bad examples; though it should be remembered how much many of the reverends *then* differed from the same class *now.* Do not all parties need a voice behind them, saying, " This is the way, walk ye in it,"—when they turn to the right hand, or when they turn to the left ?

I sometimes met at Mrs. More's house and table the celebrated Alexander Knox, who has more than noticed me as a preacher in one of his letters to Bishop Jebb. I remember well his once specially introducing his views of Justification; when Mrs. More, though less enlightened then than afterwards, made no scruple to express her dissent, and alleged several scriptures with great propriety. If he did not believe in baptismal regeneration, he talked very ambiguously upon it. Indeed, from my personal intercourse, and my subsequent perusal of his letters and papers, I have thought he helped to prepare the way for Puseyism.

At Mrs. More's, too, I also repeatedly met Sir James Stonhouse. He was formerly a physician of note at Northampton. At that time he was a hearer, and the intimate

the good of many; and, if it do good, may I give to thee the glory, and take to myself the shame of its defects. I have devoted three years to this work. Two millions of these tracts were disposed of during the first year. God works by weak instruments, to show that the glory is all His own."

friend, of Dr. Doddridge, in speaking of whom I recollect
his observing the amazing affluence and readiness of his
mind. " We sometimes," said he, " for a little excursion
and recreation, left home together, for a week or a fortnight; and, after exploring the sceneries and curiosities of
places in the course of the day, he frequently preached in
some meeting in the evening to a crowded assembly, without
time for retirement, without notes, without fatigue; with
an ease, an order, an accuracy, and a fervour, truly astonishing."—Yet he professed to prefer Orton to Doddridge as
a sermonizer, and indeed, to every other English divine! I
believe he nearly coalesced with him in sentiment.

Rather late in life, he left his professional engagements,
and entered the Establishment, and became vicar of Che-
veril, in Wiltshire; where the Rev. Mr. Steadman was his
curate, to whom, by his desire, Orton addressed a small
volume of letters, which were afterwards published, and
which are well worthy the attention of every young minister.

I first became acquainted with him while residing at
Clifton, and when serving Lady Maxwell at Hope Chapel.
He lived in ———— Row, and occasionally preached in
a chapel-of-ease in ———— Square, where he was much
followed. His access to this pulpit he assigned as the
reason why he could never appear in the place I occupied;
as prejudice might deprive him of much opportunity for
usefulness, though he paid for the sitting of his servant
and his daughter, Mrs. Vigo, who attended my ministry.
When he first came to Bath he was very schismatical himself; for I believe he always attended in our conventicle.
But religion lives, and moves, and has its being, in various
degrees. He was a good man, with too little spirituality,
and too keen an appetite for human praise; therefore Mr.
Hervey, whom he attended as a physician, said to him,
when dying, " Dr. Stonhouse, beware of the world! beware
of the world! beware of the world!" His sentiments were

the *skim-milk* of the Gospel; but he must be classed as belonging to the Evangelical Clergy, though very near the border that separates them from others.

As an author, he wrote only a few small, useful tracts for the afflicted and dying; but, as a preacher, he was famed for his eloquence, and still more for the admirable manner in which he read the prayers; in which, he said, he had availed himself of the dictation of Garrick. He was a very sensible and accomplished man, yet noted for excessive egotism, but for which he would have been a more delightful and edifying companion.

I may, perhaps, be hardly excused for introducing the following letter, the last I ever received from Mrs. More; but it pleasingly displays traits of her more private character, and affords another proof of her kind and constant friendship :—

My DEAR SIR,—I know not how to express the gratitude I feel for the very excellent works you have had the goodness to bestow upon me. To feel deeply their inestimable value, and to offer my fervent prayers to the Almighty Giver of every good gift, are all I *can* do. May he enlighten and strengthen me more and more by the constant perusal. Your last bounty, the new edition of your Prayers, with the valuable additions, is a great additional treasure. We fell upon it with a keen appetite this morning, and I hope I shall be the better for it as long as I live.

My truly pious friend, Mr. Elven, who is my chief spiritual visitor, said, when I showed him your volumes, "Mr. Jay has more ideas than any man I ever knew." I could not prevail on myself to keep this remark from you. I thought my hard necessity to leave Barley Wood was a great trial, but it has pleased my gracious God to overrule it to my great comfort and benefit. I was there almost destitute of all spiritual advantages ; here I find four ministers of great piety, who are much attached to me, and who supply my want of public attendance at church.

It was a very agreeable surprise to me to see your good lady; and I was grieved that the largeness of the party (almost all strangers,) prevented my attention to her, which was so justly her due. I beg to offer my most kind regards to her.

I hope you will have the goodness to remember me at the Throne
of Grace; no one stands more in need of your prayers than, my
dear Sir,

Your very faithful

And highly obliged

Friend and Servant,

Clifton.—Saturday, 1829.   HANNAH MORE.

The following lines have never yet appeared in print.
They were addressed by Mrs. More to the celebrated and
pious Miss Steele, of Broughton, Hampshire, during her
visit; and after they had walked to Danebury Hill, an
ancient camp, near which, according to tradition, a battle
had been fought between the Saxons and the Danes. Miss
Steele having written a poem entitled "Danebury," Mrs.
More gathered there a sprig of juniper, for which she thus
apologized :—

> Sylvia, forgive thy daring friend,
>   And do not take it ill,
> If her presuming hand has plucked
>   A wreath from Danebury Hill.
>
> Yet, though I much admire the gifts
>   Thy genius can impart,
> Far rather, Sylvia, would I steal
>   One virtue from thy heart.
>
> And who, fair Sylvia, do you think,
>   Would blame the moral theft ?
> One Virtue you would scarcely miss,
>   You'd have so many left !

At the time when Mrs. More was so cruelly persecuted
by the Rev. Mr. B——n, and the Rev. Mr. S——n, and
Mr. E——ds, (not to mention others,) Peter Pindar was in
his popularity; he also insinuated his unprovoked slanders
and ridicule, and endeavoured to rob her of her fame as an
author; upon the reading of which a member of my church
wrote the following severe and deserved address, and published it in the papers :—

TO PETER PINDAR, ESQ., ON READING HIS "NIL ADMIRARI," ETC.

This is not candid in thee, Peter Pindar;
　　'Tis a fresh blot upon thy dubious name,
To envy that applause thou canst not hinder,
　　And blast a woman's literary fame.

'Tis very contradictious in thee, Peter!
　　It looks unmanly, and betrays thy spleen,
To insult a female, and with scorn to treat her!
　　It blunts the edge of satire, else so keen.

' *More* has no genius,' Peter says; moreover,
　　' She has no claim to merit, not the least!'
Yet in her style improved, thou canst discover,
　　She must have been assisted by a priest.

If mental powers which Garrick could admire,—
　　If talents that command a Porteus' praise,
May without arrogance to fame aspire,
　　Her claim is good, whatever Peter says.

Thy judgment, Peter, comes, I guess, too late;
　　Its prompt applause a virtuous public gave her;
Nor will thy wicked wit reverse her fate,
　　Or cancel that decision in her favour.

But, let the public as it may decide,
　　There is a dread tribunal, Peter,—hear—
Where thou, and all thy actions, shall be tried,
　　And what thy doom will be I greatly fear.

Believe me, Peter, all thy ridicule
　　Will turn to very poor account at best;
Thou hast for many years but played the fool,
　　And prostituted genius to a jest.

That man's a simpleton who flings away
　　The precious grain, and only hoards the chaff;
And he's no better, flout it as he may,
　　Who squanders his whole life to raise a laugh.

Try to repair the past; reform thy plan;
　　Conscience will tell thee thou hast acted wrong;
Assume the moral dignity of man,
　　And give to virtue all thy powers of song.

Bath, Nov. 7, 1799.　　　　　　　　　　　AKYBSTON.

REV. ROWLAND HILL, A.M.

"Grant some of knowledge greater store,
    More learned some in teaching ;
    Yet few in life did lighten more,
    Or thunder more in preaching."

WHEN I preached the funeral sermon for this very singular, but excellent and useful man, immediately after the
service, Lord Hill, to whom I dedicated the sermon, several
ministers of different denominations, and some of the trus-
tees and managers of Surrey Chapel, came into the house,
and intimated that I should be expected to write a memoir
of the deceased. Some of them, I found, had taken it for
granted that I had long been preparing for such a work,
and that I had many materials by me for the purpose. I
assured them the thought had never entered into my mind;
but they pressed it upon me, on the ground that I had
been connected with him so long, and knew more of him
than any other surviving minister. I was then (and it had
affected me in the preaching,) suffering under the *influenza*,
and everything appeared trying ; and I could not be unconscious of the difficulty of doing justice to so peculiar a
character, and of giving satisfaction to many of his admirers. I, therefore, came under no other engagement
than to consider the proposal. This I did on my return
home ; and, as the formidableness of the affair lessened,
and I knew that I was not *wholly* or *comparatively* un-
qualified for the performance, I yielded, and had even
written a few pages, when I received a letter from the Rev.

Mr. Sidney, informing me that Mrs. Hill, the evening
before her death, had urged him, and that Mr. Hill by will
had appointed him, to be his biographer. I was thus, and
not ungladly, relieved from the arduous task. Mr. Sidney
soon fulfilled his appointment; and, after *his* publication,
Mr. Jones, of the Tract Society, also sent forth another
Life. I was pleased with both these works, the latter of
which had the most of specific delineation; yet the public,
never very easily satisfied, seemed to think there was
wanting more individuality. There can, indeed, be no
character without individuality; but it should have been
considered that a writer, in *this instance*, could not go all
lengths, or enter into all the *particularizations* which the
subject would supply, without offence. There is an idiosyn-
crasy in mind as well as body; and, if the one tries physical,
so does the other moral, anatomy. There are persons
uniquely framed and disposed, called, by a distinguished
author, "unclassed anomalies," and who constitute the
corps particulier of exceptions to general rules.

Mr. Hill's life would be written at some distance of time
from his death better than near it, as in the mean time
some *innocent* peculiarities and facetiousnesses, which many
observers might deem exceptionable in a sacred character,
would wane away, or strike less; whilst his great excellences and usefulness would remain, and be more prominent
and distinct.

It may not be amiss to mention two mistakes, or inadver-
tencies, which have crept into these valuable pieces of
biography. The one regards Mr. Hill's *ecclesiastics*. He
much disliked strict Independency; but he could not be
considered properly as an Episcopalian, in the common or
prelatical acceptation of the term. He might not, with
many others, have objected to such a bishop as Usher's
primus inter pares, having nothing to do with secular affairs,
appointed by the State, chosen by his brethren for his age,

talent, and piety, and residing in the midst of his diocese; and he did at first *submit* to the state of things in the Establishment, as they are, *partially*—I say *partially*, for he only received deacon's orders, not accepting those of priest, on the condition alone by which he could obtain them, viz., *regularity;* and so, as his drollery expressed it, *he ran off with only one boot on:*—nor was he an enemy to some state-provision for the instruction of the people. But from conviction he preferred Presbyterianism. I cannot be mistaken here, from my intimacy and conversations with him on the very subject. At my last interview with him, a very few weeks only before his death, he unexpectedly said, "Ah, Mr. Jay, Presbyterianism comes much nearer the original and Scriptural model than your Independency or our Episcopacy;" and, stroking his face in his usual way, added, "You *know* this was *always* my sentiment." The last time he preached in Bath, he spent the evening with a large party, before whom he explicitly made the same acknowledgment. It was hence he so much liked the Welsh Calvinistic Methodists, as their plans and measures (though not in name) approximated to the system he *most* approved.

The other piece of misinformation regards his intimacy with Mr. Whitfield. This is everywhere admitted, as if it were a generally known fact. But when and where did any personal intercourse take place between them? The truth is, though Mr. W. wrote a letter to Mr. Hill, encouraging him to continue his field-preaching, yet they never met; and I have often heard Mrs. Hill affirm, how mistaken many persons were, for that her husband had never *heard* or *seen* Mr. Whitfield. Neither of these things is of much importance, but it is better that each of them should appear as it really was.

My long acquaintance with this noted man commenced when I was yet a student at Marlborough. Before I left, or ought to have left, the Academy, he engaged me to go to supply Surrey Chapel for eight weeks. I did this with the approbation of my tutor; and, as I proved acceptable, Mr. Hill much wished me to enter immediately into an entire connexion with him, dividing my labours between London and Wotton-under-Edge, and Haverfordwest, and several other places, which were then more or less under his management and control. This I was induced to decline; but, as he seemed disappointed and rather displeased at my refusal, I promised, if he desired it, to occupy his pulpit in town for eight Sabbaths annually. This was done rather thoughtlessly; as, after I became a pastor, I found the time too long to be absent at once from the people of my charge; yet, for nearly forty years, I did this; after which I was constrained to reduce my visit to six Sabbaths, and then to four, and then to three; and, upon Mr. Hill's death, with whom my engagement was originally made, I entirely gave up the connexion, wishing also to afford more of my extra services to the demands of country applications, as well as to secure, if possible, a little relaxation and leisure in the season, at the sea-side; after the maxim—

> *" Juniores ad labores,*
> *Solve senectutem."*

Mr. Hill not only built the large Surrey Chapel, where so many souls have been brought to the knowledge of the truth, and such large sums raised in the cause of God and the poor, and where there is even now a vast congregation and church prospering under the ministry of the Rev. Mr. Sherman;* but also a large tabernacle at Wotton-under-Edge, where God, amidst much opposition at first, had peculiarly blessed his preaching. Here several individuals of respectability were converted, and a numerous church was formed, distinguished by much spirituality and zeal,

---

* Mr. Sherman has recently resigned the charge of the congregation at Surrey Chapel, and been succeeded by the Rev. Newman Hall.

and which is now in a more thriving condition than ever, under the care of the Rev. Mr. Knill.* Adjoining the tabernacle, Mr. Hill built also a dwelling-house, in which he resided the summer-half of the year. But during this season his labours were not confined to Wotton, but frequently extended to various other places in England and Wales.

My friend and tutor, Cornelius Winter, was acquainted with him years before I had seen him, and from his lips I have derived many anecdotes, especially concerning his earlier history; one of which, as I frequently heard him mention it, I will undeviatingly relate. Mr. Winter was labouring in Bristol when Mr. Hill first came there. He preached much out of doors; and, as he was young, and a gentleman's son, and betrayed no little wit and humour, which seemed natural to him, he awakened great attention, and crowds followed him. Mr. Winter much ministered unto him, reminding him of his engagements, and attending him in his movements. In another way he was serviceable to him. As he wished to go preaching from place to place, a horse became necessary; and Mr. Winter collected the money that bought one, which, when it was presented to him, and he would know whence it came, he naturally at first declined it, saying, he could not think of being under obligation to persons who could not afford it; but Mr. Winter assured him that no one would suffer by so trifling a sacrifice; and that all would feel themselves honoured by his acceptance of it for the service of Christ, and the expense was not great, for it was a poor kind of *Rosinante*. But for a while it bore this man of God about in those neighbourhoods. Mr. Winter also more than once obtained

---

* Mr. Knill has, since Mr. Jay wrote, removed to Chester, and been succeeded at Wotton-under-Edge by the Rev. J. T. Feaston, during whose residence the Tabernacle has been rebuilt, and the cause greatly prospered.

for him a little pecuniary supply for his present wants.
For at this time he had straits; and was it not to his
honour that he *subjected* himself to these, not by vice, but
in order to do good to his perishing fellow-creatures, and
when he might have been enjoying every kind of indulgence
at home? For his offended father withheld for a season all
support; and, to bring him back from his wild wanderings,
his brother (afterwards Sir Richard Hill) was sent to
Bristol. But, lo and behold! when he came, and had seen
the grace of God, he was so struck with young Rowland's
spirit and usefulness, that he not only omitted the design of
his mission, but Saul also was amongst the prophets, and he
actually began preaching himself; and I have known many
who heard him hold forth in his usual coloured dress. How
often have I seen cottages and chambers in which this
minister of God has been satisfied to eat and sleep, which
some, not born gentlemen, would be very unwilling to put
up with!

As Mr. Hill was an educated man, so his talents were
very superior to what many may imagine. He had an uncommon quickness of apprehension, which will account for
the great fund of general knowledge which he possessed;
though he never seemed to study anything, or to read any
book attentively through,—yet there was no subject upon
which he seemed unable to speak; though in discourse he
could never be kept long to any one point. His sentiments
were Calvinistic, but his Calvinism never ran to seed. He
was not so high in doctrine as his brother, Sir Richard; nor
so low as his brother, the Rev. Bryan Hill. He was not
afraid to address sinners; and when, in a particular place,
as he was leaving the vestry to go into the pulpit, one
officiously hinted to him, that they preached *there* only to
the elect: " Well," said he, " so will I, if you 'll go and set
a mark upon them."

There was nothing he was so anxious to prevent as the

abuse of Gospel-grace. Who has not witnessed his abhorrence of Antinomianism? In later years, indeed, he was led to notice its adherents too often and too much; for they were unworthy of his attention; and as they were sure from prejudice not to hear him, it was trying for others to suffer on their account. Never did a minister more deserve the character of a Gospel-preacher. Without being censorious, a hearer would sometimes be perplexed to characterize some men's pulpit performances. James the First, on hearing a discourse in which the preacher had said much of politics, turned to Bishop Andrews, and said, "My lord, is this to be considered a sermon or not?" To which he replied, "May it please your Majesty, it may pass for one by a very charitable construction." And Louis XVI. is reported, after hearing one of his chaplains, to have said, "This preacher would have left nothing out of his sermon, if he had happened to touch upon religion."

But no candour or allowance was necessary in judging of Mr. Hill's discourses. There was not one of them but more than touched upon the sole theme of the Apostle's ministry, "Jesus Christ and him crucified,"—"the Lord our righteousness and strength;" whatever his subject was, it was sure, before its close, to exhale forth something of the "savour of the Redeemer's knowledge."

As Mr. Hill is not to be tried by ordinary rules, and as he is not likely to become a precedent or example, (for who ever again is likely to be *constituted* or *circumstanced* like him?) we may the more freely speak of his character and ministry.

He has, in his own odd way, in one of his dialogues, spoken of three kinds of preachers, the *tap-cask*, the *slop-dash*, and the *slap-dash*. By the first he means preachers distinguished by tame and correct feebleness; without faults, but also destitute of all energy of thought or force of expression,—as Shakespeare would say, fit to "chronicle small beer." By the second, he means preachers marked by strong things in doctrine, but loose, and hazardous, and extravagant in representation ; aiming at great effect by the noise of manner and the conceits of folly. But by the third, the *slap-dashers*, he meant preachers whose addresses were attended by an inartificial and often abrupt manner ; with sudden and bold allusions, and stirring anecdotes ; and rough and homely familiarities of expression, and flashes of imagination and passion ; preachers who, despising formality, and aiming at impressiveness, if not, sometimes, offending taste alarmingly, yet keep within the bounds of truth and *general* propriety. This third species, as differing from the two former, was the kind of preaching which Mr. Hill intended to recommend and to practise. Let us see how far he exemplified it.

And here, while we would not plead for anything improper, by whatever authority it has been sanctioned; so neither shall we censure anything against which mere fastidiousness, or affectation, or prejudice, may object. There may be a negligence of style which betrays a nobleness of mind,—a mind too much impressed with things to be at liberty to attend to the nicety and order of words ; though here another extreme is to be avoided, and plainness of dress is not to let in the disgust of slatternliness.

The goodness (we speak now only of the goodness of their composition,) of public discourses, depends much upon their adaptation to the audience addressed, and the aim the speaker has in view. Mr. Hill always wished to be considered the apostle of the common people, in resemblance of Him whom the common people heard gladly, and in whose teaching "the poor had the Gospel preached unto them." But he who undertakes *this* work of faith and labour of love, will find that he has not to address angels, or, sometimes, hardly—men. He will need to learn the advice which Isocrates was wont to give his pupils,—" Study the

people;" or that which Cromwell gave to his soldiers,—
"Fire low." Had his men fired high, they would have done
no more execution than some of our preachers who shoot
over their hearers' heads.

The eloquence of the pulpit cannot be, in the nature of
things, philosophical; but is it rhetorical? The feelings
are always eloquent; but they cannot be learned in the
schools. "Rhetoric," says Coleridge, "is the creature of
art, which he who *feels* less will most excel in. It is the
quackery of eloquence, abounding with specious, but *mere*
pretensions. Eloquence was ruined after it began to be
taught by sophists and grammarians in the schools." If the
wish and aim of a preacher should be mere eloquence, he
would do well to remember the observation of Mr. Hall:—
" A consummate orator is a character which we despair of
ever seeing perfectly associated with that of a Christian
teacher. The minister of the Gospel is called to declare
the testimony of God, which is always weakened by a pro-
fuse employment of the ornaments of secular eloquence.
The imagination is too much excited and employed by those
exquisite paintings and nice touches of art, not to interfere
with the awful functions of conscience:—the hearer is
absorbed in admiration, and the exercise, which ought to be
the instrument of conviction, becomes a feast of taste. It
is a strong objection to a studied attempt at oratory in the
pulpit, that it naturally induces a neglect of the peculiar
doctrines of the Gospel, where the preacher feels himself
restrained; and is under the necessity of explaining texts,
of obviating objections, and elucidating difficulties, which
limits the excursions of imagination; and not only confines,
but breaks his fine expatiatings in the flowery field of
declamation."

Hume observes, that the speaker who most powerfully
affects the mass of an audience, ought to be considered the
greatest orator. And Dr. Campbell says,—"We readily

admit, and zealously contend, that nothing can be more opposite to a just notion of eloquence, than a rule to exclude familiar and very humble objects and topics from all intervention in the illustration of great subjects." Under the direction of genius, very common and even mean matters may be conjured up into marvellous appositeness and dignified services.

To return:—These remarks are not impertinent. They will prepare us to go forward, and will serve in a measure to explain, and in a degree to defend, the preacher before us.

Mr. Hill was not, as many think, who have only heard of him by report—that lying tale-bearer, a mere boisterous bawler. He was sometimes loud, and occasionally even vehement; but in common his voice only rose with his subject; and it was easy to perceive that it was commonly influenced and regulated by his thoughts and feelings. He was not like those who strain and roar *always*, and *equally*, having no more energy or emphasis for one thing than another. As the parts of a subject must vary, some being more tender, some more awful, some more plain, and some more abstruse, a uniformity of vehemence must be unnatural; it is obviously mechanical; and will, after a while, have only a kind of automaton effect.

Mr. Hill had an assistant that erred this way, and I remember how he one day reproved him. " J——," said he, " you yelp like a puppy as soon as you get into the field; but I am an older hound, and do not wish to cry till I have started something."

As many things said of him were entirely false, so, some that were true were much enlarged and aggravated. But he had many freedoms in the pulpit, which could not be entirely justified. These were commonly the effects of his engaging with little or no premeditative preparation. He never wrote anything like an outline, or even seemed to

have attempted to methodize his thoughts.   Three things
have often made me wonder at his continual neglect of this:
—*First*,—That it arose not from inability.   He *could* think,
and think consecutively and orderly; as appears from his
Dialogues,—a species of writing in which he excelled, and
which requires no small degree of reflection, forecast, and
comparison.   *Secondly*,—That he was not urged to more
previous arrangement and readiness, from his suffering so
much, which I know he occasionally, if not frequently, *did*,
from his embarrassments in his work, and his uneasiness
after it was over.   And, *Thirdly*,—That his piety did not
constrain him, by reflecting what a talent was given him, in
having the care of a thousand people committed to him ;
and what a duty it was to use it to the best possible
advantage.

His text seldom much confined him.   I heard his brother,
Sir Richard, complaining of this, and making this just remark,—" When a man gives out a text, he raises my expectation to hear *that* text explained and improved; and I feel
disappointed, though I hear as good, or better things, from
any other words."

Yet, though I think a method, in a way of divisions, (not
multiplied,) is a great aid to the preacher and the hearer,
the meaning of a text may be substantially treated without
it; and Mr. Hill would sometimes, by a few bold thoughts,
strike out most powerfully the spirit of a passage.   The
most original and brilliant sentiments I ever heard him
deliver, escaped from him in his loosest harangues, and
when his mind was void of all sense of effort.   Indeed, when
a preacher who extemporizes much is in a good frame of
mind, and thought flows freely and easily, he will feel more
fresh and lively than one who has anticipated and fami-
liarized his subject by premeditation; but, at other times,
having nothing to support him, or to start from, he is per-

plexed by effort, or reduced to very common-place.   So true
it is, as Lord Brougham says, that "he who studies, and is
most prepared, always extemporizes best."

I have observed that, while divisions of the subject were
to others only as the banks of a river, which do not hinder,
but guide and accelerate the stream; all Mr. Hill's attempts
at arrangement, if he had made any, would have been like
throwing something across the current, which impeded and
made it run astray.

He was in danger from another quarter.   *Wit*, it has
been said, is a quality which more instantly and irresistibly
pleases and captivates than any other attribute of a speaker.
We need not wonder, therefore, if the possessor of this
endowment should be tempted to use it unduly and un-
seasonably.   How hard must it have been for Mr. Hill to
leave his humour behind him when he entered the pulpit!
This was, indeed, overruled for good; and the expectation
of hearing something droll and witty drew many to hear
him, who, though they came to laugh, returned to pray.
But Mr. Hill himself was not unconscious of the danger
here.   In his sermon on the death of the Rev. Mr. Roquet,
of Bristol, he says,—" Amid all these amiable endowments,
is it to be wondered at if one hears a distant hint, as if now
and then my dear loved friend might have been supposed to
have made somewhat of a small elopement from that cheerfulness which is truly Christian towards a disposition too
nearly bordering upon a turn of pleasantry, which might
have needed a little more of the spirit of solemnity?   With
the greatest delicacy I mention this hint, and am glad to
cover it with the mantle of love, *by lamenting before you all
the same weakness.   A lively, active disposition is too apt to
lead into this mistake.   In many things we offend, and it is of
the Lord's mercies that we are not consumed.*"

A man should never dive who cannot swim.   Mr. Hill
could come up again; and we have often seen the smile

which he excited soon followed by the dropping tear. Yet these outbreaks of wit and humour sometimes gave offence, and caused his good to be evil spoken of; and it must be owned that his ideas, like rich clusters of grapes, sometimes, for want of proper support, fell down and were soiled upon the ground. But, though you could not tie the wings or guide the flight of the eagle in his preaching, it was otherwise with his prayers. There was nothing eccentric, nothing of levity there. They were even singularly solemn, serious, and devotional; and they had also two other good qualities. They were always *short*, and also free from the introduction of *very particular cases*, which endangers devotion by awakening curiosity, and embarrasses the preacher by the difficulty of properly wording them.

I do not think with some that *candour* was one of Mr. Hill's greatest qualities. Among his own immediate connexions, he expected implicit submission, and his will was law. Of other parties, who differed from him, he could speak freely.* He did not always distinguish between

---

* He was commonly not very candid or courteous towards our Baptist friends, and would use severe, if not insulting sayings, when he administered the ordinance of infant-baptism. One evening he preached at our Association at Bath. On these occasions our brethren of all denominations mingle. His sermon was not only very loose and unconnected, but irritating and reflective towards the Baptists, many of whom were present; so that their minister, Mr. P——, instantly left the place, and never could be prevailed upon to hear him again. The case was, he had come down from Chippenham in the afternoon, where they had told him of the indiscretions and bad influence of some not very well accredited Baptist preacher. This prepossessed his mind; he could think of nothing else, and for the time speak of nothing else. And this leads me to observe how much depended always, as to his preaching, upon the company and conversation of the persons he immediately left to go into the pulpit. These would commonly give a turn or a tincture to the sermon. His wisest and best friends knew this, and would be concerned to bring forward nothing but what would rather aid

bigotry and regularity, nor consider that persons were not to be run down as illiberal, because they acted conscientiously, and did not feel themselves at liberty to tread in all his steps. Johnson surprised some, when he was in Scotland, by calling a man who seemed to lay stress upon nothing, "a bigot to laxness."

But too much cannot be said of his Benevolence and Beneficence. Tenderness and kindness seemed inherent in his very nature ; and they were nourished and strengthened by the spirit of the religion which he so eminently possessed. He did good to his beast, and his feeling for the brutes sometimes showed itself in ways which many would be almost ready to ridicule; but it bespoke the sensibility of his disposition.* And not only did the enthusiast and fanatic, (as some supposed him to be,) regard the souls of men, but their bodies and outward estate. Hence his frequent collections for the poor, and his visiting their lowly sheds, and teaching them arts and habits of economy. Hence he built tenements for the indigent at Wotton, and almshouses for widows in London. Hence he even learned vaccination, and always carried lymph with him, and performed upon hundreds, if not thousands, in the towns and villages he visited in preaching.

"I have seen an end of all perfection ; " and my friend had failings. The greatest of these I ever observed in him was an extremely quick sense of any injury or offence, and allowing it to *linger* about his spirit. The offence, too, was sometimes supposed, rather than real ; or credited on the evidence of some tattler, or busybody, who too often beset

---

than injure him. Upon this principle, he always preached best of a Sunday morning, when the bloom was not rubbed off from the plum, and he only left the company of Prophets and Apostles.

* Thus he had what he called a *Frogery* and *Toadery* at the bottom of his orchard, where he said these poor creatures could marry and be given in marriage, and live an unpersecuted and merry life.

him, and was not sufficiently frowned off. His high regard for moral consistency would be enough to make one impropriety or indiscretion undo much of an opposite quality; and where there was anything actually peccable in the character of a professor, or especially of a minister, the spirituality and purity of his mind would render it more intolerable to him than it would be to many men.

With too little discrimination many of his striking sayings and allusions have been published. If I were required to add to them, I should not repeat many of his homespun, familiar, lowly, and very simple images and illustrations; but only try to distinguish the flowers he gathered off the bank from those which he occasionally drew from the ditch. Yet here, it is very probable, I should be too fastidious for some, and admit and admire too much for others.—In one of his sermons he was speaking of the value of the Gospel from its *relative* aim and influence.—"It makes," says he, "husbands better husbands, and wives better wives; parents better parents, children better children; masters better masters, and servants better servants; in a word, I would not give a farthing for that man's religion whose cat and dog were not the better for it." Every one could not have uttered this, but I received it from no less a person than Mr. Wilberforce, who heard it himself; and who remarked that, while probably everything else he said that evening was long ago forgotten, no one would ever forget this.

Not very long before his death, meeting an acquaintance who was nearly as aged as himself, he said, "If you and I don't march off soon, our friends yonder," (looking upwards) "will think we have lost our way."

Reading in my pulpit the words of the woman of Samaria at the well, "the Jews have no dealings with the Samaritans,"—looking off, as if he saw the parties themselves, he exclaimed, "But the devil has had dealings enough with both of you."

He one day said, " When I was in Scotland I found
many parties, all very clever and zealous in defending their
own tenets, and distinguishing between their *Sibboleths* and
Shibboleths. There were the Lifters and the anti-Lifters.
These were divided by the action of the minister in the
sacramental elements,—viz., whether, in the consecration
of them at the table, he should lift them up or not. One
of their pastors was ordained by imposition of hands; but
one of the elders could not reach *his* hand far enough to
impose it on the head of the candidate, and so he put along
his cane,—' This,' says he, ' did equally well; it was timber to timber.' "

I never thought Mr. Hill particularly happy in the introduction of many of his anecdotes. As far as wit,
humour, or drollery, was concerned, he invariably succeeded; but sometimes his anecdotes were abruptly brought
in, in consequence of the failure of subject-matter to go on
with; and Mr. Hill's voice, though good and strong, was
not versatile and pathetic, so as to make the circumstance
of the incident to "touch and tell." Herein he was inferior to Whitfield. Though he had more stoutness, and
firmness, and independence of mind than Whitfield, he had
not the same softness and sensibility: while Whitfield's
voice was incomparable, not only distinct and loud, but
abounding with every kind of inflection, and perfectly
under the power of the owner; so that he could render
everything he expressed, however common or insignificant
in itself, striking and affecting. How many proofs and
instances of this did I receive from my friend and tutor,
Mr. Winter, who related them from his own observation
and hearing! I lament I did not receive more of them
from his mouth. At this moment I remember two of them,
which, as specimens, I will exactly relate.

On going to preach at Bristol Tabernacle, he began his

series of sermons on the eve of Bristol fair. His text was
Isaiah lv. 1, "Ho, every one that thirsteth, come ye to the
waters, and he that hath no money; come ye, buy and eat ;
yea, come, buy wine and milk without money and without
price." The congregation was large. Thus he began:—
"My dear hearers, I guess many of you are come to attend
Bristol fair. So am I. You do not mean to show your
goods until to-morrow; but I shall exhibit mine to-night.
You are afraid purchasers will not come up to your prices ;
but I am afraid my buyers will not come down to mine;
for mine (striking his hand on the Bible) are 'without
money and without price.' "

Upon the death of his wife, he preached her funeral sermon. The text was, "And we know that all things work
together for good to them that love God, to them who are
the called according to his purpose."—Romans viii. 28. In
noticing her character, he mentioned her fortitude, and suddenly exclaimed, "Do you remember my preaching in those
fields, by the old stump of the tree ? The multitude was
great, and many were disposed to be riotous. At first I
addressed them firmly; but when a desperate gang of
banditti drew near, with the most ferocious looks and
horrid imprecations and menaces, my courage began to fail.
My wife was then standing behind me, as I stood on the
table. I think I hear her now. She pulled my gown (he
then put his hand behind him, and touched his gown), and,
looking up, said, 'George, play the man for your God.'
My confidence returned. I again spoke to the multitude
with boldness and affection; they became still; and many
were deeply affected."

Mr. Hill sometimes rendered a word of rebuke, equally
strong and witty. Thus, when a preacher of no very good
reputation was in the vestry of a place where he was going
to preach, and seemed uneasy lest his servant should not

arrive in time with his cassock, Mr. Hill said, "Sir, you need not be uneasy; for I can preach without my cassock, though I cannot preach without my character."

As he was coming out of a gentleman's house in Piccadilly, he met in the passage a minister with a begging case, who, though popular with some, had, it was suspected, been imposing for a good while on the religious public. This person offered him his hand, but Mr. Hill drew back, and looking him in his face, said, "Ah, I thought you had been hanged long ago."

A forward and conceited young man one day calling upon him at my house, asked him if he had heard that he was going to change his sentiments? "No, sir," said Mr. Hill, "I have not; but, if you have not fixed the time, I would advise you to do it as near the change of the moon as possible."

A rather talkative woman one day said to him, "I have been a good deal of late with some papists, and they have sadly tempted me to change my religion." "Indeed, ma'am," he replied, "I was not aware until now that you had any religion to change."

I once heard him repeat the Lord's Prayer, and witnessed the great effect produced when he had said, "Forgive us our trespasses," by making a considerable pause before he added, "*as* we forgive them that trespass against us;" as if he almost feared to utter it, lest he should condemn himself and others.

I remember what an impression he made when preaching for me, by an interjective parenthesis;—for when, in reading the chapter, 1 Thessalonians v., he repeated the verse, "Abstain from all appearance of evil," he lifted his eyes, and said, in a very solemn voice, "Oh, the infinite delicacy of the Gospel!"

His brother, Sir Richard, once told me of an early instance of his adroitness, remarking that he was the same from a lad. It occurred while he was at Eton College. Even then he was under deep impressions of a religious nature; and as he felt the importance of divine things himself, he was active and concerned to do good to others; and thus he did with an old female servant that frequently waited upon him. She one day rather reproved him for his zeal, saying, that persons should not be righteous overmuch, and should be careful to avoid extremes in religion. "Some," she said, "were too cold, and some were too hot." "Then," said young Rowland, "I suppose you think that we had better be lukewarm?" "Yes," she said, "that was the proper medium." He then took up his Testament, and read the Saviour's address to the Church of Laodicea:— "I would thou wert cold or hot. So then, because thou art *lukewarm*, and neither cold nor hot, I will spue thee out of my mouth;" at which his *tepid* admonisher seemed a little surprised and aghast.

He was the intimate friend of Dr. Jenner, who introduced vaccination. To this discovery he was an admiring and practical devotee. I was one day with him, when one of the company was speaking rather disrespectfully of this remedy; and said there was something very disagreeable and offensive in communicating a disease from a filthy beast into a human being. "A filthy beast, sir! why, a cow is one of the most agreeable of all animals; everything about her is wholesome and useful; we get odour from her breath; she supplies our tables with meat, and butter, and cream, and cheese; and I assure you, sir, I would rather eat a cow than a Christian."

I *know* that once at Wotton he was preaching in the afternoon, (the only time when it seemed possible to be drowsy under him,) he saw some sleeping, and paused, saying, "I have heard that the miller can sleep while the mill is going, but if it stops it awakens him. I'll try this method;" and so sat down, and soon saw an aroused audience.

I was one day walking with him through Bath. In the market-place we met an eminent clergyman, whom he much respected, but with whom he could be familiar, having been at college with him. He had for some weeks been in the city, where as to *his* not having preached in any of the churches, there existed no surprise ; but Mr. Hill thought it became him to countenance his own creed wherever he was, by his practice. He therefore began instantly : " Ah ! Mr. ———, this will never do. You know the value of the Gospel ; you have published, not only in favour of its truth, but of its all-importance. You have contended that God only gives testimony to the word of his grace ; and have said that those who preach any other doctrine are betrayers and destroyers of souls, condemning them as worse than Robespierre, who only murdered men's bodies, while these destroyed their souls." The divine began to explain and defend. " Nay," said Mr. Hill, " my dear brother, I may take you upon your own ground, and argue with you on your own principles and professions. How can you, with your *avowed* sentiments, turn your back upon the Gospel where it is preached, and go where you acknowledge it is not preached, owning, too, a great difference between things essential and not essential in religion ; and that our preferences in subordinate matters should not amount to exclusions ? What is the chaff to the wheat ? I contend that always, and wherever we are, we ought to show our regard to the truth as it is in Jesus ; and that this cannot be done by indifferent and indiscriminate attendance. Here you admonish people to abide where they are, praying and waiting till the Gospel comes there, without any promise when it will come, or whether it will come at all into their particular church, unless in the latter-day glory ; while in the mean time they are hearing words which cause them to err, and are in danger of perishing for lack of knowledge. Can you believe that one would do

this who determined to know nothing save Jesus Christ
and him crucified; and suffered the loss of all things for
the excellency of the knowledge of Christ Jesus his Lord?"
"Dear Rowland," said his friend, "I see you are Rowland
still." "Yes," said his reprover, "and I hope I shall never
change or skulk even to the end. You say I go too far.
You know in doctrine you go as far as I go; but I see you
have met with Nicodemus; and the fear of men bringeth a
snare." Mr. ——— was now glad to turn the conversation,
and to notice the grand victory of Trafalgar, which had just
been achieved. "Ah!" said Mr. Hill, "do you not admire
the strain of piety in Collingwood's despatches? I declare
I wish that some of our admirals were made bishops, though
I could not wish that any of our bishops were made admirals—unless yellow ones."

To conclude this imperfect sketch. Let us hear a voice,
saying, "What God hath cleansed, that call not thou common;" and let us honour them whom God honours, however they may differ from us. He will do his own work in
his own way; and let him do what seemeth him good. We
need instruments of all kinds, and every man in his own
order. Sharpshooters may do execution, as well as the
rank-and-file soldiers, and belong to the same army, though
their movements are detached, and they seem to act irregularly. David essayed to go in Saul's armour, and could not;
but was he inefficient with his sling and stones?

Above all, let us glorify God in him. He might well
have said, "By the grace of God I am what I am; and I
laboured more abundantly than they all; yet not I, but the
grace of God which was with me." And how exceedingly
abundant was that grace towards him, in the faith and love
which are in Christ Jesus!

Behold the strength of a principle, appearing in his ceaseless and self-denying exertions and sacrifices; keeping up

the intenseness of his ardour, and allowing nothing to drive or draw him for one moment aside.

If any (for none can *accuse* him), should be disposed to *pity* him as weak, and ridicule him as fanatical, a period will soon rectify their judgment, and lead them to pass sentence on themselves:—" We fools counted his life madness, and his end to be without honour. How is he numbered with the children of God, and his lot is with the saints !"

"They that be wise shall shine as the brightness of the firmament, and they that turn many to righteousness as the stars for ever and ever;" and in that day how many princes and heroes and philosophers will envy the man who, through good report and through evil report, followed his Lord with purpose of heart; and then hear that Saviour saying, "Well done, good and faithful servant, enter thou into the joy of thy Lord."

REV. RICHARD CECIL, M.A.

Mr. Cecil was a very popular preacher when I went first to London, though I always thought his popularity was not equal to his desert. I greedily seized every opportunity in my power of hearing him, and never without impression. The impression was not so much of the pathetic, as of the serious and solemn. He did not excel so much in the soft and tender, as in the striking and powerful.

He was perfectly free from all affectation of oratory; but everything about him in the pulpit,—his figure, his looks, his hand sometimes laid across his loins from pain, his firm and decisive enunciation—all was dignified and impressive, and never failed of commanding attention. Conscious of the divinity of his mission, and the importance of his message, he always seemed to feel what he once expressed, when with a powerful voice he said, "*I must be heard.*"

For the sake of excitement and effect, especially upon the mass of his hearers, he was sometimes, after the manner of the Nonconformists, with whose works his education made him familiar, quaint in his sentences; and sometimes also in the plan and division of his sermons. Indeed, his excellence lay, not so much in the clear and orderly arrangement of his subject, as in the fillings up and exemplifications. There was also nothing very consecutive in his discourses; no one train of thought being pursued at length, or fully argued out; and this, I remember, Mr. Wilberforce rather complained of, saying, one day, after he had been attending

him, that he seemed too much to follow after things by
starts, and sometimes failed to overtake them. This was
rather severe, especially for him ; and I could not but think
that the *senator* had been hearing rather than the *Christian ;*
and that for once, if possible, the talent and the eloquence to
which he had been accustomed made him forget what is
most profitable to a common congregation.

The eloquence of the senate, the bar, and the schools, will
never be the effective eloquence of the pulpit. All eloquence
there which does not arise from feeling, and produce it, is
as sounding brass and tinkling cymbal ; and any profound
argumentation, or long-continued illustration, will fail in
keeping up the attention, or in securing the remembrance,
in ordinary hearers.   " The words of the wise are as goads
and as nails."   What preponderates must be weighty ;
what pierces must be pointed ; what is carried away must
be portable ; and all cannot equally carry.

Mr. Cecil had always a number of striking remarks, reflections, and sentiments, which would be remembered from
their own impressiveness, independently of a more lucid or
connecting arrangement.   He seemed much at home in
treating historical passages ; in representations of common
life ; in brief sketches of character ; and in hitting off with
a stroke, a particular feature, so distinctly and strongly,
that there was no mistaking the individual to whom it
belonged.

He had few anecdotes, but these always told, and were
brief and pertinent, and uniformly offered their assistance,
instead of being introduced for their own sakes.   But he
abounded peculiarly with Scripture facts, which, without a
formal quotation, he aptly interwove in the texture of his
discourse, with singular propriety and telling effect. If a
figure would go with him a mile, he did not compel it to go
twain. He never evaporated the spirit of a metaphor, in
numerous, subtle particles of allusion. He seldom used an

entire comparison; but rather, as he passed along, by a glance, snatched from it a significant circumstance, which helped his subject without drawing off attention to itself. Instead of glossing a passage of Scripture as he repeated it, or explaining it after he had repeated it, he admirably threw out the meaning and force of the words previously; and then announced them, as a beautiful and powerful illustration, confirmation, and clinching of the argument he was treating.

Among many other excellences in his preaching, he was always brief. I never heard him exceed forty minutes. This is an excellence which did not distinguish our forefathers; and it is not, I fear, very likely to be a characteristic of the moderns; especially our younger preachers, who show, in their long harangues, the confidence they have in their own ability and acceptance.

The late Dr. Bogue is reported to have one day said to some of his students, "Do you suppose that people have nothing to do but to listen to your emptiness by the hour?" —a rebuke too pettishly given, and too severe. But there is propriety in Lamont's remark, "There is no excuse for a long sermon; if it be good it *need* not be long, and if it be bad it *ought* not to be long." Queen Anne, after hearing Dr. South, said, "You have given us an excellent sermon, Dr. South: I wish you had had time to make it longer." "Nay, please your majesty," said he, "I wish I had had time to make it shorter." Whitfield and Wesley, and most of the early Methodists, were short. Why do not many of their successors follow their example?

No man distinguished more in his mind, and in his preaching, between the essential parts of Christianity and the subordinate and circumstantial, than Mr. Cecil. With what a crushing force has he been heard to repeat the language of Jeremiah, "He that hath a dream let him tell a dream; and he that hath my word let him speak my word faithfully. What is the chaff to the wheat?" With him "neither circumcision availed anything, nor uncircumcision, but a new creature."

I believe the following incident has been published; but I was in London when it occurred, and knew it before it spread. A female, who had more of the form of godliness than of the power, one day said to him, "Sir, have you heard that I am going to turn from the Dissenters to the Church?" "Madam," he replied, "you are turning from nothing to nothing."

Hearing a person censuring a churchman for going to hear the Gospel in a meeting, (the only place in the village where it then could be heard,) he exclaimed, "Did ye never read what David did when he was a hungred, and they that were with him; how he entered into the house of God, and did eat the shew-bread, which was not lawful for him to eat, neither for them that were with him, but only for the priests?"

He had his own fixed views and convictions, (and without these candour is only indifference,) but he was moderate enough to think it no sin to attend occasionally in Argyle Chapel; and one day calling upon me, he asked where he could take two sittings for his daughters; adding, "You know I am an Episcopalian, and wish my children to go to church, that is, *if* the one thing needful be heard there. But they must take heed *what* they hear, as well as *how* they hear. If *the story* be not told in a cathedral, they must follow it into a barn; for they *must* hear it, and hear it with care."— And what practical proof can we give of our belief either of the truth, or the importance of evangelical principles, if it be nothing to us whether we hear the words which cause us to err, or those by which we may be saved?

With this man of God I had some acquaintance in London, but he frequently came to Bath for some weeks together for recreation or health, and then I had much intercourse with him.   His conversation was equal to his preaching.   It was singularly original, vigorous, pertinent, instructive, and edifying ; and none of it could easily be forgotten.   In the pleasure of the companion you felt also the presence of an oracle.

I remember his admonishing me against having too great a plenitude of matter in a sermon—an admonition which I fear I have not sufficiently followed.

He also advised me, as I was acceptable, and found people much disposed to hear, to beware of checking it by disappointment in frequently putting up others to preach.   But how is this in many cases to be avoided ?   Can a minister slight his brethren when they come in his way ?   " But they may decline his invitation ;" yes,—and this would be often wise even for themselves ; for when people hear under a baulked expectation, they seldom hear with pleasure or profit.

" *Be*," said he, " *never to be had*."   Many other hints I received from his rich mind and acute and judicious observation, by which I ought to have profited more.   I thank God that I ever heard the *preacher*, or was in company with the *man*.

Who can be ignorant of his " Remains ?"   Is there a work of the same size that abounds with such riches of understanding and wisdom, and genius and truth ?   By what a multitude of inimitable passages from them has Mr. Poynder enriched his three volumes of " Literary Extracts !"   How much of his excellence has his daughter secured and made known in her Memoirs of Mrs. Hawkes !

REV. SAMUEL PEARCE, A.M.

I HAD not a great deal of intimacy with Mr. Pearce, but I knew him, and heard him sufficiently to appreciate him ; and to make me thankful that I had not to depend on report, for my knowledge of his character or preaching. It may seem saying much, but I speak the words of truth and soberness,—when I have endeavoured to form an image of our Lord as a preacher, Pearce has oftener presented himself to my mind than any other I have been acquainted with : not, however, as he *began* his ministry. Then he was too rapid, and had a kind of tiptoe motion in the pulpit ; but after a while—when his delivery was distinguished by mildness and tenderness, and a peculiar unction, derived not only from his matter but his mind. I cannot accurately convey the appearance and impression he made, yet I can see the one, and feel the other, even at this great distance of time.

If, after days of drought, in a summer's evening, you have viewed from your window the rain from heaven, not falling in a pouring torrent, but in a kind of noiseless distillation, every drop soaking in, and sure to be useful, and you thinking of " the smell of a field which the Lord hath blessed ;"— that emblem would aid you a little in conceiving of the mode and effect of his address. He was a man of a most affectionate disposition and candid temper, having much of the meekness of wisdom and the wisdom of meekness. He

was the first Baptist minister I ever heard use the Lord's
prayer, which he did as he prayed before my sermon, when
I preached at Battersea for Mr. Hughes. There, too, I had
my last interview with him. Mr. B——e had sent his carriage to town for two others and ourselves, and it was to
take us back the next morning; but, preferring to be by
ourselves, we privately took boat, and returned by water.
In our conversation, I well remember asking him—what
views of heaven he found the most attractive and affecting?
He replied, "These have varied, (perhaps owing to some
change in my condition or experience,) at different times;
but for a good while past, I think my most delightful view
of heaven has been derived from it, as a place and state of
blessed and endeared society with Jesus at the Head.
Hence I have frequently touched upon it in my sermons,
and have more than once preached from such texts as these:
'I beheld a great multitude,' &c. 'By our gathering together unto him.' 'He will present us together with you,'
&c." Thus we reached the stairs of Blackfriars' Bridge,
and parted to meet no more till "*adieus* and *farewells* are
sounds unknown." But what a savour does communion
with such a man leave upon the spirit! And how blame-
able are we in not turning our social moments to more
account! for we never know but our *present* intercourse
may be our *final*.

What a noble and deserved Memorial of him did Fuller
publish, and what a beautiful motto did he prefix to the
work!—" O Jonathan, thou wast slain in thy high places!"
Who was not, therefore, mortified to find, in a new edition
by his son, this exquisite motto exchanged for a good, but
common-place, passage of Scripture? Fuller, all polemic as
he was, had no little genius and sensibility; and sometimes
he had expressions which verify Shakspeare's remark,—

"One stroke of nature makes the whole world kin!"

N.B.—The son promised, in case of a new edition of the Life, to replace the beautiful motto.

Pearce seemed beatified before his time. How young he died, and with what prospects of usefulness before him! and with what qualifications to serve his generation! What can we say to these things? Nothing. " Be still, and know that I am God."

But there is something peculiarly mysterious and affecting in the removal of such men, and in the midst of their days ; especially,

1st, When contrasted with the continuance to long life of many of the worthless and injurious. And,

2ndly, When viewed in connexion with the disposition and influence to do good, and the numberless calls for their exertion. Alas! for this dark world of ours. We have had a few burning and shining lights ; and can we see the most luminous among them extinguished without concern ? We want all their talents and all their zeal; and shall they perish, and *no* man lay it to heart ? or pray, " Help, Lord, for the godly man ceaseth, for the faithful fail from among the children of men ?"

When the Reminiscent informed Dr. Davies of the death of Dr. Williams of Rotherham, he burst into tears, and said, " I am almost ashamed to be alive, when so many great and good men die."

" The hoary head is a crown of glory, if it be found in the way of righteousness ;" and Job speaks of it as a privilege : " Thou shalt come to thy grave in a full age, like as a shock of corn cometh in, in his season." Be it so, and let all whose days are lengthened be concerned to " bring forth fruit in old age." Yet, is protracted life always the mark of Divine approbation and distinction ? May not the produce remain longer on the tree because of its slow ripening ?

May not persons go late to rest, because the business of the day is not yet discharged? Do not some live because they are not fit to die?

Of one thing we may be assured, that, whenever we are summoned, we shall not be detained for want of means of removal.

> " Dangers stand thick through all the ground
>   To push us to the tomb;
> And fierce diseases wait around
>   To hurry mortals home."

Though I was not a personal witness of the following occurrence, I cannot deny myself the pleasure of recording it, from the testimony of one who was. Mr. Pearce was preaching on a public occasion; the sermon was excellent and well arranged; but after he had appeared naturally to have ended it, he broke forth afresh; and what was added, though excellent, seemed not to grow out of the particular subject of the discourse.

When it was over, Mr. Fuller, who had heard it, said, "Mr. Pearce, will you allow me to ask a question? I much liked and admired your sermon; but did you make intentionally any alteration of, or addition to it, in the close? because, valuable as it was, it seemed not of a piece with the former parts." After a pause, Mr. Pearce said,— "Well, if I must answer, the case was this :—When I was uttering the last two or three sentences, I saw running up to the crowded place a poor man, wiping his face and head, and eager to hear. I thought this poor creature had come from a distance, and it would be cruel to let him go away without hearing a word of the Saviour: and so my pride yielded to my pity; and I tried to be useful, by adding a few things, regardless of connexion or order." And what said—not fastidious critics—but lovers of souls, and angels, and God, the Judge of all?

In confirmation of Mr. Jay's exalted judgment of this eminent minister and Christian, the Editors could add something from their own recollections; but prefer the insertion of a few words from the pen of the Rev. W. Ward, missionary to India, and a brief description of Pearce's character by the Rev. Andrew Fuller.

Mr. Ward says, in a letter to a friend, dated January 5th, 1799, " I am happy in the company of dear brother Pearce. I have seen more of God in him than in any other person I ever knew.   O how happy should I be to live and die with him !   When well, he preaches three times on a Lord's-day, and two or three times in the week besides.   He instructs the young people in the principles of religion, natural philosophy, astronomy, &c.   They have a Benevolent Society, from the funds of which they distribute £40 or £50 a-year to the poor of the congregation.   They have a Sick Society for visiting the afflicted in general; a Book Society at chapel; a Lord's-day school, at which betwixt two and three hundred children are instructed.   Add to this, missionary business, visiting the people, an extensive correspondence, two volumes of mission history preparing for the press, &c.; and then you will see something of the soul of Pearce.   He is everywhere venerated, though but a young man; and all the kind, tender, gentle affections make him as a little child at the feet of the Saviour."

Mr. Fuller says, " There have been few men in whom has been united a greater portion of the contemplative and the active; holy zeal and genuine candour; spirituality and rationality; talents that attracted almost universal applause, and the most unaffected modesty; faithfulness in bearing testimony against evil, with the tenderest compassion to the soul of the evil doer; fortitude that would encounter any difficulty in the way of duty, without anything boisterous, noisy, or overbearing; deep seriousness, with habitual cheerfulness, and a constant aim to promote the highest degree of piety in himself and others, with a readiness to hope the best of the lowest: not breaking the bruised reed, nor quenching the smoking flax."* Mr. Pearce died October 10th, 1799, at the early age of thirty-four, universally admired, beloved, and lamented.

* Memoirs of Pearce by Fuller, pp. 208 and 245.

REV. ROBERT HALL, A.M.

WITH this very eminent man I became acquainted when, before my settlement in Bath, I was preaching for Lady Maxwell, at Hope Chapel, at the Hotwells. Being so near Bristol, I had opportunities of hearing him, and also of visiting him in his own house, and meeting him in various companies. He was then co-pastor with Dr. Evans, of the Baptist church in Broadmead, and co-tutor with him in the academy. He had been for some time before noticed, but he was then exciting peculiar attention, and rising into great fame.

In speaking of him as a preacher, I have one advantage which Mr. Foster had not;* viz., an early, as well as a late, acquaintance with him: so that I can view him comparatively in different periods of his history.

His preaching, when I first knew him, was certainly intellectually greater and more splendid than it was for many years before his death. This was the case with sermons I well remember, from these texts,—"Ye err, not knowing the Scriptures nor the power of God;"—"The wrath of man shall praise thee, O Lord;"—"The spirit of life in Christ Jesus hath made me free from the law of sin and

* Mr. Foster wrote "Observations on Mr. Hall's Character as a Preacher." These are appended to the "Memoir" by Dr. Gregory in the sixth Volume of Mr. Hall's Works.—*Editors*.

death;"—"The inheritance of the saints in light," &c. These sermons, considered only as the productions of genius, rose above any I ever heard from him years afterwards. This, however, was not the effect of any declension of ability; and, therefore, he still occasionally brought forth a discourse far above the level of his usual performances, as if to show that he had not become unequal to his former doings; but from mere pious consideration, and a growing wish to accommodate himself to the common apprehension, and to general usefulness. Another reason, too, had some influence; viz.,—the increased number of his sermons after he became a sole pastor, which allowed not so much time to elaborate and polish.

Mr. Hall sometimes expressed himself as if he believed his real conversion was subsequent to his first awful visitation (*insanity*). We do not admit this; but it is well known that he became more and more spiritual and evangelical; and that at first, while he drew the admiration of all, he awakened the fears of some. Nor need we wonder at this, when we take into the account the occasional, (though not criminal,) sportivenesses and levities he betrayed; his freedoms in conversation, when, for the sake of a contest, in which he was always pretty sure of victory, he defended things which he did not believe; and that, for a while, he avowed *materialism*, and denied the common notion of the Trinity, by contending for a duality of Persons in the Divine Essence. With regard to the latter, the scheme had all the difficulties supposed to attach to Trinitarianism, without some of its scriptural supports. Hence, many have questioned whether he was in earnest in his belief of so strange a doctrine; but I have heard him avow it with firmness; and I remember spending an evening with him in Bath, in a company that included a Sabellian, two Trinitarians, and himself as a Dualist; and when the Reminiscent, afraid to enter into the metaphysical part of the discussion, ventured to mention the baptismal form of words as a difficulty, and to ask whether it was not very strange that—" in the name of the Father and of the Son," should intend *personality*, and, " in the name of the Holy Ghost"—only a mere *power* or *influence ;* and, also, whether it was not strange to baptize any one "in the name" of an abstraction; he acknowledged that it presented a difficulty.

Some *individuals* (for there was no *party*,) complained and frequently absented themselves when Mr. Hall preached; and there was considerable probability that the number would increase. I speak from personal knowledge at the time, and as one who, standing out of the scene, could observe and judge with less bias than those who were thus drawn into an unpleasant dispute and division. In the painful breach that took place between Mr. Hall and Dr. Evans, I must think that Dr. Evans was perfectly blameless of the *motive* which some of Mr. Hall's friends were led, by some circumstances, to impute to him. I am fully persuaded that nothing could be farther from the spirit of Dr. Evans, than an uneasiness at the growing fame of his associate. He loved and esteemed him almost to idolatry. I happened to be in Bristol for a Sabbath, but a little while before the breach. I attended Dr. Evans in the morning; preached myself in the afternoon; and heard Mr. Hall in the evening. As we were going to the evening-service, Dr. Evans leaned upon my arm, and all his conversation was of the wonderful man we were going to hear; and it was all full of what some would have deemed excessive honour and praise. "His eloquence," said he, "is unequalled, and his powers of mind seem bordering on infinite. If some are not so satisfied with regard to his piety, I have had better opportunities of knowing him; and whoever shall live long enough will see the excellence of his character. I find him distinguished, not only by his talents, but by his grace also." But, on the other hand, as from *this* motive Dr. Evans did not hail Mr. Hall's invitation, (and never did use means to *procure* it, as some have surmised) ; I believe he had no objection to Mr. Hall's removal, on *another ground*, viz., the danger of a schism, owing to some respectable persons who were suspicious of his orthodoxy, occasioned by appearances likely to operate on *some* minds. A rent in, or even a considerable secession from, such a respectable and kindly mother-church, was to be earnestly deprecated; but the evil would be prevented by Mr. Hall's translation to another sphere ;—and what place seemed so suitable as Cambridge, for the exertion and display of his mighty mind ?

There is little doubt but Mr. Hall, in process of time, saw this. He spake cordially of Dr. Evans before his death, and he has now joined him in a world where mistakes and infirmities are known no more. Yet we cannot help remarking with lamentation, what trifling causes give rise to surmisings, and strifes, and discords, even among good men, which a little seasonable explanation would hinder or heal. But there is nothing new under the sun. Paul and Barnabas contended, and parted for a season; but this was overruled for good, and caused the Gospel to be spread in several currents, when it would otherwise have been confined to one; while it served to prove the excellence of their principles in their eventual reconciliation and harmony. But how ought we to rejoice and praise God, that a man of his extraordinary ability and influence so soon had his " heart established with grace!" fully preached the peculiar doctrines of the Gospel! and through the whole of his after life, acknowledged and defended their *importance*, as well as their *truth!* His path was like the shining light, which, though it may be a little hazy in the dawn, yet shineth more and more unto the perfect day, and sets in cloudless glory.

It is needless to dwell on Mr. Hall as "the eloquent orator." But, in his preaching, there was not only eloquence which charmed numbers who sought for nothing else, but the fervour of the man of God. It was impossible to hear him, and not be impressed with his earnestness, and concern to do good, rather than to be admired; and the entire forgetfulness of himself in his subject.

His powers of conversation were equal to those of his preaching. Some have thought they even surpassed them. I remember Mr. Foster, when he had been introduced to Mr. Hall, remarking that, after being in his company, you might be comparatively disappointed in hearing him preach; for, after hearing him speak off-hand upon any subject with such ease, and force, and purity, and precision, and exquisiteness, you might be naturally led to expect something proportionably greater, after much study and preparation.

Some men's minds seem to resemble a reservoir, large and deep; yet having *been* filled, capable of *being* emptied. But Mr. Hall's mind always intimated a mighty spring; not made, but created; always full, yet pouring forth streams of clear and living water. There was not only a constant plenty, but a constant freshness of communication. Who ever heard him repeat any image, or maxim, or saying of his own? Perhaps the following is *not* an exception:—A minister has stated in print, that, in a conversation with him not a great while before his death, he called Dr. Owen's works " a continent of mud." * I am sure I heard this from him more than thirty years before, and I had often repeated it. Might not the report of an old sarcasm have been taken for a fresh one? And what was related by another be mistaken for what was so unlikely to be *repeated* by himself?

Dr. Owen was a voluminous writer, but surely he was anything but a dull one. How searching and quickening are some of his treatises! what specimens also of fine rea-

* See a note upon this anecdote in Letter XIII. of the Autobiography.

soning have we in them! how much does he carry us always
with him! and how little are we able to question his con-
clusions as we peruse them! We say not this of all his
numerous publications, but we could specify many of his
works which, for their practical bearing, and experimentality,
and evangelical sentiment, and the savour they diffuse of
the Redeemer's knowledge, we are ready to say, are incomparable; and we wish many of our young divines were
more familiar with them. I have a little work of his, I
believe very little known, (of which I have never seen any
other copy,) "Evidences of the Faith of God's Elect." It
was written for the encouragement and comfort of his wife
under her doubts and fears, and was given me many years
ago by Mr. Wilberforce, who much commended it; only
wishing, for the sake of some readers, that it had been
differently entitled. So I remember he did also with regard
to Fuller's unanswerable publication, "The Calvinistic and
Socinian Systems Examined and Compared;" remarking
that, if the word "evangelical" or "orthodox" had been
used instead of "Calvinistic," many would have read that
wonderful performance, whose narrow and prejudiced minds
had been revolted by a term unnecessarily adopted.

Mr. Hall, like Dr. Johnson, professed to believe in preter-
natural appearances; and certainly, from his manner, when
speaking of such subjects, his credence seemed to be sincere.

The first evening I ever spent with him was at the house
of Mr. W——y, near the Bristol Bridge. Of course he was
the *lion* of the company. The party broke up late, and the
latter part of the conversation turned upon apparitions. He
defended his belief, not only in the possibility, but in the
actuality, of these appearances, with much ingenuity and
ability, and seemed to convince himself, if not others; and
when we were to separate, he refused to go home at that
midnight hour unless some of us accompanied him. His

arguing and fear certainly *seemed* more than oddity or affectation.

Mr. Hall was fond of referring to Satanic power. In his sermon on this subject, taken imperfectly in short-hand, finding a difficulty in his view of such agency, as immediate, personal, and individual, without admitting omniscience and omnipresence, he seems to solve it by pleading for an infinite number of agents. Is not this strange?

It is remarkable how he noticed little incidents and circumstances, which seemed likely to escape the observation of so great a mind; and what proof he gave of this in adverting to them long after. How many instances of this have I witnessed! No one could express a compliment or a commendation more tersely and perfectly. I one day asked him his opinion of a female who attended his ministry at Leicester. " Sir," said he, " she has the manners of a court, and the piety of a convent."

He was at the Tabernacle the first time I ever preached in Bristol, and when I was little more than seventeen. When I came down from the pulpit, as I passed him, he said, "Sir, I liked your sermon much better than your quotations." I never knew him severe upon a preacher, however moderate his abilities, if, free from affectation, he spoke with simplicity, nor tried to rise above his level. But, as to others, nothing could be occasionally more witty and crushing than his remarks. One evening, in a rather crowded place, (I was sitting by him,) a minister was preaching very *finely* and *flourishingly* to little purpose, from the " white horse," and the " red horse," and the " black horse," and the " pale horse," in the Revelation. He sat very impatiently, and when the sermon closed he pushed out towards the door, saying, " Let me out of this horse-fair."

I was once in the library at the academy, conversing with one of the students, who was speaking of his experience, and lamented the hardness of his heart. Mr. Hall, as he was near, taking down a book from the shelf, hearing this, turned towards him and said, "Well, thy head is soft enough; that 's a comfort." I could not laugh at this; it grieved me; for the young man was modest, and humble, and diffident. *He* must have felt it severely; and I have no doubt Mr. Hall's reflections smote him afterwards for this *apparent* harshness and offence. There is no just excuse for such things. We must not fling about arrows, and, if any of them pierce, say it was in sport. Should not only ill-nature, but wit or humour, expose us to this evil, we know the prayer,—" Set a watch, O Lord, upon my mouth: keep the door of my lips."

A minister, popular too, one day said to me, " I wonder you think so highly of Mr. Hall's talents. I was some time ago travelling with him into Wales, and we had several disputes, and I more than once soon silenced him." I concluded how the truth was; and some weeks after, when his name was mentioned, Mr. Hall asked me if I knew him. " I lately travelled with him," said he, "and it was wonderful, sir, how such a baggage of ignorance and confidence could have been squeezed into the vehicle. He disgusted and wearied me with his dogmatism and perverseness, till God was good enough to enable me to go to sleep."

Though the Reminiscent so much admires the whole of Mr. Hall's writings, nothing strikes him so powerfully as his " Reviews." Who does not wish we had more of them? The Reminiscent also is compelled to acknowledge, contrary to the opinion of some dissentients, that he believes Mr. Foster has done justice to Mr. Hall's character as a divine and a preacher.

I cannot forbear inserting here Mr. Hall's character of Popery:—

"Popery, in the ordinary state of its profession, combines the form of godliness with a total denial of its power. A heap of unmeaning ceremonies, adapted to fascinate the imagination, and engage the senses; implicit faith in human authority, combined with an utter neglect of divine teaching; ignorance the most profound, joined to dogmatism the most presumptuous; a vigilant exclusion of Biblical knowledge, together with a total extinction of free inquiry—present the spectacle of religion lying in state, surrounded with all the silent pomp of death. The very absurdities of such a religion, render it less unacceptable to men whose decided hostility to truth inclines them to view with complacency whatever obscures its beauty, or impedes its operation. Of all the corruptions of Christianity which have prevailed to any considerable extent, Popery presents the most numerous points of contrast to the simple doctrines of the Gospel; and just in proportion as it gains ground, the religion of Christ must decline. On these accounts, though we are far from supposing that Popery, were it triumphant, would allow toleration to any denomination of Protestants, we have the utmost confidence, that the professors of evangelical piety would be its first victims. The party most opposed to them look to papists as their natural ally, on whose assistance, in the suppression of what they are pleased to denominate fanaticism and enthusiasm, they may always depend: they may, therefore, without presumption, promise themselves the distinction conferred on Ulysses,—that of being last devoured. From a settled persuasion that Popery still is what it always was, a detestable system of impiety, cruelty, and imposture, fabricated by the father of lies, we feel thankful at witnessing any judicious attempt to expose its enormities and retard its progress." *

* Rev. Robert Hall, Works, vol. iv. p. 230.

REV. JOSEPH HUGHES, M.A.

No Institution, since the Apostolic era, will bear a comparison with the British and Foreign Bible Society, whether we consider the period and circumstances of its origination; the supreme importance of its design; the catholicism of its basis; the principle on which alone it depends for its success; the unbroken harmony of its numerous adherents; the magnitude of its undertakings; the immensity of its achievements; or the bearing of its operations on the great moral questions which agitate the world.

To meet its growing and rapid demands, and to support its operations, especially by public meetings, three secretaries were appointed to defend, advocate, and recommend its claims. These were John Owen, chaplain to Bishop Porteus; Dr. Steinkopff, a German Lutheran divine; and Joseph Hughes, a dissenter. The wisdom of the appointment appeared strikingly obvious. No three individuals could more have suited each other and their work.

Mr. Hughes, besides his secretaryship, had another relation to the Society. He not only attended from the first its formation; but may be, in some respects, acknowledged (as Mr. Owen, in his history of the Bible Society, states,) as influencing the commencement of it. This was enough to ennoble and immortalize him; but he would always say, "By the grace of God I am what I am."

A good Life of this deservedly-esteemed man was published soon after his death by the Rev. Dr. Leifchild. In
that work, my opinion of him, generally expressed, is to be
found.* My acquaintance with him is there also noticed.
It was long and very intimate. We indulged in a peculiar
freedom of mind towards each other; and there seemed to
be but a single religious difference between us, and this was
not an essential one. It did not, therefore, diminish our
mutual regard. Some, perhaps, would deem *it* impossible
to be the means of increasing it. But love and liberality
have secrets which strangers intermeddle not with. And
is there no pleasure in knowing that we are able to distinguish things that differ; that we have candour enough to
allow others to think and judge for themselves; and that,
instead of being "overcome of evil, we can overcome evil
with good?" And is not bigotry such an evil?

He was a man of great simplicity of manners, and of freedom from affectation and all airs of superiority; and, though
decidedly a Dissenter and a Baptist, not only from education but conviction, yet he had a most catholic spirit; and I
do not wonder that the exercise of it, in some instances,
awakened the suspicions of bigots, who feared that, because
he was not rigid, he was not decided; and that, where there
was no exclusiveness, there was no conviction.

He kept himself unspotted from the world, and was not
only sincere, but "without rebuke until the day of Christ."

As a preacher he possessed materials and qualities, which
did not produce the advantages in his ministrations, which
might have been expected. I remember the Rev. Mr.
H——n [*Hinton*] of Oxford, (his *alter idem*, and who was
exceedingly attached to him,) once asking this question,—
"Whence is it that our valued friend, who has such an
unblemished reputation, and stands so high in public esteem,
and has so much more learning than falls to the share of

* See the addition to this paper at its close.

many of his brethren, and has such an easy command of words, and such an affluence of imagery, and such a readiness of utterance—should make so little impression in preaching, compared with persons so inferior to him, in these and other attributes?" "Send this question," said I, "to all the tutors in our academies; bring it forward also in every company of preachers; and show the propriety of learning from example as well as from precept, and from failure as well as from success, how to excel."

Some would, perhaps, ascribe a little of his want of popularity to his personal appearance. This was not prepossessing; but other preachers have succeeded without this species of attraction and impression. In part, his failure arose from his voice, which was inharmonious and weak, and, when elevated to the full, had a kind of dry shrillness, and allowed of no inflexions. But his style is the most faulty. Foster, in one of his letters to him, says, "Hall spoke much of your attainments and talents, but exceedingly condemned, what you know I always hate, the want of simplicity in your style." It was this want of simplicity, rather than a want of right feeling, that made him fail in the pathetic. His metaphors were glances rather than comparisons. His beauties were too delicate to be striking, and required some degree of previous cultivation and taste to perceive and admire them. His discourses contained too little of the phraseology of the pulpit, to be satisfactory to many of the common yet pious hearers who were most familiar with the words which the Holy Ghost useth, and whose ears were most attuned to the language of their orthodox ancestors. And why should such hearers be disappointed or perplexed? And what is there less instructive and edifying in the diction of our old divinity, than in the terms of those who would rather remind us of Johnson and Addison, than of Leighton, Flavel, and Whitfield?

It was too much Mr. Hughes's aim, not only as a writer

but as a preacher, to render his language correct and refined, rather than bold and free. His concern here was
extreme; and what Gray said of the *penury* of his " Church-
yard"-peasant may be applied to the *fastidiousness* of our
preacher—

> " *Fastidiousness* repressed his noble rage,
> And chilled the genial current of his soul."

A dread of little mistakes and improprieties, like the
sword of Damocles, hung over his head, and prevented the
relish of the banquet he would otherwise have enjoyed.

A preacher's great and obvious attention, (and where it
is great it will usually *be* obvious,) to minutenesses in his
composition and address, weakens the sympathy of his
audience, and often hardly allows of a frigid approbation of
what is deserving of praise. On the other hand, when a
man is absorbed in his subject, little improprieties, should
they occur, will either be unperceived, or as being more
than atoned for, will be disregarded by a riveted audience.

And what should be the anxiety of a man of God—to
gain *admiration* or to secure *profit?* To be favourably
noticed for memory, by two or three who have little more
to recommend them than mere intellect; or to have numbers hanging upon his lips, and " wondering at the gracious
words which proceed out of his mouth," to the use of edifying? To appear the chaste classic from the schools, or the
able minister of the New Testament, full of grace and
truth?

I always considered Mr. Hughes as one of the founders
of the Tract Society, and also as the first suggester of the
British and Foreign Bible Society. Had he been distinguished by nothing else, surely this would have been sufficient to ennoble and immortalize him. One structure has
made an architect; one poem, a poet; one battle, a hero.
But what one exploit can be compared to that which led to

the establishment of a society which has translated the
Scriptures into all languages, and is filling the earth with
the knowledge of the Lord, as the waters cover the seas ?
And how much did he, who was honoured in the suggestion
of this Godlike Institution, aid it afterwards by his Secretaryship, by his travels, and labours, and those addresses
on the platform, which so much excelled the effect of his
sermons !

Mr. Hughes was the first from whom I heard anything
of the extraordinary powers of John Foster. He was then
a student leaving Bristol Academy, where he had been only
one year. Mr. Hughes prepared the way for the spread of
his fame ; and for this he had the best opportunities, especially on his settlement at Battersea; and having access to
a variety of distinguished characters residing at Clapham
Common. He was not mistaken in his estimate of this
peculiar and original genius ; but lived to see his opinion
abundantly confirmed by the voice of the public. Mr.
Hughes himself sold several hundred copies of the Essays
when they first came out.

Mr. Hughes had the honour of being appointed to preach
Mr. Hall's funeral sermon. But how strange was the choice
of his text, on so peculiar an occasion !—" All the days of
my appointed time will I wait, till my change come." Job
xiv. 14. It was as appropriate to a private believer, as to
one of the most extraordinary of human beings. But he
had prepared a funeral sermon from those words which he
had preached a fortnight before at H——y, (*Hackney*)—
" In all labour there is profit." How much do we often
lose by sacrificing to ease ! An old discourse seldom
answers the purpose of a new occasion :

First : As something already prepared is learnt off, there
will be relaxing of study and exertion.

Secondly : There will be less suitableness and pertinence
to the event to be noticed and improved. And,

Thirdly : There will be less liveliness and freshness of feeling in the preacher's address.

Mr. Hughes was little known as an author. He published several single discourses,—a sermon before the Society for the Propagation of the Gospel, in the Highlands and Islands of Scotland;—a sermon on the Sabbath ;—and a sermon on the death of the Duke of Kent. He published also an Essay on the Excellency of the Scripture—his best performance.*

There were few men for whom I entertained a higher regard, or with whom I exchanged so much thought.

APPENDIX BY THE EDITORS.

The Rev. Dr. Leifchild, in his life of the Rev. Joseph Hughes, thus introduces Mr. Jay's opinion referred to in the preceding Article.

"With the Rev. W. Jay of Bath Mr. Hughes was more than ordinarily intimate. As far as two men, of somewhat different intellectual habits and theological views, could love one another, they did so love to the end of life. Let the survivor speak for himself, with his own characteristic *naïveté* and force :—

" ' Mr. Hughes was often and much at Bath formerly, supplying several years at Argyle Chapel for six weeks together while I was in town. I have been intimately acquainted with him for upwards of forty-three years, and have exchanged more mind with him than with any man I ever knew, except my friend and tutor, Cornelius Winter. With regard to religious things, we only differed as to Baptism ; and if we did not love each other the more for this difference, I am sure we did not love each other the less. We disagreed, too, a little with regard to composition and preaching : he too squeamish, and I too careless ; he labouring for correctness, and I for impression ; (in grasping which I sometimes erred ;) he too satisfied if he could abide criticism ; and I too careless of critical

---

* This was no doubt the Essay which prepared the way for the formation of the Bible Society. It is noticed in our Appendix to this article.

judgment, if I could secure effect. Yet though he was often kindly finding fault with me when we were alone, he was always seeking opportunities to hear me; and I cannot be ignorant how much I shared his commendation, as an author and a preacher. I am thankful for my intimacy with him. My esteem of him always grew with my intercourse. *I never knew a more consistent, correct, and unblemished character.* He was not only sincere, but without offence, and adorned the doctrine of God our Saviour in all things.

" 'His mind was full of information; his conversation singularly instructive, and very edifying; and while others *talked* of candour and moderation, he *exemplified* them. In his theological sentiments he was firm, yet sober and liberal; and not too orthodox (as I have often known this) to be evangelical. But why do I write this? You know it as well as I, and will describe it better.' "

Mr. Jay's opinion that the conception of the British and Foreign Bible Society originated in the mind of his friend, Joseph Hughes, is fully confirmed by the Memoir from which the above extract is taken; and from which we must beg to present the following elucidation of a fact which has sometimes been obscured, if not actually denied.

"The Rev. T. Charles, a clergyman of the Church of England, but frequently officiating among the Calvinistic Methodists in Wales, paid a visit to the Metropolis. He represented, with all the characteristic ardour and pathos of his native country, the dearth of Bibles in the native language of the Principality. He told of a scanty supply which had once been obtained from 'The Society for Promoting Christian Knowledge,' but which by its inadequacy had served rather to increase than allay the anxiety of the inhabitants; as the thirsty earth but pines and languishes the more for a few big drops only from the cloud which had been expected to shower down an abundance of moisture. This individual being present as a visitor at the Committee Meeting of the Tract Society, expatiated on the subject of a supply of Welsh Bibles, (Mr. Joseph Tarn, a member of the Committee, having previously introduced him,) and urged it most earnestly upon the attention of the meeting. To supply Bibles was not the professed object of the Society; yet he could hardly have been introduced to a circle of individuals in the whole world more disposed to listen to his representations, to sympathize with his feelings, and to respond to his calls. The whole meeting instantly felt the desirableness of the object; but the mind of the Secretary (Mr. Hughes) was warmed with the subject; his previous train of reflections was recalled and quickened into motion, and wrought, it may well be believed, into a high degree of energy. His views, probably in connexion with those of the Members present, went much further than the specific object proposed to them—the supply of the Welsh. The precise language in which he expressed his views, it is now difficult, if not impossible, to ascertain ; and we must, therefore, be contented with the fact.   Some, indeed, of the individuals present at that meeting who survive, recollect nothing particular ; others retain a sense of his distinct and emphatic utterance of this remark—'Why not Bibles for the whole country—for the whole world !'

" The minutes of that meeting, which were revised by himself and Mr. Tarn, under a concern to leave a perfectly accurate account of what had transpired, record that such an object of solicitude, 'AT THE SUGGESTION OF THE SECRETARY,' (*Mr. Hughes,*) was deemed worthy of attention, was suitable for the notice of that body, and should be placed on record for consideration at their next meeting. This fact he himself, though careful of not having too much attributed to him, always admitted.   It appeared in several printed accounts, while most of the members of that Committee were living, (and all had access to the minutes as well as himself,) and was never questioned.   A variety of particulars in his correspondence, as well before as after this period, *and the part immediately* and thenceforward assigned to him in all ulterior proceedings, confirm the idea.   It may, therefore, be safely concluded that the elements of the new institution were first of all deliberately conceived in his mind ;—that there its original seed was planted by the hand of its Almighty Author. The facts above related occurred on the memorable morning of December 7, 1802.   The views and feelings of all present accorded with the suggestion or suggestions made to the effect above noticed.

" Mr. Hughes was requested by the Chairman, in the name of the rest, to embody the sentiments then delivered in a written address, to be read to them at a future meeting convened for the purpose. He readily complied ; and, after several meetings of the same kind, the address, with some few emendations, was ordered to be printed with a view to its immediate circulation.   It was printed at first in *quarto,* the intention being to circulate it chiefly among persons in high station—individuals whose countenance might shield the magnitude of the scheme it proposed, from the charge of wildness or utter impracticability.   It was subsequently printed in octavo, and went through several editions.

" This pamphlet, which was entitled, ' *The Excellence of the Holy Scriptures : an Argument for their more general dispersion at home and abroad,*' was the earliest public act of preparation for the establishment of that first and greatest of our National Societies.   A document so momentous in its results, so excellent in itself, and so intimately connected with the subsequent history and everlasting renown of our friend, requires some further notice from the pen of his Biographer. A more important production, viewing the train of consequences to which it has led, and is still leading, surely never issued from the British press, saving only the Holy Bible itself."

After giving a very complete analysis of Mr. Hughes's work his Biographer thus concludes :—

"The publication of this pamphlet marks an era, undoubtedly one of the most propitious in the religious history of our country; and which will be pointed to and signalized in future ages, as the date of one of the most popular, most useful, and most important Institutions that ever blessed the world.

"The publication of Mr. Hughes's Essay took place early in 1803; and for something more than a year the project was contemplated with serious, and, it may be believed, with much prayerful thought, by pious and benevolent men of various Christian denominations. At length its first general public meeting was called, on March the 7th, 1804. Granville Sharp, Esq., in the Chair."—Memoir of Rev. Joseph Hughes, M.A., pp. 142, 194, 207, 209.

REV. JOHN FOSTER.

I HAD many opportunities of seeing Mr. Foster, from the time he was a student at Bristol to the period of his death. He was thrice settled near me, viz., at Downend, at Frome, and at Stapleton. His wife had relations in my congregation; and he sometimes passed a Sabbath in Bath; but I could never induce him to preach for me. He declined commonly by saying, (with complacency and pleasantry,) "You know neither you nor your people would ever ask me again; I am never desired to preach a second time."

The first interview I had with him was at the house of Miss Hannah More. It was attended with the incident which I mentioned in my Reminiscence of this extraordinary and excellent woman,—the producing, for the opinion of the party, of the tract entitled, "*The Shepherd of Salisbury Plain*"—as the first of a series which, it was hoped, would tend to supplant the worthless and mischievous trash in immense circulation, and to furnish something not only harmless, but useful, in its stead. It was at a breakfast; the company was select, yet rather numerous. But all I remember with regard to Foster was his taciturnity; for I know not that he uttered a single sentence. As, like myself, he had risen from (what is called, I know not why,) penniless life, and had, as yet, seen little of society, it might have been supposed that he was rather restrained when among persons above the class in which he had moved;

but even then, he had such a consciousness of his talents, as would have secured him from such influence.

Some time after this, Mr. Henry Thornton, M.P. for the Borough of Southwark, being in Bath, and having heard of his powers, desired me to engage him some day to dine with him. I did so; and, mortifyingly, he again showed his indisposition to talk; and our most excellent entertainer was not much formed to make his company easy, and free, and communicative; for his manner was peculiarly cold, distant, and reserved. Foster said, (yet I think very untruly,) that *he sat as if he had a bag of money under his arm;* but at this time Mr. Foster had a kind of silly prejudice against persons of affluence, however their wealth had been obtained. This lessened in time; and when he thought of espousals, he seemed to think *property* "was good and profitable to men;" not that, in his choice, he overlooked wisdom and goodness, but showed that he thought these were not the worse for being endowered.

And this leads me to observe, that I never knew a man possessing such a capacity for every kind of conversation, who spoke so little, unless he had an individual or two, not, (as he used to express it,) to talk *upon,* but to talk *with.*

An observable circumstance was, his omission of Scriptural expressions in his prayers : for I can hardly remember his ever using any. This could not have been from his ignorance of the Scriptures, for from a child he had known them; and, if it were designed, what could have been the motive for the omission? As this applied very much to his sermons, as well as to his prayers, (as may be seen in his skeleton lectures,) I ventured to ask him once concerning it; when he rather lamented than justified the practice, and said the fault was principally in his memory—and that he feared to repeat such expressions, lest he should fail or boggle in the accuracy of the sacred diction.

This leads me to remark another thing. In his account

of Mr. Hall's prayers, he has gently censured him for too much of personal reference and specification. The remark being rather bold and novel, and coming from such a pen, I hoped it would have excited notice, and produced a friendly discussion in some of our religious periodicals. For myself, I had always wished that less of the practice prevailed in our public devotions. I say *public devotions;* for the family altar, and the private closet, admit these, and often require them; and *there* they are not only allowable, but desirable. But against the public and frequent introduction of minute and specific cases pertaining to individuals, there lie, I think, four objections:—*First,* it often perplexes and embarrasses the preacher to bring them forward *properly.* Few have command of that fluency, which would enable them to express incidents, with readiness and with ease; and there is frequently danger in extempore prayer, lest the faculties should be employed where the affections only should be exercised; and this difficulty should not, if possible, be increased. *Secondly,* it excites improper and unseasonable attention and inquiry in the minds of the hearers. This is especially the case with the more curious and inquisitive. The devotion of many of these is at an end, as soon as such personalities are brought in; and their minds are immediately hunting through the congregation or the neighbourhood, to ascertain the family, or the individual, to whom the minister has alluded. Yet some in their devotions introduce, not only a particular fact, but its circumstantial attributes; the thanksgiving is not only for a *safe* delivery, but for that of a *son* or *daughter;* and the prayer is not only for a *safe* journey, but by *land* or by *water;* and the recovery is implored, not from *sickness,* but from *dropsy* or *fever;* and so of the rest. *Thirdly,* there is frequently in these references a kind of adulatory, complimentary strain. This is sometimes so gross that, if it be not very trying to those for whom it is designed, it must be offensive to those by whom it is heard. Hence expressions must be sought which *tell* in favour of the individual; and, when several are to be noticed at the same time, great caution must be observed not to use more respectful terms in speaking of one than of the other. So averse have I been to this, and so afraid of it in my own case, that I have commonly, especially with younger ministers, when they have been preaching for me, taken them aside before they entered the pulpit, and begged them, either not to refer to me personally at all, or in only general terms. *Fourthly*, a difficulty arises from the multiplicity of cases. And which of these can be passed by without offence? Yet how can all be distinctly referred to? I had, when preaching in the great congregation in Blackfriars Road, ten or twelve notes at a time. Who had memory enough to retain them all? And what time would all these particularizations have taken up? And—" God is in heaven, and we upon earth; therefore, our words should be few."

I always dissented from Mr. Foster's recommending preachers, (sanctioned by his own practice,) to lay aside the language of what he called religious technicalities, and speaking of divine things in the same phraseology, as that in which they would speak of other things. Would the substitution be easy? Would the advantage repay the endeavour? has it ever succeeded, where it has been tried? I have known attempters who have injured their acceptance and usefulness, especially among those who would have heard our Saviour gladly. And is the improvement of the mass of hearers to be forgotten, in trying after two or three dry-minded, perhaps captious, speculatists, or individuals, looking only for literary display, when they hear the Gospel, as well and as much as when they hear or read anything else?

Three things should be remembered. *First;* that many (and let the main of these be poor,) suppose they have not the same things, if they are delivered in new and strange words. *Secondly;* the terms and phrases to be laid aside, are generally the language of our translation (the only Bible the many have) ; and, of all our divines, the most eminent and the most known.—*Thirdly,* Is the new image preferable to the old currency ? Is *reformation* equal to *renovation?* Is *favour* as significant as *grace?* Is *forgiveness* a full substitute for *justification?* Does *a promise* supersede "*an everlasting covenant, ordered in all things and sure?*"

No one seemed to delight more in a simple, consistent Christian, or "an Israelite indeed, in whom was no guile," whatever was his condition or religious party, than Mr. Foster; but he was very indignant at the inconsistencies of many professors. I was one day visiting with him at the house of a gentleman, who, though a deacon of a Christian church, was too much carried away with the pride of life. The mansion was decorated with every kind of ornament, and the table furnished with every luxury. As we were entering the sumptuous dining-room, Foster pinched my elbow, and said, "Is this the strait gate?"

In preaching, his delivery all through was in a low and equable voice, with a kind of surly tone, and a frequent repetition of a word at the beginning of a sentence. He had a little fierceness occasionally in his eye ; otherwise his face was set, and his arms perfectly motionless. He despised all gesticulation, and also all attempts to render anything emphatical in announcement: looking for the effect from the bare sentiment itself, unhelped by anything in the delivery, which he professed to despise. He contended that all eloquence resides essentially in the thought, and what is eloquent in *any* mode of expression would be so in *every* mode. Yet he was singularly slow in composition, and fastidious in the structure of his sentences. But, upon the admission of his own principle, how needless was the solicitude of his practice! But in *what* do any of our professions and our practices ever perfectly accord?

He declined all explicit divisions in his sermons, and was never found using the numerals " first," or " second." The notes of his discourses (I have seen many of them) seemed to consist of some leading sentences, as places from which he started to enlarge. These sentences, to change the metaphor, were seminal, and contained much matter which *he* could deduce from them; and the seemingly detached parts had some real connexion or relation, in his own mind.

An anecdote here may be instructive. I remember dining with him in company, when the gentleman who entertained us, (the conversation happening to turn upon preaching,) remarked the propriety of an obvious and numerical arrangement; stating that, whatever may be the case with educated and intellectual individuals, the greater part of an audience do not perceive what is relative unless it be expressed; nor are they able, without methodical assistance, fully and easily to receive and secure what they have heard. Mr. Foster not seemingly assenting, the gentleman proceeded to ask, what no one could deny, whether that which escaped in the mere act of hearing could do much good; and whether that was not more likely to be beneficial which remained on the mind, and would be thought of alone and repeated in company. He added, " Now, sir, here is a preacher present who heard you deliver in Bristol a few days ago a sermon which he much admired; but when I pressed for a sketch of it, he said he could not recall or relate it. But, sir, I will call in my gardener. * * * John, did you hear Mr. —— last Sunday?" " Yes, sir." " Did he not preach from such a text?" " He did, sir." " Do you remember anything of the sermon?" John, after a little reflection, replied, " Why, sir, he introduced the subject by observing what a difference there was between pretension and reality in religion,—that there may be a form of knowledge and a form of godliness without the power,—and how necessary it was to remember, and be able to distinguish this, especially with regard to ourselves. He then said the text contained three things. These he stated and severally explained. He then called upon us to examine ourselves, and I shall never forget it (it thrills through me now) how he closed with Bunyan's words, 'So I saw there is a way to hell by the gate of heaven.'"

But though Mr. Foster despised the usual order and arrangement, yet he did not leave things general and indefinite in their bearings; and there was often a pointed force and appropriateness of reflection, which *seemed* suddenly called forth without design, and which fell terribly on the conscience. This may be seen in the *Lectures* which have been published; for though they are posthumous, and none of them were entirely the discourses which he delivered, they fail not to give a just impression of his usual preaching. They also show (though too sparingly) that he held what are commonly called the peculiar doctrines of the Gospel. Of these doctrines, as a Christian, he felt the truth and importance; yet not sufficiently by believing to enter into rest, and feel that peace which passeth all understanding, keeping his heart and mind through Jesus Christ; or *fully* to enjoy the blessedness of the people who know the joyful sound, and walk all day in the light of the Lord's countenance. His mind seemed too much surrounded with gloomy, rather than cheerful, images; nothing appeared to satisfy him in civil or religious concerns; and he commonly was not indulged with the peculiar associations which well suited and pleased his mind and heart.

It is needless to speak of his endowments, which have become so generally known from his works, and so justly rated. His *Essays* have excited universal admiration, and have obtained for him a very high and established position, in the estimation of all readers of judgment and taste. These *Essays* first came to my hand on the morning of a day devoted to rural jaunting and recreation; and though I was bound to be attentive to my companions, and was always fond of natural scenery, (some fine specimens of which we were visiting,) yet, having opened the work in the carriage, I was tempted to go astray more than once in the day, to dip into the contents, which I could not leave until the morrow.

Mr. Wilberforce thought his *Essay on Popular Ignorance* much inferior to its predecessors; others have thought the same. I confess I could never see any reason for this. But priority has here an advantage; and if an author does not surpass in a second attempt, he is supposed to come short of himself. The *Lectures*, without being sermons or expositions, abound with thought; but the reflections are too subtle, or profound, for the seizure of common attention or intellect; and what degree of impression or effect did *they* produce?

I love not to draw comparisons between good and great men, but I have commonly thought he was superior to his illustrious contemporary; not in every respect, by any means, especially in learning, and composition, and eloquence; but in a kind of unlaboured penetration, an iron grasp and hold of whatever he seized; a bottomless profundity of thought, and a fulness of all kinds and degrees of illustration; nothing of which ever seemed derived *ab extra*, but all springing from his treasures within. And I found, when in Scotland, that Dr. Chalmers and others conceded to him the same *partial* pre-eminence.

I have sometimes thought of the one as having more genius, and the other more judgment; the one as having more comprehensiveness of mind, the other more force and condensation; the one having more of intuition, the other of acquirement; the one more discursive, the other more consecutive; the one more distinguished by depth, the other by height. But all this is of little significance; they were both great and extraordinary men. I knew enough of each to feel competent to describe them accurately; and, if they were to be weighed, I should strive to hold the scales.

It is worthy of observation that, though Mr. Hall, as a preacher, was so much more popular than Mr. Foster, (we were always hearing of the one, and scarcely ever of the other,) yet, since the decease of both, quotations from the sermons (I mean the unpublished,) of the former are seldom to be met with; extracts and whole skeletons from the ordinary preaching of the latter, have been, and continue to be, in various modes multiplied.

In God's hand it is to make great, and to give strength "of every kind" to all; and superior talents are never given in vain. They have their use and their value; but, lest we should idolize them, and think them essential, we often have them (unlike the instances before us), unassociated with piety; and God doing his work without them, "that the excellency of the power may be of Him, and not of them." Admired, therefore, and valuable, in their way, as natural and acquired endowments and attainments are, they are not grace; and Paul would say to us, "Covet earnestly the best gifts, and yet I show unto you a more excellent way." Many without splendid endowments have been made the power of God to save; and will have to present a number of converts, their joy and crown, in the day of the Lord Jesus. It is lamentable to reflect how little this master-genius effected, at least in the higher species of good; and how every religious interest he served was diminished, rather than increased, by his labours!

The biography of Scripture is impartial, and faithfully records the errors and miscarriages of God's greatest and dearest servants; and *need* we, *should* we, overlook the errors and imperfections of wise and good men now? Especially when they have excellences, which will bear a gentle censure without snuffing them out? And is not this the more necessary where persons are elevated, and their example the more likely to be seen, and influential; where morals, like fashions, always work downwards? We should not readily concede the dispensableness of attending on the means of grace and ordinances of religion to any. Man is not purely intellectual, nor is reason the only attribute of his nature. His mind must be approached through the medium of sense; and his fellowship with things unseen and eternal must be maintained, or aided, by those which are seen and temporal. And those eminent degrees of the divine life which, some might suppose, render attendance in the sanctuary and at the Lord's Table needless, always attach the possessor more to them. But, if some individuals could supply the place of such attendance from their own stores, yet it is otherwise with the mass of persons. Without these excitements and advantages, the very appearance of religion would soon cease among them. Therefore, how desirable and dutiful is it that we should sanction and enforce such usages, even for the sake of the public welfare, by our own example! However defective the public services may be, they conduce to some profit. Nothing tends so much to socialize, and civilize, and to produce decorum and cleanliness; so that by the want of these, you may always infer the spiritual destitution of a neighbourhood.

When residing in the vicinity of Bristol, and disengaged from office, Mr. Foster usually heard Mr. Hall, (and what marvel?) but no other minister; nor, I believe, did he even then commune at Broadmead; and, when residing for some time at Bourton-on-the-Water, he always heard the pastor, yet left the table of the Lord: and Mr. C—— (*Coles*) complained, and said what a distress it occasioned to himself, and what a stumbling-block it proved in the way of some of the members. I presume, (but I am not certain,) that in the several places where he officiated as the pastor himself, he administered the Lord's Supper; but as to the other

ordinance, he never dispensed it, or attended the administration; and, after several attempts, Mr. Hughes, his most
familiar friend, assured me, he never could get him to
express himself upon the subject; but had a full persuasion
that, with the *Friends*, he did not believe in the perpetuity
of water-baptism.

I never knew a person, (with the exception of Mande-
ville and Rochefoucault,) who had such views of the badness
and depravity of human nature. He seemed to regard it
as a mass of entire corruption, and especially of *aversion*
in *everything* towards God; so that he saw nothing in it
capable of being altered, or *improved* into something better;
and religion was not with him a transformation, by the
renewing of the mind; but a perfect reproduction and substitution of other powers, through the power of God. His
views also of ministerial and missionary labours, far from
being sanguine, were scarcely hopeful; and his expectation
of a better state of things did not arise from the blessing of
God on the use of the means we possess, but from an express interposition of Almightiness coercing its effects.

And who can commend his wish to break up all church-
institutions and orders, leaving religion to individual influence and exertion; or at most to domestic? In several
of these things he was joined and aided by another remarkable and talented character, a member of my congregation,
Mr. Thomas Parsons, of whom I have spoken in my published funeral sermon.

But is it wise to abandon the present methods of doing
good because of their defectiveness, instead of gradually
endeavouring to improve them? Who knows what may be
the result between the giving up of the old means, and the
establishment and prevalence of the new; for the change
may not be easily, and, therefore, not speedily accomplished;
and who can be certain of its greater benefit and usefulness? We actually know what is now doing, and may

hope for greater things than these, by the blessing of God upon our wise and active use of our present instrumentalities. "To him that hath shall be given, and he shall have more abundance; but from him that hath not shall be taken away, even that which he *seemeth* to have."

Mr. Foster, though great in all his productions, appears to me greatest in his *Reviews*. The more I read them, the more I am astonished at the quickness and clearness of his perceptions; the power of his discrimination; his detection of sophistry; his love of fairness, rectitude, and truth; his sly, yet just sarcasms; his stinging satire; his abomination of pedantry and pretence. Nor is my admiration abated by comparison, when I read the contributions of Macaulay, Jeffrey, and Mackintosh; and nothing surprises me more, than that the purchase of the two volumes of his contributions has not been rapid and extensive enough, to induce the editor to send forth the large remainder, now shut up in the *Eclectic Review*.

But the production of his pen, the most spiritually important, and the most adapted to awaken the conscience and to urge the heart to God, (perhaps, too, the best written,) is the *Essay* prefixed to Dr. Doddridge's *Rise and Progress of Religion in the Soul*. Why is not this more known? Why is it not published separately?*

Yet, as to himself, the choice of that work for this prefix (for the subject was at his option,) was remarkable. As in scenery he could not endure the old forms in which gardens were laid out, in squares, and parterres, and yew-trees cut into formal figures; but something bordering on rude, in which *nature* was seen rather than art; something rather wild than neatly cultured; ever yielding freshness and having no bounds,—so it was as to his taste with regard to publications; especially also as to the commencement of

---

* It was published separately,—probably after Mr. Jay put this question.—EDITORS.

religion. He conceived that it began by some one powerful emotion or impression, and never from any plan or scheme laid out in long and regular perspective. He would say, "I love a scene in which nature keeps much in her own hands."

Mr. Cottle (Foster's friend, and, I am happy to say, my own also,) once showed me a letter of Mr. Foster's, concerning this prefixed *Essay*. It may be curious and gratifying to subjoin a copy. It will serve, as the receiver remarked, to show the complex motives and manner in which important productions originate and are perfected.

My DEAR SIR,—Dr. Chalmers some three years since started a plan of reprinting, in a neat form, a number of respectable religious works of the older date, with a preliminary Essay to each, relating to the book, or to any analogous topic, at the writer's discretion. The Glasgow booksellers, Chalmers and Collins, the one the Doctor's brother, and the other his most confidential friend, have accordingly reprinted a series of perhaps now a dozen works, with essays, several by Dr. Chalmers, and several by Irving, one by Wilberforce, one by Daniel Wilson, &c. &c. I believe Hall and Cunningham have promised their contributions. I was inveigled into a similar promise more than two years since. The work strongly urged on me for this service in the first instance, was 'Doddridge's Rise and Progress;' and the contribution was actually promised to be furnished with the least possible delay; on the strength of which the book was immediately printed off, and has actually been lying in their warehouse as dead stock these two years. I was admonished and urged again and again; but, in spite of the mortification and shame which I could not but feel, at thus occasioning the publisher a certain positive loss, my horror of writing, combined with ill health, invincibly prevailed, and not a paragraph was written till towards the end of last year, when I did summon resolution for the attempt. When I had written but a few pages, the reluctant labour was interrupted and suspended by the more interesting one of writing those letters to our dear young friend, your niece (Miss Saunders). Not, of course, that this latter employment did not allow me time enough for the other; but by its more lively interest it had the effect of augmenting my disinclination to the other. Soon after her removal, I resumed the task, and am ashamed to acknowledge such a miserable and matchless slowness of mental operation, that the task held me confined ever since, till actually within these few days. I believe that nothing but a strong sense of the duty of fulfilling my engagement, and of not continuing to do a real injury to the publishers, could have constrained me to so long a labour. It is most mortifying to think of so slender a result of so much time and toil. The article is, indeed, of the length of one half of Doddridge's book; but many of my contemporary makers of sentences would have produced as much with one-fifth part of the time and labour. I have aimed at great correctness and condensation, and have found the labour of revisal and transcription not very much less than that of the substantial composition. The thing has been prolonged, I should say spun out, to three times the length which was at first intended, or was required. It has very little reference to the book which it accompanies, has no special topic, and is merely a serious inculcation of the necessity of religion on young persons and men of the world. In point of merit, (that, you know, is the word in such matters,) I rate it very moderately, except in respect to correctness and clearness of expression. If it do not possess these qualities, a vast deal of care and labour has been sadly thrown away. I suppose the thing is just about making up, to be sent from the publishers' warehouse. I shall have a little parcel of copies, and shall presume to request the acceptance of one in Dighton-street.

"My dear Sir, I am absolutely ashamed to have been led into this length, of what is no better than egotism, when I was meaning just five lines, to tell what has detained me from the pleasure of seeing you.

"My dear Sir,
"Yours most truly,
"JOHN FOSTER."

LADY MAXWELL AND THE REV. JOHN WESLEY.

I HAVE mentioned in another place my meeting with Lady Maxwell in Bristol, and her engaging me to preach at Hope Chapel, at the Hotwells. (1789.)

This place of worship had been founded, and the cause advanced, by Lady Hope and Lady Glenorchy. The former (whose name it bears,) died before its completion. This was also the case with her successor, Lady Glenorchy, on whose death it came into the hands of Lady Maxwell. She finished it, and opened it for the service of God; and had it supplied for some time by a succession of ministers; and managed by a selection of gentlemen from the several congregations in Bristol, two of whom in succession always attended on the Sabbath, to arrange the affairs of the infant interest. But this plan was soon found very inconvenient and troublesome. It seemed desirable that the chapel should have a fixed minister. The trial was made, and it commenced with the Reminiscent.

Lady Maxwell was a very holy and pious woman, with a considerable tinge of enthusiasm in her constitution. Her Memoirs have been published in two volumes. Some of her religious views were peculiar, or not easily explained. She had a notion of communing with the Persons in the Divine Nature *individually* and *separately*, i.e., one day more particularly, if not exclusively, with the Father, another with the

Son, and a third with the Holy Ghost.   Has not Dr. Owen
a little verged towards this in his work on "Communion
with God?"   But here it was not only admitted, but pleaded
for, as of great importance, and reaching the very *acme* of
Christian experience.

Her ladyship was peculiarly attached to Mr. Wesley.
Her doctrines, unless in the above articles, accorded entirely
with his; but as these were not precisely the sentiments of
the two foundresses of the place, who were Presbyterians,
she determined it should not be said that she availed herself
of her privilege to introduce them; and, by a very scrupulous delicacy, admitted none of Mr. Wesley's preachers to
officiate there, and not even himself.

The place had not long been opened when I undertook
the service.   A congregation was to be raised.   Though
young and immature, my labours were acceptable and useful; and while there the Lord gave me three converts, all
of whom entered the ministry and laboured well.   Here I
remained for nearly twelve months; and, being pressed by
her ladyship as well as the congregation, here I should perhaps have continued, but for a dispute with a good female,
whom her ladyship left to manage the secular concerns of
the place.   It regarded her interfering with the ecclesiastical also.   In this disagreement we were both to blame.   Two
things I learned from it,—

First, To prefer the government of females in the family,
rather than in the church; and,

Secondly, To observe on what slender things often hinge
the most important events of our lives.   This disagreement
determined me to accept the invitation I had just then
received from Bath.

During my stay at Hope Chapel, I had the honour and
pleasure of dining at her Ladyship's house, with the venerable Mr. Wesley.   He kindly noticed me, and inquired after
Mr. Winter, adding, "Cornelius is an excellent man."   This

was the more candid; as Mr. Winter, in a letter, a copy of which I have, had testified freely against some of Mr. Wesley's opinions. At the first interview, there were in the company the Rev. Mr. Moore, one of Mr. Wesley's biographers, and several other preachers in his connexion; and among these was a Captain Webb, deprived of one eye at the battle of Bunker's Hill, who held forth commonly without-doors in regimentals. As I wished to hear Mr. Wesley talk, nothing could be more mortifying than the incessant garrulity of this fanatical rodomontader; and I much wondered Mr. Wesley, who had such influence over his adherents, did not repress, or at least rebuke, some of his spiritual vagaries and supernatural exploits. Did this master in Israel think it harmless to tolerate a kind of visionary agency, and suppose that it was better for the common people to believe too much rather than too little?

At my second interview, among others was the Rev. Mr. Easterbrook, the Vicar of Temple parish; one of the best men I ever knew; and at whose death, it is said, some respectful notice was taken of him in every pulpit in the City. He denied himself to an extreme to give to him that needeth, and was always going about doing good. As evidential of his liberality of mind, as well as of heart, when Mr. Hoskins, a dissenting minister, opened a large room for preaching in his extensive parish, he himself attended the opening; and embracing him before the people as he came out of the pulpit, said, " I thank you, my brother, for coming to my aid." This very good man, (for so he was,) erred a little on the side of credulity and superstition. A few weeks before this, an extraordinary service, with fasting and prayer, had been held in his church, attended by several ministers in the Methodist connexion, to dispossess a supposed demoniac. This was John Lukins, who had exhibited some strange appearances, and uttered some kind of singular sounds, which his friends were unable physically to account for. The man was present at the service, and the spirit supposed to be in him was addressed, and in the name of Christ was ordered to come out of him. After some shrieks and contortions he became gentle, and exhibited nothing more of his former malady. I knew the man afterwards, and more than once relieved him. The case naturally excited even public attention, and gave rise to several pamphlets; the chief of which was written by an eminent surgeon in Bath, in whose native place Lukins was born.

I should not have related this, but it unfortunately engrossed the conversation for nearly the whole of the afternoon; and because, to my great surprise, Mr. Wesley seemed to admit the reality of the possession and dispossession, and to consider it as nothing less than a wonderful work of God. After tea I went with him in his carriage into Bristol, and heard him preach from Ephes. v. 8—" Ye were sometimes darkness, but now are ye light in the Lord: walk as children of light." It was the only opportunity I ever had of hearing this truly apostolical man. The whole scene was very picturesque and striking. Several preachers stood in the large pulpit around him: the sermon was short, the language terse and good, but entirely devoid of expansion and imagery, while the delivery was low and unanimated. This surprised me. Was it the influence and effect of age? If it was originally the same, how came he to be so popular, among the rude multitudes which always attended him, and so hung upon his lips? Whitfield's voice and vehemence, and strong emotions, will in some measure account for the impressions he produced, even regardless of the grace of God which accompanied them. How popular and useful was Berridge! yet he had nothing of the vulgar orator in his manner; it was plain and unimpassioned. This was the case also with many of the original corps of evangelists.

—— HOLMES, ESQ.

WITH this gentleman I became intimately acquainted early in my ministry. He then resided at Ide, in the vicinity of Exeter. He had good natural talents; was well educated; read the Scriptures familiarly in their original languages; and could speak French fluently. He was also, without assuming the ministerial office, occasionally a preacher. For though he had retired from merchandise, in which God had prospered him, he did not consider himself as thereby justified in living a life of ease and indolence; but as the more bound (as in some respects the more able,) to do good; and to serve his own generation, according to the will of God, especially in their spiritual interests.

He possessed an ample fortune, kept his carriage, and lived in a genteel style becoming his circumstances; but expended nothing in gay extravagance, and saved up nothing by sordid hoarding. He viewed himself as a steward, used his property as a talent, and kept in mind the day of account.

I pass by his private benefactions, in which he never sought to be seen of men, to notice two or three things of a more public nature, by which being dead he yet speaketh; and in which, I hope, he may be instructive and exemplary.

Observing the people in the villages so exceedingly ignorant and irreligious, he found out individuals of good character and decent capacity; and employed them as schoolmasters during the week, and as preachers on the Sabbath, and supported them at his own expense. He was the means of reopening some meeting-houses which error had shut up, of repairing others that were decaying, and of enlarging others that had become too small.

He erected, exclusively at his own cost, a large and commodious chapel at Teignmouth; and principally, if not entirely, supported it for some years. When he resolved on this, there were no pious individuals in the place. I only remember (and I had opportunities of knowing,) one person who made any pretension to serious religion. And here I differed from my friend, thinking that, in all cases of this kind, we should first make trial of the will of God, and see if there is a disposition to hear, and then build. But the founder said, he was strongly impressed with the importance of the measure, and was fully persuaded in due time much good would be done by means of it. His expectation, however, was not immediately accomplished. Some years passed before there was any considerable appearance of success. It must indeed be allowed that, for a good while, the preaching was not much suited to the station, or adapted to convert or to edify. But in process of time things changed for the better; a good congregation was raised, and the church made to prosper, and continue to be a flourishing interest. I preached at the opening. My subjects were, Psalm xciii. 5, "Holiness becometh thine house, O Lord, for ever;"— and 1 Sam. i. 13, "Now Hannah, she spake in her heart; only her lips moved, but her voice was not heard: therefore Eli thought she had been drunken."

Owing to its being opened on the Lord's-day, ministers could not attend without leaving their own places. One brother only was there, but he took no part in the service, except the introductory prayer. Being a hypochondriac he had left his pastoral office. I never had the pleasure of seeing him again. But I heard afterwards of his misfortune, shall I call it?—or happiness? He was a man of sober years, and was going to be conjugated to a dame of discretion; but happening to pass a fortnight with her at the house of a relation previously to their union, they gained such a mutual increase of knowledge, as induced them to be satisfied to remain *in statu quo*.

The first six Sabbaths I remained to officiate. Mr. Holmes himself preached in the afternoon, and I in the morning and evening. We came from his house on the Saturday, and returned on the Monday. Our accommodations were always at the inn.

Mr. Holmes had children by his first wife, but they all died young. His second wife was the daughter of the Rector of W——n. She had then two brothers in the church, evangelical preachers, but afterwards turned away from the truth. I trust she was a good woman; but though she had married a rich Dissenter, her heart was left behind. I could perceive, the six weeks I resided in the house, that she did not relish what her husband was doing out of the Establishment; and I foresaw what would be the consequence, if she survived him. The event took place, and the apprehension was realized. It is desirable when persons marry, to marry as much as possible in their own religious community. To justify a contrary course, two things are at least necessary:

First: That they hold the sentiments in which they differ with moderation, and feel them to be subordinate: and

Secondly: That they consent to attend the same place of worship. Worshipping together cherishes and promotes social and devout affections; and has a lively and favourable effect upon children and servants. What evil consequences have I often seen arising from husbands and wives, fathers and mothers, always repairing to separate sanctuaries, or worshipping alternately at different places!

I do not herein condemn myself. I married the daughter of a clergyman, but there was no separation in our devotions, or differences in the training of our children. We united with each other much more as Christians, than Episcopalians and Dissenters; and never had we, in a long and happy union, one word of discord, or even dispute.

I happened, in my way to the opening of a Meeting-house at Tavistock, to spend a week at Paignton. The people of Teignmouth hearing of this, sent a deputation to urge me to preach for them on the following Sabbath, as it was the very day of my opening their sanctuary thirty years before. This I did, and was pleased to see the state of things, so prosperous and promising. Two days after, when I had reached Totnes, as the chaise was at the door to take me forward to Tavistock, I was recalled home by a messenger announcing the apprehended death of my youngest daughter, whom I had left perfectly well. I was only in time to see her expire. How much do times and places derive from association and recollection! What have been my feelings in passing through Totnes since!

To proceed with this Reminiscence.—On my return from the dedication of the chapel at Teignmouth to Bath, Mr. Holmes brought me in his carriage as far as Taunton, where I took coach. He had made engagements for me to preach on my way back at Chudleigh, Tiverton, Wellington, and Taunton. At Taunton I preached for Mr. Reader, then the Tutor of the Western Academy. He was a very pious and spiritual man; but had for some time past been led inordinately to the study of the Revelation of St. John. His wife assured me, that, sometimes, for nearly an hour together, would he be agonizing with God in prayer, when he found difficulties in the Book, and could get no satisfaction from human authors. Hence he too readily concluded, that what came into his mind after these prayers, was the meaning of the Holy Ghost; and this made him too positive in his interpretations. As " out of the abundance of the heart the mouth speaketh," his reference to the Apocalypse was almost incessant. My friend apprized me of this addiction, and desired me to observe, as we were approaching his house, how long it would be before he brought forth his favourite topic. Within a quarter of an hour, the name of Mr. Newton was incidentally mentioned; when he said, "Ah, Mr. Newton is a very good man, but God will correct him before his death." Wherefore? it was asked. "Because of his indifference," said he, "towards the blessed Book of the Revelation." I asked wherein he had shown this indifference. "Sir," said he, "when I had finished my Exposition of that Book, I sent him a copy for his acceptance, and begged his opinion of the work; and this," said he, pulling a letter out of his bureau, "is his answer :—'Dear Sir,—I am much obliged by your kindness in sending me the volume on the Apocalypse; but you must excuse me for not criticising the contents, for which I have neither leisure nor ability. I hope God has for some years given me a word in season for him that is weary, but he has not given a capacity to open the seals.—I am, &c., John Newton.'"

Now, I do not go the length of South, nor admire the unhallowed wit that says,—"The Revelation always finds a man mad, or leaves him so:" yet we may learn from this good man; and what I say concerning him, I speak as with affection, so I speak only what I could verify :—this kind of prophetical zeal gave a sort of new and unhappy turn to his preaching. It injuriously affected the congregation :—

"The hungry sheep look'd up and were not fed;"

and sinners heard less of repentance towards God, and faith towards our Lord Jesus Christ, than before.

We are not ignorant of *his* devices who is not only the accuser of the brethren, but the tempter too. Had he addressed this excellent man with anything obviously erroneous or sinful, he would have said, "Get thee behind me,

Satan." But it was otherwise when he approached him in a sacred attire, with the Bible in his hand, and this text in his mouth,—" Blessed is he that readeth, and they that understand the words of this prophecy."

Would it not be well if professors, and especially preachers, were not only to think of the difficulty, (not to say impossibility,) of deciding many things in dispute—but remember their little value, comparatively, if demonstrated? —" What is the chaff to the wheat ? "

After preaching for this good old man, and returning into his house, he said, " Sir, I did not like what you said of candour this evening." I answered, " I think I sufficiently guarded it, and distinguished it from indifference with regard to essential truth." " Sir," said he, " you have had many apostates to hear you, and they will think too favourably of you." While he was thus speaking, Mr. (afterwards Dr.) Toulmin was introduced into the parlour, asking me to preach for him, like Robinson, saying, his pulpit was open to all good men. At this, Mr. Reader pounced upon me—a confirmation of what he had said; nor did he ask the applicant to sit down, or even speak to him. And is this the meekness of wisdom? If we cannot love persons as Christians, are we to refuse them civilities as men? Is this the way to win souls? Not that I was disposed to preach for him. I never officiated but twice in a Unitarian pulpit; and in each instance I took care not to be asked under an ignorance of my sentiments. I said, " The thing with me is not *where* I preach, but *what* I preach. I must speak according to my own principles. Allow me this liberty and I will comply. I shall not go out of my way to insult or oppose; but I cannot forbear to deliver what my conscience tells me I should deliver from the same text in my own place."

Having said all that honesty and fairness required, I spoke with freedom; but one of the two ministers who invited me the first time, went out in the middle of the discourse, and the other before I began had rather cautiously intimated that—" it was always better to avoid abstruse doctrines, and teach our people how to keep God's commandments and find their way to heaven." I told him I always made this *my* ultimate aim.—Yet I felt not at home. I seemed not to be among my own people, and was not a little embarrassed in the intercessory part of my prayer for the ministers; for under what character could I pray for them as *Pastors?*

I was only once after this coldly asked, and I refused; for, besides the difficulty I had felt in the performance, I considered how liable it was to misconstruction; and how careful we should be not to offend against the generation of the upright. Upon the same principle Mr. Hall acted. He had occasionally, when he came to Bristol, preached for Mr. E——n, the Unitarian minister; but after a while, with godly prudence, he declined; and saved from surmise, fear, and distress, some who, if not his most intelligent, were yet his most pious and prayerful hearers. The last sermon he preached there was against Atheism!

I see in his Diary, Mr. Toplady (who lived not far from Exeter,) though a beneficed clergyman, was most cordially intimate with Mr. Holmes.—Here I insert two short extracts from Mr. Toplady's Posthumous Volumes, pages 279 and 285.

" Spent about an hour and a half with good Mr. Holmes, whom I found in great distress, on account of his only surviving son being given over in a fever. During our interview, God so opened my mouth and so enlarged my heart, that I trust both my friend and myself found our spiritual strength renewed, and were sensibly and powerfully comforted from above."

" After breakfast, rode to Exeter, where I dined at Mr. Holmes's. Found that dear and excellent man not only more resigned to the will of God, but even more cheerful than I could have conceived.—Mrs. Paul, of Topsham, and Mr. Lewis, a worthy Baptist minister, dined with us. Our conversation at table was on the best subjects; and I found our Christian discussions sensibly blessed to my soul. After tea, myself and four more followed the remains of Master Holmes to Cade, about two miles out of the city, where they were interred. Mr. Cole, curate of the parish, read the funeral service. I preached a sermon, suitable to the solemn occasion, to a large auditory, and one of the most attentive ones I ever saw."

—— WELSH, ESQ.

I AM the more inclined to speak of this good man because I *believe* no account of him, even in a funeral discourse, has been published. I can assign no reason for this; but, as we proceed in this brief narrative, the omission will raise our wonder, and show us that the excellency ánd usefulness of persons, are not to be always estimated by the noise they make, or the notice they excite at the time. I say "*at the time*," because, as the thing is only partial, so it is often only temporary. In due season, and in a way which *marks* the providence of God, he brings forth their "righteousness as the light, and their judgment as the noonday." How many of the Nonconformists are now admired, whose names were even cast out as evil! When Cowper wrote, he seemed forbidden to mention Whitfield by name;—

> "Leuconomus, (beneath well-sounding Greek,
> I slur a name a poet must not speak)."

Is there a man now in the kingdom but considers him an upright, honest man, who lived only to do good? But Bunyan! poor Bunyan! that ignoramus, that fanatic, that rebel, that traitor to his country, insulted on his trial, infamously condemned, cruelly imprisoned for twelve long years; what—where—is he now? His book is acknowledged the first of allegories, and his Statue has been voted into one of our parliamentary niches!

Good men should be willing to leave their reputation, like everything else, with God; and it is well if, when little is said of *them*, yet their works praise them in the gate. By these "the *memory* of the just is blessed."

Mr. Welsh was a considerable banker in London. One of the partners in the firm was Mr. Rogers, the father of the poet. His wife was a daughter of the famous Thomas Bradbury, of political, polemic, and facetious memory; and she had much of her father's humour about her. She often mentioned some of his witticisms. I wish I had recorded them. Two of them at this moment I just remember. One day, meeting with a man who was going to push him from the wall, saying, "I don't choose to give the wall to every fool I meet,"—says Mr. Bradbury, "I do, and so pray take it." Another day he was at the coffee-house, where several gentlemen were reading the papers; and one of them having read that, the Sunday before, a man who was violating the Sabbath fell from his horse, and fractured his leg and thigh; upon which he said, turning to Mr. Bradbury, "I suppose, Mr. Bradbury, you deem this a Divine judgment?" "Why, sir," said Mr. Bradbury, "if you deem it a Divine mercy, we will have no dispute about it."

The church over which the Reminiscent has so long and happily presided, owed very much to the zeal and liberality of Mr. Welsh. He unceasingly nursed it in its infant state; and, when it had only a small and incommodious place to assemble in, he, principally at his own expense, fitted up the old Roman Catholic chapel, which had been left very much in ruins, from the Protestant riots in 1780. He also, from their having only a successional and uncertain supply of preachers, recommended to them an able pastor, who could feed them with knowledge and understanding, and engaged to support him, till the congregation should be capable of bearing the burden themselves.

Mr. Welsh commonly passed some weeks, if not months,

annually in Bath; and nothing in these visits afforded him more pleasure, than to observe the cause he had so patronized increasing and prospering; and this was the case even after the loss of my predecessor, the Rev. Thomas Tuppen, whom he had introduced; and especially after the opening of our new chapel in Argyle-street, and which even then required to be enlarged.

But this was not all, but comparatively little, of what Mr. Welsh accomplished. I was once passing the evening with him; he was in a very solemn and feeling mood; and after a while he said, with tears, "I am growing old, and I ought, and I wish, to do something more to glorify God, and serve my generation, according to his will, than I have done; and I have the means." Several schemes passed under our review; and at last he mentioned what (as I entirely approved of) I did all in my power to enforce. I will simply specify the case.

At this time, our country was in a state very different from its present condition. It was generally under the greatest of all curses, the curse of an unregenerate ministry; especially in the smaller towns and villages, where many of the people, though in a land of vision, and with an Established Church, were yet perishing for lack of knowledge.

We, therefore, thought (for it was the King's business, and required haste,) that it was desirable immediately to search out, and educate, a number of young men of gifts and grace for the ministry, and place them in a kind of domestic academies. These seminaries were not to be in opposition to any larger and higher establishments, but rather in addition to them. They were to give these young men a less literary training, but a more theological and practical one; or with a fuller reference principally, though not exclusively, to divinity and preaching. These students were to be placed for some years under the care of ministers of piety, experience, and competent learning, residing in separate localities;

and where they could be, even during their tuition, employed in teaching the poor, and ignorant, and vicious; and, while employed, to be also improved, and *actually* prepared for their work, like those who are taught to run by running, and to walk by walking, and not by mere rule and lesson.

Of seven tutors, Mr. Welsh chose three, engaging to support several students under each. Cornelius Winter was one of them. He had, indeed, been engaged in such work before; though without any *regular* and *certain* provision for expense, like Professor Franke, at Halle, in *his* work of *faith* and labour of *love*.

The Reminiscent was not one of Mr. Welsh's students, but belonged to an earlier class under Mr. Winter's care; and principally supported by John Thornton, Esq., Sir Richard Hill, and others.

Mr. Welsh married a second time, late in life, the half-sister of Dr. Evans, of Bristol. He lived to a good old age, and died very suddenly. I had preached before him in the morning, from the words of our Lord to the Church at Ephesus :—" To him that overcometh will I grant to sit with me on my throne." It was the last sermon he heard; and, one hour after, rising from dinner to return thanks, he fell down upon the floor, and expired :—

> " A soul prepared needs no delays;
>   The summons comes, the saint obeys;
>   Swift was his flight, and short the road,—
>   He closed his eyes, and woke with God ! "

To conclude this brief and imperfect memoir.—We read of " the spirit of judgment and the spirit of burning." This is a fine and an advantageous union; fervour enlivens prudence, and prudence qualifies fervour. Therefore, says the Apostle, " Let your love abound yet more and more, in all knowledge, and in all judgment." As if he should say, " Be not weary in well-doing, but in your benevolence exercise discretion as to time, and place, and means, and manner; and as your ability is always but small, endeavour to make a little go a great way." I cannot but think a more judicious course of usefulness could not have been chosen than that which Mr. Welsh encouraged; and, though some were disposed to contemn it at first, and though more may now deem it too humble for *modern* Dissent, yet how many opportunities have I had, and thousands more, of witnessing its blessed effects, in turning sinners from darkness to light; in evangelizing heathen neighbourhoods, and even in forming congregations, whose beginning indeed was small, but whose latter end greatly increased!

And here, without the least wish to check or undervalue superior degrees of literary attainment, may not the Reminiscent be allowed to ask a few questions? Is there no distinction between an educated and a learned ministry? If—(and the Apostle says, " Christ sent me not to baptize, but to preach the Gospel,") if the chief design of the ministry is to preach, and faith cometh by hearing, should not everything in the preparation be made to bear principally upon *it*? And is *this* unceasingly and obviously the case in all our existing institutions? Are mathematical and classical acquirements, especially in their higher degrees, equally necessary in *all* stations, and for *all* teachers? Are there not cases in which these distinctions may relatively even disqualify, more than help; *first*, by their aptness to draw away the preacher too much into the pursuit of things in which he excels, and in which, therefore, he delights? and, *secondly*, by betraying him into a manner of address less intelligible, familiar, and impressive, to the mass of his audience? Is not a minister of the Gospel to be the teacher of religion, the subjects of which are matter of pure testimony and not of reasoning; and, therefore, little depending on talent and science? for " by faith we stand." Is there no difference in the department of preparation, between a kingdom which is "not of this world," and one which is? Is the minister to be laboriously qualified to meet the casual, intellectual few, rather than the *certain many*, that may attend his teaching? Is the church the proper and express sphere for the highest cultivation of genius and literature; or for studying and striving for degrees and titles derived from the arts and sciences? Far be it from the Reminiscent to domineer or dictate; but may he not again ask, Is there any mode of address, so little likely to be popularly useful as that of a dry, cold intellectuality? Is there no difference between the press and the pulpit? May not that which is proper for the one, be unsuitable for the other? Is there no difference between a treatise and a sermon? I will buy the former, if it be published, and read it with pleasure; but I will never hear it under the form of the latter, if I know it. Can a discourse adapted to general improvement, safely admit more than a certain portion of intelligence and argument? Can that be felt, which is not understood? And that carried away which is not portable? And is there no danger of rendering the Scriptures in time, a mere book for criticism, and to be treated scientifically; without regarding it for the sole purpose for which it was given,—to guide our feet into the path of life, and to answer the inquiry, "What must I do to be saved?"

But to return. Let us redeem our time, and use our resources and abilities, whatever they may be; and let us never forget that, if we have not ten talents, we have one; and that the man with one talent was the unprofitable servant, and therefore the wicked servant, and therefore the *punished* servant. He hid his talent in a napkin. And let us see what a *single* individual may accomplish, when (as it is said of the builders at the Temple,) he has "a mind to work." What good did this man effect, by the natural and simple instrumentality which he set in motion! Why, "there is joy in the presence of the angels of God, over one sinner that repenteth." He that saves one soul from death, does more than he who rescues a country from civil bondage. And how many were hereby turned from the error of their way, and made partakers of that "godliness, which is profitable unto all things, having promise of the life that now is, as well as of that which is to come!" Yes; and how *extensive* was the good done to all these! for it not only saved their souls, but blessed their bodies, and the labour of their hands, and their relations and families. And then, how *perpetuated* was this good! The subjects of it themselves were the medium of it to others; and now, even now, it is operating in various influences and effects, and will continue to operate till the last day.

And by what was he rendered most a benefactor? By the consecration of a measure of his substance to the service of his God and Saviour. One is almost afraid to speak in favour of money, lest avarice should hail the remark, and capture the praise, and apply it to perverted purposes. But, the truth is, that while the love of money is the root of all evil, the use of it may be made the root of all good. In one respect, it is the most important of all agencies, because it can employ in its service *all* other instrumentalities—labour, genius, eloquence, learning, and even piety itself. The lawful acquisition of it, therefore, should never be neglected; a penny of it should never be wasted; nor a farthing of it be sordidly or needlessly hoarded up. "Charge them," says the Apostle, "that are rich in this world, that they do good; that they be rich in good works, ready to distribute, willing to communicate." Again, he says, "To do good, and to communicate, forget not, for with such sacrifices God is well pleased."

Thus did Mr. Welsh. He was in a good degree his own executor, and had the satisfaction to see the seed he had sown ripened and reaped. Nor was it a small sum, which

he only in this one instance employed, in defraying the
expenses of the tuition and boarding of such a number of
students, from year to year.

But what shall we say of some, yes, even professors of
religion, who perhaps began with little, accumulated much,
did nothing with their abundance while they lived, and
secured by their accursed treasures the depravity and destruction of their descendants when they died! Shame be
to those pliant ministers who, in compliment to their connexions, will preach funeral sermons for such characters,—
unless they take for their text, "But whoso hath this world's
good, and seeth his brother have need, and shutteth up his
bowels of compassion from him; how dwelleth the love of
God in him?"—There are two suppositions concerning these
men. The first is awful, and we shrink back from it. "Lo,
this is the man that made not God his trust, but trusted in
the multitude of his riches."—"With these words," says the
Jewish Rabbi, "the angels sing down to hell the soul of
the wealthy sinner, when it leaves his body." We do not
believe this; we have a better opinion of those heavenly
beings than to suppose they rejoice and sing at the misery of
any creature, though they may acquiesce in it. But says
Young—

"Hell's loudest laugh—the thought of dying rich."

The second is perplexing. It regards the supposition,
(how hard to be realized!) that those persons who die in
such affluence are received up into glory. We naturally
think that grief and shame can never enter heaven; and yet
Christians are never more happy now than when they are.
most ashamed, and mourn after a godly sort, under a sense
of the Divine goodness. It seems improbable, that those
saints who died so rich will then be free from certain reflections. There is a relation between the present and the
future; and not a relation of sequence only, but one of

cause and effect; for "whatsoever a man soweth, that shall he also reap; he that soweth to the flesh shall of the flesh reap corruption; but he that soweth to the Spirit, shall of the Spirit reap life everlasting." No one can deny, that there will be in another world a consciousness of our state and conduct in this; but the consciousness must affect us, according to the nature and quality of the recollections themselves. In that world, things will be seen clearly and perfectly; and, in the morality and holiness of heaven, there must be righteousness in our feelings, as well as in our conceptions. What, then, we should be ready to say, must such an individual think and feel, when he knows what a power of every kind of usefulness his wealth gave him, and remembering what good he neglected to do with it;—the many poor he might have fed and clothed; the children he might have educated; the academical institutions he might have endowed; the Gospel he might have extended; the souls he might have saved! And when, in addition to this, he reflects upon the evil his property is now doing,—surrounding his children and dependants with temptations, providing for their evil passions; so much going to the gaming-table, so much in riotous living, so much swallowed up in the pride of life; the evil still extending and multiplying, and operating in its effects, perhaps for generations to come! And when he remembers, how the Book he was constantly reading and hearing, charged him to be *a good steward of the manifold gifts of God!* And when he sees face to face Him, who, "though he was rich, yet for our sakes became poor, that we through His poverty might be made rich;" who was always going about doing good, and who said, "It is more blessed to give than to receive," and gave His life a ransom for us. We leave the subject,—" *Consider of it, take advice, and speak your mind.*"

ROBERT SPEAR, ESQ.

SOME considerable notice of Mr. Spear appeared, after his death, in the papers and magazines. There was also a larger memoir of him by Dr. Raffles, in a quarterly periodical. The writer was very adequate for such a work, as far as talent was concerned, but he was not intimately acquainted with the person who was the subject of it. And when I was in Edinburgh, where Mr. Spear died, Dr. Stuart, with others, who all well knew and much esteemed him, wished a fuller and more particular account of him could be sent forth; and desired the Reminiscent to undertake it; but this he declined from some peculiar circumstances in the family, and also from too much engagement, and too little leisure and health at the time.

Mr. Spear, under the blessing of Providence, had risen to affluence by his own exertions and skill. He was a cotton-merchant, residing at Manchester. He stood very high in the commercial world for ability and integrity, for fairness and honour. I remember a very clever American, who had long known him, and had large dealings with him, saying, that while he preferred English merchants to those of any other nation, he preferred Mr. Spear to any even of his own nation.

Having met at Cadiz with a quantity of cotton of a fine and superior kind, he very advantageously purchased the whole; and soon introduced its growth into Georgia, where he kept and employed an agent of his own, sent from Manchester to encourage the culture, and purchase the produce. He loved not speculation, yet in his line of business it could hardly be avoided. He, therefore, laid down this rule for his own government therein,—that he would keep a certain sum appropriated to this purpose; and that it should be no more than he thought he could afford to lose, without injuring his *family* or his *temper*.

"He that maketh haste to be rich shall not be innocent;" and "they that will be rich fall into temptation and a snare, and into many foolish and hurtful lusts." But when the acquisition of property is not made an absolute aim, but is a consequence left with the providence of God in the discharge of duty, it will not be found so commonly corruptive and injurious. Mr. Spear knew it became him not to be slothful in business; and God blessed the labour of his hands. Yet as riches increased, he set not his heart upon them; but viewed them as a talent for which he was responsible, and by which he was "to do good and to communicate." And who can estimate the measure and degree of his benevolence and beneficence? His bountifulness was *impartial*. He loved all who loved our Lord Jesus Christ in sincerity; and aided many institutions and charities, which belonged not to his own immediate connexions. His beneficence was also very *extensive*. He devised liberal things. He gave largely to the Bible Society, and to the London Missionary Society. With regard to the latter, at the first public collection at his own chapel in Moseley Street, Manchester, designing it to be secret, he slipped a £300 note into the plate, which was only discovered accidentally. He contributed generously to several of our academies for the education of young men for the ministry;[*] and as, "owing to the spiritual de-

---

[*] A valued correspondent says, "Mr. Spear supported entirely the education of a considerable number of pious men for the Christian ministry, under the judicious care of the late Rev. W. Roby,

stitution of the people, especially in the villages and smaller towns," many laymen were engaged in teaching,—to render them more acceptable and useful, he remunerated an able minister to instruct them in the evenings, as they had leisure; and even from this humble source of improvement issued several able preachers, who in time became pastors of churches.

There was another thing with which I was struck, (for after my intimate friendship with him I knew much of his liberal measures,) and I mention it as rather original, as well as exemplary. He looked out and employed in several parts of thickly-peopled localities pious men and women, whose houses were to be day-schools to which any children might come, at any time, as they could be spared from their home or their labour; while the owners were to be always present and ready to teach them.

While thus going on, Law's "Call to a Devout and Holy Life" fell into his hands, and unduly impressed him. The book might be useful to some, but it might lead others astray, by not distinguishing things that differ, as to their order and place in the scheme of the Gospel. It has too little of Evangelism in it; and is sadly wanting in that "free spirit" by which the subjects of Divine grace are upheld in their goings, and enabled, with enlarged hearts, to run in the way of God's commandments. It is John preaching the baptism of repentance, rather than Jesus proclaiming the glad tidings of the kingdom of God.

Some mistaken zealots, too, at this time urged him to leave his secular calling, and dedicate himself entirely to the service of God; as if he was not entirely serving Him while trading for God, and by means of it doing so much good to

of Manchester. The fullest account that has come to my knowledge of the Institution under Mr. Roby's care, may be found in Mr. Slate's "Brief History of the Rise and Progress of the Lancashire County Union."

men.   What we do *by others*, is as much our agency as if we did it in our own persons.   By nothing can a man be so useful as by property, for this enables him to employ every kind of instrumentality, including piety itself.   Few, comparatively, have it in their power to gain substance largely.   When, therefore, a man has the opportunity and the means of attaining it, he should not needlessly resign it, amidst so many calls for pecuniary assistance; and especially if he can trust his benevolent bias.   When a tradesman called upon the rector of St. Mary Woolnoth, and told him he was going to leave off trade, for he had gained enough for himself and family,—" Why, then," said Mr. Newton, " now be the Lord's journeyman, and carry on business for him."   And, says Isaiah, " Her merchandise and her hire shall be holiness to the Lord : it shall not be treasured nor laid up ; for her merchandise shall be for them that dwell before the Lord, to eat sufficiently, and for durable clothing."   This is the text from which I should have preached his funeral sermon, had he died at Manchester, but he died at Edinburgh.   The title would have been " The Christian Merchant."

But there were some who pleaded, and in a measure prevailed, that he should forsooth leave merchandize, and go about personally relieving the poor, and consoling the afflicted, and distributing tracts, and preaching the Gospel to souls perishing for lack of knowledge.   During these excursions he sustained considerable losses in business, which he acknowledged afterwards to me might have been prevented, had he remained at home, with God's blessing, in his calling.

On two other grounds these erratic efforts were wrong : for, First : Though he was exceedingly qualified for business, he was (not for want of talent, but *suitable* talent), as unfit for his new work, especially teaching : and,

Secondly : He had a tinge of lowness of spirits, which required active scenes of employment, rather than solitude and study, to which he was much driven by his supposed calls.

Accordingly he soon began to fall under dejection, which was rapidly increasing, and from which he was with difficulty rallied by the visit of the Reminiscent, and by travelling with him and his wife. Few in doing good ever more fulfilled the command, " Let not thy left hand know what thy right hand doeth."

He was generally a man of much reading and reserve, so that it was impossible to know the interior riches of his character, but by being much with him, and observing him when he was a little off his habitual guard. I hardly ever knew a man who seemed to make so much conscience of his speech. He was cautious and careful in the extreme, not to err or mistake, especially in relating things which he had heard, and in speaking of persons. He daily made David's resolution and prayer his own :—" I said I will take heed to my ways, that I offend not with my tongue.—Set a watch upon my mouth, keep the door of my lips."

It was a pleasing trait in his character that he loved to raise those of low degree, and to set forward in life industrious and deserving individuals. A clerk or a person in his employment, who for a few years had acted confidentially, and diligently, and respectfully, was sure to be aided and elevated; and, therefore, he was always well served.

On the occasion of his second marriage, I preached and published my Sermon on " The Mutual Duties of Husbands and Wives." The acceptance and commendations which this discourse met with, (for it soon went through six editions,) encouraged and induced me to become more familiar with the press ; and to issue in time a large number of publications. Several other events also rose from my connexion with this excellent man—such as a relative alliance; and especially my acquaintance and connexion with the family of Mr. Bolton of America, from which most important consequences to me have resulted.

Such a concatenation and dependence is there in occurrences and circumstances, which may seem to be casual, but are really providential: "And whoso is wise and will observe these things, even they shall understand the loving-kindness of the Lord." Life should never be separated from the agency of God in all; but in retracing it, how often do we find a particular event, otherwise not distinguished, pregnant with results, the birth of which fills us with surprise and astonishment; and teaches us that "the way of man is not in himself."

In general, we see that the generation of the upright is blessed;—but this implies imitation and conformity. The seed of the righteous have many advantages, arising from the prayers, instructions, examples, and influence of their pious parents; but these *may* be disregarded, and even turned into a curse; for "where much is given much will be required;" and "to him that knoweth to do good, and doeth it not, to him it is sin." And if there are children who have forsaken the guide of their youth, and are, after all their early opportunities and advantages, walking in ways that are not good, who shall read this page, let them tremble at the thought of separation from, and of condemnation by, those parents who so anxiously sought to save them!

MISS ELIZA PROTHEROE.

I HAVE never entered into the dispute concerning the comparative powers of the sexes. We naturally and unavoidably judge of the whole by parts, and of course by those parts which come within the circle of our own observation. Either (which I have no reason to believe,) I have met with a series of very favourable *exceptions*, or I ought to think highly of the female character. I am sure I cannot be mistaken with regard to many, with whom I have been intimately acquainted, in various seasons and circumstances of my life. I have found in them a kindness, a tenderness, a purity of affection, a disinterestedness of friendship, a readiness to oblige, to serve, and to sacrifice; and these, with their gentle manners, and lively conversation, and sprightly correspondence, (next to the influence of the dearest of all connexions,) have been my peculiar excitement and solace, under anxious duties and trying afflictions, and a tendency to depression of spirit, to which, though perhaps little suspected, I have been always liable.

As my children had all left me by death, marriage, or professional engagement; and as my beloved wife had some growing indispositions which limited her activities, I much wished for what I soon obtained, in a very valuable and inestimable friend. This was Miss Eliza Protheroe, whose uncle was member of Parliament for Bristol, and whose cousin is member for Halifax.

I knew her first, by visiting her as a minister, when she was suffering under an enervating malady, which had much reduced her. She was then under medical care in Bath. Upon her recovery, she left this place for Cheltenham; but she soon returned, and we had frequent interviews with her. These prepared Mrs. Jay and myself for a more intimate connexion. So she accompanied us to the sea as our only companion; and this excursion of six weeks together gave us such an insight into her qualities, that, after our return home, she soon became an inmate under our roof. She was well brought up, genteel in her manners, very intelligent, an excellent reader, pleasingly sociable, with a degree of the humorous and comic in her conversation. Above all she was truly pious, entirely free from everything low and mean, and singularly unselfish and generous, never seeming to be ·so much in her element as when denying herself to do good to others. What a treasure did we find in her! What a companion, helper, and comforter did she prove! And what a mutual regard did we all increasingly feel towards each other!

The most pleasing weeks I ever spent on earth were passed in four successive excursions to Lynmouth, in the north of Devon. No little of the exquisite pleasure I experienced was derived from the mixed, sublime, and beautiful scenery, and from the solitude and tranquil retirement; but how much of it did our associate contribute in our mutual walks, and readings, and discourse! And not only so. Here I prepared my Lectures on the Christian Character for the press, and wrote the long preface prefixed to it. And here also I wrote many of my Morning and Evening Exercises, one of which, as I wrote them, I daily read at our family worship. These familiar compositions, which have had such an extensive circulation, I owe much to her stimulation and encouragement; without which I much question whether I should have persevered.

Watts tells us,

> "We should suspect some danger near
> Where we possess delight;"

and Cowper tells us,

> "Full bliss is bliss divine."

My entirely esteemed wife, while at Lynmouth, was unable fully to enjoy the attractions of the retreat, and the week after our return home from the last visit, she was seized with apoplexy and paralysis, which, though life was spared, broke up much of my domestic happiness. Our friend was so attached and devoted to us, that she was ready to die for us—yea, I cannot but think that this was the case, in a great degree at least; for, in consequence of my affliction, I immediately wrote to her at Cheltenham, whither she had gone for a few days to see her mother; upon which she instantly hastened back while under medical treatment and considerable indisposition, and much mental suffering from affection and fear; so that the day after her arrival she was seized with delirium, and after a week of frenzy she expired. At the time my wife was insensible, and thus ignorant of an affliction that would have exceedingly added to her own; and which did add much to it, when she became capable of learning the event. As for myself, I hardly felt more at the death of my own daughter;—by whose side she lies in my own family vault.

After mentioning several natural relations, Moses says,— "Or thy friend which is as thine own soul." Is this an anticlimax? or does he mean to say that sometimes friendship rises above kindred?

> "The tear
> That drops upon this paper is sincere."

Few deaths could have affected me more. It was the termination of a life of perfect unselfishness, no little of which had been lived for the welfare of myself and mine.

" Scarcely for a righteous man will one die; yet peradventure for a good man some would even dare to die." Power may cause a man to be feared; learning to be admired; wealth, to be flattered; but goodness naturalizes one heart in another, and renders it "more blessed to give than to receive." Mrs. Jay was equally affected when recovered enough to be able to bear the report of our loss.

> " Friend after friend departs :
>   Who has not lost a friend ?
> There is no union here of hearts,
>   That finds not here an end.
> Were this frail world our final rest,
> Living or dying none were blest.
>
> " There is a world above,
>   Where parting is unknown ;
> A long eternity of love,
>   The good enjoy alone ;
> And faith beholds them, dying here,
> Translated to that glorious sphere."

MRS. SMITH.

WITH this very excellent woman I had a long and intimate acquaintance. My youngest daughter, of whom I was bereaved in the bloom of her youth, was named Statira after her. During many of my annual visits to Surrey Chapel, I spent with my wife much of the time I could spare from my services in London, at her house at Woodford. Her name was then Pool, and her husband was a merchant, and had been prosperous, and was rich. She was a woman of a superior understanding, and had a cultivated mind. She had lived in the levities and gaieties of genteel, commercial society, (generally the most vain, profane, and vapid,) and so she knew enough of the ways and friendships of the world, to be, in a measure, weaned from them; or at least to be fully convinced of their vanity and vexation of spirit; while she felt her need of something better than earth could offer, without knowing what it was, or where it could be obtained.

With these views and feelings she came with her husband to Bath; and as they were acquainted with Mr. H. Thornton, M.P., she inquired of him what place of worship he would recommend them to attend. He answered, "You know I am a Churchman, but there are persons who may be occasionally heard to advantage out of the Establishment." *He* knew what was *then* the state of Bath, and he also perceived the state of her mind. What he said induced her to visit Argyle Chapel; and the first sermon she heard the Reminiscent preach, brought her in sight of the relief and satisfaction she had ignorantly, but really, been seeking after. She now made herself known, and a mutual and growing friendship ensued.

Upon her returning home to Woodford, her lamentation was that she could not hear the truth which had made her free indeed. But one of her servants rather casually heard the Rev. George Collison of Walthamstow, and eagerly informed her mistress that she had found a minister who preached just like the minister they had heard at Bath. She forthwith the next Sabbath ordered out her carriage, and went to hear him herself. She much relished the preaching of this man of God; and from thenceforth made it the place of her constant attendance.

From the commencement of her religious career, she had morning and evening prayer, with the female domestics of her household; but her husband was not as yet favourable to the establishment of *family* worship. But when is a woman, whose heart is right with God, at a loss to carry a good point, for want of motives, methods, or means?

Some months after, Mr. Thornton and the Reminiscent were to spend a week together as their guests. So she said to her husband, " These friends who are coming, always have the worship of God in their families; and they will expect it here, and will think it very strange, if they could not find it." He replied, " Well, then, we must conform to their custom *while* they are here." So I was desired to conduct the service every morning and evening, reading the Scriptures, now and then dropping a very few words; and always praying *short*, and as *wisely* as I could. But no sooner had we departed than the good wife said to her husband, " Will it not appear very odd to the servants, if we now give up this exercise? Will they not think that we have been endeavouring to appear to our friends more religious than we really are? And do you not think the performance itself is

likely to do good, if not to ourselves, yet to our domestics?"
So the practice was allowed to be continued, on the condition of *her officiating*. This she was qualified to do; but
she took it up, not by choice, but as a trial, and from a
sense of duty, arising from a peculiar condition of things.
She always had a form of prayer before her, but she occasionally interspersed some expressions of her own. And
would not this be the best way of using forms of devotion?
I once heard Mr. John Shepherd of Frome, recommending
it from his own example and experience.

Are Christians ever useless? When blessed themselves
they prove blessings to others; and in various degrees, in
some way or other, serve their generation by the will of
God. Who can tell the good this woman accomplished in
her own place and neighbourhood by her example and influence, in visiting the rich; feeding and clothing the hungry
and the naked; instructing the ignorant; establishing
schools; and forming a club for the poor females to aid
them in their illnesses and lyings-in, whose meetings she
accompanied with moral and religious addresses, without
however excluding their little homely and innocent festivities?

When she was bereaved of her husband, as her means
remained, the widow equalled, sustained, and carried on what
the wife had begun and established.

Some years after she married again. It was to a very
accomplished gentleman, a serjeant-at-law, a fellow of the
Antiquarian Society, a scholar, and the father of the authors
of the "Rejected Addresses," "Horace in London," and
various celebrated novels.* At first his doctrinal sentiments widely differed from her own. This created great
difficulty on her side; and for some time a refusal of mar-

---

* I once dined with these gifted young men; and was sorry to
remark that, if religion was not the object of their contempt, it was
not "the one thing needful."

riage was the result. At length some peculiar circumstances led her to yield, though not *perfectly* in accordance
with her convictions. But God overruled it for good, in
more evangelizing his sentiments, and bringing some of his
daughters into the way of life. Yet the connexion was not
without its trials. It occasioned the loss of a large part of
her property. But herein again her gracious principle continued to operate and show itself. Though she much reduced her establishment, she resolved that her charities,
sacred and civil, should not suffer. These continued the
same. In what are not the subjects of divine grace a *peculiar* people? Trying events befall them, and evince that
they are not conformed to this world, but transformed, by
the renewing of their mind; and so proving " what is that
good, and acceptable, and perfect will of God."

It is pleasing to know that her husband, whom she had
once characterized in a letter to the Reminiscent, as "having all the wisdom of the Greeks, and their foolishness too,"
—after a while, received the Kingdom of God as a little
child; died in the faith of the Gospel, a member of the Independent Church at Wandsworth, looking for the mercy
of our Lord Jesus Christ unto eternal life. "Not many
wise men after the flesh are called;" but there have always
been a few to falsify the prejudice, that the religion of the
cross is fit only for the vulgar and illiterate.

JOHN POYNDER, ESQ.

MY acquaintance with this good and distinguished character was continued for considerably more than fifty years. It commenced from a letter I received desiring me to inform him from what author I had given an extract, in my sermon preached upon the formation of the London Missionary Society. This inquiry was prefatory to something else,—and he soon expressed his gratitude to God that he ever heard that discourse, as " it had had such an effect upon him as he hoped would never wear away." And this was the case; for from that period he was found a decided, avowed, consistent, undeviating, and zealous follower of the Lamb.

After this letter, upon my going to London to fulfil my annual appointment at Surrey Chapel, I had my first personal interview with him. The meeting was affecting; and we exchanged some pleasing thoughts and feelings. After this we seized every opportunity to meet and converse; and though, as he was a Tory and a firm Churchman, and I a Whig and moderate Dissenter, and we, therefore, differed in some of our political and ecclesiastical views, this, instead of gendering alienation, rather endeared us the more to each other. Harmony is better than unison—" Yes," says Lord Bacon, " and it is so, not only in *sounds* but in *affections*."

Hence during my annual weeks of labour in London,

Mr. Poynder frequently heard me, and has given most ample proof of his kind approbation of my services, by his multiplied quotations from my preaching and publications, in his three volumes of "Literary Extracts." In these three volumes he shows much reading, judgment, and taste; yet they would have borne abridgment or reduction. It is natural for persons when they read to remark and transcribe. But what strikes them peculiarly at the time, owing to its novelty, or something in their own circumstances or feelings, may appear very differently afterwards; and the wonder is that, in the cool review, more freedom was not here used in selection, and articles *weighed* rather than *numbered*.

Though these volumes are large, they are not all his issues from the press. His publications were numerous, in all of which usefulness was the obvious design and tendency. As he was a *Christian*, many of them turned on religious subjects:—The evangelization of our Eastern dominions.—The Paganism of Popery.—The sanctification of the Lord's Day, &c.

As an *East India Proprietor* he spoke much in favour of the abolition of Sutteeism, or burning of widows. In this work and labour of love, many of his speeches were very able and eloquent, and several of them were published. Several years before his death he had the satisfaction of seeing his exertions crowned with success.—He was equally earnest and persevering in opposing the accursed tax arising from the idolatrous worship of Juggernaut. But he died without seeing this foul stain wiped off from our government; and "hope deferred made the heart sick." Yet he had roused the public indignation, and awakened a cry that he knew must be heard in due time.

Never was there a warmer advocate of evangelical truth, and the doctrines of the Reformation.

Never was there a more determined enemy to Popery, and its half-sister, Puseyism.

Never did man more strive to serve his generation by the will of God.

And, as to his private and relative character, who ever excelled him—as an attached husband, a devoted father, a faithful friend, or a helper of the needy?

Behold what may be done by a single individual when disposition, ability, and opportunity concur!

" The memory of the just is blessed."

N.B.—I wrote this brief sketch the very day I was informed of his death, lest, at my time of life, I should be prevented from bearing even a very inadequate testimony to a man of so much varied worth.

RAMMOHUN ROY.

I was but little acquainted with the Rajah, but I feel inclined to notice him, not only because I was struck with him, as a man of prodigious powers of mind, and treasures of knowledge, and readiness of address ; but because I think justice has not been done to him, in another and far more important view.

I first saw him at the Mansion House, London, to which I was invited to meet him, by the then Lord Mayor, with whom, as an author, I had had considerable dealings. The dinner was early and the company select, though not entirely religious; and I was allowed to bring any of my acquaintance with me. Several accompanied me, one of whom, John Poynder, Esq., could turn the intercourse to account, in conversing with the Rajah, on a subject in which he was then so zealously labouring, and did not labour in vain, (the abolition of Sutteeism,) and which the Rajah himself, before he left India, had nobly advocated.

Of course this man was the *lion* of the company. He spoke freely on several topics, especially of Mahometanism, which he considered as an improvement on Paganism, and of some considerable advantage to Christianity itself, whose professors were yielding to a kind of idolatry, in worshipping masses and relics. He also expressed himself with regard to Mahomet himself, as possessing greater talents, and some better qualities, than had been commonly ascribed to him.

This was not suffered to pass without some hesitation and dissent, especially by the Rev. Mr. Melvill.

The Lady Mayoress asking his opinion of the comparative estimate of the sexes, he promptly replied, " *Physically* considered, men are superior to women. *Morally* considered, women are superior to men. *Intellectually* considered, they are on a level, admitting the same opportunities and advantages :"—a confession which, if not questioned, was deemed remarkable, as coming from a quarter where females are commonly, if not universally, undervalued and degraded.

When he spoke of the Gospel, he frankly avowed his full belief of it; adding, " But I consider this as no merit of mine, for I found it impossible to peruse the Book itself, and not be convinced that it was the work of a Being of perfect wisdom and benevolence." The Rev. Mr. Dale, who sat next me, could not help expressing rather audibly his approbation and admiration of the sentiment, and the manner in which it was delivered; and Mr. Melvill, who principally led the discourse with the Rajah, acknowledged, as I went away with him, that he had a much more favourable opinion and hope of him than he had before.

On the following Sabbath-evening he came with the Lord Mayor and the rector of St. Olave's to hear the Reminiscent. He gave proof of his liking, not only the preacher, but the subject, by coming into the house afterwards, and soliciting a copy of the discourse to print for distribution among his friends. As the sermon was taken down in short-hand, I was able to comply with his desire. I procured him a transcription, and he printed it at his own expense. (The sermon is to be found in the seventh volume of my Works.*)

I fear this is too personal to be excused; but it tells upon what I have in view; for though the discourse was not

* See page 100 of that volume.

strictly doctrinal, it contained allusions and statements only to be found in "the truth as it is in Jesus."

He had engaged to accompany Mr. Poynder to Surrey Chapel again the Sunday after; but, before its arrival, he wrote Mr. P. a note, (which I keep, and value as an autograph,) saying he was afraid he should not be able to attend, owing to a degree of indisposition, and the pressure and heat of the congregation; but lamented the loss the less, as he should soon have an opportunity to hear, so he expressed it, that truly evangelical minister in Bath.

This was denied him, as, the week before his intended visit to Bath, he died in Bristol. There he was, by invitation, at the house of a lady belonging to Lewin's Mead Meeting, where he attended on the morning of the Sabbath, but heard an evangelical clergyman at Clifton in the evening. During his short stay in Bristol, a party of several distinguished individuals met him. Among these was John Foster,* who, upon my inquiry, said that nothing on this occasion very striking or definitive came from him. He probably began to feel the approach of the disorder which so rapidly carried him off.

Soon after his private interment in the premises of his friend, an extolling account of him was published by Dr. Carpenter, assuring the public that he was a Christian, in the Socinian translation of that word. Here I am persuaded Dr. C. was mistaken. He was this on his conversion to Christianity in India, when he only considered Christ as a moral Teacher, and wrote accordingly. But we have reason to hope and conclude, that, on his coming to this country, his views varied, and were approaching evangelical sentiments. At first, (and it was not wonderful, with such talents and reasoning powers,) on emerging from heathenism, he felt difficulties with regard to some of the more

* Mr. Foster's interesting account of this interview, and of the Rajah's death, we shall subjoin to this article.

mysterious doctrines of the Gospel; but there is no littl
proof that his mind was beginning to open to the doctrine
of the cross and grace of our Lord Jesus Christ. He commonly in London attended the preaching of an orthodox
clergyman.

Earl Gainsborough was not only much pleased with him,
but much encouraged concerning his state and character, by
the Rajah's visit to Barham Court. When he dined with
Mr. Poynder he begged to be allowed to attend his evening family-worship, after the company were gone; and
next day he came also to attend his morning-worship; and
expressed much delight at the blending with prayer, the
reading of the Scriptures and singing. Mr. Poynder engaged the Rev. Mr. Knight to conduct these services, by
means of which this pious and judicious minister became
acquainted with this prodigy; and he also had good hope
concerning him, both from his interviews and correspondence; for the Rajah often addressed notes to him respecting
passages of Scripture, with the solutions of which he
seemed satisfied, and often called upon him; and in his
last interview with him, finding him very serious and
tender, Mr. Knight said to him, " Sir, I trust you do not
less prize Christianity since you came amongst us." He
rose, and, taking him by the hand, said with tears, " Mr.
Knight, I feel such a regard for the truth and importance
of Christianity, that I think I could die for it."

This account, we presume, will not be satisfactory to
some; they will ask for more evidence; and we could have
wished we had been able to furnish more. We cannot be
too anxious and inquisitive, where our *own* religious state is
concerned; but with regard to others, there is a charity,
which, with due discrimination, " hopeth all things, believeth
all things, endureth all things." We may know what
heresy is without being able to ascertain the state of a
heretic. We know not what disadvantages *he* has been

under; what struggles he has had with difficulties and
doubts, to which others have been strangers; and what
prayers he has offered, which, though they cannot be lost,
may not have been immediately and consciously answered.
But we know who hath said, "Seek, and ye *shall* find."
"He that doeth His will shall know of the doctrine
whether it be of God:" and—"Then shall we know, if we
follow on to know the Lord."

Why cannot we admit in connexion with Christian safety
and sincerity, doctrinal as well as moral deficiencies? And
why cannot we imagine, that where there is less enlighten-
ment, there may be more excellence of another kind to
balance it—more humbleness of mind, more benevolence,
and more active zeal? I have met with instances in which,
where there was little speculative and systematical clearness and accuracy, there has been much of that "wisdom
which is from above, and which is first pure, then peaceable, gentle, and easy to be entreated, full of mercy and
good fruits, without partiality and without hypocrisy."
When the blind patient in the Gospel first looked up, he
only saw men as trees walking; but he was under the
operation of a Divine Restorer; and a second touch enabled him to see everything clearly. How little of the
Gospel-salvation did Peter know at the time; yet upon his
confession, our Lord pronounced him blessed; and affirmed
that flesh and blood had not revealed this unto him, but his
Father in heaven!

From this case we are led to another reflection. How
readily and eagerly are the advocates of religious parties induced to claim and avow extraordinary men as belonging to
them; as if their faith stood in the wisdom of men, and not
in the power of God. But let no man glory in men. We
should be thankful when any of superior intellect and endowment are found walking in the truth; but we are not to
have the faith of our Lord Jesus Christ with respect of

persons. The poor and the common people are generally
the evangelized. These "things are hidden from the wise
and prudent, and revealed unto babes!" Not many wise
men after the flesh are called; and these are often in our
churches more glaring than useful members; yea, it is well
if they do not become like Diotrephes—loving to have the
pre-eminence.

Mr. Foster gives the following interesting particulars of the
Rajah's visit to Bristol, in a letter to Mr. Hill, dated Oct. 8th, 1832:
—"The most remarkable thing of late is the visit, so soon to end in
the death, in the house behind our garden, of the Rajah Rammohun
Roy (the title of rajah, of no very definite import, was conferred on
him by the king of Delhi, the remaining shadow of the Great Mogul).
I had entertained a strong prepossession against him, had no wish
to see him, but could not avoid it, when he was come to the house
of my young landlady, Miss Castle.

"My prejudice could not hold out half-an-hour after being in his
company. He was a very pleasing and interesting man; intelligent
and largely informed, I need not say,—but unaffected, friendly, and,
in the best sense of the word, polite. I passed two evenings in his
company, only, however, as an unit in large parties; the latter time,
however, in particular and direct conversation with him, concerning
some of the doctrines of the Indian philosophers, the political, civil,
and moral state of the Hindoos. In the former instance, when the
after-dinner company consisted of Dr. Carpenter, and sundry other
doctors and gentlemen, Churchmen and Dissenters, he was led a
little into his own religious history and present opinions. He
avowed his general belief in Christianity, as attested by miracles,
(of which, I had understood, that he made very light some ten or a
dozen years since,) but said that the internal evidence had had by
much the greatest force on his mind. In so very heterogeneous a
company, there was no going into any very specific particulars.
Carpenter, in whose company I have since dined at Dr. Pritchard's,
very confidently claims him as of the 'Modern Unitarian' school.
* * * * It may be that he was finally near about in agreement
with that school, but I do not believe that they have any very exact
knowledge of his opinions. * * * * Here he went to several
churches, and to hear Jay on a week-day at Bridge-street, as well as
sometimes to Lewin's Mead, where the family, in which he was visit=

ing, constantly attended.   There is, or a few days since there was, a great perplexity how to dispose of his remains.   He had signified his wish not to be committed to any *Ecclesiastical* burying ground, but, if it might be so managed, deposited in some quiet corner of the mere *profane* earth.   His principal London friend (a Mr. Hare, from India) thinks it the most desirable that he were conveyed to India.   During the greater part of his short illness (it was an affection of the brain) he was in a state of such torpor as to be incapable of any communication.   Dr. Pritchard, who attended him during the latter days, says he did not utter, while he was with him, ten distinct sentences.   As far as I have heard, there was *nothing* to indicate the state of his mind.   There were actions (of his hands, &c.) which his own attendants said were the usual ones that accompanied his devotional exercises.   To me, and several of our order of friends, who were, the latter evening to which I have referred, (at Mrs. Cox's,) in such close and interesting conversation with him, then apparently in perfect health, but then within hardly two days of the commencement of his fatal illness, it was emphatically striking, nine or ten days after, to think of him as no longer in our world."— Foster's Life, Vol. II. p. 218, &c.

REV. THOMAS TUPPEN.

He was my predecessor in the pastorate of the Congregational church in Bath. He was originally in trade; and in his earlier days had deviated from the paths of righteousness and peace. Living then at Portsmouth, he went to hear Whitfield, who was to preach on the neighbouring common, and (which was so often the case under the ministry of that extraordinary herald of the Gospel,) the word came to him not in word only, but in the demonstration of the Spirit and with power. He had gone to hear, not so much from curiosity, as from the worse motive,—to oppose, insult, and interrupt. "I had," said he, "therefore, provided myself with stones in my pocket, if opportunity offered, to pelt the preacher; but I had not heard long, before the stone was taken out of my heart of flesh; and then the other stones, with shame and weeping, were dropped one by one out upon the ground."

The change, then commenced, was carried on, and evinced itself to be of God, by its continuance and its effects. In process of time, the receiver of the Gospel became also the publisher; and was ordained over a church in the place where he resided. Some years after he ruptured a blood-vessel, and resigned his charge, as unable to meet safely its numerous services; but after a considerable suspension, his recovery allowed of his taking another sphere, with less public duty. Mr. Welsh, a rich banker from London, (as may be seen in my reminiscence of him,) who had much aided our rising cause, brought him to Bath while the interest was young and weak; and engaged to support him till the congregation should be able to meet the expense.

Here his labours were peculiarly acceptable and useful. Many were awakened under his ministry, and added to the growing church; which was soon required to enlarge the place of her tent. He was, therefore, excited and encouraged (much by Lady Glenorchy) to take ground and build. Argyle Chapel was the consequence. But the founder, though he set his heart upon it, was not permitted to open it for the Lord's service. This was performed by the Reminiscent, who had been introduced by Mr. Tuppen to his people as an occasional supply during his sickness, and recommended to them as their pastor when he was dying.*

* In the Life of the Countess of Huntingdon, Vol. II. p. 75, is the following notice of Mr. Tuppen :—" The Congregation assembling in Argyle Chapel, Bath, originated in the secession of a few pious individuals who did not approve of the forms of the Established Church, and who formed themselves into a church on Independent principles. The first person to whom application was made to preside over this infant church was the Rev. Thomas Tuppen, who had been a preacher in Mr. Whitfield's connexion, and afterwards minister of the Tabernacle at Portsea; he arrived in Bath in the year 1785, when the interest rapidly increased; from about 25 persons who at first attended him, the number rose in a few years to seven or eight hundred. The place in which they worshipped being now too small for the congregation, a new chapel was begun in 1789, and opened Oct. 4, 1789; but Mr. Tuppen's health was then so much reduced that he was never able to preach a single sermon there,—he could only attend the services of the day, which were performed by the Rev. Wm. Jay, who has been the minister of the place ever since.

"During the few years that Mr. Tuppen exercised his ministry at Bath, his manner of preaching was very striking: he was often heard to say, 'If the attention be gained, half the business is done.'

"It was never his wish to empty other places where the Gospel was preached in order to fill his own; for, after observing the large-

He was a man of great seriousness and exemplary piety; he talked little, but his speech was always with salt and ministered grace to the hearer. Mr. Cecil once said, a minister should not be " a man to be had,"—and Mr. Tuppen was most observant of this rule of any man I ever knew. This grew not so much out of disposition as out of circumstances, as he had had only a common education, and never had the advantage of any regular preparation for the ministry, and yet was very thirsty of improvement. Through desire he separated himself, seeking and intermeddling with all wisdom. He was a most laborious student, and by assiduous and self-denying application he gained much general information; acquired a tolerable knowledge of the original languages; excelled in theology; and became one of the most distinguished preachers of the day, in his own connexion. He, therefore, lived very retired, not only from society at large, but also from his own congregation; and to such a degree as would not have been justified or excused, but for the value he attached to time, and the necessity he felt for diligence.

This is not always the case. I have been sorry to have observed in no few instances the reverse of this. Where the iron has been blunt, less strength has been put to it; and where there has been no advantage of preparatory fitness, preachers have been *less* anxious and active in their exertions. It is one of the benefits of training for the ministry that, however imperfect it may comparatively be, it creates a habit of order, a tone of application, and a heedfulness of time and opportunity. I have known individuals

ness of his own audience, he would often inquire whether the other places were full. When he was answered in the affirmative, he seemed to be much pleased, and would say, ' Well, we may now hope something is doing.'

" After a lingering illness, which he supported with great resignation and patience, he entered into his rest on the 22nd of February, 1790, aged 48."

of no enviable talents, and of no previous acquirements, who have even given less time and attention in preparing their three sermons for the week, than Robert Hall, with all his powers and education, employed in preparing one, and that only his week-evening lecture before the Lord's supper. And are there not people who prefer this remissness, and lounging and sauntering in a preacher, provided he favours them with a portion of it, in what they call pastoral visits, than in letting his profit appear unto all men, in giving himself to reading, meditation, and prayer?

Mr. Tuppen's face was peculiarly intelligent; his eye remarkably piercing; and his look frequently insufferable. The skeletons of his sermons (for he wrote none at full length,) were written with uncommon neatness, order, and precision: and generally filled two octavo pages. They were in long-hand, with a few contractions. His library was arranged according to Locke's Common Place Book; so that when he had to preach on any particular subject, he could turn to any volume, and every volume, where that subject was treated in a way of proof, illustration, or improvement. Whenever he added a book to his collection, he thus immediately arranged its topics for reference; and this rendered the work of consultation easy, which would, otherwise, have been a tiresome task.

He was a widower, and had only one child, a son, residing with him, and articled to a solicitor in Bath. This son had more than his father's natural talents, and was a good scholar, and gave much promise of rising above many in his profession. He also seemed much inclined to walk in those ways which are pleasantness and peace. When, therefore, he had arrived at age, on his birthday, he wrote a paper, entitled, "Rules for my Conduct." It began thus: "I am now come of age, and hope for the favour and blessing of God upon my future years. But in order to this, I know I must adhere to certain principles and rules. The first of which is *piety*. ' Behold, the fear of the Lord, that is wisdom, and to depart from evil, that is understanding,' " &c. But, alas! this goodness was as the morning cloud, or early dew which passeth away. These hopeful appearances were in a few months blighted, and in a few more entirely destroyed.

" Evil communications corrupt good manners : and a companion of fools shall be destroyed." This fine youth became acquainted with some sceptical, or as, by a patent of their own creation, they call themselves, free-thinking young men ; gave up the Sabbath ; forsook the house of God which his father had built ; abandoned the minister to whom he had been greatly attached ; and boldly " left off to be wise and to do good." But as his fall was rapid, so his new course was short. Swimming on a Sunday for amusement and experiment, he caught a chill which brought on a consumption. This for months gave him warning, and space for repentance, but it is to be feared this grace of God was in vain. During his gradual decline, he refused all intercourse with pious friends or ministers ; and when his good nurse entreated him to call me in, as I lived close by, and there had been such an intimacy between us, he frowned and rebuked her, and ordered her to mind her own business. On the last day of his life, unasked, I ventured into his dying chamber. He was sensible ; but exclaimed, " O Voltaire! Voltaire!" He then raised himself up in the bed, and wringing his hands, again exclaimed, " O that young man! that young man!" I said, "My dear sir, what young man ?" With a countenance indescribable, he answered,—" I will not tell you."

How was my soul agonized, for I had loved him much, and had endeavoured in every way to render myself agreeable and useful to him. But " one sinner destroyeth much good." What have I seen, in a long ministry, of the dire effects of evil associates, and licentious publications ! He kept moving about, and grasping the bed-clothes; and after a disturbed silence muttered something about his seeing fire, and then suddenly expired. On the last circumstance I laid no stress; it was probably from a sparkling of the eye, affected by the imagination or by disease; nor did I publish a narrative of the event from the press or the pulpit; or attempt to make of it an imitation of Dr. Young's " Centaur not Fabulous." In many cases we know too little for explanation or decision; and it is our wisdom to " be still, and know that he is God,"—both as to the exercise of his mercy and justice. We are to avoid rash judgments, but it becomes us to *hear and flee*.

Should this solemn and true statement fall under the notice of any youth who has had godly parents, and a religious education; and not only outward advantages, but serious convictions and resolutions; from all which he has turned aside,—surely here is enough to awaken his reflections and fears, and to enforce the language of inspired wisdom and love.—" My son, if sinners entice thee, consent thou not. Enter not into the path of the wicked; and go not in the way of evil men. Avoid it, pass not by it; turn from it, and pass away. For they sleep not except they have done mischief; and their sleep is taken away unless they cause some to fall. And thou mourn at the last, when thy flesh and thy body are consumed; and say, How have I hated instruction, and my heart despised reproof; and have not obeyed the voice of my teachers, nor inclined mine ear to them that instructed me! Rejoice, O young man, in thy youth; and walk in the ways of thine heart, and in the sight of thine eyes: but know thou, that for all these things God will bring thee into judgment."

⸻ YESCOMBE, ESQ.

⸻

THE following brief history of this rather singular character I derived from himself; and, as far as my information goes, it principally turns upon his two conversions, the one from Protestantism to Popery, and the other from Popery to Protestantism.

Of his family I am ignorant, though I think he once mentioned, that he had a brother who commanded a government packet to Lisbon. As it is a considerable time since his death, I may have mis-remarked a few trivial circumstances; but I am certain, from the impression the case made upon me at first—my repeated relation of it since—and my lengthened acquaintance with him, that the following statement is essentially correct:—

He was travelling in Wales. In the neighbourhood of Abergavenny he met with a Romish priest, who immediately and sedulously sought an intimacy with him. He succeeded; and they soon became familiar friends; since, though a nominal Protestant, he knew very little of the rudiments of his own profession. He was shortly, by the zeal and art of his new associate, drawn over to Popery, and fell so entirely under the control of this man, that he was prevailed upon to deliver up his Bible, (of which, alas! he had made little use,) and to live a kind of monkish life in a sort of mountain-cave; and though he had often witnessed the occasional intemperance of this priest, he went weekly, and regularly, and solemnly, to confess before him for penance and pardon.

In process of time, in his complete devotedness to Popery, he thought of entering the monastery of La Trappe, the inmates of which were so renowned for denying themselves even the use of the speech, which God has given us for enjoyment and profit. But, as it was required of the convert, as the terms of his admission, that he should divest himself, in favour of the holy body, of all he had, he hesitated a little, and resolved to judge by a personal inspection. For this purpose he set out to visit the institution, and "he must needs go through" Bath. On the Thursday-evening, walking by Lady Huntingdon's chapel, he heard the singing after the prayers, and went in, and continued during the whole of the sermon. The preacher was the Rev. Mr. Kemp, of Swansea. I forget the text; but, in the course of his sermon, he spoke against the errors of Popery, especially transubstantiation, and the idolatrous worship of the Virgin Mary. His remarks so powerfully struck Mr. Yescombe, that, when the service was over, he went into the chapel-house, and asked to see the minister, and said he wished much to have some conversation with him. Mr. Kemp was surrounded with friends who were taking their leave of him, as he was setting off for London early the next morning. He, therefore, excused himself from a conference; but learning that the applicant's desire arose from some impression of what he had just heard, he recommended him, mentioning my name, to call upon myself. This he did on the day following. He apologized for calling by mentioning this recommendation, and stated the occasion of it, in the doubt which had been raised in his mind from the sermon he had heard, avowing himself to be a Roman Catholic. If true, I was glad of such an opportunity, and lifted up my heart to God, that I might continue and complete these doubts, and make him know the truth, that the truth might make him free.

And this, I have every reason to hope, was the case; for after several interviews (not without prayer,) he expressed with gratitude and tears his full conviction—brought me his beads and books, constantly attended my ministry, and communed with us in the dying of the Lord Jesus, spiritually and by faith, eating the flesh and drinking the blood of the Son of God.

He soon now furnished himself with a Bible, and indescribable was the pleasure he found in it, after never having dared to look into it for sixteen years. How often and significantly would he say with Jeremiah, "Thy word was found, and I did eat it; and thy words were to me the joy and rejoicing of my heart."

Yet he said, as he was single, and had now been so long accustomed to *solitude*, and from habit enjoyed it, he hoped he might still be allowed to live much in retirement; and this he did, occupying two rooms away from all interruption and intercourse; walking with God, and confessing himself a stranger and pilgrim on the earth.

He always called me—"Father." I had many pleasing and profitable interviews with him, and saw him growing in grace and in the knowledge of the Lord and Saviour till he reached the end of his faith, and that end was peace.

Three inferences are derivable from this brief memoir: *First:* We see the spirit of Popery, and its fear of the Scripture. If we could separate the zeal to make proselytes, from the cause, how worthy would it be of imitation!

Secondly: Let young persons, when they travel, be careful of the company they keep, lest they get a snare to their souls, and be led away by the error of the wicked.

Thirdly: See on what little, and, to us, casual circumstances, important events hinge; and how the purposes of

Him are accomplished " who worketh all things after the counsel of his own will."

I bless God that, in the sixty-three years of my pastoral life, I lost no one of my flock by perversion to Romanism; while I received into my communion two converts from Popery, who walked in the truth, and " adorned the doctrine of God their Saviour in all things."

DR. THOMAS COGAN.

DR. COGAN, celebrated as a physician, author of " Views on the Rhine," and many other well-known works, was originally a Dissenting minister, educated at Homerton Academy, and officiating first at Southampton. But changing his sentiments, and abjuring his Calvinistic Creed, like an honest man, he informed the church of his new convictions, and resigned his pastorate. For some time he was subsequently a preacher at the Hague, but afterwards he was led, as the condition of a matrimonial alliance, to study medicine, and practised as a physician at Rotterdam. When the French poured into Holland, he feared, (as he had offended them by some public strictures,) and fled to this country with the Prince of Orange, Mr. Hope, the Malvers,* and others.

He took a farm at Wraxall, in Wiltshire, but soon found that the scientific agriculturist could not succeed so well as his plain practical neighbours. He then fixed his residence in Bath, and occupied a house of his own opposite the Reminiscent's Chapel. He had married in Holland. His wife, being an orthodox Presbyterian, communed with our church. He always attended the Unitarian Chapel; but in the evenings he was seldom absent from Argyle Chapel. When my subject was of a more general and practical nature, he was pleased and sometimes flattering; at other

* An esteemed correspondent thinks that this should be Maclaines.

seasons he was silent, but never seemed offended, and was never censorious or severe. He allowed the liberty he assumed : but I presume he thought we were not very well off in Bath, for he said more than once that, of the two ministers he heard, one of them preached about God as if there had been no Christ; and the other about Christ as if there had been no God; but he hoped from the pulling on each side he should be kept upright.

I sometimes found it trying to preach before such a superior man, and so often; but I am perfectly conscious I never yielded to the temptation of pleasing, by altering my matter or style.

Though he passed, and wished to pass, generally as a Unitarian, he did not give that community in all things his preference or commendation. He wished they would give up reading their discourses, as less exciting and impressive; and often spoke of republishing a pamphlet, entitled— "Reading not Preaching." He complained of their disuse of the awful terms of Scripture, such as *fury*, *vengeance*, *the lake of fire and brimstone*, observing they were words employed by the only wise God himself, and were adapted to strike the careless and arrest the thoughtless. He disliked their glossing Scripture, when read or quoted, and wished the language of revelation to be always left to speak in its own unmixed simplicity. He also acknowledged that they never seemed to ascribe importance enough to the mediatorial work of the Messiah; especially to his sufferings and death, as the (in some way or other) medium of Divine forgiveness.

He had the habit of too many of his party, and which may be deemed worse in its cause and effects than pure error itself: viz. the speaking lightly of Divine things, and even sporting with them. He also often joked about Satan. He kept back his attack on the agency and even existence of the apostate spirit in the last volume of his works, because he knew his more orthodox friends would never forgive him for the offence. He mentioned that, when he was in Holland, a minister put forth a pamphlet deemed by many atheistical in its tendency, yet he was not anathematized by the Synod to which he belonged; but afterwards, when he published again, denying diabolical influence and existence, they immediately suspended him,—as if not caring what became of God, if they could but retain the devil. But it was not a bad thing he uttered, when in the fields I met him after a return from town, (though it was a little inconsistent with his avowed opinion,)—" When I am in London I believe in the devil, and when I am in the country I believe in God." He was a great and consistent admirer of Nature, and I believe drew more of the materials and excitements of his devotion from wood and lawn than from Bethlehem and Calvary.

He was truly generous and benevolent. As a companion he was most amiable and interesting; never obtruding or insinuating his sentiments among those who differed from him. Like other great men, he was not so ready with his tongue as with his pen, nor so definite and lucid in his speech as in his writings. Nothing indeed can surpass the crystal clearness apparent in his works, for which see his " Treatise on the Analysis and Influence of the Passions," and his " Theological Disquisition on the Characteristic Excellences of Christianity."

The following is rather a curious circumstance. One evening at Argyle Chapel, he sat in the same pew, and close by the side, of Mr. Wilberforce. After the service Mr. Wilberforce coming into the vestry asked me, who that very agreeable looking man was, who sat at his left hand. " Sir," said I, " that gentleman is your opponent, who has just published an answer to the Chapter in your work on Hereditary Depravity."—"Indeed!" said he, " had I known it I would have shaken hands with him, for he is a fair and able disputant." Two days after this, dining at Dr. C.'s house with Mr. Fuller, of Kettering, (who was his guest,) Dr. Cogan soon asked,—"Who was that odd and very moveable gentleman, who sat last evening at my right hand?"—"What, Sir, did you not know that that was Mr. Wilberforce?"—"Was *that* Wilberforce! I should much have liked to have been introduced to him; for though I have written against his sentiments, no one can admire his character more, as one of the best of men, and one of the greatest philanthropists:"—and went on justly eulogizing him.

Not being inclined or qualified for controversy, I never entered into dispute with him, but I sometimes dropped a few words from experience or observation, to which he listened, and which seemed to strike him, especially when I spoke of persons who had recently died in confidence, peace, and comfort, commending and recommending those truths which they said were all their salvation and all their desire. And when I had mentioned what I had lately met with, viz., a female young and beautiful, agreeably espoused, with two lovely babes, with everything that could render life desirable, dying of a consumption, (which destroys so many of our roses and lilies,) and when, reduced by the lingering disease almost to a shadow, she asked an attendant to hand her the looking-glass,—after glancing at which she returned it, saying with a smile—

> " Then while ye hear my heart-strings break,
>   How sweet my moments roll !
> A mortal paleness in my cheek,
>   But glory in my soul !"

and soon expired,—he could not avoid weeping.

When also I sometimes mentioned instances (and, blessed be God, I could mention such instances under my own preaching) of persons converted from a sinful course to a life of morality and holiness ; and where the change has not been produced by practice, but the practice has been the effect of the change : and sin has not only been left but loathed; and duty has not only been performed but delighted in; his silence and manner have seemed to say, " Why—*we* hear and see nothing of this !"

He went to see his learned brother, the Rev. Eliezer Cogan, (whose name so often appears as a contributor in the "Gentleman's Magazine,") and who was the pastor of the Presbyterian Church at Walthamstow. Before his return home he died. I know not the manner or circumstances of his departure; but have been informed only, that he ordered his tomb-stone to be inscribed with these words : " I am the resurrection and the life : he that believeth in me, though he were dead, yet shall he live : and he that liveth and believeth in me shall never die. Believest thou this ?"

I cannot help observing, that while Dr. Cogan was in Holland, from the existence and usefulness there of the Humane Society for the recovery of drowned persons, he recommended the institution of it in this country to his friend Dr. W. Hawes of London, an elder of Dr. Rees's church. In consequence of which, that gentleman had the honour of establishing a similar society here, by means of which so many lives have been restored and given back to their agonized connexions.

Shall I remark,—that when Dr. Hawes called upon the Reminiscent to engage him to preach for the Society, our discourse naturally turned upon the subject of suicide ; and he expressed it as his opinion, that self-murder *commonly* sprang not from *infidelity* or *insanity*, but from some *impression* intolerable for the moment, but which might have been diverted or dissipated by some timely change of company, place, or action ; and the event been prevented. And who has not felt a temporary, gloomy depression, which had it been increased tenfold, or fivefold, might have issued in some fatal deed, (and it might have been easily so increased,) but which might have found relief by some means within reach ?

He also remarked, contrary to a common opinion, that those who once attempt self-destruction repeat the attempt, and commonly succeed at last; but that the Humane Society had found comparatively few of those they had happily resuscitated chargeable with the repetition of the offence.

I remember Dr. Cogan's saying he was once, when abroad, walking with a young Portuguese lady, and saw at a distance a fire surrounded by a number of persons; and when he was disposed to notice it, she pulled him on, saying: "O, I suppose it is only the burning of a Jew!" "Yet," said he, " she was not wanting in humanity, yea, she was even tender and benevolent." But see the effect of persecution, education, and custom !

REV. BENJAMIN DAVIES, D.D.

DR. DAVIES was originally tutor of the Dissenting Academy at Oswestry, where he had for one of his students Dr. Edward Williams, afterwards president at Rotherham College, and a writer of no little celebrity, especially in the Baptismal and Calvinistic controversies.

I was anxious to learn from him, whether this pupil of his, when under his care, had anything peculiar or superior about him, indicative of his future eminence. "Nothing," he said, "but more of a solitary disposition, a greater addiction to study, and a special seriousness of reflection."

Do constitutional propensities, or accidental circumstances, lead men into those departments of action and science in which they have mostly figured? In many instances, perhaps, this cannot be decided; in some, it is obvious, both these causes unite and co-operate.

I remember eagerly perusing Dr. Williams's famous work on "Divine Equity and Sovereignty," but I found little satisfaction in reading it: perhaps I did not thoroughly comprehend it. I certainly did not feel, in consequence of it, more disposed for such investigations than before; and I had always felt a full persuasion that there are depths in which the mind is swallowed up, and that Pope's advice is wisdom here,—

> " Wait the great teacher, Death;
> And God adore!"

Did not Bacon say, "I am no metaphysician, for I am not an owl, I cannot see in the dark!" Do not some good men impose upon themselves and others? They feel and express great confidence and certainty as to the result of their own perceptions and discussions: but—

First:—Are they not governed by terms and phrases of their own, hallowed, and significant probably with those who use them; but as to others, are they not words without knowledge, and which darken counsel rather than enlighten it? For what are they when they come to be explained? Or what satisfactory explanation are they capable of receiving?

Secondly:—They imagine they have solved difficulties, when they have only shifted them. They push them into holes and corners, but after a while they are met with again, by accidental approach, or revived research, to the awakening of their doubts, but seldom to the acknowledging of their mistakes.

Would it not be better for us to seize and improve the inviting and glorious truths of revelation, which are so plain and important, (and of which there are so many,) the experience of which we find useful to ourselves, and the communication of which we know to be useful to others? "The secret things belong unto the Lord; the things that are revealed are for us and for our children."

And what a difference must a Christian and a minister feel, between the trammels of some systems of divinity and the advantage of Scripture freedom, the glorious liberty of the sons of God! The one is the horse standing in the street, in harness, feeding indeed, but on the contents of a bag tossed up and down; the other, the same animal, in a large fine meadow, where he lies down in green pastures, and feeds beside the still waters.

But I remember hearing Mr. Owen, the Secretary to the Bible Society, say, after a long interview and discussion with Dr. Williams, that he never met with a systematizer, who seemed to have so clear a view, and so ready a command of his system.

To return. Dr. Davies was afterwards, for some years, Theological Tutor of Homerton Academy; alluding to which he often complained of the difficulties and trials of the situation and office, especially as they arose from the insubordination and manners of the young men, and which frequently induced him to exclaim, " Ye are too strong for me, ye men of Zeruiah."

He was also pastor of the church in Fetter Lane ; but he was compelled to resign his public and pastoral labours, owing to an extraordinary pain in his head. After (in a remarkable manner) being relieved from this, he resided for a time at Reading, and preached often there. He then resided with his niece, who had married the Independent minister of Wells. There too he often preached, and was very useful. Lastly, he came to Bath, and became a member of my church. Here he married again, and continued to reside to the end of life.

He occasionally preached for me, and always with much acceptance ; and it is remarkable that, though for many years he had always read his discourses, he latterly laid his notes aside ; and never, as it might have been supposed, felt embarrassment. His preaching was of a more evangelical and experimental and simple order than that of some of his contemporaries in London ; and he was one of the few who, in contrast to the stiffer and drier brethren, openly countenanced and commended Whitfield and his assistants.

He was a man of very considerable learning, of great theological knowledge, and of pre-eminent piety and spirituality.

I derived much benefit from him, (I might have derived more,) as a hearer, a companion, an admonisher, and an example.

He published but little. I had some of his manuscript

sermons, and also his course of Theological Lectures, (exceedingly clear and good,) and a Treatise on Human Depravity and Regeneration; all of which are now in the possession of my grandson, the Rev. Cornelius Winter Bolton, a clergyman in the United States.

His reading towards the last was almost entirely of one kind; and his favourite authors were Leighton, Baxter, and Newton. Newton's Letters in particular he delighted to re-peruse; for, he observed, what a double advantage he enjoyed, (owing to the declension of his memory,) as the same works seemed again new to him.

When I informed him of the death of his distinguished pupil, Dr. Williams, he burst into a flood of tears, and said, " I am almost ashamed to be alive, and eighty years old, when so many good, and great, and useful men are taken away in the midst of their days." He still lived considerably beyond this period, dying in a good old age, and gathered in like a shock of corn fully ripe in his season. His end was peace, but partaking more of trust than triumph. And I like best such modes of dying experience. Few can expect ecstacy and rapture, but many may die saying, " Let me not be ashamed of my hope,"—

> " A guilty, weak, and helpless worm,
>   On thy kind arms I fall;
> Be Thou my strength and righteousness,
>   My Jesus and my all ! "

REV. THOMAS HAWEIS, M.D.

DR. HAWEIS, in various respects, was a character well known in the religious world. He was for a time cotemporary with the founders of Methodism, though he was not a student at Oxford till Wesley and Whitfield had left that University. I have heard him mention that, during his residence at the College, he sometimes went over on the Sabbath to Weston-Favell to hear the celebrated James Hervey; and observing (what I had heard also especially from Mr. Newton and others, viz.) the dull aspect of his congregation, and the difference there was between the liveliness of his writings, and the unimpressiveness of his preaching. This rather strange fact may excite wonder; but it furnishes matter for a twofold remark.

First:—How divided and individual endowments and excellence are! and,

Secondly:—How the sovereignty of God appears, not only in his choice of instruments, but the way and work in which he employs them! and herein the Lord does not often conform to the judgment, or gratify the wishes of his servants themselves. They prefer a particular place or line of operation; but they find themselves unexpectedly in other situations and engagements; and though the providence may be trying at first, after a while grace produces acquiescence, and enables the man to be thankful if, in *any* mode or degree, he is honoured to be useful.

I enter not into the case of Dr. Haweis's obtaining the Living of Aldwinkle; concerning which there was a great difference of opinion, and several pamphlets published. The late Dr. Bridges and my father-in-law, the Rev. Edward Davies, also a beneficed clergyman, always defended him; and this was probably the case with others. I understood from Mr. Winter, that Mr. Whitfield indeed much wished him to resign the living; and Lady Huntingdon advanced a very considerable sum to satisfy or silence the complainant. I have more than once heard the Doctor say, that he offered to do anything for the complainant, if he would accept it as a *distressed* man, and not as an *injured* man; but as he demanded remuneration as a *right*, he could do nothing without condemning himself.

The Doctor himself always avowed that the living was put into his hands, after he had clearly, and fully, and repeatedly stated the only way in which he ought, and only could, consent to receive it, without an act of simony. But it made an impression generally against him; especially among those who judge not according to the rectitude of the case, but the usages of church-jobbing. Some, not wanting in impartiality, asked,—Was it the avoiding the (perhaps) appearance of evil? and—Was it lovely and of good report?

The Doctor may, perhaps, be considered the first man in the South Sea Mission. Some years before the London Missionary Society was established, from the accounts published by Captain Bligh and some other navigators, he was induced to choose, and bear the expense of preparing, two young men to go as missionaries to Otaheite; but who, as soon as they were educated, ignobly and deceitfully preferred staying at home. This exceedingly disappointed and distressed him; but he never drew off his attention and desire from the project and the place. When, therefore, this great and successful institution was formed, he rejoiced, and early attached himself to it. He preached the first sermon, at the first meeting in Spa Fields Chapel, on its behalf; and as the Directors and Managers were at a loss where to begin, he naturally and promptly directed their view to scenes of labour, which had become familiar to his mind, by much thinking and some effort and expense. And these were Otaheite and Tongataboo, the most central and advantageous stations for communication and extension.

As an Author, he published a volume of sermons and several single discourses, with some essays and tracts. But his principal works were, an Exposition of the whole Bible, in three volumes folio, and a Church History, in three volumes octavo. The former of these has often been supposed to be an abridgment of Henry, but it was not so designed, and is in reality a Commentary of his own, possessing no little value. The latter has been considered as a very hasty and superficial performance; but it has the recommendation of always nobly and simply looking after real and vital Christianity; and of frequently finding it, and showing it where partial or prejudiced ecclesiastics have overlooked it, or anathematized it. The work always breathes a most liberal spirit towards his brethren among the Dissenters and Methodists. He animadverts freely and judiciously with regard to Constantine, and the consequences of his conversion to the Christian Church; while his arguments against Milner, with regard to penal enactments in an Establishment, are unanswerable.

He had a peculiar confidence in himself, and a readiness of address which never failed him. But this rather injured him as a preacher, (and where has not this envied talent injured the owner?) so that leaning on his facility, he neglected retirement and study; and commonly had company on the evenings of his preaching, from which he seldom withdrew, till the clerk arriving with the robes and three-bushel wig, reminded him that the time was up. Hence, though able to do so much better, his sermons not only wanted method and consecutiveness, but were common-place and unctionless.

It is a bad case when a man has acquired the knack of preaching, and can talk on for an hour in the pulpit without effort and without *effect*. In proportion as the truths and doctrines we preach are well known and familiar, so much the more necessary is it to retire and meditate on them much, that our own minds may be affected by them, and that we may render them impressive and interesting to those that hear us.

It is well for a young minister to feel difficulties; and if these induce him to retirement, study, and prayer, he will in time surpass, at least in efficiency and usefulness, many who proudly towered above him at the beginning. This is one of the cases in which the first shall be last, and the last shall be first. To whom was the admonition addressed,—"Meditate upon these things, give thyself wholly to them, that thy profiting may appear unto all?" Yet young men, who are not Timothys, talk of the time when they finished their studies!

As before the Gospel was preached in the churches in Bath, Lady Huntingdon's Chapel was a place of fashionable resort, and as many careless creatures attended, especially on the Lord's Day evenings, the Doctor's style of address was too invariably terrific; and derived from such texts as these, —"It is a fearful thing to fall into the hands of the living God,"—"Who among us can dwell with everlasting burnings?"—"Depart, ye cursed," &c. But was this the more excellent way? Is there not danger that such tremendous expressions will lose their force by constant repetition? Is such horrifying declamation preaching the Gospel, and bringing good tidings of great joy? It would be well to endeavour to ascertain what is the legitimate employment of terror in an evangelical ministry. The use of it should not be a preacher's *pleasure*, but *pain;* and as an old writer says, "He should always utter a Divine threatening as a judge would pronounce sentence of death upon his son." Our subject is " the faithful saying and worthy of all acceptation, that Jesus Christ came into the world to save sinners ;" and the value of terror only is as an auxiliary or motive, to enforce the reception of our message of pardon and peace. So the apostles employed it: " Knowing the terror of the Lord, we persuade men," to accept the mercy and grace we hold forth. He hath " committed to us the ministry of *reconciliation*. Now then we are ambassadors for Christ, as though God did beseech you by us, we pray you in Christ's stead, be ye reconciled to God."

The Doctor's manner also was high, and not sufficiently courteous to the common people. Hence, after preaching long in Bath, the dissatisfied congregation induced him to decline his ministry among them, and also his attendance at the chapel. From this time he constantly worshipped with us, till his death. I attended him in his last illness, if it deserved the name, for, as he had no fears, so he had no pains,—so entirely was his end peace.

One thing he desired, and it was in character with his love of the missionary enterprise. On the very day of his death, one of the first set of missionaries sent to Otaheite was expected in Bath. It is hardly possible to express the earnestness with which he wished to see him, before he breathed his last. He sent again and again to my house, begging that, if he called upon me first, I would instantly bring him to his dying bed. The missionary came—he called upon me ; and, without asking him to sit down, I hurried and introduced him. We found Dr. Haweis like the expiring Simeon, saying, with tears, " Now, Lord, lettest thou thy servant depart in peace."

He left a large diary, which would have thrown much light on the earlier periods and events of the revival of religion in our own country ; but his son, a clergyman, of very opposite views to his father's, prevented the use which I wished to have made of it.

By the way, how was it, when Evangelism was so persecuted in the nation, and our bishops were so averse to its doctrines, that so many of the obnoxious clergy were suffered to act so irregularly, as to preach for weeks and months together, in places unconsecrated and unlicensed, yet retaining their livings; which was the case with Berridge, Venn, Pentycross, Glasscott, Haweis, &c. ?

Dr. Haweis, speaking one day of Whitfield's wonderful voice, and of its force as well as sweetness and variety of tone, said, he believed on a serene evening it might be distinctly heard for very nearly a mile.   Was this possible ?

PART IV.

SELECTIONS FROM THE CORRESPONDENCE

OF THE

REV. WILLIAM JAY.

SELECTIONS FROM CORRESPONDENCE.

Mr. Jay to Miss Davies, afterwards Mrs. Jay.

MY DEAREST LOVE,—
I always used to have a disinclination to preach at Bath, but I now
think it long to Sunday week. You know the reason. May we
have a happy and sanctified interview! I find the longer I stay here
the more I like the situation, and the harder it will be to dissolve the
connexion. But I wish to live having my conversation in heaven,
and then every place will be in some measure indifferent. Yes, my
love, let us determine to live as strangers and pilgrims here, and
plainly declare by our profession and conduct that we seek a better
country, that is a heavenly. Not when we shall be incapable of
pursuing this world, and when our gust for earthly pleasure shall be
abated by old age; but now while our affections are so warm, and
when so many are carried away by the vanity of the world and the
pride of life, let us unreservedly dedicate ourselves to God, and present ourselves as a living sacrifice, holy and acceptable to God,
which is our reasonable service. Nothing but real religion can make
us holy and happy in any situation or relation. In proportion as it
prevails we shall find heaven begun below. If you could come to
Bath, Saturday, should be glad. Let us, if possible, visit Prior one
day. Best respects to Mr. and Mrs. D., to Mrs. Hall if yet with
you, and Miss Isabella. The Lord bless you and help you, and

Yours most affectionately,

W. JAY.

Clifton, Feb. 2, 1789.

If you write, should be glad to know how dear Mr. Tuppen is,
and whether I may apprise Prior of our coming.

Rev. Cornelius Winter to Mr. Jay.

Painswick, Jan. 22, 1790.

MY VERY DEAR BILLY,—It is enough to have a pretext of necessity to write to you, and my pen moves freely. You have awakened all my tender sensations by your late visit, and given me occasion to prove that I cannot say to you as a great man once said to me at the close of a family connexion,—"I cast you off, now sink or swim." No, my dear friend, to carry on the idea, I believe if you were to sink, I should attempt to dive for you; but blessed be God, you swim: may you always keep your head above water, till you set your feet on the shore of that wealthy place where you shall find an everlasting abode. I hope you got safe and comfortable to Hope Chapel on Saturday, and found all well. Take proper care of your health, and employ it for Him who hath loved you and given himself for you.

I have employed some thought about *Paul* and *Saul*, and find Beza and Dr. Doddridge very candid. Doddridge adopts Beza's criticism on Acts xiii. 9. * * * * * * While writing this, yours came to hand, and is a conviction to me of our attachment being mutual. Friendship well grounded cannot be easily alienated. Through various interruptions I have been prevented from proceeding with my letter from the day I received yours till now. To be sure the sermon is in the press, and the Advertisement which precedes it not to be altered or improved.

I wish it may not appear too consequential, if not trifling. I repent that I have not spoken of you by an epithet expressive of the affection of my heart, for the world should know that you are dear to me. There is a delicacy in the use of terms, and they sometimes excite envy. My desire is that, in us, Cicero's remark on Friends may be exemplified: "Absentes adsunt, et egentes abundant, et imbecilles valent, et quod difficilius dictu est, mortui vivunt."

Yesterday se'nnight Mr. Surman gave a call, and preached a sermon to us. I declare I was surprised to hear him, and wonder not that he was invited to Plymouth. What cannot the Lord do? May He condescend to give me a farther proof of his power in my present family. They all unite in love to you with myself and Mrs. Winter. Mr. Griffin is under inoculation, and I trust will be brought abroad again. Recollect the hint I gave you about your parents, and when you write to or see them, give my love to them. I have a disposition to fill up the sheet, but I cannot. I therefore only add, come and see us when you can, and thereby add to the pleasure of, my very dear Billy,

Ever yours affectionately in our dear Lord Jesus,
CORNELIUS WINTER.

I saw Mr. Ashburn the morning you left me, who dropped a hint expressive of his approbation of what he heard the night before.

Mr. Jay to Mr. Withers.

London, 1793.

MY DEAR FRIEND,—Having a leisure half-hour, I said to myself, I'll embrace this opportunity to write to Mr. Withers. No sooner said than done, or at least begun. I thank you for your letter, but not for your apologies, as to your manner of writing, &c. &c. These I put amongst Mrs. Withers' kind ceremonies and cares when I am at your house. They are all bad things belonging to good persons; otherwise I should be more severe with them. You may depend upon it that I shall always be glad to see you and hear from you, but you must treat me with less compliment. I do not desire it, and I know I do not deserve it. I must be under strange infatuation indeed to think highly of myself. I have much to humble me. I am everything that's bad. "In me dwelleth no good thing." Whatever distinguishes me from others is the undeserved gift of God; and if, in any degree, I am useful to my fellow-creatures, 'tis "not I, but the grace of God which is with me."

What fine weather we have had for the ingathering of the fruits of the earth! How has our blessed God crowned the year with his goodness, and how lamentable is it that our world, so full of his mercy, should be so empty of his praise! Our fears were awakened, but they have been more than disappointed, and may we not hope that the same God will crown plenty with peace? Though the prospect is not favourable, all things are possible to Him, all things are under his control. The hearts of kings are in his hands. This is all the comfort I have as to present affairs.

I had a blessed time last Sabbath-day morning in preaching from these words: "Casting all your care upon him; for he careth for you," 1 Peter v. 7. I could not help wishing that a certain friend of mine who resides under your roof had been with us. Well, if Providence spares us to meet again, she may probably hear it second hand. Mrs. Jay unites with me in kind respects to her; thanking you all for your very great kindness towards our dear boy, to whom through you, we transmit a few kisses, and a promise not only of a horse but a whip too. We have spent half of our visit here, and shall be glad, after four more Sabbaths, to return *home*. O why do I not long equally to leave this bustling world, to go to my heavenly and everlasting *home?* Why do I not long to depart to be with Christ, which is far better? I have sometimes such views of this world and the next, that, if they were realized in experience, I think I should be in some measure what I ought to be; but alas! I have much more religion in my head than in my heart: and, with all my fine notions, I feel myself prone to cleave to the dust, and to neglect my Saviour. But my paper reminds me of the propriety of drawing to a close. Has Hymen yoked Mr. James yet? Tell him he must inform me, if he expect anything like an Epithalamium. I love both of them, and hope God will bless them. I know he will if my prayers are answered. I have not seen your daughter since I wrote last. Desire her, when you write to her, to call upon us again, and as often as she pleases. We know not where to direct for her. You see I sometimes write to yourself, and sometimes to Mrs. Withers, but I always mean both. You are, I trust, not only one in the common sense of the term, but one in Christ Jesus. May your union, begun upon earth, continue in heaven.—I am, dear Sir, yours, &c.

Mr. Jay to Mrs. Jay.

London.

MY DEAREST LOVE,—Last night I preached for the Sunday-morning Lecture, and in honour of the accession of this family to the throne. Dr. Hunter prayed. The congregation was large; and just as I was concluding the sermon there was a general consternation and outcry. All was confusion, the people treading on one another, &c. It was rather dark, and the pulpit candles only were lighted. I saw something moving up the aisle towards the vestry. It was a bull! we presume driven in by pickpockets, or persons who wished to disturb us.—We were talking on the affairs of the nation, and John Bull very seasonably came in. But imagine what followed:—the bull could not be made to go backwards, nor could he be turned round: five or six persons, therefore, held him by the horns; while the clerk, as if bewitched, gave out, in order to appease the noise,—

" Praise God, from whom *all* blessings flow,
Praise him, *all creatures* here below," &c.

O that the bull could but have *roared* here in compliance with the exhortation! I looked down from the pulpit, and seeing the gentlemen who held him singing with their faces lifted up, as if returning thanks for this unexpected blessing, I was obliged to put my hands before my face while I dismissed the congregation. This I think is enough for once.—I long to receive a line from you to tell me all your plans. Love to the dear children.

Yours, &c.

The Same to the Same.

My dearest Love,—You may imagine that I am always full of matter, but I assure you I have been sitting a considerable time with my pen in hand not knowing what to say. Love indeed would dictate a thousand fond things, but I am not certain that they would be most acceptable; and I hope they are not necessary. I would love, not in word only. I wish to make my whole conduct a proof of my affection and esteem. Tuesday evening I preached upon family religion, and as an inference from the importance of it, I exhorted young people to beware how they formed connexions:—"How can two walk together except they be agreed?" Here I hope we are agreed, and I trust we shall always "walk together as heirs of the grace of eternal life, that our prayers be not hindered." But I have been thinking, that, notwithstanding there is no disagreement between us, in our sentiments and dispositions respecting religious exercises in the family, as is the case with many, we may be more useful to each other in our relation than we have been; and watch over, pray for, rebuke, exhort, teach, and comfort each other, more than we have done. I know not indeed why I should class you with myself herein. But I am conscious of deficiency. I am to blame;—nor in this instance only. I seem all wrong, I have not half religion enough in my own soul to make me useful to others or happy in myself: I frequently doubt the truths I preach to others, and frequently fear lest, after having been useful to save others, I myself should be a castaway: the conviction of my judgment goes far beyond the experience of my heart. You cannot conceive in what an inferior light all sublunary objects frequently appear to me; and still I am looking to and depending upon creatures. I might enlarge. In the midst of all this there is some relief. O 'tis well to have light enough to see our darkness, and softness enough to feel our hardness: 'tis well that Jesus Christ saves sinners; that unworthiness is no bar; and that he provides *strong consolation for those who have fled for refuge.* O examine this character of the righteous, when, O my soul, thou canst not derive comfort from any other,—" *Hast thou not fled for refuge?* "

*   *   *   *   *

Yours, &c.

ON THE DEATH OF TWO CHILDREN.

To Mr. Newall, who was for upwards of fifty years a Member of Mr. Jay's Church, and for many years Deacon and Treasurer.

(Dated about Sept. 1805.)

MY DEAR FRIEND,—By a letter Mrs. Jay has this morning received from Mrs. Lockyer, I am informed of the very severe trial with which the Lord has been exercising you. Had I been at home I would have hastened to comfort you at your dwelling, and have mingled my tears with yours at the mouth of the grave, under the loss of two dear children,—lovely children, removed almost at a stroke! But I hope that, though a poor worm has been absent, He has been present, who has promised to be with us in trouble, whose property it is to comfort them that are cast down; and who while He *chastens* can *teach* us out of his law. Intervening objects are often removed that He may be seen, and even death commands silence that He may be heard. And the *blessed* sufferer, the *sanctified* sufferer, is the *humble supplicant*, who wipes his eyes and says,— " Speak, Lord, for thy servant heareth." " Lord, what wilt thou have me to do?" In our judgments we readily acknowledge His right to us and ours; but when He comes to take His own, how hard do we find it to say practically, "The will of the Lord be done!" But I am persuaded this is your disposition,—this has been your prayer; this will be your experience. He who knows our frame, *means* us to feel. He who designs our profit by our pain, *requires* us to feel. But he expects that we should qualify and regulate the feelings of the creature by the grace of the Christian. And why? Because he has provided for all our wants, knows that His grace is sufficient for us, and that if we ask we *shall* have. My prayers shall attend you through all this gloomy scene, and if they are answered you will never be afraid of trouble again. You will soon perceive reason to say,—" It is good for me that I have been afflicted." In the multitude of your thoughts within you, *His comforts* will delight your souls. You will be enabled to say,—" Well, my darling infants are not lost, but provided for. The Shepherd has gathered my lambs with his arms, and now carries them in His bosom. I shall find them again in yonder happy world. I shall embrace them all perfect and immortal."

> " Our journey is a thorny maze,
>   But we march upwards still ;
> Forget the troubles of the ways,
>   And reach at Zion's hill."

I cannot do justice to your affliction or my own feelings ; but I have snatched a few moments from company and engagements, to show you that I sympathize with you, and am, my dear Friend, yours to serve in the Gospel of our dear Lord Jesus,

WILLIAM JAY.

To his Daughter Statira when very young, and while he was in London.

[We give the following as a beautiful specimen both of his condescension to the capacity of a child, and of the tender and pious affection with which he watched over his children.]

MY VERY DEAR STATIRA,—I assure you I intended writing when I left home, and before I knew you had desired your mamma to ask me to do it, but I was much pleased to learn that you wished it. It shows that you value my notice, and proofs of this notice you shall never want, while you continue to act as you have done. * * * Oh, if children did but consider the satisfaction they give their parents by being good, they would never be naughty. But their good conduct is not only attended with pleasure to their parents, but with peace and comfort to their own minds. It gains them the approbation of all around them ; yea, it pleases God, who gives us all we enjoy, and on whose favour and blessing all our happiness depends. I do not know anything so lovely as a little girl of your size when she is good-natured, and not selfish, fond of reading and improvement, obedient to her mamma, and when she loves the Scriptures, and the Sabbath, and God's house ; and often prays,

> "Make me to walk in thy commands,
>   'Tis a delightful road ;
> Nor let my head or heart or hands
>   Offend against my God."

And such, I have a full persuasion, I shall always find my dear and last-born child. I promise myself much pleasure for years to come, in endeavouring to train you up in the nurture and admonition of the Lord, and in making you an amiable and useful member of society. But you, my dear Statira, may die, or papa may die, or mamma may die, and no more feel the kisses of their darling upon their cheeks morning and evening, but be laid in the cold grave ; yea, we must all die, and so part sooner or later; and, therefore, we must so live here as not to be parted hereafter, but indulge the pleasing hope of living together for ever in heaven.

I hope you feel much obliged to Mr. Bolton for his attentions. Tell him I thank him much on your behalf, and shall be glad to repay him in any way in my power, in addition to my having given him (I hope she is) a good wife.   *   *   *   *

I long to see Percy Place again, and one of the principal reasons is to see and embrace again my dear Statira, and to prove by more than a hasty and imperfect letter, that

I am, my darling girl, your affectionate and devoted Father,
London, Oct. 30, 1812.   WM. JAY.

To the Same.

MY DEAR SWEET PEA,—How I long for the time when I shall see thy image and thyself once more in my garden ! But "to everything there is a season :" and we must learn to deny ourselves and wait. Neither should I object to view some other flowers in my little Eden, or even one or two birds. O when will that spring or summer arrive? But I must not sin against the rule I have just laid down; and, therefore, instead of giving way to impatience, I will try to write on. I hope you will find this journey useful and improving. It is in your power to render it so by keeping your attention awake, and suffering nothing to pass unobserved. Listen to what is said by persons of any talent in company, especially when they speak upon those subjects with which they are most familiar ; and they who have no general information may be well versed in their own line, and commonly talk well concerning it. I some time ago overtook a little sweep. I did not suppose he could criticise Milton, nor Locke, but there was one thing he understood better than I did ; and before we separated, I knew how to climb a chimney. Not that I mean to set up in this calling. I am too big, too old, and fully occupied with some other things ; but I love to learn, and I meet with few but are able to teach. Search your head all over, and if you find two ears, and only one tongue, be always more ready to hear and slow to speak; and when you speak, speak with diffidence and modesty. A forward, bold, decisive tone is never agreeable in a man; in a youth it is always offensive, but in a girl it is intolerable. You know how Miss —— was disliked and neglected after her father's death, for the freedom with which, in every circle, she delivered her opinion of men and things. Always say little of characters, and let this little as much as possible be in a way of commendation. Be less disposed to remark blemishes than excellences; and let it appear that you can discern and acknowledge merit of any kind with pleasure. Gain some little addition every day to your mental stores, and remember the axiom, "To him that hath shall be given;" that is, diligence and use increase what is good, both by their natural tendency, and the Divine blessing upon our endeavours. Be fond of composition; accustom yourself to write down, with as much accuracy and clearness as you can, every interesting occurrence, or any train of thought. I wish you to have a resource of pleasure through life, not only in reading, but in writing. I am glad you go on with your French. When you come home you must teach me to pronounce and speak it. I should be glad to receive a letter from you in this language. I am sure you are able to write it, especially under the eye of Mr. Bolton. How would it surprise Bella and mamma, and sharpen their curiosity when they opened it, as they always do so greedily every letter from Liverpool! How dependant will they feel, and come and beg of me the contents! I hope you rise early and take proper exercise. I hope also you *walk* well and *sit* well; for I know, a few weeks back, some considerable improvement was required in both. Some attention to each of these is the more necessary as you seem determined to be tall; and the want of gracefulness is more observed in a tall figure than in a short.—Mrs. William Evill is rapidly declining, and funeral rites will early follow nuptial solemnities. At present she seems to decline seeing any one; but I hope she is becoming sensible of her condition, though this flattering disorder may well be called "a slow sudden death," and that by-and-by I shall have some improving intercourse with her. In the space of four days I attended no less than four funerals. I endeavoured to improve them all in a sermon from 2 Corinthians v. 1,—"For we know that if our earthly house of this tabernacle were dissolved," &c., in which I observed, we have—

1. An object contemplated—"the earthly house of this tabernacle."

2. An event supposed—the destruction of it—"if it be dissolved."

8. A privilege apprehended—"a building of God, a house not made with hands, eternal in the heavens."

4. A confidence expressed—"we know" that we have this—a confidence of belief—a confidence of hope—a confidence of possession—not we *shall* have, but we *have*, &c.

When I mentioned Mr. ——, I said "he was unknown to many of you; but he was well known in the world of sport and dissipation. He formerly distinguished himself on the turf, and obtained a subsistence by horse-racing. But this course of life for many years back he had abandoned; and reviewed it with that godly sorrow that worketh repentance unto life, not to be repented of. The revival of early instruction from pious parents, by the death of a beloved and only son, brought him to religious reflection. He was a man of a most warm and generous disposition, and delighted to do good, especially in visiting the fatherless and the widows in their afflictions, and attending the bed of pain and sickness;" and when I added, "in the afternoon he passed my house,—in the evening, ordered his nephew to read the 6th chapter of St. John,—prayed with his family,—retired comfortably to rest,—awoke at eleven,—complained of a pain in his stomach,—said, 'Come, Lord Jesus,'—and in the twinkling of an eye expired,"—there was a half-fetched involuntary groan through the audience, that made it very solemn.—What I said of —— was this,—"She was an interesting infant; a sufferer from the hour of her birth; her early and continued affliction she endured with a patience above her years, and often spoke of God and heaven in language very unusual for one under five years of age. This is an event of congratulation rather than of condolence. At the grave of a child we always feel a peculiar satisfaction, arising from the persuasion that they are disposed of infinitely to their advantage. Under the protracted illness of this little martyr, the Saviour said to the parents—'Suffer this little child to come unto me, and forbid her not, for of such is the kingdom of heaven.' The Shepherd has gathered this lamb with his arms, and now carries it in his bosom."—Of Mrs. —— I said, "She was for many years a member of our Church, and walked consistently with her profession. She was a plain, inoffensive, upright character. There was nothing distinguishing in her life, and her dying experience was the same. Through her lengthened disease, she was patient and submissive, often complained of herself, and felt alternately the prevalence of fear and hope; and I am persuaded, that HE who does not 'break a bruised reed nor quench the smoking flax' has received her."

"Mr. J——," I said, "many of you were acquainted with. I see several of his companions in iniquity here this evening. O that your former associate could now address you. We have reason to hope and believe that he saw and deplored the errors of his conduct, and has obtained the mercy for which he so earnestly prayed. His language was penitential. His concern to warn and admonish others was striking, and he drew whatever relief he felt from the Friend of sinners. But O, ye bereaved neighbours, friends, and relations, my business lies not with the dead, but the living. *They* have done with all below. Their state is now fixed, and their happiness or misery cannot be affected by your opinions, or my representations, were I disposed to condemn or eulogise. They are beyond the reach of the Gospel, but you are yet in the land of the living, and have another opportunity to hear the merciful admonition—'Seek the Lord while he may be found, call upon him while he is near.' What is your duty but to retire, and falling upon your knees, pray with Moses, 'So teach us to number our days that we may apply our hearts unto wisdom!' And what is wisdom? What is that wise part creatures circumstanced as you are ought to act? Is it not to prefer your souls to your bodies, and the realities of eternity to the vanities of time? Is it not to seek without delay pardon and renovation? a title to heaven, and a meetness for it? You talk of happiness, uncertain as you are of life. I defy you to be happy without a hope beyond the grave. He—he only is happy who can look forward with humble confidence, and say—'We know that we have a building of God, a house not made with hands, &c.' "

You complain of inability to fill *your sheet.* Look at the size of my paper, and see *my* lines, not wide apart like the hedges of a London-road; nor the whole begun two or three inches down from the top. But how am I to fill up the remainder of this folio? I have no other *news* to communicate, except, indeed, a subject that is always *new,* and which I hope you love, the love of Jesus—the love of Him who, though he was rich, for our sakes became poor, and died that we might live. You have often heard me repeat his encouraging assurance, "Him that cometh unto me I will in no wise cast out," and you know, (O what a privilege!) that to come to him is to believe his word, and call upon his name. But while he rejects none, he peculiarly regards some. "Feed," says he, "feed my *lambs.*" "I love them that love me, and they that seek me early shall find me;" that is—find him as others never *will,* never *can.* And the case speaks for itself; for if religion can preserve us from snares and embarrassments; if it can make us amiable and useful; if it be profitable unto all things; if it yields the truest pleasure, the sooner it is possessed, in the same proportion the more are we privileged; and, next to the reality of their conversion, I am persuaded the people of God daily bless him for the *earliness* of it, if they have been thus favoured : and the greater part of them are called long before they are advanced in years. O, my dear Statira, what a season is youth ! of the day of life it is the morning : of the year it is the spring. And how much depends upon seizing the one, and improving the other. How desirable is it to sanctify the present in every kind of preparation for the future ; and before the journey is begun, such a journey as we have before us, to secure a guide, a guard, a friend who will never leave us nor forsake us. I trust, my dear child, that you are placing yourself under His conduct, and saying—" I will go forth in the strength of the Lord."

My time of going to London is now fixed. My visit commences the last Sabbath in May, and takes in the first three in June. Either in my way thither or back, I am to preach a sermon at Newport Pagnel, in favour of Mr. Bull's Academy there ; and I am also requested at the same time to preach before the Bedfordshire Union, at Bedford, along with Mr. Hall.

Your affectionate and devoted Father, &c.

To the Same.

Bath, May 23, 1816.

My DEAR SWEET PEA,—Though the last blown, yet not the least loved of all my flowers. I wish I had more time to write ; but my preparation for the approaching journey to London leaves me very little. But the length of my last must atone for the brevity of the present ; and remember you have to boast of receiving the longest letter papa ever wrote. I suppose, by this time, Mr. Spear and his daughters who accompanied him to Bromsgrove, are returned, and you are probably thinking of returning to Liverpool. But you must not suffer the little nephew or niece to make you impatient. If you should feel it to be a self-denial to be absent from them, you must exercise it. This virtue is indeed of such constant and universal utility, that we cannot begin to cultivate it too soon. We cannot expect to have everything according to our mind, as we pass through a world like this : it is not fit we should, and, therefore, we must learn to bear disappointment, and be able easily and gracefully to accommodate ourselves to every changing scene. Hitherto your way has been smooth, the lines have fallen to you in pleasant places ; your wishes have been generally, if not invariably, gratified.

" All without thy care and payment,
All thy wants are well supplied."

But you cannot reckon upon a perpetual exemption from- inconvenience and trial. "Truly the light is sweet, and a pleasant thing it is for the eyes to behold the sun: but if a man live many years, and rejoice in them all; yet let him remember the days of darkness; for they shall be many. All that cometh is vanity." I would not by future forebodings prevent your enjoying the kindnesses which Providence affords you at this pleasing period of life; but I know youth is sanguine, its hopes are too glaring, and require to be sobered, by that prudence which results from experience and observation. You ought ever to be thankful for the comforts and indulgences of your condition. But do you not feel your need of something better? Is there not an emptiness in the midst of all? Yes, and the world will never fill it; but He can who mercifully cries—"Seek ye *me*, and ye shall live." And those dissatisfactions which attend all creature-good are the inspirations of the Almighty to give us understanding, and to make us wise unto salvation. I hope, my precious girl, that you are listening to his voice, and dedicating yourself to his service, which they who have tried know to be perfect freedom. Having given yourself unto the Lord, I trust I shall have the pleasure, after your return, to witness your "giving yourself also to his Church, by the will of God." In Dr. Doddridge's little volume of Sermons to Young People, there is a discourse on the subject of "Early Communion," which I wish you to read. I dare say Mr. Spear has it. I hope wherever you are, that you not only devote some time to private devotion and reading the Scripture, but that you look over the books you meet with in the house where you visit, and read as much as possible of those you have not seen before. Of course I do not mean that you should shut yourself up from enjoying the prospects of nature at this season, and the society of your friends; but there are many moments to be seized which carelessness overlooks. It is by making use of these, and by early rising, that I have obtained much of the little I possess. Like the *Bee*, always be extracting materials for honey.—Yesterday morning, I was invited to breakfast at Mr. Hallet's, and to give the new-wedded pair my advice and blessing. But how changeable and chequered is every earthly scene. No sooner had the party returned from church, than Mr. Griffith, sen., was called out of the room to be informed that his only brother at Frome was just killed by leaping from a *sociable*, the horses of which had taken fright. This damped the joy of the season. But he was a very holy man—an occasional preacher in Mr. Wesley's connexion, and, at the time of the accident—so people call it, I should rather say *appointment*—he was returning from preaching in a village. He was a widower, and has left no child; but the poor will exceedingly miss him, for he was a father to them, and a fine image of Him who went about doing good.

On Saturday morning we set off for London. Miss Shepherd goes with us as far as Hammersmith. We are all longing for the time when we hope, under the smiles of a gracious Providence, to "meet and mingle into bliss," to kiss, and cry tears of joy.

Your affectionate and devoted Father, &c.

To his Son Edward at Wymondley College.

Bath, March 2, 1816.

*   *   *   *   *   *

I charge you be sparing in your remarks on character. They who hear them, may report them inaccurately, and with exaggeration; and as the consequence you will, when charged with them, be tempted to deny, or perplexed to explain and qualify. But I wish to deter you by a better principle, the command of Him who has said, "Speak evil of no man." "Be swift to hear, and slow to speak." "Love every one, and every one will love you." "Who is he that will harm you if you be a follower of that which is good?" While you talk little (especially concerning persons), *observe* much. Be continually adding a little to your mental stores. Accustom yourself to composition; put down your thoughts on paper with as much accuracy, and clearness, and celerity, as you can be master of.—I long for you to be able to *sermonize*. Whenever a text strikes you, turn it over in your mind, and endeavour to divide it. If you cannot satisfy yourself, the effort will do you good,—exertion will prepare for exertion; and thought will produce thought. While you attempt much you must not be discouraged, if at first the result be little. The infant bird practises his wings, as he stands up in the nest; then gets upon the edges of it; then upon the neighbouring boughs; and then takes short excursions, before he flies his more daring lengths; and "to him that hath shall be given," as the natural consequence of use and improvement, and as also the effect of the Divine blessing. You cannot begin so low as I did, but I felt a love to study bordering on enthusiasm; and despaired of nothing; not from a high opinion of my capacity, but an apprehension that diligence, with the Divine assistance, (which he had graciously disposed my heart to seek,) would do wonders. I was placed indeed in a situation peculiarly suited to the cast of my mind, and never wanted for excitations and encouragements. And you, my dear boy, have great advantages at present, and the prospect of every future help and direction. Trials you would have in any line of life; but in the sacred calling to which you are looking forward, you will be sheltered much from a stormy and wicked world; you will have opportunities for intellectual and pious improvement; you will enjoy the pleasure of being useful, and of doing good: and if you act from principle, " when the Chief Shepherd shall appear, you shall receive a crown of glory that fadeth not away." Let me know whether you are able to read my writing. I shall feel a pleasure in corresponding with you. Write when you have an opportunity, and write with freedom. All join in love.

Your very affectionate Father, &c.

To the Same.

Bath, March 2, 1818.

I WRITE according to my promise, but I believe I must in future alter my epistolary day, and make it Tuesday instead of Monday; as of late I feel so enervated by the anxieties and labours of the Sabbath, that on the Monday I *exist* rather than live. I wish also not only to please you by a few lines monthly, but to render my letters instructive and useful; and when I feel as I do to-day I can scarcely command a thought, and every effort fatigues. I believe, should my days be prolonged, that I shall be a very premature old man. I began early. I was emulous to advance. I laboured under a thousand disadvantages from which you are free; and being, from the first, thrown into popular and trying situations which had great claims upon me, I applied myself with more unrelaxing tension of mind than my frame (never remarkably strong) could bear; and I now begin to feel peculiarly the effect of it. This I think I may say without vanity regarding myself, or ill-nature towards others. This is not the common failing of the students and younger ministers of the present day. I wish to perceive in them a habit of greater application and diligence, a greater sense of the value of time, and the importance of their work,—as also more of a humble and devotional spirit. I can make allowances for some things in young ministers, which I could not tolerate in older: but still, as the apostle says, "A bishop must be grave,"—a general sedateness of speech and behaviour is so becoming in him, that, whatever be his talents, he will never inspire respect without it. It was to *young* Timothy Paul said, "Let no man despise thy youth;" but for this purpose, "Be thou an example of the believers, in word, in conversation, in charity, in spirit, in faith, in purity. Give attendance to reading, to exhortation, to doctrine. Neglect not the gift that is in thee. Meditate upon these things; give thyself wholly to them, that thy profiting may appear unto all. Take heed unto *thyself*, and unto the doctrine, *continue* in them; for in doing this, thou shalt both save thyself and them that hear thee." It is a great thing in all our private and social intercourse to be cheerful without being light; and serious without being sad, or appearing sanctimonious. Some few ministers, even in earlier life, have attained this excellency. Let *them* be your models, rather than pulpit flirts and fiddles, and your story-telling parsons, whose sole ambition in company seems to be to make mirth; and who generally succeed so well, that they are not only laughed *with*, but laughed *at*. Nothing is more lovely in a student and a minister, than a freedom from everything dictatorial and dogmatical, in his manner of address. It becomes him rather to listen than to speak,—to inquire than to controvert. Not that he is obliged to believe everything that he hears, even from a senior, or to admit without evidence; but he must dissent with seeming reluctance, propose his doubts with modesty, and appear to distrust his own judgment rather than depreciate that of another. Speak with warmth, (and let it come from the heart,) as much as you can, in commendation and praise of others;—but—"Speak evil of no man;"—"Love all, and all will love you." "Who is he that will harm you, if you are a follower of that which is good?"—and though spiritual religion can never be relished by depraved minds, yet "he that in these things serveth Christ, is acceptable to God and approved of men."

I have been a Sabbath to *Marlborough, where the prospect is delightful. Mr. Williams of Shrewsbury (*now Sir J. B. Williams*) is publishing memoirs from the diary of Mrs. Savage, daughter of Philip, and sister of Matthew, Henry, for which I have written a pretty long preface, at his desire, &c.

To the Same.

Bath, May 9, 1819.

* * * I AM sorry for the interruption your studies will again sustain in your long absence from Wymondley. The plan of attending lectures in London, too, does not strike me as of much importance; as, however, it is appointed, and seems a privilege shown to a few of you for good conduct, you must avail yourself of it; and you may turn it to advantage. It is a great recommendation to be able to *read* and *pronounce* well; but then it must appear to be natural; primness and affectation always displease more than *simple* and *earnest vulgarity*. The great thing is to forget *one's-self*, and to speak with *seriousness* and *affectionate feeling*. Feeling is always eloquent: and if the preacher be obviously affected, and appears concerned to do good, and not to gain applause, he will always be felt, and always approved. Nothing also is more becoming, in a young minister especially, than an apparent consciousness of the importance and difficulty of his work; an *un*forwardness to engage; a diffidence and modesty; in a word, the very reverse of what we see in many of the assuming, pert, bold, fearless, self-sufficient, and self-admiring academics of the day. Keep this to yourself. I take care how I reflect upon the sprigs of divinity before others, as there is too much readiness to censure young ministers among modern hearers already: and I am thankful to see that all are not alike, and I can reprove when I do not wish to condemn. I hope tutors will be increasingly attentive to the *spirit* and *manner* of students, both in the pulpit and in the parlour. Let me beseech you, my dear son, to keep your eye upon the best models, and pray for grace to conform to them. With regard to what is exceptionable in others, keep as far from it as you can, but never talk about it. It can do no good, and may be easily ascribed, (before a man's character is highly established,) to ill-nature or envy; and one of the worst features of many of the students and young preachers of the day, is an unbounded license in speaking of others, especially their brethren. Speak evil therefore of no one, but let the law of innocence and kindness dwell upon your tongue. But to mark the improprieties of others for your own improvement, —that is, in order to avoid them,—this is a different thing; and while you keep your mouth shut, you must keep your eyes and ears open.

*   *   *   *   *   *

Your devoted Father, &c.

To Sir J. B. Williams.

On the very sudden Death of John Lee, Esq., the Gentleman to whom several of Mr. Winter's Letters, introduced into Mr. Jay's Life of Winter, were addressed.

Bath, October 9th, 1818.

MY DEAR SIR,—You will doubtless wonder that I have not noticed your very affecting letter earlier; but I was from home when it arrived, and I have been again from home on pressing business; and while having more to do than usual, I have been very unwell, first in my head, and then in my bowels, so that I have dragged on heavily, and been fit for nothing. But be assured your communication was not received, without producing that interest which a sincere and warm friendship requires. I wept with those that weep, and I prayed with those that pray. Tell the bereaved family how much I sympathize with them, and what a persuasion I have, that the God of my departed friend will be "the Father of the fatherless, and the Husband of the widow in his holy habitation," and in their own. How surprising was the event! How well he seemed when I shook hands with him, alas! for the last time, at the coach door! I knew the year before he sometimes complained, but was not aware that the least danger of such an issue was attached to the complaint. Well, nothing has occurred by chance; a sparrow falls not to the ground without our heavenly Father, and the very hairs of our head are all numbered. And be it remembered ever, that while He does all things, He does all things *well*. His dispensations are not only sovereign, but wise, righteous, and kind—kind even when they seem to be severe. We may be unable to explain them at present; but "we know that the Messias cometh, which is called Christ, and when he is come he will tell us all things." Till then let us walk by faith, and give him full credit for the goodness of his designs, and the manner in which they are accomplished. This is the way—the only way—to reach rest in a world like this. "Thou wilt keep him in perfect peace whose mind is stayed upon thee, because he trusteth in thee." Though we must not dictate, but leave it to God to determine by what death we shall glorify him, such a dismission as our lovely friend was favoured with has always appeared to me very enviable. The partings,

> "The pains, the groans, the dying strife,
> Fright our approaching souls away," &c.

Here all this was prevented; and we can say over his grave,

> "A soul prepared needs no delays,
> The summons comes, the saint obeys;
> Swift was his flight and short the road,
> He closed his eyes, and woke with God."

I felt, too, for the shock your good wife must have felt in her delicate situation; and hope she is now disburdened, and has forgotten her anguish for joy that a man is born into this world. Remember me to her; and to all the dear afflicted house, where I was so cordially entertained. I do bear, and I will bear them all upon my mind at the throne of grace—that refuge, that source of benevolence and friendship. I had three funeral services to perform last week only.—What a dying world!

Your's to esteem and serve, &c.

To Miss Harman.

Lynmouth, August 11, 1830.

MY DEAR MISS HARMAN,—Your very acceptable parcel arrived just before we set off from Bath. I am much obliged by both the works, but you should not have had them bound so expensively. Baxter's "Life" we took with us, with some other mental and spiritual provender; but when we got out of the coach at Bridgewater, we left the parcel in the boot, and as there was no direction upon it, we did not recover it till two days ago. Though generally acquainted with Baxter and his works, I find much that is new and interesting in the "Life," for you must know I have nearly devoured it already, and even the charms of this God-made spot could not draw me off from the perusal. Your lamented friend and pastor * has, I think, done much justice to this extraordinary man; to his *character*, and to his *publications*—to the excellences and infirmities of the one, and the orthodoxy and errors of the other; and I hope the book will be largely circulated. Henry says—it is impossible to read the book of Psalms and not be inflamed or ashamed by the perusal. I say the same of this work. But I fear I shall be more shamed than fired. What piety! what diligence! what sufferings! what patience and submission! Well, by the grace of God he was what he was; and the God of all grace remains the same, and is within our reach in all that we call upon him for.

* Rev. W. Orme, of Camberwell.

Instead of growing tired of this Swiss village, we admire it more than ever. Mr. and Mrs. Kingsbury have been here four days with us; and though they have travelled much over our country, they prefer this to everything they have seen. They occupied the room *you* would have slept in, could I have had power enough to overcome your good father's objections. Give my kindest love to him notwithstanding, for we are bound to *forgive;* nor forget your dear mother, who, I believe, pleaded for us. We all lament your absence; and Mrs. Jay and Miss Protheroe send their most loving regards. I wish I could give a better account of my most dear wife; but she is very poorly, and can hardly enjoy any of the pleasures of the place. This is a sad deduction. "Full bliss is bliss Divine." The weather, too, at present is much against her. To supply your place imperfectly, a young pious lady, and an old acquaintance, Miss Browning, from Ilfracombe, has come over to take lodgings near us, and we find others are coming. But I wish not for more. I wish to be entirely disengaged; not, however, to be idle, but to be at liberty to use my pen,—and I do use it daily, as much as comports with the design of the excursion. What a work is this in France! I trust no violence and excess will mar it; yet I could wish that the wretched family of the Bourbons was entirely excluded. I always felt a persuasion that Providence would destroy it. Much yet remains to be done in the Popish countries. Adieu, my dear Miss Harman. The Lord bless thee and keep thee.

Your's, &c.

To *his Son Edward.*

London, July, 1832.

I FULLY intended returning home to-morrow, but circumstances have determined us to go round by Henley, as Mr. Bolton is not very well. I cannot, therefore, be at home before Thursday evening; and, therefore, it will be necessary to engage some one to preach. We shall be taken up at Reading by the new company's coach. I have secured our places. Anne comes by the same coach to-morrow; let her be looked out for, and see that her parcels be safe. Your precious mother is pretty well upon the whole; but she has been too much excited, and I long to get her home. We have been much crowded. Last Friday I dined at the Lord Mayor's, and met a very agreeable and interesting company, the *lion* of which was His Highness the Rajah Rammohun Roy. You cannot imagine what a full-minded, and clever, and agreeable man he is; always more than a match for any one who disputed with him, especially the Tories—and we had several of them. As it was known that he was to hear me at Surrey Chapel last evening, we were not only full, but hundreds went away. He came in his carriage, ten minutes before six, with Dr. Henry and Archdeacon Stopford, and was conducted to a good place for seeing and hearing. His fine figure, and his rich and elegant costume, attracted every eye. He was observed to give great attention, and frequently jogged his companions, without taking off his eye from the pulpit. I preached an hour and a quarter, raised above the fear of man by previous retirement. When it was over, he said, loud enough to be heard by many, "I must have this sermon, and publish it." He came into the house, with immense difficulty pressing through the crowd in the yard, all waiting to see him. The house also, in both rooms, was full. The pleasure he expressed from hearing the sermon, before all the people present, was really affecting. It so completely met with his sentiments, he said, that he hoped I would not deny him the sermon to publish himself, and circulate among his friends. I tried to decline, till delicacy would permit it no longer; and so I have committed myself, and must write it out as soon as I come back, for he is going to the continent in a few weeks. Dr. Henry and the Archdeacon were especially delighted; and when I said to the former, "Doctor, I fear you have suffered from the crowd and the heat," he replied, "Sir, I felt nothing but the sermon." You see, my dear boy, I keep back nothing from you; but I could not say all this to others. Garfit does not seem amended. I have just walked with him to the Mansion House. The Lord Mayor could not attend yesterday, but the Lady Mayoress was present, with a very splendid carriage. Kindest regards to Mrs. Burton; and kiss Margaret for me, if you do not object to it.

Your affectionate Father, &c.

To the Rajah Rammohun Roy.

Sir,—I herewith transmit the manuscript of the sermon you so candidly heard, and, so unexpectedly to the preacher, wished to see and to circulate. I could not send it earlier, owing to my travelling, and the numerous engagements and interruptions I met with immediately on my return. Your Highness will observe that I had not written the sermon previously, but delivered it from short notes only; and, therefore, I should have had more difficulty in recalling the language as well as the sentiments, had not a friend furnished me with a short-hand copy. In consequence of this the discourse will be found more than *substantially* the same with what was spoken from the pulpit. In the very *trifling alterations* I have made, I did not attempt to reduce the *free and popular* mode of address I assumed, and which was so requisite in so very large and mixed a multitude of hearers. For want of this many preachers preach inefficiently, or sacrifice impression on the mass to the gratification of the few. The manner of the Great Teacher sent from God may be inferred from the reproach, which was yet an eulogium,—"the common people heard him gladly."

It is presumed that there may be some few things in the discourse in which your Highness may not entirely coincide; but it afforded me pleasure to conclude from your request that, upon the whole, and as having some useful bearings, it has met your Highness's approbation. I commend it to the Divine influence; and, imploring the blessing of God upon your Highness, permit me to subscribe myself,

Your Highness's obliged and humble servant,

Bath, June 29, 1832.   WILLIAM JAY.

To his Son Edward.

Weymouth, August 22, 1832.

I DROP you a line to say we received the basket of fruit safe and sound. *   *   *   * So your precious mother instantly made up a nice little present for Lord and Lady W——, who were at the Royal Hotel, in their way back from Guernsey to Sidmouth, and who, hearing of us, called, and said, if I preached on the Sunday they would stay over the day. They did so; and this gave me an opportunity of several interviews. I like them both much, as far as I have conversed with them. Lady W—— knows the truth, and I really believe feels the power of it; and is resisting all the fanaticism that rages in the West of England, and all around Sidmouth. Lord W—— seems very amiable and promising, and is exceedingly attached to his wife. He is a thorough Whig; says he was a member for one of his father's rotten boroughs, but was bound hand and foot, and obliged to vote on the wrong side, and would not endure the farce any longer. He says he reads my "Exercises" every day, and uses my "Prayers." They much wish to come and live in the near neighbourhood of Bath. *   *   *   *

Give my best regards to our elders and friends, and let them be immediately informed of my return. They will see that I have not encroached upon their kindness, taking in fact but two Sabbaths, for the other pertained to my month of privilege. But where love actuates, we do not need restraints and rules. I love home, and never preach with so much pleasure as in Argyle Chapel, where I have employed for God the flower, yea, the far larger part, of my whole life. And, blessed be His name, he has not withholden tokens of his approbation. I refer not only to my own church, but to strangers also who occasionally attend there. A lady who lives in a neighbouring village called in her carriage the other morning, and said, that eighteen years ago she was at Bath with her gay companions, but felt an inclination one evening to leave them and go to Argyle. I preached, she said, from—" Is not this a brand plucked out of the fire ?" From that time she left the world, and has been ever since not only blessed but a blessing. She came to hear me on Sabbath morning, and I have been to her house.

To Miss Harman.

June 29, 1832.

MY DEAR MISS HARMAN,—We got home safe and well. My precious invalid was very little tired. She now, in very strange language, (for I know her meaning,) begs to be remembered to you, and says, it is very hard the *woman* won't let *him* come. Amidst many engagements and interruptions, always multiplied on returning home, I have just finished my transcript for the Rajah, and am now (it is Friday evening,) preparing for the Sabbath. Preaching is trying work this weather ; so you say is hearing, unless the pastor makes us lie down in green pastures, and feedeth us beside the still waters. How delightful the *five points* would be now treated in the jargon of the school theology ! O my charming Bible, how I love thy simplicity, and grandeur, and grace ! Prov. vi. 21, 22.

One of my best members died the day after my return. She was "an old disciple," whose life was goodness, and whose end was peace. With best respects to your good father and mother, I have but just time to subscribe myself,

Your's, &c.

Lord Barham to Mr. Jay.

London, December 31, 1834.

MY DEAR MR. JAY,—You will be glad to hear that we arrived safely in town, though the fog was so thick on Saturday-evening as

we approached London, that we were in some danger of an overturn
by driving up a bank. Parliament, you see, is at last dissolved.
Some Tories I have seen think that this is a very unwise measure
for their own interests. They have now nothing to fall back upon,
which they would have had, if they had first endeavoured to meet
the now late Parliament. May the Lord direct the ensuing election
as shall best promote the nation's good!

We were very sorry not to see you the morning we left Bath.
We hope dear Mrs. Jay continues pretty well. We beg our most
kind regards to her. Will you accept our little offering for the
rich gratification and edification we have enjoyed from our late
attendance upon your much-valued instruction? And believe me,
my dear Mr. Jay,

With much respect and affection,
Your obliged Friend,
BARHAM.

Mr. Jay to Lord Barham.

Bath, July 11th, 1835.

MY DEAR LORD BARHAM,—I was out when your letter arrived,
and I have been since engaged, even to engrossment. As your Lordship says nothing of your own or Lady Barham's health, I hope you
are both in the enjoyment of that greatest of all temporal blessings.
My dear Mrs. Jay has not been so well for the last month as usual,
and seems to grow weaker. Of course my trial is increased, and I
live in constant alarm and anxiety. But He, whose we are and
whom we serve, knows what we need, and has engaged to make our
strength equal to our day.

Did your Lordship see, in the "Christian Observer" about three
months ago, an extract from the "Reminiscences of Dr. Valpy"
concerning Mrs. More, and the account which he says *she* gave him
of her communing once in Argyle Chapel? Never was there such a
tissue of misrepresentation; and, could I believe that Mrs. More
had been capable of uttering it, I should never feel respect for her
memory, or read her works with pleasure again. But she had a
mind too good and honourable to express what, as coming from her,
would have been no less than falsehood, to serve the purpose of what
she hated—*bigotry*. I was urged to write to the editor, but I declined. All these things will get rectified and known in due time:
and *then* some illiberals may feel a little mortification, though it is
almost unreasonable to expect a thorough-paced ecclesiastic to blush.

I hardly know what to say to your Lordship's question. I have always considered high Churchism and low Popery as nearly the same; or the difference between them as the difference between the tadpole and the toad. None of our passions so readily assumes the mask of rectitude and religion as *anger;* but "the wrath of man worketh not the righteousness of God." Many, I fear, "know not what manner of spirit they are of;" or forget that it is said of our Example as well as Saviour, "He shall not strive nor cry, nor cause his voice to be heard in the streets: a bruised reed shall he not break, and the smoking flax shall he not quench." If "the servant of the Lord must not strive, but be gentle towards all men," violence, and defiance, and scorn, and insult, are not the weapons of *our* warfare. "He that winneth souls is wise:"—and the best way to convert men, or at least to induce them to attend to what we advocate, is to convince them that we love them, and desire to do them good. Between ourselves, I have always thought that these Reformation Meetings do more hurt than good; and I am persuaded they have already increased Popery, by awakening zeal and courage in its defence; and flattering its adherents, (for they must feel delight in such announcements,) as if they were amazingly multiplying, and endangering Protestantism and the church. But if the church be in danger, it is not the church of Christ; or He was mistaken when He said, "On this rock I will build *my* church, and the gates of hell shall not prevail against *it.*" "Secret things belong to the Lord," but we must act according to his will, and do justly, and do unto others as we would have others to do unto us. I cannot, therefore, but believe we have done what God approves, in "loosening every yoke and letting the oppressed go free." I was, therefore, a friend, and I am still a friend, to Catholic Emancipation. Everything like persecution is hateful to the meek and lowly religion of the Lamb of God; as we see in his rebuke to James and John, with regard to the Samaritans who had not received him;—"The Son of man is come not to destroy men's lives, but to save them." I should be ashamed to take a liberty to think and act for myself in religion, which I was unwilling to grant. Neither am I afraid of Popery,—nor do I believe in its increase, but as papists increase relatively with other parts of our population, or in some few and particular places, by occasional influxes of Irish. But why are not *some* individuals ashamed to let out what they believe to be a fact,— "Popery increasing, amazingly increasing," without the encouragement of the State! without an Establishment! against an Establishment! and a richly endowed church doing nothing! Yea, retrograding and in danger of coming to nought! What! has this pure and

Apostolical institution been tried so long in Ireland, and found wanting? And while we abhor Popery, we must be candid enough not to *wonder*, that upwards of six millions, brought up in the religion of their forefathers, should *feel* an Establishment over them consisting of so small a minority; for how small is it when all the other Protestant parties are deducted! Was there ever such a state of things in any other country under heaven? With regard to some of the wretched and alarming tenets of Popery, (though these are seldom war-whooped by *many* churchmen, till some movement seems to threaten the loaves and fishes,) we may ask how would some other parties appear, if some of their former and abstracter principles were to be published among them now? Take Knox's pleading for destroying papists as idolaters; and the church of Scotland's confession of the duty of exterminating prelacy; and Dr. Dopping's Sermon, (Bishop of Meath,) that no faith should be kept with papists, &c., and trumpet this at Exeter Hall, and run down those who are regarded as brethren!

Besides, if Popery is the same, the times, the state of society, and public opinion are not the same. Papists, however disposed, could not put a heretic to death, or imprison him in any country, even where it prevails. Neither will it be ever able to do it again;—the power is gone for ever. Look at Germany—look at Switzerland, where some cantons are popish and some protestant; and some consisting of both intermingled; and exercising alternately the same places of worship. See America. Is Popery, civilly and politically, more dreaded than any other denomination? The reason is, they are all tolerated, and none exclusively favoured. How true is your Lordship's remark, that—" political opinion tinges all information." But let us judge as well as we can for ourselves. Let us be zealous in doing our Lord's work while it is day; but let us do it in his own spirit. I am no croaker. I am persuaded real religion is advancing; and I know that " the knowledge of the Lord shall cover the earth," &c., " for the mouth of the Lord hath spoken it." How glad I should be to talk over many of these things with your Lordship, but I have not time to enlarge this letter.

We all unite in best regards to your much esteemed Lady Barham.

And believe me, &c.

————————

[*Note by the Editors.*]

THE reader of this letter must not fail to observe its date, and to remember that it was written nearly twenty years ago; a circumstance, which, if, in the perusal, he felt any surprise at the tone in which Mr. Jay speaks of Popery, will tend considerably to explain the tone used, and abate the surprise of the reader. The movements on behalf of Protestantism at that day were of a totally different character from those of our own. Had Mr. Jay been alive, and required to express his opinion on the subject of Roman Catholic claims and emancipation now, especially in view of Dr. Wiseman's elevation to the Cardinalate, and the creation of an ecclesiastical hierarchy, based on, and designed to enforce, the infamous Canon Law of Rome, we believe he would have somewhat modified his language and opinion. He might not, any more than ourselves, have changed his opinion on the expediency of admitting Roman Catholics to equal civil and political privileges; but he would certainly have expressed his indignation, disgust, and alarm at the turbulent, encroaching, and intolerant spirit of the Papacy, and of its abettors in Ireland, which, instead of remaining satisfied, as it was understood it would be, with the concessions of the Relief Bill, has used it only as a vantage-ground, from which to urge further demands, till it has become but too apparent, that it aspires at nothing less than a political and ecclesiastical supremacy. Nor would Mr. Jay, had he written upon the subject at the present time, have expressed himself so confidently of the safety of concession, after what has taken place in Tuscany, and even in Ireland. An intolerant religion is always and everywhere an enemy, and even the greatest of enemies, to the well-being of states. Those who execrate liberty of conscience, and would extirpate heretics by the secular sword, ought to be indulged with only a limited power; but never intrusted with the liberties of England, while they declare that their object is to introduce the *Canon Law*, which is thoroughly intolerant, and bitterly persecuting against subjects, as well as treasonable against royalty. In contemplation of such facts Mr. Jay would have deemed the whole Roman hierarchy as merely an organized conspiracy against the liberties of the world. Their view of liberty is a freedom granted to ecclesiastics to enslave the laity: while they proclaim themselves persecuted, if they are restrained from persecuting others.

We wish also to offer a remark upon Mr. Jay's views of the Irish Church. As Nonconformists ourselves, we cannot but coincide generally with his remarks on this subject; and yet we are not forgetful, that a more devoted and laborious ministry does not exist, than may be found in many of the parishes of the Established Church in Ireland. Their successful efforts for the conversion and emancipation of the miserable slaves of Roman Catholic superstition and tyranny, as set forth in the statements of the Society for Irish Church Missions, entitle them to the highest praise; while the pitiless persecution endured by their agents and converts should call forth the sympathy of the Protestant world; and at the same time convince it, that Popery, either at home or abroad, is the inexorable enemy of all liberty, whether civil or religious, though the loudest clamourer for both, when it is deprived of the means of encroaching on the liberty of others.

Lady Barham to Mr. Jay.

1838.

DEAR MR. JAY,—You will have seen by the papers the loss my dear husband has sustained in his father, who died last Wednesday, leaving behind him many pleasing instances of his heart having been renewed; and to us the delightful hope of his having entered into glory,—entered upon that endless life of bliss.—I shall indeed be very happy to present your " Morning and Evening Portion" to the Queen. I think it would be well to write a note *with them*, expressing your humble hope that Her Majesty will condescend to accept of your book, which has already had the honour to have been graciously received at the court of Petersburgh, &c.

I have written this to you to give you an idea (as you wished) of the manner in which Her Majesty generally is addressed; and then you will of course write what you like, only after this fashion. I think it would be better not to write the Queen's name in the books. Perhaps mentioning where they had been received would be an additional inducement to her to read them.

Will you give my kind and Christian love to dear Mrs. Jay, in which Lord Barham joins, and also in best remembrance to yourself? When I see Mrs. Welman I can deliver your message to her. She is now staying at Eston.

Believe me, dear Mr. Jay,

Yours respectfully and sincerely,

Catmore Lodge, Feb. 26, 1838.   F. BARHAM.

TO THE QUEEN.

On presenting to Her Majesty a copy of the " Morning and Evening Exercises."

Bath, March, 1838.

MADAM,—Will your Majesty pardon the freedom of one of your loyal subjects, and graciously condescend to accept this humble offering at his hand?

The Author has long been honoured with the intimacy of Lord Barham, and his excellent Lady has kindly and readily offered to present the work to your Majesty.

The publication is designed to furnish the reader with a text of Scripture for every morning and evening in the year, accompanied with very brief reflections; the better suited to those who have multiplied engagements, and yet are concerned to feel their dependence upon God, and not lose his approbation in the discharge of them.

Though the writer is very sensible of the imperfections of his work, yet he is not a little encouraged by hearing of its continued circulation; the reception it has met with in some of the higher walks of life; the approbation of it expressed by Her Majesty the Empress of Russia; the notice it has obtained from several of your Majesty's illustrious House; and, above all, the blessing of God, which has honoured it with many tokens of usefulness.

Though he will be unknown to your Majesty, there is not one in all your applauding Empire who more sincerely and earnestly prays for your Majesty's safety and happiness, than,

May it please your Majesty,

Your Majesty's most humble servant and dutiful subject,

THE AUTHOR.

To Miss Head.

*   *   *   *   You see from her information, *(from America,)*
and she is not querulous, that religion is not in such a state as we
could wish; and that the preaching is defective, because the preachers
there, (as too often *here*) wish to appear to be learned and intellectual,
and so the common people, who heard our dear Lord gladly, and
understood and felt him, "look up and are not fed." What can the
mass of an audience do with nice distinctions, and abstruse reason-
ings, and long argumentative paragraphs? A preacher may as well
take a fiddle into the pulpit, and better too, especially if he could
make the people dance; this bodily exercise would profit a little.
"The *words* of the wise are as goads and as nails." Let ministers
read Bunyan, and Leighton, and Henry, and Flavel, and many more,
under whose ministry "the poor had the Gospel preached unto them."
However well composed, (according to a certain standard,) *I* could not
sit patiently under many an American and many an English preacher;
though I should not do as I knew a man, (for *I* can vouch, and many
more now living, for the truth of the fact,) at Avebury some years
ago. He, one Sunday afternoon, after listening for some time to a
sermon, correct enough, but perfectly dry and uninteresting, rushed
up from the aisle, and pulled the man,—the Rev. Mr. G.—by the
collar out of the pulpit, and then with his iron-tipped shoes kicked
the pulpit in pieces, for which he was confined five months in Fisher-
ton gaol, but for which he ought to have had a statue erected to his
memory. Poor fellow, I well remember him. The last time I saw
him, after *mowing* all day, he had walked six miles, and had the same
distance to return, to get something to *affect his poor heart*, and which
he could think of when whetting his scythe, or eating his crust upon
the new-mown swath. Our old divines and the Methodist preachers,
when they had just sprung up, had something to *rend* or *melt*, to
strike and *stick*,—to lead their hearers to think of again and again
when alone, and to talk of again and again when in company. But
what is the recommendation of many of the moderns? Oh, they
glitter,—they do—but, as Foster says, "with *frost*."—You know my
fondness (amounting almost to idolatry,) of dear *John Bunyan*. What
a pretty sentiment is this which I recently met with from one of his
pilgrims! I give it the more readily because I am sure my dear
friend can make it her *own*. "I always loved to hear of my Lord,
and wherever I saw the print of his shoe, I wished to put my foot."
There,—is not that as good as some sermons? Do you think there
was ever such another tinker in all the world? When I was last

week with your friend, the blind clergyman, (his sister-in-law now comes to our Monday-evening meetings,) I was speaking of Bunyan's "Holy War." This he had never read. I long to hear how he liked it. I was going foolishly to say, I wish *I* had never read it, but had the *entire* pleasure to *come*. How I should like to read it through to your uncle and aunt, and weep over parts of it together! Though the image of war is not so agreeable as that of a pilgrimage, and though, as a whole, the "Holy War" is not equal to its predecessor, yet I am surprised that it is not more read, and I cannot but think some parts of it are peculiarly affecting—witness the sending of the letter to Immanuel by *Mr. Wet-eyes;* the *difficulty of destroying the Doubters,* &c. I cannot endure transcription, and therefore I send you (preserve it, for I have no copy) a passage which Mr. Bedford had just found in, and translated from, Milton's Second Defence, in Latin, of the people of England in putting Charles to death. He felt it, dear man; it came home to his own affliction; and I observed he was not a little moved when his daughter read it for him.*

I am, &c.

* Mr. Jay does not transcribe the passage in his letter, though no doubt it was sent in a separate form. We venture to guess it must have been the following, which is to be found in Dr. Symmon's *Edit.* of the Prose Works, vol. vi. p. 385. Its exquisite beauty and sublimity entitle it to a place here, since it most probably formed a part of the above letter.

"There is, as the apostle has remarked, a way to strength through weakness. Let me then be the most feeble creature alive, as long as that feebleness serves to invigorate the energies of my rational and immortal spirit; as long as in that obscurity in which I am enveloped the light of the Divine presence more clearly shines ; then, in proportion as I am weak, I shall be invincibly strong ; and, in proportion as I am blind, I shall more clearly see. O! that I may thus be perfected by feebleness, and irradiated by obscurity! And, indeed, in my blindness, I enjoy in no inconsiderable degree the favour of the Deity, who regards me with more tenderness and compassion in proportion as I am able to behold nothing but Himself. Alas for him who insults me, who maligns, and merits public execration! For the Divine law not only shields me from injury, but almost renders me too sacred to attack; not, indeed, so much from the privation of my sight, as from the overshadowing of those heavenly wings, which seem to have occasioned this obscurity; and which, when occasioned, he is wont to illuminate with an interior light, more precious and more pure."

To Miss Head.

Bath, Nov. 27, 1838.

Now for a little news for maiden ladies ;—and even good and pious maiden ladies like a bit, let them say what they will ; and why, in the name of wonder, should they not ?—To-day we had a letter from Lord ——, who is on a visit to the Queen at Windsor. He says, "he thought dear Mrs. Jay would like to have a line from *thence*, and learn how well our amiable and excellent Queen is, and also Lady ——." He laments the bigotry of Wilberforce's Life ; and says, "I have just seen Miss ——, who says, ' Mr. Wilberforce said to me, a few weeks only before his death,'—' my sons are sad high churchmen—all trumpery and nonsense.'"—Sunday, I was again in Bristol, and preached at Brunswick Chapel, to immense congregations, for the Sunday-school. I called on the Dean, Dr. Lamb, but he and his wife are now at Cambridge. I dined with Mr. and Mrs. Hare, who will not be satisfied till you and Mrs. Jay have paid them a visit.

I only add that I love a laugh when it leaves no sting in the conscience, or stain upon the mind ; and that such a laugh cannot be disagreeable to your uncle in his long solitudes, and (I love to hear him laugh, he does it so heartily) tell him, therefore, I lately heard of an Irishman who was very ill, and who, when the physician told him he must prescribe an emetic for him, answered, "Indeed, doctor, an emetic will never do me no good, for I have taken several, and could never keep one of them upon my stomach." Walter Scott says, " When in Ireland a poor man did something for me, and having no change, I gave him a shilling instead of a sixpence, saying, ' Now, Paddy, remember you owe me sixpence.' ' God bless your honour,' said he, ' and may you live till I pay it.' "

" I walked," says a gentleman, " into one of their fields, and to try him, I said to one of the haymakers, ' Well, Pat, if the devil was to come and fetch one of us, which would he take first ?' ' O surely,' said he, ' myself.' ' Why so ?' ' Because he's sure enough of your honour at any time.' "

Mrs. Jay joins in all loving-kindness with, &c.

To Miss Harman.

Bath, Jan. 7, '24.

Upon the reception of your letter with a second sorrowful announcement, I thought I would not write to you again for some days till you would have gone through a fresh painful service, and be a little more composed, and be able to receive an epistolary visit. But after our long and endeared friendship, I cannot refrain from breaking in upon you immediately, lest you should think we do not sympathize with you so much as I am sure we really do. I say *we*, for my precious invalid, to whom your letter was addressed (as well as myself), deeply feels for you, under these sudden and closely successive losses of a father and a mother. May He, whose property it is to comfort those who are cast down, be a very present help in this time of trouble. I know your judgment will immediately acquiesce in this trying dispensation, because He has done it; and if your feelings are not so easily ruled, and nature now and then seems ready to repine, do not condemn yourself as destitute of submission, while your desire is to the Lord, for He knows your frame, and looks to the heart. You have, too, and these must not be overlooked, many alleviations and comforts to mingle in your affliction, especially that the dear departed are disposed of infinitely to their advantage, and after being continued to you so long, while you have a good hope through grace that, in due time, you will be received by them into everlasting habitations. Were I near, how gladly would I call and weep with you; but Mrs. Jay and myself do hope that you will relieve the scene as soon as possible by a change, and let us have the great pleasure of welcoming you under our roof for a season. The travelling is now nothing, and the old—I will not call it an *excuse*, for I am sure it was not, but *prevention*, is removed. You shall interpret my dear wife's language, which you can do better than any other, and ride out with her in the carriage; and I will give you as much of my company as I can afford, and you shall detect me if I preach old sermons, &c. Mrs. Ashton is now with us, as her husband, through business, was obliged to return before her, and will return, I expect, to-morrow week. But should you be able to journey before she goes, we have plenty of accommodation, and she will be delighted to see you here. She joins with her dear mother and myself in every kind and tender regard.

My dear wife says you must come, and you know her husband seldom differs from her.—In haste, &c.

Rev. T. Grinfield to Mr. Jay.

Clifton, Feb. 6, 1841.

DEAR SIR,—I am sure the well-known kindness of your nature will pardon the freedom I take, (as an unknown stranger,) in sending a transcript of some lines which appear in the "*Bristol Journal*" of this morning. They were almost an irrepressible effusion of feeling on the occasion mentioned. And, having just perused the beautiful account, in the same journal, of the Jubilee proceedings of Tuesday last, I cannot refrain from begging your acceptance of my mite among so many worthier offerings. Born at Bath, about two years before the commencement of your ministry, I well remember having often heard a beloved mother speak with pleasure of your early popularity and usefulness. And though I have enjoyed but four or five opportunities (few and far between) of hearing you, (once years ago at Bridge Street, for the Moravian Missions, once at Broadmead, on "Grace and Truth coming by Christ," once at Lady Huntingdon's, on the fine analogy between the influence of the *Rain and Snow* and that of God's Word,) I have retained a most pleasing impression of your preaching, and congratulate those who could statedly enjoy it; while I cannot wonder at their zeal in expressing their regard for one who had so well secured it. Excuse this trespass upon your time and attention, and permit me to subscribe myself, with every sentiment of respect and esteem,

Yours sincerely,
THOMAS GRINFIELD.

P.S. I rather think you remember my schoolfellow at Mr. Simons's, of Paul's Cray, Kent—Cornelius Neale, who used to see you at his father's, and to speak of you to myself as early as 1804. Your "Christian Contemplated" I read with admiring delight.

Lines occasioned by the perusal of the very interesting Sermon delivered on Sunday, Jan. 31st, 1841, in Argyle Chapel, Bath, by the Rev. William Jay, on the completion of the Fiftieth year of his ministry in that Chapel.

Dear venerable Pastor! whose career
Of labouring zeal hath closed its fiftieth year
Within those favour'd walls, where once thy youth,
Where still thine age, hath taught celestial truth;
Well did thy flock, with grateful love agree
To celebrate thy Pastoral Jubilee;
Honouring their friend, their father, honouring Heaven,
Who such a father, friend, so long had given.
Oh! in this changeful world, how few, like thee,
Have train'd *one* church through half a century;

With undeclining constancy like thine,
Alone, unaided,—save by strength Divine !
How well in thee was piety combined
With kindly converse, and a master mind ;
How well thy natural eloquence impress'd
Wisdom, devotion, on the listening breast !
A spreading throng caught manna from thy lips,
Thy popularity knew no eclipse ;—
The wise, the good, still hail'd thy faithful course,
And with thy foremost friends, the sweet-soul'd Wilberforce.
Happy like him in enviable age !
With Canaan opening on thy pilgrimage !
Oh ! golden sunset of a beauteous day !
Soon in the clime of glory, thou too, Jay,
Midst the bright host shalt shine, a star of loveliest ray !

THOMAS GRINFIELD.

To Miss Harman.

Bath, Dec. 1841.

WHAT a blunderer am I? I read in your extract "Home" for "Rome." This puzzled me, and under the perplexity I instantly wrote to prevent hinderance ! In future, I will (if anything perplexes me,) read a letter a second time before I answer it.

But now, in reply to your proposal. It does strike me that your brother's offer should be readily accepted. Your motive would not be unjustifiable were it only rational gratification ; but it may be useful to your health and spirits. You will also turn many things (with your mind) to moral and pious account, while you will yield satisfaction to a worthy youth whose relations in America and in Bath will thank God for the providence. As far, therefore, as the decision depends upon me, I say, Go, and the Lord be with thee. You *will* not, you *cannot*, suppose that I wish you at a greater distance than London, (*that* being too far away,) and nothing will be dearer to me than your return. But I see no one objection of weight, especially as you will meet with Mrs. E. Jay, and her brother and sister ; and your expenses will be defrayed by one whom I long to thank on your behalf. But oh, to think how you will glory over us when you come back, and " once more mingle with us meaner things !" But to prevent your despising us too much, you must remember who maketh you to differ, and that some of us have not had the same opportunity or means. Let this be an answer to Jay's note. As I presume you cannot set off before the beginning of the week, could you not see Bella, who comes up on Monday? If so, appoint her by a line a place of interview; but if you can set off sooner, do not delay; but let me have a line as soon as you have arranged things, and blow me a salutation in it. Shall the books be still sent? Have you seen the engraving? I heard from Bartlett last evening that Jay dislikes it. How sad should it not answer! You must not forget to correspond with me, and I will do my *goodest* in return. Regards to Mrs. Dore, &c. My respects to the Pope, but do not kiss his toe. Get Paul's old lodgings if you can, Acts xxviii. 30. And the "good-will of Him that dwelt in the bush" be with you, in going out and coming in.

Ever yours truly, &c.

I think you know Mark Wilks at Paris, otherwise get a line from Mr. Burnet.

To Miss Harman.

Bath, Dec. 21, 1841.

I HAVE just received your kind letters to my wife and to her husband. They are like your whole self, or at least, like all you have exhibited towards us, ever since we were indulged with your friendship. I was a little anxious whether you would have made up your mind so easily and so soon, till I heard again from you, not-withstanding your obliging deference to my opinion; as in such cases, after all, we must judge for ourselves. But I cannot conceal my satisfaction at your decision; and not entirely on a kind of selfish account, but hoping that one so dear to us as you are will derive pleasure and profit from so interesting a prospect. Oh, that I could be your companion and your chaplain, and be able by-and-by to say as you will, "I have seen Rome"! But the providence which approves of your going requires me to "sit still." But spirits like bodies are not fettered, and I shall think of you much, and follow you much, and shall expect a visit from you as soon as ever you return, to tell us about it; and to hold up your head above us all while doing it. As you write short-hand, it will be inexcusable not to keep a kind of journal; and if you should wish to publish, who knows but I may write a preface, and so our names be blended together before the world! Be attentive to your health, and brace up your mind by some daily retirement for meditation and prayer. Idle away none of the short time you will be there; and be sure to see and hear what you cannot see after your return. Especially observe whatever is connected with the sacred volume; and neglect not to go "as far as Appii-forum and the Three Taverns;" and for any expense you may incur there *I* will be answerable. Whether any one at Rome ever prayed for me before, I know not; but I shall prize your remembrance of me much more than his Holiness's,—yet if you can get him to frank your letters to a heretic, you will induce him to do one good thing in his Pontificate. To induce him to do this, or to enclose them with any of his missives, please him by telling him how favourably things are going on in the Church of England; and how many are longing to return home from their Reformation wanderings!

What a feeling I have to see you both before your departure! and I assure you I have been trying to arrange things so as to allow of the pleasure; but I find it is not practicable. So I embrace you at a distance, and commend you to the God of our mercy. Read this to-day, with my love and concern,—and believe me,

Yours most truly, &c.

To Miss Head.

Worthing, August 21st, 1842.

I AWOKE this morning with the words upon my mind, "I was in the Spirit on the Lord's day." "The Lord's day," as you well know, means the day of our Saviour's resurrection; and is so called because it was dedicated and observed to the glory of his name, and the service of his people. John's being "in the Spirit" on this day, *immediately* intends a state of inspiration; and this was abundantly exemplified in the visions he received and reported. But we do well to use the phrase, (as we do in our prayers,) to mean a peculiar frame of mind under the ordinary agency of the Spirit; and what is a Lord's day without this? Yet it struck me that there are two mistakes to which we are liable concerning it. *First*—We are not to think we are not in the Spirit because we are not in a *lively and comfortable frame.* Such a frame is not to be undervalued; but it may be overvalued, and it is so when we make it exclusive. For we want many things besides consolation; and we shall be "in the Spirit" if we feel much of His enlightening, or convincing, or humbling influences, and are more empty of self at the end of the Sabbath than at the beginning of it.

And, *Secondly* :—We must not suppose that such a Lord's day is impossible, unless we are favoured *with the usual, and social, and public means of* grace. John was away from all these in the mines of

Patmos; yet he never had such a Sabbath before: and the Lord, who always teaches his children to love the temple, will show them that he is not confined to it. Not that we are to expect his presence when we *can* repair to his sanctuary; but if we are *his prisoners*, he will not despise or forget us; but will render the house of mourning or the chamber of sickness, "none other but the house of God and the gate of heaven."—I know not whether your present duty deprives you of the whole, or a part only, of your sanctuary-privileges; but in either case, apply to yourself, my beloved friend, the remarks I have made; and be sure to apply them also to your precious sufferer under every secret, silent, sightless Sabbath she may be called to endure. I trust her confidence, and calmness, and comfort continue; and that as her day, so is her strength.

I did not, however, mean to preach; but only to call upon you in a letter for a few moments, and to exchange a few words; though I forget that you always in these written visits leave all the talk to myself,—but is this quite fair? "Bell's Daily Advertiser" will doubtless inform you of all that may be called *news*. We all go on much the same; only by the goodness of God I feel much better, and seem to hope that I may become, not a young man again, but what I was before my several late indispositions; and should this be the case, I trust I shall improve the blessing, by doing more than I have done for some time past. Oh, what a privilege is health and strength, when we not only *enjoy* but *employ* them !

My reading has been various since I have been here; my present engagement is with the life of "Billy Dawson," the celebrated Wesleyan preacher. It is not well written, but it contains interesting and profitable matter. He was truly a great man; not equal to our divine Bunyan; without learning, or at least without academical preparation for the ministry.   *   *   *
        *   *   *   *   *

I have just received a letter of three sheets from my spiritual daughter, Miss Harris, at Caen in France. Had I a private hand, I would send it for your perusal; as it would afford you pleasure to see how much decision and yet gentleness and prudence she displays; and how useful, in a land of barrenness, she is likely to be. I wish you had known her when she was in Bath. Should she come there again, I must bring *her*, or fetch *you;* and you will soon be like two drops of water on a table, when they touch and run into one.

                                        I am, &c.

To Mr. Rice Hopkins.

Bath, Dec. 10, 1849.

MY DEAR SIR,—I duly received your kind letter, and also the pamphlet. In addition to all your former kindnesses, I am much obliged by your remembering my wish, and taking pains to gratify it. If the publishers (Jackson and Walford) would have no objection to inform you of the author, I should be glad to be informed. But whoever was the writer, the work is masterly, and cannot be easily answered. It falls in with my views, which have never altered upon that subject.*

I am glad you are in prospect of settlement with a pastor, and pray for a blessing upon the approaching union; but I must decline your application, for my attending at the reopening of your chapel. I do not like to refuse in anything such peculiarly kind friends as Mr. and Mrs. Hopkins,—but Mr. and Mrs. Ashton will be here at the time, and, &c. &c.

My dear Mrs. Jay is sitting by, and begs to join in everything that is kind and loving to Mrs. Hopkins and yourself, with,

My dear Sir, yours most truly,

WILLIAM JAY.

To the Same.

Bath, Jan. 7, 1850.

MY DEAR SIR,—I believe I thanked you for the discovery and present of the letters I so much wished to see, and I ought to have thanked you last week for tracing out the clever author. The work is well written, and the point well argued. Some things perhaps may be added, and would require to be so, as the subject has excited so much attention *since* the publication. The works, however, I have not read; but when in Cambridge I met with Professor Lee,

---

* The work here honoured by the notice and commendation of Mr. Jay, is entitled, " Objections to the Doctrine of Israel's Future Restoration to Palestine, National Pre-eminence, &c. In Twelve Letters to a Friend. With an Appendix. 1828." Mr. Jay's strong language, used so late as the year 1849, informs us of his matured opinion upon a subject which has long divided the judgment of the Christian Church, and upon which it will probably remain divided so long as the two opposite modes of interpreting prophecy are followed—the figurative and the literal; or till the decisions of history shall supersede the comments of opinion. Mr. Swaine's Work has received the commendation of many other eminent divines besides Mr. Jay.

who is very strong on Mr. Swaine's side, and has lately published a
work on prophecy, in which there is much which I should like him
to see.   So also is there, I am told, in Professor Stuart's work on
the Revelation.   I should be glad to see a new edition of the Letters,
and would do what I could *orally* to notice and recommend them in
private and public ; but some rules which I have laid down, and
some fears of being at my time of life drawn into controversial publicity forbid my *writing* a Preface. Give my best respects to Mr.
Swaine, though personally unknown, and hope he will accept, not
my excuse, but reason.

The Ashtons are now with us, and with Mrs. Jay join in best
regards to Mrs. Hopkins and her husband, with, my dear Sir,

Yours truly, &c.

To Lady Ducie.

Bath, Dec. 29th, 1846.

MY DEAR LADY DUCIE,—I thought I heard a jingle, and examined
the floor, but, finding nothing, I concluded it was a *lapsus auris*.
But does such honesty grow everywhere ?   Certainly wherever it is
found it ought to be rewarded.   But to whom am I indebted ?   As
Lady Mary Wortley Montagu says—" In all my travels I never met
with but two kinds of people—men and women," so the finder must
be, I presume, male or female ; and as your ladyship *can* decide this,
will you present to *him* or *her* the little publication I have enclosed
—" Clarke's Memoirs ?"   I would have inscribed it, but, again, I
know not the name.   Should I have the pleasure of a future visit to
Tortworth, and the servant be still with you, I will then do it.

Along with the "Short Discourses for the Use of Families,"
which I begged your ladyship to accept, I have put into the parcel
the " Charge to a Minister's Wife," and the sermon to a bad husband, not for you to keep, but just if you like to throw your eye
over them, and then dispose of them where you think they are most
called for.

By the way, when I spoke to your ladyship of my having *delivered*
and *written out* a course of lectures on Scripture Female Biography,
and that my plan would be completed by four lectures more,—two
on Hannah, and two on the Mother of our Lord,—I intended to ask
whether, (if I should have health and leisure to finish the series,) your
ladyship would allow me the honour and favour of dedicating them
to *yourself?*   Should you be disposed to yield this request, your
ladyship may be assured I would not offend by dedicatory fulsome-

ness. "I know not (with Elihu) to give flattering titles to any; for in so doing my Maker would take me away:" yet I wish to bear my witness to goodness and excellence, and to remember the words of Solomon—"a gracious woman retaineth honour."

I was sorry I was too tired to give you words of exposition, and to leave your kind roof without a *devotional and social* benediction; but I did not forget the family in my chamber; and if my prayer be heard, Lord Ducie's health will be restored and established and perpetuated; and he will be a growing and public blessing in his day and generation; and will much and long walk together with his estimable companion, both "as heirs of the grace of life;" and see their fine and lovely children "as plants growing up in their youth, and as corner stones polished after the similitude of a palace." Amen and amen.

My best respects await Lord Ducie (not forgetting Mr. Watts, if yet with you).

I am, my dear Lady Ducie,

Yours to esteem and serve, &c.

I got home safe a quarter after 10. My wife (one of the best women God ever made) begs her most *esteemful* regards.

To Lady Ducie.

Bath, Feb. 3rd, 1847.

MY DEAR LADY DUCIE,—I ought to have written earlier to thank you for your very kind present, every article of which proved very good; and as, being a teetotaller, I could not *drink* your ladyship's health, (unless in an element which all do not value as I do, and as Samson did,) I *ate* it, heartily wishing your ladyship (and the Earl too) much of that blessing which is the salt that seasons, and the honey that sweetens every temporal comfort; praying also in a better exercise, that bodily health may be accompanied with every kind of spiritual welfare. This sentence would be almost long enough for Dr. Chalmers.

"By love serve one another." What a beautiful little text is this! the practice of which would turn this vale of tears into a paradise; and as your ladyship, I know, does not consider it an interpolation or wrongly translated, I venture to give you a little trouble. The Dean and Mrs. Lamb would be much obliged, if your ladyship could say, "whether you could recommend a governess who once lived with you of the name of ——, as to her character, accomplishments, piety, and good temper." The wish has been transmitted through my daughter, Mrs. Ashton, from Cambridge, where the Dean now is. A line to her, or him, or myself, will suffice.

Is the Mr. Wyat, near Stroud, mentioned in the papers as dead, the very pleasant and amiable gentleman I met at your house so recently? I presume it is; and, if so, the circumstance is affecting. Ah! if we had all foreknown it then, would not our intercourse and conversation (I am blaming nothing) have been more specifically religious, and bearing upon his (and indeed our own) spiritual welfare? Should we not meet and part more as mortals and immortals; and would this injure the allowed sociabilities of life?

What awful accounts still from Ireland and Scotland! I pleaded for them successfully on Sunday. My text was, "A cloak of covetousness;" and I, *First*, described the evil—*covetousness*. *Secondly*, proved that its folly, baseness, and sin, by common feeling, needed a covering. *Thirdly*, I showed some of the cloaks it was accustomed to wear. Here I led them into the devil's wardrobe, where they would see a fine assortment of articles to suit any purchaser,—cloaks of every colour and shape, size and price. Here a scarlet one, fringed with fur; there a velvet one, lined with silk; here a shorter, and there one reaching quite to the ground; there new ones, and here some only a little injured by wear; some a little soiled and mended, but then cheaper. That was introduced by Lady ——; and this is now much admired by ——, &c. I then passed from irony, (justified by the sacred writers,) to seriousness, and from figure to fact, and exposed four of these excuses and disguises, which I have not time on paper to do justice to. *Fourthly*, I inquired how far these cloaks would conceal the things? and answered—1st. They cannot always conceal it from the wearer *himself*. 2ndly. They cannot *commonly* conceal it from *others*. 3rdly. They can *never* conceal it from *God*. I then concluded—1st. By calling upon them to take heed and beware of covetousness. 2ndly. Admonishing them to seek the true riches, in which there could be no excess in their desires, or failure in their hopes, &c.*

As I am not sure whether you are in the country or town, I direct this to Tortworth House, supposing, if I am mistaken, it will be immediately forwarded on. I trust Lord Ducie is quite convalescent. Please to present to him my best regards. Earl Gainsborough and

---

* We cannot entirely approve of this specimen of ingenuity in preaching; and trust that the insertion of it will tempt no one to imitate it. We agree with the Reviewer in the Christian Observer, (June, 1855,) that though it is ingenious, clear, comprehensive, and even complete, in point of argument, yet that " it gains attention at the expense of reverence."

the Countess are here. He has had a severe attack since they came.
God bless you, my dear lady,

And believe me, &c.

The Jay's *love*
To the *Dove*.

To Lady Ducie.

Bath, Jan. 8, 1848.

MY DEAR LADY DUCIE,—We duly received your very kind present
of game, and return many and very sincere thanks. They would
have been transmitted earlier, but I only returned this evening after
a week's absence from home, and during which I have had an attack
of the very common complaint. It has not indeed been severe, but
sufficient to lay me by for some days, and to qualify me to sympathize with much greater sufferers. As ministers we frequently
escape what others endure, not because we do not deserve or need
personally the same trials with others, but because of the duties we
owe to others; for if physicians were to experience all the ailments
of their patients, they could have neither time nor strength to practise; and, as our exemptions are often relative to others, so also are
our inflictions. Ezekiel heard the knell—"Son of man, behold I
take away the desire of thine eyes with a stroke;" not because of
any offence of his for which God would chastise him, but that he
might be "a sign unto the people." It is the doctrine of Paul,
2 Cor. i. 6. Indeed this will, in some measure, apply to Christians
as well as ministers : we are all parts of some little whole, more or
less affected and influenced by us. "None of us liveth to himself,
and no man dieth to himself."

For some good while back I could not make out where your ladyship and the Earl were. Some said you were at home,—some at
Malta,—some in Syria. But, though I knew not how to follow you
locally in my prayers, I could address One who saw where you were,
and could afford you whatever blessing you needed from him as the
God of providence and of grace. If the excursion has been in search
of health, (the salt that seasons and the honey that sweetens every
temporal blessing,) I trust it has not been sought in vain, and that
the Earl has returned with renewed strength, and growing disposition to "walk before the Lord in the land of the living."

Neither do I now know whether the family is in the country or in
town; but I venture the present direction, knowing this thanksgiving will surely reach persons so well known, wherever they are.

It is rather late to send the congratulations of the season. But
another year is gone, and by far the most important we ever passed
through, because it is the nearest to our "long home," and the bar
of God; and we have entered on a new period of our time, not
knowing what a day may bring forth; but, as Cowper sings, if we
give up ourselves to Him,

> " It can bring nothing with it,
>   But he will bear us through."

My text last Sunday morning, in reference to the season was,
"These days should be remembered." What days? Days of un-
regeneracy—days of conversion—days of persecutions—days of bereavement—days of providential interposition—days of particular
speciality, viz., birth-days—nuptial days—new-years' days.

I beg my best regards to Earl Ducie, with my prayers for his
entire welfare. I presume he approves of the Bill for the Removal
of the Jewish Civil Disabilities; and condemns the conduct of those
who have opposed Lord John in one of his noblest actions. Many
are not aware as yet how much the spirit of popery has prevailed
of late years in the Church of England, (for we have nothing of it
among all other parties). May it be detected and *thoroughly* en-
countered before it be too late.

Mrs. Jay begs to join in best thanks and regards with,

My dear Lady Ducie, yours, &c.

To Lord Ducie.

MY DEAR LORD DUCIE,—Yesterday Mr. Bidwell called upon me.
The interview was very agreeable in itself, but particularly so as I
learned from it that Lady Ducie was well, and your lordship so
much improved in health, and, as usual, active in doing good.
And how much obliged am I to your lordship for the beautiful
present, and for such a kind proof of remembrance, and that out of
sight is not always out of mind! I hope I can also say, that I sometimes thought of your lordship in your absence and distance, and—
where I think your lordship would most value my remembrance,—
at the throne of grace. I had but just begun this letter before
the hare and the birds came, requiring another qualified acknowledgment.

Another year is rapidly closing; and what an eventful year has it
been! Among its most remarkable, (and I am persuaded influential,)

events, in our own country, have been Mr. Noel's secession and his Essay on the Union of Church and State. The book, in many respects, is one of the most extraordinary I ever read. It is written with great ability, and with much Christian spirit. It must make a great impression in favour of our free churches. Will it lead to any improvements in the Establishment? yet, if something be not done there, I think that church is in danger.

I am sorry that, by several little indispositions, and also by engagements and interruptions, my visit into Gloucestershire has been prevented; and for some time longer must be postponed, as my daughter and her husband from Cambridge are soon coming to see us.

Soon after this reaches Tortworth we shall enter on a new period of time, not knowing what a day may bring forth; but under the care of him who sees the end from the beginning, and has said, "I will never leave thee nor forsake thee." Allow me to send (in which Mrs. Jay joins me) the congratulations of the season to Lady Ducie and your lordship, with our prayers that all grace may abound towards the whole family.

I am, &c.

To Lady Ducie.

Bath, October 23, 1849.

MY DEAR LADY DUCIE,—You will think it strange and probably blame-worthy that I have not answered your letter earlier; but I was from home when it arrived, and I have been variously absent nearly ever since,—not for my pleasure, but on my great and good Master's business, doing a little, and wishing to do more; but I find the old man rapidly coming on, and the infirmities of eighty keeping me from doing the things that I would. One of my excursions was to Kingswood, occasioned by the death of my old friend Mrs. Long. I much wished to have gone over to Tortworth; but I was hurried for time, and the weather was wet, and I heard that the Earl was suffering confinement. I long to hear that his Lordship is released, and able as he is willing to be well-doing. I was thankful to be informed of your ladyship's fresh deliverance; and pray that the life spared and the life given may be precious in the Lord's sight, and sacred to his service and praise. " Lo, children," says David, " are an heritage of the Lord ; " and some have a much larger portion than others. But, says Henry, " Children are certain cares, and uncertain comforts, and possible crosses." In these matters, however, we are not left to our own choice; but are under the management of Him "who performeth all things for us," and "doeth all things well." But there is a part belonging to us, and if we discharge it in dependence upon Him, we are entitled to expect the exemplification of the *proverb*, if not the *promise*,—"Train up a child in the way that he should go, and when he is old he will not depart from it."

At Budleigh Salterton, where I spent a month, I met with good Dr. ——, of America, who spoke with pleasure of his visits to Tortworth. I heard him preach (*i. e.* read) several times, and was *pleased;* but when I hear, I love to be *rent* or *melted*. I do not like for a preacher's mouth to be lined with velvet. When will ministers remember what the mass of every congregation consists of, and learn to preach *ad populum?* By whom was He heard "gladly" who spake as never man spake? The words of the wise are as goads and as nails, they pierce and remain. What are fine smooth periods that slip off from the conscience like water from a duck's back? What evaporates in the mere article of hearing can do little good; but that which is carried away to be again and again thought of alone, and talked of in company. "Let the word of Christ dwell in you."

Mrs. Jay and myself are tolerably well. I wish we could see you in Bath. With best regards to Earl Ducie, believe me, &c.

To Lady Ducie.

Bath, December, 1851.

DEAR LADY DUCIE,—How kind and good you were to think of us, and furnish our table with such fine game; the last of which we have only recently dispatched, and during our partaking of which, I more than once drank your ladyship's health, in a bumper of the purest water the neighbourhood affords. By the way, the American ambassador (Mr. Stephenson) told me that when he dined with the Queen, he made her smile by drinking her Majesty's health, as a Teetotaller, in the same beverage,

I ought to have written earlier,—but this morning, I said, with a blush, "I will write to Tortworth." No sooner said than done, or at least begun. But now, whether I shall finish as I wish, depends much upon "Satan," who often interrupts and hinders, by favouring me with calls of indefinite length, from persons senseless of the value of time, and who, having nothing to do, discharge some of their idleness and curiosity under a cover of business.

But now, after our acknowledgment and thanksgiving, what can I write about? There is, indeed, one subject of supreme importance which is always at hand, and on which we should be always ready in our thoughts and communications. It is the Name above every name. But with this your ladyship is graciously acquainted, though in a rank of life in which He is so little known and honoured;— otherwise how could I speak of Him both from office and experience as "fairer than the children of men;"—as "altogether lovely;"— as having "given himself for us an offering and a sacrifice to God for a sweet-smelling savour;"—as remembering us now he is come into his kingdom;—as "ever living to make intercession for us;"— as "the Lord our righteousness aud strength; all our salvation and all our desire, our glory and our joy."

> "Such Jesus is, and such his grace;
> O may He shine on you;
> And tell Him, when you see his face,
> I long to see Him too."

I was delighted to see Lord Ducie's letter to the chairman of the Protestant Alliance. It did him much honour, both as showing his aversion to the "mother of harlots and abomination of the earth;" and also nobleness of mind in being willing publicly to retract an opinion. A very learned man has said, "The three hardest words to pronounce in the English language are, '*I was mistaken;*'" and when Frederick the Great wrote his letter to the Senate, "I have just lost a great battle, and it was entirely my own fault,"—Gold- smith says, "This confession displayed more greatness than all his victories."

I should much like to hear his lordship's opinion with regard to the New Revolution in France. He must, I think, dislike the character of the usurper; though, perhaps, one tyrant is better than twenty agreed in nothing but mutual opposition for selfish ends. If he suc- ceeds, as is most probable, the effect I fear will be favourable to Popery: yet, if he allies himself to a cause doomed to perish, he will place himself in the way of God's judgments, and be easily brought down. Our comfort is, that "the Lord God omnipotent reigneth;" —and that "He will overturn, overturn, overturn, until He comes whose right it is, and it shall be given him."

You were, my dear lady, misinformed as to my objection to the Liturgy. I even like much to hear it occasionally, though I cer- tainly should like it better were it curtailed, and stripped of its repetitions. That I am not an enemy to all forms of devotion is obvious from my volume of Prayers for the Use of Families; and for the publication of which I have great reason to bless God. Nor, though a firm Dissenter, am I unfriendly to the Established Church. My connexions have been very much among its members and ministers, as you will see from my Reminiscences, which will be published at my death. But I do *hate* all exclusiveness; and I *lament* that a church should be less tolerant and liberal *now* than when it first left Rome, and could be excused some mother-marks upon it. But *then* it did not unchurch other churches, nor invalidate other ordinations, but even allowed preferments to some who only had had on their heads, " *the hands of the presbytery.*" But see the mess the good Archbishop of C—— gets himself into ! Oh that he had *avowed* and *gloried* in what he conceded to his deceiver ! But instead of *this candour,* he applies what he said *only to these Foreigners ;* and not to any here, though standing on the very same terms. The fact is, the wretched notion of Apostolical Succession so far *unites the Church of England to the Church of Rome, and dissociates it from all other churches,* however orthodox or useful. Some must break through, and lead in a better way. I, therefore, rejoice, and thousands beside, that Lord Ducie and a few more are serving the Lord Christ in a mode which will please God, and draw down his blessing, whoever may censure or condemn. Bolton speaks of your visiting Bath. Is it so? I wish it may be,—and that we may be favoured with a little of your company. Mrs. Jay unites in kind regards to yourself and Lord Ducie.—I am, &c.

To the Same.

Bradford, June 10, 1853.

DEAR LADY DUCIE,—

" If thou shouldst stay e'en as thou art,
　　All cold and all serene,
I still might press thy silent heart,
　　And where thy smiles have been :
While e'en thy chill, bleak corse I *have,*
　　Thou seemest still mine *own ;*
But *there,*—I *lay* thee in the grave—
　　And now *I am alone.*"

Such was the language of Wolfe, who wrote the fine monody on the death of Sir John Moore. In more instances than one I have felt the truth and force of the tender and touching sentiment. While the remains of the dear departed are only in the coffin, and not in the grave,—and we can yet go and look, and gaze, and weep, we seem to possess him still; but when we have laid him in the tomb, and return to the lonely house in which we have taken sweet counsel together, and walked to the house of God in company; ah, then we feel its emptiness, and know what real *solitude* is. I, therefore, would not write during the engagements and distraction of funeral preparations, but resolved to wait upon you with a few lines when you would be saying—" And *now* I am *alone*."

And yet in another, and more important sense, your ladyship will not be alone, because the Father will be with you; for He has said, and " the Scripture cannot be broken," " I will be with thee in trouble." And surely you are now entitled to claim and plead that promise. But you must not expect it to be miraculously fulfilled, or in a way that will raise you above the sense of the greatness of your loss. There is no patience in bearing what we do not feel, or resignation in giving up what we do not value. But you may expect from it support under the affliction, however great; and that you shall be able to say, (or endeavour to say—and the Lord looketh to the heart,) " It is the Lord, let him do what seemeth him good." " The Lord gave and the Lord hath taken away, blessed be the name of the Lord." What a state was David in when he came to Ziklag! All was gone! and, hero as he was, he lifted up his voice and wept. " But David encouraged himself in the Lord his God." *He* was left —and never left *him;* and after every distress enabled him to say, " Come unto me, all ye that fear God, and I will declare what he hath done for my soul."

You also will prove a witness for God, and be able to acknowledge that it is good for you that you have been afflicted. Great as your trial is, remember, my dear Madam, how much greater it might have been. Only consider what the God of all grace has done for the deceased, whom we all loved, and all will miss. I confess the late development of experience did not surprise me. I entertained from the time I knew him a good hope through grace; and latterly I felt a deep and constant impression which ever excited my prayer on his behalf. Well, his pains are now over; and the days of his mourning are ended; and though he was not permitted to enter his exquisite earthly mansion, he is now in " a house not made with hands," but " eternal in the heavens." Your loss, therefore, is his infinite gain; and under this loss may you know that God is the husband of the widow in his holy habitation and in her own, and also the Father of the fatherless! May the affliction be sanctified to them! and may they prove that "it is good for a man to bear the yoke in his youth;" and from this time cry unto *Him*, "My Father, thou art the guide of my youth!"

I hope that none of the religious resources of such a family will be dried up; or any of its useful institutions, and exertions, and influences cease, or be impaired.

Thus, while you have attended the entombment of the dear Earl, I have communed with you in spirit, in writing these few lines.

Believe me, my dear Lady Ducie, &c.

Mrs. Jay joins in all this. I long to know Lord and Lady Moreton; and will not cease to pray for them.

My state is much the same as to health and strength as when I was at Stone. I am able to do but little; but the spirit is willing, though the flesh is weak. "Let her alone, she hath done what she could."

To Dr. Bowie.

Percy Place, January 24, 1853.

MY DEAR DOCTOR,—Uncertain whether I should see you this afternoon, I write a few lines, and they must be few, as I find writing, like every other exertion, a trying task. You know not only my sense of obligation for all your kindness, but the confidence I have in your judgment, and what a submissive patient I have been. But I am now venturing a step of my own accord, and hope if you reprove you will strike gently. I have felt the last few days worse, *i. e.* lower in my strength, and more painful in my complaint. I am, therefore, going, if possible, to Bradford to-morrow morning, thinking whether the change may not probably affect me. My stay, I presume, will not be long; and if anything peculiar arise, I or Mrs. Jay can inform you.

But I forget not the nature and character of the ensuing Sabbath, when sixty-three years ago I was ordained over the people of Argyle Chapel, after occasionally labouring among them full twelve months before. On the next Sabbath, this long, happy, and endeared connexion terminates; and pastor and people have to look *backward and forward* under awful responsibilities.

Should Mr. Dyer see fit to have any reference to the event, I wish him to inform the Church and Congregation how much I have all along hoped to have been able to address them on the occasion; but the Lord has prevented it, as I could not undertake any public service, much more a service which would rend me to pieces!

He may also assure them, that, though my pastoral relation has ceased, I shall be delighted if a degree of ability should enable me occasionally to address them again from my old chair and pulpit.

I am much concerned for their proper settlement, and pray that the Lord may direct them to the choice of a pastor after his own heart; and that peace and prosperity may ever be within their lovely borders. They may be assured that, in proportion as the people of his late and long charge are satisfied and edified, *he* will approve and rejoice, who, in finishing his ministry, can say—

> " E'er since by faith I saw the stream
> Thy dying wounds supply,
> Redeeming love has been my theme,
> And shall be till I die."

I wish I could write more and better, but I am as weak as I am willing.

Believe me, my dear and beloved physician,

Yours, &c.

ANECDOTE.

Conversion and subsequent History of Mrs. Ulph.

WHEN I knew the subject of this brief notice first, she was living at the White Hart Inn, Bath, then kept by Mr. and Mrs. Pickwick. My acquaintance with her commenced very incidentally. I was going to Chippenham. The London coach from Bath took me up at my own door. I found in it only one passenger. This was a young female, in whose countenance and manner of speech there was something very pleasing and interesting. I felt a wish to say something during our journey that might be useful, though she was an entire stranger; remembering the assertion and admonition of Solomon—" A word fitly spoken, how good is it! In the morning sow thy seed, and in the evening withhold not thy hand : for thou knowest not whether shall prosper, either this or that, or whether they both shall be alike good." I had an opening for this without the impropriety of forcing religious reflection upon my fellow-traveller, as is often done, abruptly and offensively.

This arose from my mentioning the design of my journey, which was to preach a funeral sermon for a very good man, who had died in such a blessed manner as to exemplify the words of David—"Mark the perfect man, and behold the upright, for the end of that man is peace;" and which must have induced all who witnessed it, or heard of it, to exclaim—"Let me die the death of the righteous, and let my last end be like his."

I noticed also something of the excellency of character with which such a decease well harmonized. I soon perceived that, instead of wishing this kind of discourse broken off, she encouraged its continuance. I therefore spoke on till I left the coach. I was glad to see she was going on alone, hoping solitariness would help impression, and that what had been spoken might be useful in days to come.

I was happy enough to learn afterwards that this was the case. In consequence of what she had heard, she was favourably disposed towards me; and finding that I was a minister, and preached in Bath, she resolved upon her return to go and hear me. She did so, and it was not in vain in the Lord; for one day, some months after, I received a note from Mrs. Pickwick, saying, that a young person whom she much valued was very ill, and was anxious to see me, and begging that I would visit her. I immediately went. As I approached what was supposed to be a dying bed, she wept much. When she had recovered herself, and I saw her face, "Why, surely," said I, "I have seen you before." "Sir," said she, "blessed be God, you have;" and then called to my remembrance our transient intercourse when we travelled together to Chippenham at such a time, and the benefit (she hoped she was not deceiving herself,) she had derived from it.

The difficulties and hinderances we meet with in the things of God arise not so much from the subject as from ourselves; and when the heart is once opened and humbled, and we are brought to the foot of the cross, and to the foot of the throne, we are soon led forward in the right road. I found, therefore, the mind of the sufferer much advanced for the time in spiritual knowledge and experience: and knowing what I now learnt, had she then died, I should have had the fullest satisfaction concerning her eternal state; but she soon surprisingly recovered, was finally restored, and continued attending at Argyle Chapel.

Her opportunities of attendance were soon enlarged, in consequence of her having made it a condition of her remaining in her place, and which was readily conceded from a regard to the value of her services, rather than from any wish to favour the object of her desires. Oh, how much may those who are in official situations accomplish, by walking in wisdom towards those that are without! They may put to silence the ignorance of those who are ready to accuse them, remove their prejudices, and win them without the word. And who ever walked uprightly without walking surely? and when did God ever falsify his own word—"Them that honour me I will honour"?

Not long after these occurrences, a passenger through Bath stayed a few days at the White Hart Inn. He was a truly good man, possessed of landed property, and also carrying on a large business at St. Ives, near Cambridge. Being a Dissenter, and having heard of my name, he inquired of the bar-maid, on the Sunday morning, where Mr. Jay preached. She answered,—"I am just going to his chapel; and, if agreeable, I will show you the way." He accepted the offer. After the service, meeting her in the house, he thanked her for directing him, and spoke concerning the sermon; and again and again he noticed her.

And now another leaf in her book of providence was to be turned over without any thought of hers. Though she was very modest and retiring, (and indeed very much because she was so,) she much impressed him. Owing to this impression, he prolonged his stay; and the impression continually increasing, he offered her his hand, and she, after reflection and proper inquiry, saw no reason to refuse it.

She now, of course, removed to his residence at St. Ives, where, for many years, she exemplified the excellences of the wife, the mother, the mistress, the friend, and the neighbour—in the Christian. Her conversation was such as became the Gospel. She bore richly of the fruits of the Spirit, and adorned the doctrine of God her Saviour in all things. Having now the command of property, she added beneficence to benevolence; and, instead of only saying with many,—"Depart in peace; be ye warmed and filled!" she gave them liberally such things as were needful; and, while not forgetful of the body, she showed herself still more concerned for the soul; and by her prayers, and influence, and example, the diligence and gentleness of her instructions and invitations, and the uniformity and loveliness of her character and conduct, she was always endeavouring to bring souls to the Saviour, and in some way or other to promote his cause.

Some years after her marriage, and at her earnest and repeated request, (her husband cordially joining in it,) I visited St. Ives. She was a good *trumpeter*, and had prepared the way for my coming. My preaching proved peculiarly acceptable, and I hope and believe good was done in various instances. To add to the effect of my public addresses, she pressed persons to come to her house to attend the domestic worship. But, as the number increased to the inconvenience and disordering of the family, and as the meeting-house was near, I proposed that, during the rest of my visit, I should perform the service there every morning. This I did, beginning at seven, and continuing then, and in all my after visits, a little more than half-an-hour, adding to the psalm and prayer a short exposition of Scripture. Though the exercise was early, the attendance commonly filled the place ; and surely God was in the midst of us, of a truth.   The services were informal and simple, and the spirit of devotion was certainly felt.   With what pleasure does the writer call back those delightful engagements, in which many joined in saying, " Lord, it is good for us to be here" !

The pastor of the church at this time, instead of feeling jealousy or indifference, was himself most pleasingly excited, and did everything in his power to increase a brother's acceptance and success.   He was the excellent Mr. Crisp, who is now, and has been for many years, the president of the Baptist College in Bristol ; and his removal to that important station was one of the results of the writer's intercourse with St. Ives.   Nor can he forbear mentioning another event originating from it, viz., the marriage of his second daughter to W. Garfit Ashton, Esq., an event very interesting to his feelings, and which has furnished one of the greatest satisfactions of his life.— After a life, blameless, exemplary, and useful, in no common degree, this follower of the Lamb finished her course in peace, and fell asleep in Jesus ; and is had in applauding remembrance of all that were about her.

A minister should feel peculiarly honoured and grateful when God gives him a convert that not only obtains good, but also perpetuates, multiplies, and diffuses it.   We believe that none of the subjects of divine grace are entirely barren and unfruitful in the knowledge of our Lord and Saviour ; but some of the good ground brings forth, not only thirty, but sixty, and even a hundred fold.

CONCLUDING OBSERVATIONS

ON THE

REV. WILLIAM JAY,

AS A PREACHER AND AS AN AUTHOR:

BY THE EDITORS.

CONCLUDING OBSERVATIONS.

HITHERTO the reader's attention has been mainly directed to Mr. Jay's own account of himself—his history, his progress, his recollections. The Editors have felt that their services to his memory ought to be chiefly regulated by the documents placed in their hands, and limited to such passing annotations, or supplemental matter, as seemed to be required for conveying a just view of their subject, and a complete narrative of his history.

But judging that so interesting and remarkable a character well deserves a separate sketch from another hand beside his own, and supposing that the reader will expect something of this sort, as a conclusion to the volume, which in the main may be said to be his own representation of himself, the Editors have ventured to subjoin the following observations, on the two principal views of his public character, for which he was admired by his contemporaries, and will be respected by future ages.

MR. JAY AS THE PREACHER.

A preacher who, from his first appearance in the Pulpit, at the age of Sixteen, till he retired from it when Eighty-four years old, fixed and held the attention of the Public; who during this lengthened period was heard with equal interest by the aged and the young, the learned and the illiterate, who always crowded, whenever he presented him-

self, to listen to his teaching; who was eulogized by such
men as Wilberforce, Beckford, and Sir William Knighton;
by Hall, Chalmers, and Foster; who, whether he preached
in the city or in the village, drew after him his ministerial
brethren, both of his own church and most others; who was
esteemed and admired by all denominations of professing
Christians; and who, when his sermons were sent forth from
the press, raised for himself in both hemispheres, a reputation such as few of his own day, or any other, ever obtained,
—must have possessed elements of power, after which it is
worth while to inquire, not only for the purpose of gratifying curiosity, but to prompt and guide the spirit of lawful
emulation. Such a preacher was Mr. Jay: and it is the
object of this Sketch to show, in what his attractions principally consisted, and to what he owed his extensive and
permanent popularity.

It may be stated, as a preliminary remark, that the
arrangements of Providence, as regards his personal appearance, his endowments both of body and mind, the circumstances of his conversion, the peculiar nature of his professional education, as well as the state of the Christian Church
when he first appeared in public, were all preparatory to his
future eminence as a preacher of the Gospel. This, with a
kind of instinctive sagacity, he perceived; and, from the
commencement of his Christian career, fixed his eye exclusively upon the Pulpit, and cherished a hallowed desire to
excel as a Minister of Jesus Christ. He clearly saw that,
if he would do one great thing well, he must concentrate his
powers upon *that;* and make everything else give place, or
become subservient to it. He had from the beginning an
almost intuitive perception of what constituted pulpit excellence; he studied the attractions and defects of other
preachers; felt the promptings of a holy ambition after
eminence and usefulness; and with that consciousness of
power which usually attends genius, and inspires it with

the foresight of success, he determined by God's grace to attain to distinction as a *preacher*. This, however, was not the mere yearning of youthful vanity, but the prompting of a heart throbbing with a solicitude for the salvation of souls. True it is, that his attention was first of all directed to this object by Mr. Winter. This excellent man discerned at once, what a bud of ministerial promise there was in that mason-lad whom he saw among his hearers ; and who afterwards came in his apron to converse with him on the subject of religion and of the ministry. But the boy Jay embraced with his whole heart the sublime object, as soon as it was presented to him ; and consecrated himself to it, from the moment that it rose in its full-orbed glory upon his mental horizon.

His academic curriculum was of too short duration, and too limited in its literary advantages, and too often interrupted by preaching, to allow much hope of his ever being a scholar, a metaphysician, or a philosopher. But preaching of a very high order, he was assured, could be attained without these things. And he was right.—As a general principle, learning is of essential importance to the ministers of religion ; and, other things being equal, *he* will make the best preacher who is most thoroughly educated. Nor should our young ministers suffer themselves too hastily to conclude, that they can never attain to eminence in literature ; and be induced to abandon it under the notion, that, as they have neither taste nor aptitude for it, they will concentrate all their attention on preaching. Still, we contend it is not indispensable that every preacher should be an eminent scholar. Where, as in the case of Mr. Jay, opportunities for literature are denied to the eager aspirant after ministerial success, and yet there are all the other essential elements of a good preacher, there let a strong determination be formed, by all possible diligence in the use of such means as are afforded, to excel in that holy career, to which

the leadings of Providence invite, and the impulses of a
longing heart prompt.

Mr. Jay's whole character as a public man may be
summed up in that one word, THE PREACHER; and it is in
this view he must be contemplated by all who would conceive of him aright. True, he was an Author, and one of
the most popular writers of his day, both in America and
this country; yet nearly all his works consisted of sermons;
or what, as in his "Morning and Evening Exercises," bore
a resemblance to them. So that he was still a silent
preacher, even in his books. Such a mind as his could,
however, doubtless, by dint of resolute determination and
close application, have attained to eminence in any department of study. He himself tells us, that his taste at one
time led him to abstruse speculation; but that, finding it
engrossed too much of his time, and interfered with more
useful pursuits, he laid it aside, and addicted himself to
matters which bore more directly upon his ministerial duties.
We have no doubt, however, that while conscience had
something to do with this, mental aptitude was not wholly
excluded. What was practical was far more congenial with
his order of mind than what was speculative; and his
choice of the former was as certainly and, perhaps, as much,
the result of temperament as of principle.

Mr. Jay as a preacher owed not a little to his personal
appearance, and undoubtedly much to his voice. In the
earlier periods of his history, his countenance was eminently
prepossessing. The Portrait affixed to this volume, copied
from a painting taken when he was about forty-nine years of
age, and which was considered a good likeness at the time,
proves this. His black hair, dark eyes, florid complexion,
and an expression of features in which intelligence and
benevolence, mingled with somewhat of archness, at once
attracted and interested his hearers. As he advanced in
years, he became much stouter, which, as he was never tall,

destroyed in some measure the symmetry of his frame. A graphic writer thus describes his appearance in the decline of life :—

"It is not very long since," says Dr. James Hamilton, "we heard him with wonder and delight, and in our own as well as in myriads of memories is still depicted that countenance whose sunshine furnished its own photograph; so wise and so witty, so wrinkled yet so radiant; with so much of youthful ardour welling up in the fountains of those deeply fringed, softly burning eyes; and with words so holy and so tender, dropping from those lips in whose corners lurked all that was quaint or caustic; whilst like an oak-thicket on an old rampart-summit, that strong visage and firm brow rose and were lost in the shaggy wilderness which covered all with its copsy crown."

Mr. Jay's voice was certainly one of the charms of his preaching. It was sonorous but not loud—alternating between bass and tenor; strong yet soft; musical and flexible; and more adapted to give expression to what is tender, pathethic, and solemn, than to what is lively, impetuous, and impulsive. If it did not stir you as with the blast of a trumpet, it soothed and delighted you, as with the soft tones of a flute. This indeed was the general character of his preaching, in which the manner was suited to the matter. You sat in sweet stillness, luxuriating under those beautiful trains of quiet thinking, and gentle, holy, and evangelic emotion, uttered in tones so mellifluous, that you seemed to be listening to music which came from another world, and which lifted your soul to the sphere from which it emanated. An involuntary, unbidden tear occasionally suffused your eye, and a gentle emotion filled your heart, as some touching passage, in plaintive sounds, swelling like those of an Eolian harp, passed over your spirit and moved it, just as a summer's breeze ruffles the surface of a lake, without deeply or violently disturbing it.

He entered the pulpit in a grave, collected manner, apparently absorbed in his mission, and with a step rather quick, yet solemn, and without hurry ; and after sometimes casting a glance round upon the audience, retired into himself, and seemed to be gathering up his thoughts and energies to negotiate between God and man the weighty affairs of judgment and of mercy.

In the preliminary exercises of public worship, reading the Scriptures and prayer, Mr. Jay never forgot that, in one of these, he was enunciating the words of the Most High ; and in the other, that he was addressing himself to Him before whom the seraphim veil their faces. It has been sometimes thought and said—that very little spiritual, or at any rate saving effect, is produced by the public reading of the Scriptures. Is not this to be traced up to the careless, unimpressive, irreverend, and unfeeling manner in which the exercise is often performed? The tones, emphasis, and actions of a good reader, who is neither elaborate, artificial, nor theatrical in his manner, convey both instruction and impression, and are a kind of exposition of the sacred text.*

* In illustration and confirmation of what is here stated, we beg to introduce an extract from a letter received since the publication of the first edition of this work, from the Rev. G. Greatbatch, of Southport, recording the opinion of the late Rev. Dr. M'All, of Manchester :—"The subject of always reading the Scriptures in all religious services was mentioned, to which he gave his most decided approbation ; and remarked, that during his ministry at Macclesfield, it had come to his knowledge, that some of the most powerful impressions which had been made on the hearts of his hearers, had been wrought by the simple reading of the Word of God. After a solemn pause, he added, 'If the Lord had appointed two officers in his Church, the one to preach the gospel, and the other to read the Scriptures ; and had given me the choice of these, I should have chosen to be a Reader of the inspired Word of Jehovah.'

"May our reverence for the Word of God greatly increase ; and may our ministers be more devout and solemn in publicly reading the Scriptures of Truth."

In prayer Mr. Jay was often singularly felicitous in his expressions, and always devout in his manner; his devotions were richly scriptural and strictly appropriate. He was slow and solemn in his utterance, and his feelings were so far under control as never to hurry him into that rapidity and vociferation, which, we regret to say, occasionally characterize addresses to the Almighty made from some Nonconforming pulpits. If reform be necessary in the liturgical services of the Church of England, it is equally necessary in the extempore ones of some among the Dissenters. Occasionally there is too much of preaching in prayer; too much of theology; too little of petition and confession. There is a happy medium between that elaboration which, by its artificialness, represses religious feeling, and that negligence which disgusts good taste : between that muttering and trembling which betoken slavish dread, and the loud or even boisterous manner which indicates want of feeling and displays unhallowed familiarity. We do not wonder that Church-people of refinement, who occasionally attend Dissenting worship, complain of a want of solemnity and devout feeling in some of our public prayers; yet were extempore prayer performed as it should be, they would retire with a conviction of its superior appropriateness, earnestness, and adaptation to the various classes of the congregation, and the changeful experience of the Christian heart.

In the selection of his texts, Mr. Jay was often very ingenious. His extraordinary acquaintance with his Bible gave him great advantage in this. His hearers were often surprised by a passage which was so novel to them, that they did not know there was such a verse in the Scriptures. His canon was, that to secure and hold attention, to produce impression and do good, the preaching must be something that will "*strike* and *stick*." Perhaps, in carrying out this, he sometimes erred on the side of quaintness, both in the selection of texts and in his illustrations. Yet

a quaint text, if one may thus characterize any portion of
God's word, if it contain an important lesson, and if it be
fairly dealt with, and be not by an ingenious fancy tortured
upon the rack, to extort from it a meaning which it would
not otherwise acknowledge, tends to secure attention and
enliven the preaching. But this must not be done too
often, or it will lose its effect, and subject the preacher to
the imputation of being a pulpit-jester.

Mr. Jay's introductions to his sermons were sometimes
as striking as his texts. We remember once hearing him,
when preaching on Pilate's question put to Jesus Christ,
—" What is truth ? "—commence his sermon thus :—" It is
A truth, Pilate, that thou art a cowardly, guilty wretch, in
surrendering Christ to be crucified, when thou wert convinced he was an innocent man." This *ex abrupto* method
of introduction is, however, a hazardous one ; since it is
somewhat difficult to keep up the attention to that altitude
which it has reached by such an exordium. It is like
spicing the first dish at a feast so highly as to render all
that follow in some measure insipid.

The prevailing character of Mr. Jay's sermons, considered
as to their matter, was the mixture of evangelical doctrine,
experimental feeling, and Christian practice. His memoirs
mention the fact, that on his first visit to London he had
the character of several ministers described to him : one as
a doctrinal, a second as a practical, and a third as an experimental preacher. With the good sense, tact, and discrimination belonging to him, he said to himself, " I will be
neither exclusively, but all unitedly." So he was. His
evangelism, so far as doctrine was concerned, was never
very prominent as a thing separate and by itself, in the
form of a dogmatic statement, with proofs from Scripture
and controversial arguments ; but was held in solution
in his general course of preaching. To borrow an illustration from his reminiscence of Mr. Newton, that good man,

in speaking of his own Calvinism, said it was, in his preaching, as sugar in a cup of tea; that which sweetened the whole, but which is not to be taken in the lump.

By some persons Mr. Jay has been thought somewhat deficient in not giving greater prominence to the chief truths of salvation in their dogmatic form. He acknowledged he was so in early life; but it may be satisfactorily explained without impeaching his evangelism. When setting out in his ministry, he saw the errors into which many of the newly-formed evangelical school in the Church of England ran, in dwelling too abstractedly and exclusively upon dogmatic theology, and the bad effect it had in some instances upon their conduct;—and, in avoiding this extreme, he, partially and for a time, inclined to another. He was in sentiment, however, decidedly evangelical, and also in his preaching, but not formally and controversially doctrinal. It was his evangelism, which constituted no small share of the attraction of his preaching. His confession of faith, if such it may be called, delivered at his ordination, though drawn up when only twenty-one years of age, is one of the most complete and beautiful compends of evangelical truth in the English language.

He was, to a very great extent, an experimental preacher; and though his preaching seemed to touch chiefly upon the experience of those who were tried by the ordinary cares and sorrows of human life, and to suggest the usual topics of consolation adapted to such cases, yet it did not fail sometimes to analyze the deeper workings of the human heart, when struggling with all the powers of darkness, and all the strength of its own corruptions. It was, however, the widow mourning over her bereavement, the mother weeping for her dead child, the man of broken fortunes, the orphan youth, the perplexed pilgrim, or the soul under the common temptations of our probation, that his preaching was mainly calculated to help and comfort; and hence the wide range of his popularity. But the intellectual doubts and difficulties, the profounder depths of mental distress, the sterner conflicts of the soul with unbelief, were, perhaps advisedly, not so much, nor so frequently, made the subjects of his discourses. Hence, amidst the crowd of his hearers and admirers, were not so many of those who wanted the stronger consolation, which a heart bruised and broken in the spiritual conflict requires. But equally true is it, that he never administered to inconsistent professors the ardent spirit of Antinomian comfort; which was but too common at the commencement of his ministry; or to imaginative believers, the cordials of a sentimental comfort, no less common at the close of it. It was, however, as a practical preacher that Mr. Jay chiefly excelled; and here his excellences were transcendent. No man perceived more clearly the obligations of the Christian life, and no man urged them more earnestly or more attractively. It was his happy art to make men feel, that wisdom's ways are ways of pleasantness, and that all her paths are peace.

Perhaps there is scarcely a single word which will more aptly describe Mr. Jay, as a preacher, than the term *naturalness*. This constituted, we are sure, no small part of the attraction of his *manner*. His voice, his tones, his action, were all inartificial, and displayed the gracefulness of nature. It was not an imitation of nature on the stage, but nature's self in her own walk and place of action. He spoke to you as you felt he should do, without any uncouth awkwardness or caricature which disfigures nature, or any studied affectation which destroys it. To much action in the pulpit, in the use of the hands and arms, he was strongly opposed, and seldom used any, except an occasional elevation of the hand. Here we think he was somewhat deficient, for nature prompts in strong emotion to bodily action. But this was the least part and the lowest manifestation of his naturalness. He spoke *from* his own nature *to* the nature of others. He was himself a most inartificial man. All his tastes, his habits, and his pursuits proved this. He knew human nature well. He studied it in himself and in others. He knew *man*, how he thinks, and feels, and acts. He drew his knowledge, not from copies in books, but from the living original. Men felt when they heard him, that they were listening to a preacher who knew not only books, and theories, and systems, but humanity, both in its fallen and in its restored state; in its wants, woes, diseases, remedies, and varieties; one who could sympathize with them as well as teach them. When on a Sunday-morning they came, worn and weary with the trials, toils, and cares of the six days' labour, and placed themselves under the sound of his mellifluous voice, they felt sure of not being tantalized and disappointed with a cold intellectualism, or a mere logical demonstration, or a metaphysical abstraction, or a wordy nothing, which would have been giving them a stone when they asked for bread; or with something religiously poetic, which would have been offering them flowers when they wanted meat;—but he fed them with food convenient for them, and satisfied the cravings of their nature with what satisfied his own.

This quality of his preaching was very strikingly displayed, in the *illustrations* with which his sermons abounded. He never suffered the attention of his hearers to doze over dry abstract disquisitions, or dull, didactic, and prosaic harangues, but kept it perpetually awake by appeals to their imagination. His talent for illustrative allusion was extraordinary. His sermons were not only by his beautiful fancy illuminated, like the ancient missals; but illustrated, like modern books, by descriptive scenes. They contained all the glowing colouring of the one, with the more correct and graceful forms of the other. Here his naturalness constantly appeared, and in close resemblance to that of our Lord, who drew his similes and metaphors from the works of nature, and the relationships of humanity. The great Teacher's discourses were replete with images borrowed from the beasts of the field, and the birds of the air ; from rural sights and rural sounds ; from the ties of parentage, and the reciprocal obligations of husband and wife, master and servant. So were Mr. Jay's. A natural simplicity and beauty, polished yet artless, pervaded his discourses. There was comparatively little of the grandeur and sublimity of the great masters of eloquence ; but a constant succession of chaste, tender, and smiling allusions. His preaching did not produce the effect of the lofty and fervid utterances of Robert Hall, which, with their elegant diction, mighty conceptions, and glowing imagery, raised you into a fellowship of rapture with the speaker's own mind : nor did it bear any resemblance to the gorgeous language, exuberant fancy, and dazzling splendours of Chalmers, which overwhelmed you with such mental opulence. The eloquence of the two latter fell upon you as music from a full and perfect orchestra. It came with the rush of a mountain torrent, and sounded majestic and awful like thunder booming over the ocean : but the eloquence of Mr. Jay was as the gentle flow of a beautiful river through a verdant landscape, or like the solemn and soothing tones of the organ. In hearing him you were brought near by a sweet and resistless attraction. You felt you could approach him, and be at home with him, and were in a state of affinity with him ; while a feeling of awe came over you as you listened to the others, which at once fascinated you, and transported you with delight, and yet made you almost tremble. It seemed, in listening to Hall and Chalmers, as if you could no more always bear such mental excitement than you could always endure the roar of a thunder-storm, or of the falls of Niagara : but to Mr. Jay you could for ever listen, just as you never feel burdened by the waves of ocean, gently breaking upon the shore on a summer's day ; nor by the

gurgling noise of a brook, meandering among stones. In-
numerable instances of this naturalness of allusion and
illustration might be selected from his printed sermons,
which, when uttered with all the effect given to them by
the music of his pathetic tones, must have melted down the
hearts of his hearers into a state of highly pleasurable
emotion.

Mr. Jay was a master of the true pathetic. Ministers
have too much neglected this. Some have thought to do
all in religious teaching, by forceful appeals of logic
addressed to the intellect. The understanding is the only
faculty they seek to engage. Their logic is clear, but it is
cold. They deal with man in only one view of his nature,
as a rational being, who has only to apprehend ideas, but
forget that he is also an emotional being, who has a heart
to feel, and who often needs rather to be moved than convinced. His sensibility, sometimes the best, the only,
avenue to his soul, is left unobserved, unoccupied. If the
true order of nature be—for the head to guide the heart;
yet, in our disturbed and disordered condition, it often
happens that the heart is the avenue to the intellect. Men
love to feel, as well as to think; and hence we speak of the
luxury of tender emotion. Mr. Jay knew this, and entered
very deeply into Christian æsthetics. His voice gave him
great advantage here. His very intonations touched and
opened the springs of feeling. When the people were in a
prepared state of mind, he has sometimes melted them by
his manner of uttering an interjection, or a single word.
His pathos, however, was not at all confined to his manner,
but extended itself to his matter. In this there were often
the most tender and touching allusions and descriptions.
Who, that ever read, can forget that beautiful passage in
his sermon to husbands and wives, in which he represents
woman, pleading on the ground of her weakness and
dependence, for sympathy, kindness, and protection? To

have heard this passage uttered by his pathetic tones, and
enforced by his plaintive looks, must have been followed by
an effect more than dramatic :—

"Milton has finely expressed the difference in the original
pair :—

'For contemplation he and valour form'd ;
For softness she and sweet attractive grace.'

Her bodily strength is inferior, her constitution less firm
and vigorous, her frame more tender, her temper more
yielding, her circumstances more generally depressing. A
rose, a lily, allows of no rough usage. Tenderness demands
gentleness ; delicacy, care ; pliancy, props. Has a condition
fewer resources, and is there much in it of the afflictive and
humbling ?—the more does it need succour, and the more
necessary is every assistance to maintain and increase the
consequence of it ; especially, where so much depends upon
the respectability of the character who fills it.—Where is
the man who is not alive to this consideration ?—Where is
the husband, who, reflecting on her peculiar circumstances,
would not be disposed by every possible means, to promote
the dignity and the satisfaction of a wife ?—What is the
language of these circumstances ?—'Honour us ; deal kindly
with us. From many of the opportunities and means by
which you procure favourable notice, we are excluded.
Doomed to the shades, few of the high places of the earth
are open to us. Alternately we are adored and oppressed.
From our slaves you become our tyrants. You feel our
beauty, and avail yourselves of our weakness. You complain of our inferiority, but none of your behaviour bids us
rise. Sensibility has given us a thousand feelings, which
nature has kindly denied you. Always under restraints,
we have little liberty of choice. Providence seems to have
been more attentive to enable us to confer happiness, than
to enjoy it. Every condition has for us fresh mortifications ;
every relation, new sorrows. We enter social bonds ; it is

a system of perpetual sacrifice. We cannot give life to
others, without hazarding our own. We have sufferings
which you do not share—cannot share. If spared, years
and decays invade our charms, and much of the ardour produced by attraction departs with it. We may die. The
grave covers us, and we are soon forgotten: soon are the
days of your mourning ended, soon is our loss repaired:
dismissed even from your speech, our name is to be heard
no more,—a successor may dislike it.—Our children, after
having a mother by nature, may fall under the control of a
mother by affinity, and be mortified by distinctions made
between them and her *own* offspring. Though the duties
which we have discharged invariably, be the most important
and necessary, they do not shine: they are too common to
strike: they procure no celebrity: the wife, the mother,
fills no historic page. Our privations, our confinements,
our wearisome days, our interrupted, our sleepless nights,
the hours we have hung in anxious watchings over your sick
and dying offspring—' "

There was an individualizing effect produced by Mr. Jay's
preaching. He not only preached *before* his congregation,
but *to* them; and not only to the multitude, but to the individuals who composed it. His sermons formed a kind of
mirror, which reflected the image of those who approached
it, and in which every one saw himself as distinguished
from others. Each of his hearers felt as if the preacher's
eye were fixed on *him*, and his discourse addressed to *him*.
This is a happy art in preaching, and, indeed, in all public
speaking; and in order to which it is necessary to approach,
without descending below ourselves or our subject, or even
the more intelligent of our auditors, yet as nearly as we can,
to the easy comprehension of the mass of our hearers.
When the preacher soars into the clouds where their understanding cannot track him, or diverges into a wood where
they cannot find him, they will soon give over all attempts

to follow him, and leave *him* to his wanderings. Mr. Jay's simplicity, clearness, and intelligibility to all, were most commendable, rarely equalled, and never surpassed. It were desirable that these qualities should be remarked, and, as far as possible, imitated by all preachers of the Gospel. His beautiful conceptions, expressed in good, plain, Saxon words, were easily understood by the bulk of his hearers ; in fact, none could misunderstand them, while the most cultivated and refined could not feel displeased with them.

It is recorded of Arago, the celebrated French astronomer, that he had a peculiar facility of bringing down the high parts of astronomy to the comprehension of ordinary minds, —a faculty so rare, that some of the most distinguished astronomers have failed in making their science intelligible or interesting to a public auditory. Arago adopted a method which we believe had never been tried before by any of his predecessors. When he began to give his course of lectures on astronomy, he glanced round on his audience, to look for some dull aspirant after knowledge with a low forehead, and other indications that he was among the least intelligent of his hearers. He kept his eye fixed upon him ; he addressed only him ; and by the effect of his eloquence and powers of explanation, as exhibited in the countenance of his pupil, he judged of their influence upon the rest of his audience. When *he* remained unconvinced, the orator tried new illustrations, till light beamed from the grateful countenance. Next morning, when Arago was breakfasting with his family, a visitor was announced. A gentleman entered—his pupil of the preceding evening, who, after expressing his admiration of the lecture, thanked Arago for the very peculiar attention he had paid him during the delivery. "You had the appearance," said he, "of giving the lecture only to me."—Shall it be the ambition only of the astronomer, and not also of the preacher, to be under-

stood by the convert, and to make every individual feel *he*
is the party addressed ? Shall they who preach salvation
think only of pleasing the cultivated few, to the neglect of
the ignorant multitude ? Let the minister of religion take
a lesson, aye, and reproof too, from the lecturer on astronomy. Mr. Jay had learnt this lesson, and practised it
well. It is not meant, of course, that the preacher is always
to dwell on elementary truths, and ever to accommodate his
discourse to the poor and illiterate; but he ought never to
forget that our Lord said, "the poor have the gospel
preached unto them;" and that it was observed of his own
preaching, "the common people heard him gladly." True,
we ought not to be always in the nursery feeding babes with
milk; but then the babes ought not to be forgotten or
neglected.

The character of strong, sound sense, which pervaded
Mr. Jay's sermons, contributed very largely to his popularity, combined, as this uniformly was, with the practical.
There seems to be in the public mind an intuitive perception
that religion is not mere science or theory, but that it contains much that has to do with men's business and bosoms.
There is an innate conviction that it is not only something
to know, but something to do. They may not be always
very willing to do what is enjoined upon them; but still
they expect to hear it, and are dissatisfied if they do not.
They are aware that it is a matter which has to do with all
persons, states, and circumstances. Hence they feel somewhat of surprise, and even disgust, with the preacher who
deals much in abstractions that lie remote from human
nature and life. They expect to be told not only how they
should think, but how they should act: and one good sound
maxim of spiritual wisdom, which will guide them through
the intricacies of life, and the perplexities of casuistry, will
be far more valued, than many an airy speculation, or elaborate investigation of some profound and abstract question

in theology. Mr. Jay's practical directions possessed much of the terseness, the wisdom, and the force of proverbs. In a single sentence, he often expressed what others would expand into a paragraph or a page. Few ever had, in such perfection, the happy art of saying much in few words. They who could not carry away a whole sermon could remember a single sentence, which perhaps contained the pith of the whole. They may not have been able to secure the entire string of pearls; but they could retain one which was complete in itself, and a specimen of all the rest. He always preached as if he wished his sermon to be remembered as well as heard; and it was this which led him to condemn the essay-form of sermonizing, and to adopt so uniformly the methodical arrangement of his discourses into the usual divisions and subdivisions of a sermon. He aimed not merely at present effect, but at permanent advantage; and his arrangement of his subject, which sometimes was fanciful,—aiming at antithesis and parallelism, and approaching almost to the metrical,—was intended to assist the memory, and thus to promote usefulness. Mr. Hall, a master and high authority on such subjects, speaks of the narrow trammels to which in these latter days discourses from the pulpit are confined, "so different from the free and unfettered airs in which the first preachers of the gospel appeared before their audience. The sublime emotions with which they were fraught," he says, "would have rendered them impatient of such restrictions; nor could they suffer the impetuous stream of their argument, expostulation, and pathos, to be weakened by being diverted into the artificial reservoirs prepared in the heads and particulars of a modern sermon." The analogy, however, of the two cases will not hold. There are occasions, no doubt, when the sermon may with propriety and effect assume the form and character of an oration, though rarely of an essay, especially when concentrated impression, rather than instruction, is the design of the preacher; but as a general rule, considering the heterogeneous nature of our congregations, the plan of heads and particulars, if they are not too numerous, is most for edification; and it was certainly the method which Mr. Hall himself adopted: his Sermon on Infidelity, and on the Death of the Princess Charlotte, being the only ones which are printed, in which the usual announcement of heads and particulars is omitted. Mr. Jay's divisions, though always announced, were never unnecessarily multiplied; and thus, while he aided the memory, he did not burthen it.

Mr. Jay, though generally grave, chaste, and dignified in his composition, occasionally somewhat violated the law of propriety, in regard to these excellences, by a quaintness of expression not perfectly reconcileable with good taste. This applies almost exclusively to his *preaching*, and was most probably purely extemporaneous. He has extruded nearly all of it from his printed discourses. This tendency to quaintness grew upon him in his declining years, when, perhaps, under some consciousness of decaying force, he thought he would supply the deficiency by what was fanciful, and odd, or quaint. He was, perhaps, somewhat sensible of this when, in his preface to his "*Short Discourses*," he wrote the following sentence: "Though he does not wish to indulge a bad taste, the Author would ever remember that the preacher ought to have compassion on the ignorant, and on them that are out of the way. That which is too smooth easily slides off from the memory; and that which is lost in the act of hearing will do little good. It is desirable to get something that will *strike* and *abide;* something that, recurring again and again, will employ the thoughts and the tongue; and if this cannot be accomplished in certain instances by modes of address which perhaps are not classically justifiable, should not a minister prefer utility to fame?"—Certainly, to be useful is the great end of preaching; but even when that end requires "great plainness of

speech," everything that offends the strict laws of propriety
may be avoided.

This great preacher threw a sacred charm over his sermons by a profusion of Scripture phraseology, and allusion
to Scripture facts. They were adorned with the beauty and
redolent with the fragrance of flowers culled from the garden
of inspiration. Indeed the beauty and the perfume were
almost in excess. The passages were not so much selected
for proof as for illustration; they were brought forward, as
classic quotations are by public orators, to grace a speech,
and to convey the speaker's idea in the apposite language of
a high authority. While listening to his discourses, and re-
galing themselves with his pleasing thoughts, his hearers
were often surprised by his repetition of Scripture, so appropriate that it seemed as if it had been written for the occasion. He rarely ever referred to the book, chapter, and verse
which he thus used, as he imagined that the hearers would
be diverted from the subject, and disturb their neighbours
by turning over the leaves of their Bibles, and by the rust-
ling noise, if many did so, which this would occasion. Here
we think he was a little in error in point of excess. Fewer
passages, some of them explicitly quoted as well as repeated,
with a passing remark which would bring out and impress
their whole meaning, must do more good than so many passages interwoven, without reference or remark, into the texture of the sermon.

Another excess in which he indulged in his later years,
and in his ordinary ministrations, was in the way of poetic
quotation, especially verses of hymns. He was fond of
poetry. His was a poetic mind; and though he rarely cultivated his talent for this species of composition, yet he
wrote some good hymns, which appear in the collection used
in his chapel.* In the last sermon he preached in Argyle

* It may be gratifying here just to give the numbers of these, as
they are not distinguished in the Hymn book by any particular mark.

Chapel there are no less than thirteen of these poetic scraps. The greater part of them, however, he would no doubt have omitted had he prepared the sermon for the press.

Mr. Jay, through the whole of his ministry, was much in demand for public occasions. For such services he always carefully prepared, and rarely disappointed the expectation of his audience. He felt that it would be unworthy of himself, his subject, and his audience, to come forth with an ill-digested, crude, and hasty effusion of meagre thought, set forth in slovenly language. While, on the other hand, though aware he was surrounded by his ministerial brethren, he did not sacrifice the interests of the people to them, and, instead of producing sermons for edification, attempt to astonish by a display of profound and profitless speculation, or dazzle by an exhibition of vapid elegance, resembling the flash, the rush, the lofty flight and vanishing light of the sky-rocket, but withal as useless as that pyrotechnic exhibition.

He often surprised his audience by the ingenuity he displayed in the appropriation of texts to particular occasions. As specimens of this take the following examples :—On the death of George the Fourth—"Another King, one Jesus." —On the re-opening of his chapel after a temporary closing —" A door was opened in heaven."—After an enlargement of the chapel—"Be ye also enlarged."—For a Communion address—" One of you is a devil." Who but he would have thought of such a passage as this, for the text of a funeral sermon for a great man : " Howl, fir tree ; for the cedar is fallen." From this passage he preached first, after the death of the Rev. R. Hall ; and then again at the death of the Rev. Rowland Hill. How poetic, how striking, how appropriate to express the Church's lament over the grave of one of her most illustrious pastors !

As far as can be ascertained they are the following :—79, 151, 161, 230, 270, 360, 370, 422, 441, 443, 446, 455, 458, 462, 465, 471, 483, 498, 501, 503.

Mr. Jay considered it a solemn duty to take advantage of the times and of public events, to make nature and providence subservient to religious instruction. He generally preached on the seasons of the year; and on national mercies, calamities, and great political occurrences;—but he did not bring politics, in the conventional meaning of that term, into the pulpit.

It need scarcely be said to those who knew Mr. Jay, that he made no use of notes in the pulpit, except occasionally at the very close of his ministry, when he could no longer so implicitly confide in his memory. In his earlier days he wrote his sermons pretty fully, and even where this was not done, most of the leading thoughts had passed through his mind in his previous meditations upon the text or the subject. He did not, however, so closely adhere to his prepared matter as to shut out suggestions that arose at the time; those "living thoughts," as Mr. Newton used to call them, which came warm and glowing from the heart while he was preaching. He very strongly reprobated the practice of pulpit-readings, and lamented the growing disposition for this among the young ministers of the present day. Where is the practice of reading tolerated except in the Pulpit? Not on the Stage; not in the Senate; not at the Bar. In the time of Charles the Second it was forbidden by statute to the University of Cambridge, which says—"the lazy way of reading sermons began in the time of the Civil Wars."

It will be seen by this description, that we do not claim for this eminent preacher any dazzling brilliancy of genius, any profound originality, any power of philosophical analysis, any logical acumen, or even great theological research. To those who can only be pleased with such things, or to others who resolve all pulpit excellence into abstract generalizations, or lofty speculations, or subtle argumentation, Mr. Jay's sermons presented few attractions. His sound evangelism, his practical wisdom, his rich experience, his strong sense, his melting tenderness, his touching pathos, his beautiful illustrations, his sweet antitheses, his poetic fancy, which procured him, while a living preacher, such wide and continued popularity, and which in his published works will never cease to delight the readers, who can be pleased with strong intelligence and true piety,—were held in light esteem by those who love to soar in the clouds, or delve in the dark mines of German mysticism.

If Mr. Jay attained to such excellence as a preacher, it was not without great self-culture and laborious endeavours. No doubt there is some truth in the opinion, that there are natural tendencies which lead to distinction in any branch of human pursuit. We need not believe phrenology to admit this. In a qualified sense, Mr. Jay was born a preacher; person, voice, physiological temperament appropriate to this occupation, were all given to him in his physical constitution. But this was not all. If he owed much to those gifts lavished upon him by the hand of God, he owed much also to his own sagacity, diligence, and unwearied endeavours after improvement and distinction. He was a preacher from a boy. His choice of this line of action grew out of his religious convictions and emotions, and was sustained and stimulated by them. He longed to be useful in saving sinners from the condemnation which he had escaped; he saw the power of the pulpit as God's great instrument for accomplishing this end; and, almost from the time of his first entering it, he made it, as we have already said, the object of his hallowed ambition to excel there. In after-life, all his reading, his reflection, and his writing centred in that object. He studied the best models of preaching; learnt French chiefly to read the sermons of Bossuet, Bourdaloue, Massillon, and Saurin, in their own tongue; and attentively perused the Puritan and Nonconformist writers, together with more modern authors of sermons, the better to qualify himself to be a preacher. At home and abroad, when travelling or recreating himself at some watering-place, he was in one sense always sermonizing. He rarely returned to his own house, after a retreat for a while to the coast, without bringing back with him some plans of sermons or texts that had struck him, in his reading or meditations during this season of innocent relaxation from pastoral duties. To be a useful preacher was his aim; and it was thus, by constant and unwearied effort, he became one.

And if this were the habitual study of all who are called to occupy the pulpit; if with an intense longing after the salvation of immortal souls, and an unwavering determination to know nothing among men, but Jesus Christ and him crucified; if with a truly philosophical view of the adaptation of preaching to awaken attention and produce impression; if with a recollection of what has been done by the great masters in the art of preaching,—all ministers were to study the best models of evangelical pulpit eloquence, and were to take extraordinary pains to acquire, by the aid of Divine grace, a commanding and interesting style of pulpit address; and while cherishing a sense of absolute dependence for efficiency upon the work of the Holy Spirit, they were to recollect the Spirit works by appropriate means; and took half the pains to make their speaking in the pulpit as impressive, as the actor does to make his successful upon the stage; if, concerning the powerful preaching of the Gospel, they said, "*this one thing I do,*" and called in all collateral aids to do it in the best manner,—we should not hear, as we sometimes do, of the declining power of the pulpit. It is for a wonder, a lamentation, and a reproach, that they who have to do the most momentous work under the sun, give themselves the least pains to do it effectually. Mankind are wrought upon by manner as well as matter. It is an interesting, earnest style of address that engages attention, reaches the heart, and accomplishes the end of preaching; in the absence of which, learning the most profound, and theology the most scriptural, will fail to secure popularity, or to obtain success. It will not do to say, we are so engrossed with the matter of our discourses, as to be indifferent to the manner of them. The more important to men's interests is the matter, the more anxious should we be that in our manner there should be nothing to hinder, but, on the contrary, everything to aid, the success of the matter. That minister who feels called by the Holy Ghost, to be a preacher of Christ's blessed Gospel, ought to feel himself no less called, to take all possible pains to do it in the best possible manner.

How eminently Mr. Jay's efforts to excel in this matter were crowned with success, the reader of the foregoing pages has seen amply illustrated, as he has advanced through this volume. We shall here, however, add one more testimony, which, from its impartiality and high respectability, is entitled to much weight. Bishop Shirley, in a letter to the Rev. C. Bridges, says: " I spent two days at Bath, and heard Mr. Jay preach. He is a very extraordinary man. There is a commanding energy in his manner, and a weight in his style which give authority to what he says, and secure attention ; for he is evidently in earnest, and utters the result of much thinking and prayer."*

If the publication of Mr. Jay's life should serve no other purpose, than to stir up the ministry to a more earnest and anxious endeavour to excel in this, their momentous sphere of official duty, and to present to them a model which they shall aim to copy, then it will be a subject of congratulation and thankfulness, that to the world has been given this memoir of one whom Foster designated—" *The Prince of Preachers.*"

* Memoir of Bishop Shirley, p. 58. The letter is dated " Ashbourn, February 18th, 1823."

MR. JAY AS AN AUTHOR.

AFTER having expressed our opinion of Mr. Jay as a preacher, we have felt some doubts whether our readers may not think it quite enough, without referring particularly to his authorship. But still there is a sufficient diversity in the two departments to justify a separate notice. The talents which secure success in the one, can by no means be taken as a pledge of success in the other. It is a rare thing for a man to excel in both characters, even though the authorship may lie mainly in the line of sermons. Of this Mr. Jay himself seems to have been perfectly conscious; for he did little in the way of authorship, except in connexion with his preaching, as he also did little in the way of public speaking, except from the pulpit. Under a just sense of the limitation of human faculties, he concentrated his upon one object; and that object, gained so conspicuously and successfully, supplied the first and chief inducement to appear as an author; and this rather as an extension of the preacher's office, or as an enlargement of his audience.

Mr. Jay's labours as an author were principally pursued at watering-places, during a *relaxation* of a few weeks in summer. He gives the following brief but interesting account of these labours, in an Advertisement to the last volume of the "Exercises:"—

"At Sidmouth, he began his 'Domestic Ministers' Assistant,' and wrote many of the Family Prayers. In the Isle of Wight, he composed 'A Charge to a Minister's Wife,' and 'The Wife's Advocate.' At Lynmouth, he finished his 'Christian Contemplated,' and wrote the Preface; with 'Hints on Preaching.'

"But this latter place must be a little more noticed. There, for several years successively, he passed a month, the most perfectly agreeable and happy he ever experienced in a life of loving-kindness and tender mercy.

"Linton and Lynmouth are nearly connected—the one being at the top and the other at the bottom of a declivity, covered with trees

and verdure, interspersed with several houses. Linton has been remarked for its sublimity, and Lynmouth for its beauty, and their
united aspects have been called Switzerland in miniature.

"Lynmouth was to the author the most interesting spot. Here,
two narrow and craggy valleys, obviously once ruptured by a con-
vulsion of nature, terminate; and down these, tumbling from rock to
rock, two streams—one running from the east and the other from the
south—unite, and then, in a small distance, empty themselves into
the sea.

"At the time of his first going there it was hardly known or considered as a watering-place. It had not, therefore, as yet fallen into
the corruptions of such receptacles; nor had the inhabitants been
taught to make visitors a prey. The villagers were very respectful;
and strangers felt a sense of perfect safety.

"Here the author fixed his residence. He took a whole cottage;
it was far from elegant, but it was neat and agreeable; it wanted
some accommodation and comforts; but he had what he more prized,
rural and enchanting scenery and solitude. Yet not without some
to hear the exclamation, 'How sweet this solitude is!' for he had
society too: his company was small, but chosen, and suitable, and
improving:—

> ' Where friendship full exerts her softest power,
> Perfect esteem, enlivened by desire
> Ineffable, and sympathy of soul—
> Thought meeting thought, and will preventing will,
> With boundless confidence.'

"His associates consisted of his wife and a female friend. It
would be vain in him to extol the former; but as for the latter—
especially as she was soon removed from our world—he may be allowed to say, we hardly could have had her equal in everything we
wished. She was of a very respectable family; well educated,
polished in her manners, intellectual, sprightly, witty, truly pious,
full of sensibility and benevolence, and an entire stranger to everything like selfishness. What, with regard to this friend, before our
first excursion together, was acquaintance, was now rendered intimacy the most cordial; and she became a dear resident in the family
till her lamented death. The cottage we occupied was near Mr.
Herries's beautiful villa. It has since been spoiled by improvements,
and is now a kind of tawdry little mansion; and the whole of Lynmouth itself, which taste might have altered, and yet left it a village
still, is aping a paltry town.

"Here our party felt themselves at liberty to meet or to separate—

to read or to write—to converse or to walk—as inclination prompted. As to himself, the author opened his parlour, and spoke on the Sabbath-day evening to any of the neighbours who would attend. But having been struck with the design, and also having been urged to undertake something of the kind, he now began his 'Morning Exercises.' Of these, he here often wrote two, and sometimes three, a-day; and always read one of them in the morning and another in the evening devotion, and not often without the approbation of his companions, which most excited and encouraged him to proceed.

"Here he composed the greater part of these *Morning* Exercises, and here also, in after visits, he wrote the greater part of the *Evening*. He once thought of distinguishing by a final mark all he had written in this retirement; but not doing it immediately, his recollection soon became too indistinct for him to divide with certainty. The first 'Exercise' he wrote was that which is entitled, 'The Unlonely Solitude,'—John xvi. 32: 'And shall leave me alone: and yet I am not alone, because the Father is with me.'

"He wished also to have marked those which he wrote as he journeyed to and from Lynmouth. At the 'Plume of Feathers,' Minehead, where he slept as he was going down, he composed the Exercise, called 'The Pious Excursion,'—1 Sam. iii. 9: 'Speak, Lord; for thy servant heareth,' especially in reference to such a journey of recreation. At the same inn, as he returned, he composed the Exercise entitled 'The Call to Depart,'—Micah ii. 10: 'Arise, and depart hence; for this is not your rest.' He also wrote a third Exercise at the same inn, *viz.*,—'Changes in the wilderness not a removal from it,'—Numb. x. 12: 'And the children of Israel took their journeys out of the wilderness of Sinai; and the cloud rested in the wilderness of Paran.'

"The author cannot conclude without observing two things: the *first* is, That relaxation is never so perfectly enjoyed as in connexion with engagement.

> 'A want of occupation is not rest;
> A mind quite vacant is a mind distress'd.'

"Relaxation, indeed, can have no existence separate from employment; for what is there then to relax *from?* On the other hand, action prepares for repose, and labour not only sweetens, but justifies recreation; so that we feel it to be, not only innocent indulgence, but a kind of recompense. The *second* is, That, as of such a precious talent as *time* nothing should be lost, so, much may be done by gathering up its fragments."

The peculiar charm which his sermons derived from his oratory and elocution could not, of course, attend his publications; and yet, when divested of this fascination, they exhibited other charms and excellences, which secured for them, not only attention, but admiration, popularity, and usefulness. His compositions, when they came from the press, were greatly improved and chastened, both in thought and diction. What they lost of effect given them by his delivery, they gained in correctness, condensation, and point. Mr. Jay well understood that sermons printed must be skilfully prepared for the eye, which is a more critical judge than the ear. The single sermons which he first published were, no doubt, greatly aided in their success by the popularity of the young preacher. Moreover, his promotion so early to the pulpit of Surrey Chapel placed him on a pinnacle before the religious world of London; so that when he sent forth his first volume of sermons, which was as early as 1802, a wide circle of readers was anxiously waiting to peruse them. The moderation of sentiment these sermons displayed, as contrasted with the Antinomianism into which some were running, both in the Establishment and among the Dissenters,—their originality, simplicity, ease, and general adaptation to the state of the public mind, commanded for them a measure of success which rarely attends volumes of sermons in the present day; and still more rarely those from the pens of Dissenters. It may be fairly alleged, that, at the period when Mr. Jay first appeared as an author, there was a new and growing desire to peruse good and evangelical sermons; and that Mr. Jay's were eminently suited to the taste of the day: and it would be no disparagement to admit further, that, in some respects, they are less suited to the taste of the present day; or, rather, that as good sermons are now so abundant from the pulpit, there is less need of supplying them from the press; and, in consequence, few volumes of sermons now obtain popularity, unless they are

highly elaborate, on novel subjects, or characterized by eminent genius or transcendent eloquence.

Whitfield and Wesley, with their co-workers and followers, had given the people a taste for something better than
they had been accustomed to, in the dry, ethical essays of
the clergy, as void of effect upon the audience, as of heart
and life in the preacher. Mr. Jay's sermons, therefore, were
perhaps as much used in pulpits as in private houses, and
might have been heard in many a church, and found attractive
to many a congregation of Churchmen. Some of the more
liberal of the clergy recommended them to their brethren,
and to their people; and this was especially the case with
those who were alarmed at the spread of Antinomianism.
The appearance of the successive volumes of Mr. Jay's sermons, and their increasing popularity, was a pleasing omen
of the sounder views which were beginning to prevail. Indeed, it may be stated, that the influence of the Antinomian
preacher began to decrease about this time, and has been
sinking till it can scarcely be said to retain an existence,
either in the Church or out of it. A few scattered individuals
are all that can now be found, where formerly hundreds congregated to listen to high doctrine; and among other useful
works, no doubt Mr. Jay's have had a share of influence in
promoting sounder views and a more scriptural taste. An
evidence of this is seen in the fact, that Mr. Jay was singled
out by Bishop Jebb, and recommended to his friend, Alexander Knox, as a pattern of sobriety and moderation of sentiment. He says in one of his letters:—

"It seems to me as if the more sober Calvinists, both in
and out of the Church of England, were not a little alarmed
by the prevalence of virtual, if not as yet practical, Antinomianism. There has been a good deal to that purpose, I
mean expressive of that alarm, in the 'Christian Observer.'
But the Independent minister at Bath, Jay, has lately published a volume of lectures, called 'The Christian Contem-

plated,' in the preface to which are some pertinent, and I might say happy, remarks. It will be worth your while to get the book, were it only for the sake of the preface; but the book itself is worth looking over, for, though it has its defects and failings, it abounds in matter which tends to edify the reader, and do real honour to the writer."*

In speaking once upon this subject, he observed, that, though election was true, it did not appear to him a truth of equal importance with perseverance; and that in preaching we must not only distinguish between truth and error, but between truth and truth. It was a truth that our Saviour died under Pontius Pilate, and a truth that his death was an atonement for sin; but who would attach the same importance to both? So was it here. He did not conceive that there was any danger in preaching election in its effects; and that it must always be remembered that perseverance was a duty enjoined by 2 Pet. i. 5—10, &c., and as a privilege promised in Phil. i. 6, &c.; and that this two-fold view ought always to be remembered.

He said that Mr. Newton, at one of those breakfasts where he received ministers of all denominations, among other observations, made the following:—he said, that " Calvinism was one of the worst of systems preached theoretically, but one of the best preached practically." Mr. Jay added, that if he called any man master on earth, it would be Leighton or Newton.

This just and scriptural moderation of sentiment, which through life distinguished Mr. Jay, both as a preacher and an author, commended him to the approval of the best part of the Christian body, both in the Established Church and among Dissenters. For this sobriety and comprehensiveness of view he was probably greatly indebted to his excellent

* Thirty Years' Correspondence between John Jebb, D.D., F.R.S., Bishop of Limerick, and Alexander Knox, Esq., M.R.I.A., vol. ii. p. 567.

tutor, whose large experience and acute observation, in the days when there existed considerable conflict and contention among theologians of adverse schools, in connexion with his loving spirit and persuasive manner, qualified him to guard young minds against excess and extravagance. The same moderation of sentiment seems to have distinguished most of Mr. Winter's students. It is, moreover, a remarkable fact, that this sobriety was far from being associated with tameness or indifference. It was rather accompanied with eminent zeal, devotedness, and usefulness. It was very evident that Mr. Jay's supreme aim was to be scriptural in all his religious sentiments. He bowed submissively to the Divine authority. Every statement is both illustrated and confirmed by the most apposite and striking quotations. Hence, too, Mr. Jay seems never to shrink from the appearance of paradox, when it arises from the strength of Scripture language, in enforcing important truths separately. He had, from the commencement of his course, kept himself clear of the trammels of systematic theology; and was only concerned to bring the truth of God, as it appears in the Bible, to bear upon the hearts and consciences of men. Hence the constant interweaving of Scripture in every sermon,—a practice which he avows and defends in the preface to "The Christian Contemplated," where he quotes, with warm approbation, the following judicious and beautiful defence of this practice, from the pen of Robert Hall, in his strictures upon Foster's Essay, which at that day stirred up no little controversy, and which was entitled—" On the Aversion of Men of Taste to Evangelical Religion." Mr. Jay hailed this vindication of the use of Scripture language, from so high an authority, though he suspects the same authority might censure himself for using it to excess; yet that he would still allow it was an error on the safer side.

" To say nothing," observes Mr. Hall, " of the inimitable beauties of the Bible, considered in a literary view,—which

are universally acknowledged,—it is the book which every
devout man is accustomed to consult as the oracle of God;
it is the companion of his best moments, and the vehicle
of his strongest consolation. Intimately associated in his
mind with everything dear and valuable, its diction more
powerfully excites devotional feeling than any other; and,
when temperately and soberly used, imparts an unction to a
religious discourse, which nothing else can supply. Besides,
is there not room to apprehend, that a studied avoidance of
the Scripture phraseology, and a care to express all that it
is supposed to contain, in the forms of classical diction,
might ultimately lead to the neglect of the Scriptures themselves, and a habit of substituting flashy and superficial
declamation, in the room of the saving truths of the Gospel?
Such an apprehension is but too much verified by the most
celebrated sermons of the French, and still more by some
modern compositions in our own language, which usurp
that title. For devotional impression, we conceive that a
very considerable tincture of the language of Scripture, or
at least such a colouring as shall discover an intimate
acquaintance with those inimitable models, will generally
succeed best."

The copious use which Mr. Jay made of Scripture language, both in preaching and writing, gives his compositions
a peculiar character. It is a feature which strikes every
one as prominent, and we think, while it yields the highest
satisfaction to every reader, who peruses his books for edification and instruction, it can excite displacency in no one.
There can be little doubt that the eminent success of Mr.
Jay in all his publications is a sufficient vindication of his
practice, especially when it is considered, that the success
of such writings must be taken as an indication of their
usefulness. They minister nothing to the amusement of
mankind; nothing to the gratification of a mere literary
taste, or fondness for speculation; nothing to elegant scho-

larship, or dialectic skill, or a fervid imagination; but as
the plain and forcible statements of evangelical truth, "not
in the words which man's wisdom teacheth, but," to a
great extent, "which the Holy Ghost teacheth;" and as
such, their extensive and continued popularity both vindi-
cates the judgment of the writer, and commends the good
sense and piety of his numerous Christian readers.

Mr. Jay may not be an author suited to the taste of every
reader, but he wrote for the many, and they have been his
readers. He is not learned enough for some, nor profound
enough for others; not critical enough for one, nor rhetorical
enough for a second, nor imaginative enough for a third;
but had he commended himself to the approbation of such
readers, he would have had a much narrower circle than he
has had, and still has. Nature, or rather the God of nature,
formed his mind in one of its most current types; and to
serve the greatest number, by exhibiting to them, in the
most impressive, instructive, and successful forms, not the
rarities of intellectual treasures, not the elaborations of
human thought, nor the choicest and most sparkling gems of
genius, but truths of universal importance and of daily
practice. He aimed at the useful and substantial, and had
little taste for the subtle, the recondite, or the profound.
His mission was to preach the Gospel of the grace of God,
which he had received; and to extend the benefit of what
he had preached, by books, for the service of those who had
not the privilege of hearing him.

In his compositions, the critic may find many faults which
passed unobserved from the pulpit. But though sometimes
his style would admit of improvement, in respect of refinement and polish; yet, in perspicuity, simplicity, and force, it
is admirably adapted to the purpose of instruction. It is
perfectly transparent and intelligible to all; and though
occasionally, through his anxiety to be impressive, and to
fix the truth in the mind, he indulges in an expression or a

word that is too coarse or beneath his subject, yet it is so obviously for the sake of *point* and *effect*, that good taste can hardly be offended, while the less fastidious reader is better pleased with the homeliness and point, and possibly feels the truth conveyed more effectually to his mind.

Eminently practical in all his views of Divine truth, he derives useful lessons from almost every part of Scripture ; and places duties in new lights and relations, which impart fresh force and interest to them. He had no doubt profited much, in his composition in later years, by the long and extensive practice he had undergone ; and which, from the advice of Mrs. Hannah More to write much and fast, he seems early to have adopted.

Every Christian reader of Mr. Jay's works must be impressed with the pleasingly devotional turn of his mind. His reflections lead the pious and devout to the most elevated views of the Divine character, as a Father to be loved, and a Friend to be trusted. Every page seems to exercise over the mind an attraction to the Source of all wisdom, blessedness, and grace ; and every sentiment seems bathed with the spirit of devotion, and designed to win the heart for God and truth.

Another feature in Mr. Jay's writings is the skill with which, without apparent effort, he throws new beauty into the text, and, by a few happy sentences, sets the sacred word in a novel and interesting, and often strong, light. It is as if he placed the reader in a position, from which he could discover new lustre in the jewel of Divine truth. He makes it flash its radiance upon the mind's eye, with a power and beauty unperceived before. And, moreover, not simply as thus condensing the force of isolated truths upon the mind, but in the important and most useful capacity of an *expositor*, he is conspicuously successful. His large knowledge of the Scripture, and his intimate insight into its special import, and his holy ingenuity in discovering uses to which its facts and lessons may be turned, qualify him in a high degree to expound the sacred word. With an unrivalled force and effect does he bring out the hidden beauties of revelation, and enchain the mind to the truths of God's word. There was a startling originalty sometimes in his application of texts, which interested and delighted the auditor, and fixed the attention more on the word of God than on the preacher or the writer. But he never pursued originality for its own sake, nor sought, as many have done, and are still doing, to affect novelty of thought by mere novelty of phrase. The new idioms and the new terminology are found, when translated into pure English, to contain little more than old and common ideas ; often they are a mere wrappage of grotesque or pompous phraseology, thrown around poverty of thought and vulgar superficiality. But, in his own department, Mr. Jay was really an original thinker ; and his thoughts engage, instruct, and delight the mind. His aim is always exalted, his means always legitimate, his motives always pure, and his success often distinguished.

In confirmation of our own estimate of his publications, it will probably now be interesting to the reader to be informed, upon the best authority, how his works have been received among the Christian bodies of the New World ; and where, never having heard his voice, they judge of him exclusively as an author. Mr. Jay himself sometimes alludes to the extensive sale and usefulness of his writings in America, and we shall, therefore, here introduce some extracts from the pen of a distinguished American divine, who published an article more than twenty years ago in an American periodical, in which he reviewed the principal works of Mr. Jay, which had then been reprinted in that country. In pointing out these peculiar excellences, he thus concludes his review :—(*The article is from the pen of the Rev. W. B. Sprague, D.D., and appeared in " The Quarterly Christian Spectator." It was afterwards published separately.*)

" If the estimate which we have formed of the character of Mr. Jay's publications be correct, it must be obvious to every one that they are designed to have an important influence in forming the religious character of the age; to say nothing of the more remote influence which they must exert upon posterity. We will consider, under a few distinct particulars, what are the effects which have followed, or may be expected to follow, from the labours of this popular and excellent author.

" Mr. Jay's writings, if we mistake not, are peculiarly adapted *to promote the study of the Bible*. Not only are the ' Morning and Evening Exercises for the Closet' directly of a biblical character, being designed as a sort of practical commentary on various portions of divine truth, but nearly all his other writings abound in scriptural illustration, and are pre-eminently fitted to invest the study of the Bible with strong attractions. No writer of the present day makes a more copious use of Scripture than Mr. Jay; and we might say, that in his sermons he sometimes carries this to an extreme, were it not for the uncommonly felicitous manner in which his quotations are made. It would seem as if the whole Bible were in his memory, and he had ·the power, on every occasion, of selecting the very passage that is most to his purpose; and when a writer quotes Scripture with such an advantage, we can scarcely call any degree of quotation excessive.

" If Mr. Jay should be thought by some to urge to an extreme in respect to the direct use which he makes of Scripture in his public discourses, we are constrained to believe that there is a tendency among many preachers, in this country at least, to the opposite end. We certainly do not wish to be brought back to the practice of some of our venerable fathers, who not only were accustomed to string together many passages of Scripture, often without much regard to connexion, but detained their hearers by turning over the leaves of the Bible to look these passages out; but we do wish that every sermon should have so much of the Bible in it, either as it respects language or spirit, that it shall be obvious to every hearer that it is drawn directly from that sacred book. It were reasonable to expect that God should put special power into his own word; and hence we find that the frequent introduction of Scripture language into a sermon imparts to it, in the view of the pious, a kind of unction which it can derive from nothing else. So, too, all experience proves, that there is no argument so strong as ' thus saith the Lord;' and many a mind which has warred through a long course of metaphysical reasoning, has been fixed in its convictions by one plain declaration of the Bible.

* * * * * *

"Mr. Jay's writings are also eminently distinguished for their *Practical Tendency*. They are indeed by no means deficient in the exhibition of Scripture doctrines, but whenever doctrines are discussed, it is always in a practical way. They are not taken up as abstract propositions, but are presented just as they are found in God's word, and as they stand related to the experience and conduct of men. They are more commonly adapted to make men acquainted with their own hearts; to carry them back to the very springs of their actions; and to impress them with the conviction that the whole of religion is a practical reality. We are not aware that Mr. Jay has written anything of a merely speculative character; whatever has come from his pen, so far as we know, has an important bearing upon practice, and is fitted to exert a benign and elevating influence upon human character.

"It has been a characteristic of some periods of the Church, that they have been distinguished by a rage for speculation. No one can go back to the time of the latter Christian fathers, or to the days of Thomas Aquinas, without being forcibly struck by the endlessly diversified and hair-breadth distinctions which were then resorted to, in illustration and defence of Scripture doctrine; and it were hardly necessary to say, that an age which had so much in its character that was speculative could not be distinguished by religious action. It was common, in those days, for men to exhaust all their powers in endeavouring to settle points which did not admit of being settled, and which, if they had been, would not make one hair white or black, as it respects the salvation of men, or the advancement of the kingdom of Christ. The lamentable result was, that, while men were spending their lives in metaphysical quibbling, the great cause for which the Saviour shed his blood seemed to stand still, if not to be on the retrograde; and the revival of the spirit of religious action did not take place until the rage for vain speculation had begun in some measure to die away. If we do not greatly mistake, wherever the doctrines of the Gospel are exhibited in connexion with much of human philosophy, and encumbered by the technology of the schools, they will be found to a great extent inefficacious, and the Church will be found proportionably listless and inactive. But when these truths are presented in their naked simplicity, and brought home to the mind and heart as common-sense realities, without having their influence in any degree neutralized by foreign admixtures, they will be found quick and powerful; and it may reasonably be expected that in such a community there will be a waking from the dreams of carelessness, and a spirit of benevolent activity going forth to bless the world.

*   *   *   *   *   *

" One great secret of the charm which pervades Mr. Jay's writings is, that he ranges through every department of human experience, and shows that the Spirit has its appropriate teachings for every condition. Their tendency is not only to make man do right in all circumstances, but to do right intelligently and upon principle.

" It is another characteristic of Mr. Jay's writings, that they are eminently fitted *to cherish a devotional spirit.* We have already had occasion to remark, that his ' Family Prayers,' while they show the fertility of his mind, the purity of his taste, and the originality and beauty of his conceptions, also breathe, in an uncommon degree, the spirit of genuine devotion. But most of his other writings, though they are designed primarily to instruct, and are indeed, in a high degree, instructive, are delightfully pervaded by the same spirit. His ' Morning and Evening Exercises ' are particularly designed to be the companion of the closet ; and it would seem scarcely possible that they should be used by any Christian, as they were intended to be, without bringing him into an appropriate frame for communion with God.

" It will be obvious to any one who reflects how much the present age is characterized by the spirit of active enterprise, that there is danger that it will suffer in its devotional character ; danger that, while Christians have their hands full of work, their hearts will be comparatively barren of devout exercises ; that their active efforts in building up the kingdom of Christ will be suffered to interfere with the more retired business of keeping their hearts and communing with God. We do not complain that the religious character of the age has too much in it that is practical ; but we have much reason to fear, that many Christians of the present day sometimes render apologies to their consciences for a partial neglect of their closets, on the ground that their time is so much engrossed by duties of a public nature, that they have little left for anything else. Whenever this state of things exists, it is an evil which ought at once to be corrected ; for not only does it indicate an approaching decline of the spirit of piety, but it looks as if the spirit of benevolent action would not endure ; and whenever the Christian loses sight of his dependence on God, in his benevolent efforts, he may rest assured, either that his zeal will soon languish, or that his efforts will be unsuccessful.

" Another striking characteristic of Mr. Jay's writing is, that they exhibit, in the best sense, *a truly catholic spirit.* Not that there is anything in them that looks like lowering the standard of Christian doctrine or practice, or of yielding up anything that is essential in religion,—far from it. The great doctrines and duties of the Gospel are constantly stated and urged in all their importance ; and erroneous doctrines and practices meet with their deserved condemnation. But, after all, the author never seems to be trammelled by sectarian peculiarities ; and scarcely ever occupies ground upon which he would not be cordially met by Christians of every evangelical denomination. This, no doubt, is one great reason of the universal popularity his writings have gained both in Great Britain and this country ; and hence, too, we have found many who had been long conversant with his writings, who yet had never been able to discover to what denomination he belonged, and some who had always had the impression that, instead of being an Independent, as he actually is, he is a (low church) Episcopalian. No doubt he has his attachment to Independency ; but it is so far from being a bigoted attachment, that he opens the arms of his charity wide to every evangelical Christian, let his denomination be what it may. Men may differ from him in many unimportant particulars, and yet, instead of standing aloof from them, as errorists, he cordially welcomes them as fellow-disciples of a common Master. |

" The spirit of Christian catholicism which Mr. Jay's writings evince, is what we wish to see more and more extensively pervade the religious community. We are by no means disposed to plead for an annihilation of sects, or for any attempt to range all the followers of Christ under the same human banner. On the contrary, we fully believe that the division of the Christian world into various denominations is not without some important uses ; and that, if its legitimate influence is not neutralized by unchristian jealousies and alienations, it may hasten rather than retard the ultimate triumph of the Church.

  *   *   *   *   *   *

" Let the delightful spirit which Mr. Jay has exemplified in his writings pervade all the different communities of the followers of Christ, and, though we may still have different denominations, yet it will be manifest that there is but one body. Under such an influence, the world will be compelled again to the exclamations which were made in the early ages of the church, ' Behold how these Christians love one another ! '

" In the writings of Mr. Jay there is a remarkable consistency, and they are fitted, in an eminent degree, to form *a consistent religious character*. One principal reason why most of the professed followers of Christ exert so little influence in favour of his cause is, that their Christian character is marred by such palpable inconsistency. This inconsistency results from the very estimate which they form of the comparative importance of different duties ; and from the neglect of some, or other, or all of the duties of the Christian life.

  *   *   *   *   *   *

"Now if we do not mistake, Mr. Jay's writings are not more remarkable for anything than their tendency to counteract this evil.
They bring before us with great felicity, and without any apparent
reference to system, the various duties of men, just as they are inculcated in God's word, giving to each its proportionate importance.
There is no elevating faith at the expense of works, or zeal at the
expense of morality, or alms at the expense of prayer; but each
duty stands forth with its own claims, holding its appropriate place.
In short, we know of few writings which are fitted to make an impression more, in this respect, like that of the Bible itself, than
those of Mr. Jay. Whoever reads them attentively, and imbibes
their spirit, will not be punctilious in respect to one set of duties,
and lax in regard to another; but he will be attentive to all; and
under such an influence, his Christian character, instead of being
unsightly and monstrous, will develop itself in fair and beautiful
proportions.

"After what we have already said of Mr. Jay's writings, we
scarcely need add, that they are fitted *to form Christian charactèr on
the most lovely and attractive model*. It cannot be disguised, that, as the
beauty of Christian doctrine has sometimes been marred by human
philosophy, so the loveliness of Christian example has been obscured
by what has almost seemed a cold and lowering melancholy. There
have been those, and they are yet to be found, who appear habitually
gloomy from principle ; who set down the playfulness and buoyancy
of the animal spirit to the account of an inveterate waywardness ;
and who never venture to speak on the subject of religion at all, but
with what seems an air of affected solemnity.

*　　　*　　　*　　　*　　　*　　　*

"If irreligious persons are liable to be confirmed in their irreli-
gion by the careless and trifling deportment of professed Christians,
they are not less exposed to the same evil by seeing a Christian profession constantly associated with a morose and forbidding gloom.
Let religion be exhibited in all its cheerful attractions, while yet it
retains its appropriate seriousness and dignity, and it cannot fail to
commend itself to the judgment, and conscience, and better feelings
of all who witness such a manifestation.

"There are few men probably to whom the present age is more
indebted for whatever of consistent cheerfulness its religious character
may possess, than to Mr. Jay. Other writers, as we have already
intimated, may have done more than he to rouse the slumbering
conscience of the sinner, and bring him into the attitude of conviction and repentance ; but few, we think, have done more to hold
up religion to the world in all its divine and beautiful attractions.

We cannot take leave of this interesting and popular writer, without commending his writings to every class of our readers. We would commend them especially to the young Christian, as being eminently fitted to form him to a high degree of religious enjoyment, activity, and usefulness. We would commend them to the man who would know most of the windings of his own heart, and would have maxims of true practical wisdom in his own mind, to regulate every part of his conduct. We would commend them even to the man who scoffs at religion as a fable; for if he can contemplate that view of the Gospel which these writings present, without acknowledging that it is consistent, beautiful, even glorious, then it is because he belies his own convictions, or because his infidelity has made him a madman."

Though this extract is long, yet it seemed the most appropriate, complete, and satisfactory testimony we could supply of the popularity and usefulness of Mr. Jay's writings in that extensive and populous country, where they are, to say the least, as widely known and as much admired as in Great Britain. The long-established and well-earned reputation of the writer, adds weight to his judicious and discriminating observations. Our own opinions and remarks, previously given, coincide, in the main, with those of Dr. Sprague. Mr. Jay studied, and preached, and wrote for the Christian community at large. He wished the whole world to hear and to read, in the most intelligible and impressive terms, the Gospel of the grace of God; and he wrote, therefore, in the *common dialect*, as the best vehicle for the truth of God; but this he wrought into a polished shaft, and gave it a direct and successful aim.

The admirers of sustained and impassioned eloquence, or of a magniloquent style, or even of a purely classic diction, will find little to satisfy them, much less to fascinate them, in the volumes of Mr. Jay's works; but all who desire to see the truths of Divine revelation treated in their variety and comprehensiveness, their admonitions enforced in winning and persuasive words, with manly dignity, Christian simplicity and apostolic earnestness; all who read religious books for instruction and improvement, to have the heart warmed, and the life corrected,—will find Mr. Jay's works a treasury which will never disappoint them, and which they will not soon exhaust. Beckford, of Fonthill Abbey, in a passage quoted in an early part of the Autobiography, compared Mr. Jay's mind to "a clear, transparent spring, flowing so freely as to impress us with the idea of its being inexhaustible;" and such is but a just description of those volumes which so powerfully affected that versatile and exquisite genius, considered, as he probably was, the most accomplished and keen-sighted man of his day:—but not him only; for thousands and tens of thousands, in almost every rank of life, are daily benefited, and will continue to be benefited, by the writings of William Jay. We can desiderate for them no happier or greater success than that which the man of taste, already mentioned, indicated as their characteristic—"the voice which calls us to look into ourselves, and prepare for judgment, is too piercing, too powerful, to be resisted, and we attempt, for worldly and sensual considerations, to shut our ears in vain."

INDEX.